Maimonides' *Guide of the Perplexed*

Moses Maimonides' *Guide of the Perplexed* (*c.* 1190) is the greatest and most influential text in the history of Jewish philosophy. Controversial in its day, the *Guide* directly influenced Aquinas, Spinoza, and Leibniz, and the history of Jewish philosophy took a decisive turn after its appearance. While there continues to be keen interest in Maimonides and his philosophy, this is the first scholarly collection in English devoted specifically to the *Guide*. It includes contributions from an international team of scholars addressing the most important philosophical themes that range over the three parts of this sprawling work – including topics in the philosophy of language, metaphysics, epistemology, philosophy of law, ethics, and political philosophy. There are also essays on the *Guide's* hermeneutic puzzles, and on its overall structure and philosophical trajectory. The volume will be of interest to philosophers, Judaists, theologians, and medievalists.

DANIEL FRANK is Professor of Philosophy at Purdue University. His publications include *The Cambridge Companion to Medieval Jewish Philosophy* (with Oliver Leaman, Cambridge, 2003), and *Spinoza on Politics* (with Jason Waller, 2016).

AARON SEGAL is Lecturer in the Department of Philosophy at The Hebrew University of Jerusalem. He is co-editor of *Jewish Philosophy Past and Present: Contemporary Responses to Classical Sources* (with Daniel Frank, 2017), and *Jewish Philosophy in an Analytic Age* (with Samuel Lebens and Dani Rabinowitz, 2019).

CAMBRIDGE CRITICAL GUIDES

Titles Published in this series:

Hume's *An Enquiry Concerning the Principles of Morals*
EDITED BY ESTHER ENGELS KROEKER and WILLEM LEMMENS

Hobbes's *On the Citizen*
EDITED BY ROBIN DOUGLASS AND OHAN OLSTHOORN

Hegel's *Philosophy of Spirit*
EDITED BY MARINA F. BYKOVA

Kant's *Lectures on Metaphysics*
EDITED BY COURTNEY D. FUGATE

Spinoza's *Political Treatise*
EDITED BY YITZHAK Y. MELAMED and HASANA SHARP

Aquinas's *Summa Theologiae*
EDITED BY JEFFREY HAUSE

Aristotle's *Generation of Animals*
EDITED BY ANDREA FALCON and DAVID LEFEBVRE

Hegel's *Elements of the Philosophy of Right*
EDITED BY DAVID JAMES

Kant's *Critique of Pure Reason*
EDITED BY JAMES R. O'SHEA

Spinoza's *Ethics*
EDITED BY YITZHAK Y. MELAMED

Plato's *Symposium*
EDITED BY PIERRE DESTRÉE and ZINA GIANNOPOULOU

Fichte's *Foundations of Natural Right*
EDITED BY GABRIEL GOTTLIEB

Aquinas's *Disputed Questions on Evil*
EDITED BY M. V. DOUGHERTY

(Continued after the Index)

MAIMONIDES'
Guide of the Perplexed
A Critical Guide

EDITED BY

DANIEL FRANK
Purdue University

AARON SEGAL
Hebrew University of Jerusalem

Shaftesbury Road, Cambridge CB2 8EA, United Kingdom

One Liberty Plaza, 20th Floor, New York, NY 10006, USA

477 Williamstown Road, Port Melbourne, VIC 3207, Australia

314–321, 3rd Floor, Plot 3, Splendor Forum, Jasola District Centre, New Delhi – 110025, India

103 Penang Road, #05-06/07, Visioncrest Commercial, Singapore 238467

Cambridge University Press is part of Cambridge University Press & Assessment, a department of the University of Cambridge.

We share the University's mission to contribute to society through the pursuit of education, learning and research at the highest international levels of excellence.

www.cambridge.org
Information on this title: www.cambridge.org/9781108727600

DOI: 10.1017/9781108635134

© Cambridge University Press & Assessment 2021

This publication is in copyright. Subject to statutory exception and to the provisions of relevant collective licensing agreements, no reproduction of any part may take place without the written permission of Cambridge University Press & Assessment.

First published 2021
First paperback edition 2023

A catalogue record for this publication is available from the British Library

Library of Congress Cataloging-in-Publication data
NAMES: Daniel Frank, 1950– editor. | Aaron Segal (Aaron David), editor.
TITLE: Maimonides' Guide of the perplexed : a critical guide / edited by Daniel Frank, Aaron Segal.
OTHER TITLES: Cambridge critical guides.
DESCRIPTION: New York : Cambridge University Press, 2021. | Series: Cambridge critical guides | Includes bibliographical references and index.
IDENTIFIERS: LCCN 2020041988 (print) | LCCN 2020041989 (ebook) | ISBN 9781108480512 (hardback) | ISBN 9781108727600 (paperback) | ISBN 9781108635134 (epub)
SUBJECTS: LCSH: Maimonides, Moses, 1135-1204. Dalālat al-ḥā'irin. | Jewish philosophy. | Philosophy, Medieval.
CLASSIFICATION: LCC B759.M34 M3245 2021 (print) | LCC B759.M34 (ebook) | DDC 181/.06–dc23
LC record available at https://lccn.loc.gov/2020041988
LC ebook record available at https://lccn.loc.gov/2020041989

ISBN 978-1-108-48051-2 Hardback
ISBN 978-1-108-72760-0 Paperback

Cambridge University Press & Assessment has no responsibility for the persistence or accuracy of URLs for external or third-party internet websites referred to in this publication and does not guarantee that any content on such websites is, or will remain, accurate or appropriate.

Contents

List of Contributors	*page* vii
Introduction DANIEL FRANK AND AARON SEGAL	1

PART I FORM

1 The Structure and Purpose of the *Guide* DANIEL FRANK	11
2 The *Guide* as Biblical Commentary IGOR H. DE SOUZA	29

PART II HUMAN BEGINNINGS

3 Paradise and the Fall SHIRA WEISS	51
4 Maimonides on the Nature of Good and Evil DANIEL RYNHOLD	60

PART III THE CREATOR

5 The Scope of Metaphysics DANIEL DAVIES AND CHARLES H. MANEKIN	83
6 His Existence Is Essentiality: Maimonides as Metaphysician AARON SEGAL	102
7 "Whereof One Cannot Speak" SILVIA JONAS	125

PART IV THE CREATED

8 Creation and Miracles in the *Guide* — 143
T. M. RUDAVSKY

9 The Prophetic Method in the *Guide* — 161
DANI RABINOWITZ

10 Maimonides' Modalities — 184
JOSEF STERN

PART V HUMAN FINITUDE

11 Maimonides' Critique of Anthropocentrism and Teleology — 209
WARREN ZEV HARVEY

12 Maimonides and the Problem(s) of Evil — 223
DAVID SHATZ

PART VI HUMAN ENDS

13 The Nature and Purpose of Divine Law — 247
MOSHE HALBERTAL

14 Maimonides on Human Perfection and the Love of God — 266
STEVEN NADLER

Bibliography — 286
Index — 306

Contributors

DANIEL DAVIES is Research Associate in the Institute for Jewish Philosophy and Religion at Universität Hamburg

IGOR H. DE SOUZA is Lecturer in English and Humanities at Yale University

DANIEL FRANK is Professor of Philosophy at Purdue University

MOSHE HALBERTAL is Professor of Philosophy and Jewish Thought at The Hebrew University of Jerusalem

WARREN ZEV HARVEY is Professor Emeritus of Jewish Thought at The Hebrew University of Jerusalem

SILVIA JONAS is Marie Skłodowska Curie Fellow at the Munich Center for Mathematical Philosophy at Ludwig-Maximilians-University Munich

CHARLES H. MANEKIN is Professor of Philosophy at University of Maryland

STEVEN NADLER is William H. Hay II Professor of Philosophy and Evjue-Bascom Professor in Humanities at University of Wisconsin–Madison

DANI RABINOWITZ is a solicitor at Clifford Chance LLP

T. M. RUDAVSKY is Professor of Philosophy at The Ohio State University

DANIEL RYNHOLD is Professor in Modern Jewish Philosophy at the Bernard Revel Graduate School of Jewish Studies at Yeshiva University

AARON SEGAL is Lecturer in Philosophy at The Hebrew University of Jerusalem

DAVID SHATZ is Ronald P. Stanton University Professor of Philosophy, Ethics, and Religious Thought at Yeshiva University

JOSEF STERN is William H. Colvin Professor of Philosophy Emeritus at The University of Chicago

SHIRA WEISS is Academic Fellow at the Center for Hebraic Thought

Introduction
Daniel Frank and Aaron Segal

Moses Maimonides' *Guide of the Perplexed* is the greatest and most influential work in Jewish philosophy. It directly influenced Aquinas, Spinoza, and Leibniz, and the history of Jewish philosophy takes a decisive turn after the appearance of the *Guide*, in the wake of its Hebrew translation. Aquinas refers to "Rabbi Moyses" when he develops his own theory of analogical predication, and Spinoza has Maimonides and the *Guide* squarely in focus in the *Tractatus Theologico-Politicus*, when he presents his own theory of biblical interpretation.

Few works in the history of philosophy have been so fraught with interpretive difficulties as the *Guide*. Not too often do such difficulties play out as they did with the *Guide*. Completed by 1190, written in Judeo-Arabic under the title *Dalalat al-Ha'irin*, translated into Hebrew by Samuel ibn Tibbon in 1204 (the very year of Maimonides' death) under the title *Moreh Nevukim*, the book was, along with the first book of his legal code, *Mishneh Torah*, incinerated in northern France (in Montpellier or perhaps Paris) in 1232/3 at the behest of religious authorities. Why? In general, the worry was that readers of the *Guide*, under the influence of Maimonides' reputation and the persuasive power of philosophy itself, would be led astray and that the authority and validity of the Torah and the rabbinic tradition would be undermined. Why? What is so special about the *Guide* that so unnerved the religious authorities? A major worry is that the work reinterprets the divine in a very austere way, so much so that only a few (philosophically-inclined) members of the community could gain sustenance from its arguments. The rest of the community would be left behind, confused. Perhaps philosophy, the use of human reason unaided, might supplant judicial authority.

It was the anti-Maimonideans who, in their own way, dichotomized between philosophy and religion. It is far from clear, however, that Maimonides himself held this view. Indeed, adjudication of this *is* the major interpretive difficulty alluded to. Are philosophy and religion fundamentally at odds with each other, or is there some way to understand Judaism, the religious tradition, as itself philosophical? We hope our readers will be better positioned to answer this question after working through the essays of this volume. One thing is for sure. If the tradition is fundamentally philosophical, if monotheism is as austere as Maimonides suggests, then one comes away with a conception of religion and its classical subject matter – creation, prophecy, providence, the nature of good and evil, the grounds for obedience to the law – in ways very different from what the lay reader gets from an easy acquaintance of the Bible. The anti-Maimonidean worry is understandable, perhaps however not justifiable.

The *Guide* is a very long work, over six hundred pages in the standard English translation of Shlomo Pines. A notable Maimonides scholar has written, "... though the topics of the work are clear enough, their arrangement does not always follow an easily discernible order."[1] This point is usually paired with the presumption that Maimonides proceeds by indirection, driven by a felt need to obscure the real (philosophical) message of the work from those, including its perplexed young addressee, not fit to receive it. While conceding the Platonic (and Farabian)-inspired point about an awareness of natural differences in intellectual abilities and the political implications of this, we believe that the arrangement and presentation of topics in the *Guide* does in fact follow a "discernible order." Our volume replicates this order, and inspection of our table of contents reveals that the work is bookended by the Fall and potential redemption of humankind. In between are sandwiched discussions of the nature of divinity and His creation. In sum, the *Guide* is a very "human" work, from beginning to end, offering "guidance" to one in the grips of an existential crisis. It is a "practical" work in Aristotle's sense, aiming at the human good and presenting a strategy for its attainment.

In turning to the specific essays, the first two deal with formal features of the *Guide*. In "The Structure and Purpose of the *Guide*," Daniel Frank outlines the overall trajectory of the work and the goals it wishes to achieve. In brief, the *Guide* serves a practical goal (in Aristotle's sense of "practical," as noted), the goal of attaining, for its addressee and for any serious reader, the true human good. The trajectory of the work over its three parts is directed at this. Topics in (what one would describe as) philosophy of language, metaphysics, epistemology, cosmology, philosophical psychology, philosophy of law, ethics, and political philosophy

---

[1] Hyman (2010, 360).

are indexed to this practical goal, and in so proceeding, Maimonides' *Guide* can be understood as a guide for achieving the human telos, a life of rational excellence. Viewed this way, the *Guide* is no more a 'theoretical' work than is Plato's *Republic* or Spinoza's *Ethics*. While it is undeniable that embedded in these masterpieces are rich discussions of metaphysics, cosmology, and mind, all of a theoretical nature, all such discussions in these works are not offered for their own sake, even as we today may so pursue them as such by ripping them from their contexts in the work as a whole. Rather, the metaphysics, cosmology, and epistemology support, in ways to be considered, a view of human perfection. In his essay, Frank first delineates the nature and source of the perplexity that disables R. Joseph, the addressee of the *Guide*, and then turns to the particular way that the text attempts to dispel it, thereby advancing R. Joseph toward the human good.

In "The *Guide* as Biblical Commentary," Igor De Souza analyzes the kind of exegetical work the *Guide* is. He notes first that a strict, formal commentary is a text that analyzes or explains another text, and the formal structure of a commentary is dictated by the order of the text that it investigates. Under this definition, the *Guide* is not a commentary, yet the *Guide* is an exegetical work that fulfills several of the functions associated with the practice of commentary. De Souza proposes viewing the *Guide* as a "conceptual" (functional) commentary on the Jewish Bible, one that functions to confirm the authority of Scripture, while concurrently problematizing the text and rendering it difficult to prevent facile readings. Given the long, rich tradition of biblical commentary, De Souza addresses the question of why Maimonides chose not to write a formal commentary on the Bible. In large part, the answer to this question reveals the revisionary nature of the *Guide* as an exercise in biblical exegesis. Unlike a formal commentary that serves as a study guide for the reader, the *Guide* itself is less concerned with offering easy answers than with guiding the reader along a path of intellectual and spiritual stimulation and transformation.

Among the most celebrated chapters of the *Guide* are the opening chapters on the Garden of Eden and the beginnings of humankind. In her essay "Paradise and the Fall," Shira Weiss presents a taste of Maimonides' innovative readings of biblical terms and narratives through which he reveals his philosophical views. In part I, chapter 2 of the *Guide* he discusses the normative status of morality by addressing the apparent contradiction in Genesis 3 of Adam's and Eve's *reward* of knowledge of good and evil after their *violation* of God's prohibition of eating from the forbidden tree. Why, after all, should one be rewarded for disobedience? Maimonides' resolves the worry by invoking a strong distinction between truth (*emet*) and falsehood (*sheqer*) on the one side, and good (*tov*) and evil (*ra*) on the other, interpreting humankind's newfound moral discernment as a *fall* from their created state of intellectual perfection, in the "image of God." Weiss notes that this reading of the biblical episode in the Garden of Eden, with which Maimonides commences his philosophic work, reflects his Aristotelian conception of human perfection, the topic of the concluding chapter of the *Guide*. As a result of the first sin in paradise, humanity must strive to develop itself in an effort to transcend (conventional) moral judgment and achieve communion with God, a theme that Maimonides expounds throughout his philosophy.

In his essay "Maimonides on the Nature of Good and Evil," Daniel Rynhold notes that Maimonides appears to spend most of the *Guide* speaking of good and evil in terms that render them, at best, bit-part players in the quest for what really matters – knowledge of the natural and divine sciences. In what could be read as an anticipation of the appendix to part I of Spinoza's *Ethics*, good and evil are relativized to human concerns, and presented as matters of convention or "common opinion," which compare unfavorably with the intellectual norms of true and false. And yet, denigrating the ethical values of good and evil – or even relativizing them to the ultimate intellectual endeavor to which "there do not belong actions or moral qualities" (*Guide* 3.27) – appears to be at odds with both Maimonides' unwavering commitment to a life of Jewish practice and the much-discussed practical twist with which he appears to end the *Guide*. Rynhold's essay explores the various interpretive options available in the *Guide* regarding the nature of good and evil, and the extent to which Maimonides turns out to be a moral cognitivist or a non-cognitivist, a moral realist or an anti-realist.

The next section consists of three essays on interrelated themes concerning God and metaphysics, discussion of which occupies much of the first part of the *Guide*: Maimonides' demarcation of inquiry into the "divine sciences" and the relation of that inquiry to metaphysics, the question of just how austere a conception of God Maimonides argues for, and the question of what sort of knowledge of God might be possible if God is indeed properly conceived in radically austere (and negative) terms.

In their essay "The Scope of Metaphysics," Daniel Davies and Charles H. Manekin address the issue of what Maimonides takes metaphysics to be – what its defining features are and what sets it apart from other disciplines – and the precise relation between metaphysics, "divine sciences" (and "divine matters"), and what the Rabbis called "the work of the chariot." After tracing the attitude of Maimonides' Arabic Aristotelian predecessors to the scope and nature of metaphysics, they turn to certain difficulties in developing a uniform Maimonidean take on these questions. Why is that an important task? Why does it matter, for Maimonides, where everything else leaves off and metaphysics begins? Here Davies and Manekin answer, as against a proto-Kantian or skeptical reading of the *Guide*, that it is because (a) possessing certain or near-certain knowledge of metaphysical truths is essential to a good life, while (b) it is so easy to fall prey to false metaphysical beliefs, especially if one's inquiry proceeds in the wrong order.

What are the metaphysical truths that Maimonides maintains are so essential to believe? It is easy to state the most paramount ones: God's existence, unity, and incorporeality are central to Maimonides' worldview. But they are as easy to state as they are difficult to pin down precisely. In his essay "His Existence Is Essentiality: Maimonides as Metaphysician," Aaron Segal lays out what Maimonides appears to claim about these and other divine attributes, raises some serious puzzles about such claims, surveys a couple of extant resolutions, and then proposes a resolution of his own. On Segal's reading, Maimonides holds a coherent and sophisticated package of metaphysical views, and his negative theology and doctrine of pure equivocation are a lot less austere than they are ordinarily taken to be.

But what if they *are* as austere as they are ordinarily taken to be? What room is there, then, for knowledge of God, which Maimonides seems to prize so much? In her essay "Whereof One Cannot Speak," Silvia Jonas takes up this question head-on: How can there be *knowledge* of God without any *comprehension* of God? Jonas answers that knowledge of God, for Maimonides, is *non-propositional*. After canvassing a number of paradigm cases of such knowledge from the contemporary literature in epistemology and philosophy of mind, Jonas argues that what unifies these cases is that they are all "enabling states" that allow us to interact with the external world. Jonas contends that, for Maimonides, knowledge of God is likewise a state that enables to take a particular attitude, a *religious* attitude, toward the world.

Three essays follow on different aspects of God's relation to the created universe, ones that take center stage in part two of the *Guide*: the nature of creation itself and the proper interpretation of putative miracles, the prophetic methodology and the consequent epistemology of prophecy, and the disentanglement of various notions of possibility and necessity in the Maimonidean corpus.

In *Guide* 2.13, Maimonides himself lays out three options for understanding creation: the Scriptural view, the Platonic view, and the Aristotelian view. But while he ostensibly endorses the Scriptural view, scholars have fiercely debated what Maimonides' true view is. In her essay "Creation and Miracles in the *Guide*," T. M. Rudavsky makes the case that it isn't the Scriptural view. In her interpretation, Maimonides holds a somewhat skeptical stance regarding the whole issue – as no view could be demonstrated to be correct. But he nonetheless seeks to reconcile his Aristotelian naturalism with elements of the Scriptural account, and so his own tentative conclusion is neither the pure Scriptural view nor the unadulterated Aristotelian view, but rather the "middle-ground" Platonic view. Rudavsky shows that Maimonides' commitment to Aristotelian naturalism shapes his view of miracles, even as he appears in the *Guide* to attenuate some of his earlier pronouncements on the subject.

Maimonides' naturalism comes to the fore not only regarding creation and miracles, but regarding prophecy as well. In his essay "The Prophetic Method in the *Guide*," Dani Rabinowitz argues that non-Mosaic prophecy is a cognitive feat that will naturally be experienced by certain people as a dream or vision. He reconstructs in detail the belief-forming method employed in cases of prophecy, and locates the precise point at which the prophet forms a belief. In light of epistemological theories, both contemporary and ancient, that place belief-forming *methods* at the heart of epistemological evaluations, and his analysis of the prophetic method itself, Rabinowitz goes on to argue that prophecy is fallible, and that the distinction between Mosaic and non-Mosaic prophecy, so important to Maimonides, is itself problematic.

Rounding out this section is Josef Stern's essay, "Maimonides' Modalities." Stern isolates and analyzes five different conceptions of the modalities – possibility, necessity, and impossibility – in Maimonides' writings. While modality is not a subject whose secrets Maimonides explores directly or for its own sake, it emerges that a proper understanding of the various conceptions is essential in order to appreciate the arguments of the *falasifa* for eternity, Maimonides' own conception of God, how Maimonides understands the controversy between the *falasifa* and the *mutakallimun*, and, in Stern's view, the full extent of Maimonides' skepticism regarding metaphysics.

Maimonides is keenly aware of human finitude, and in his essay "Maimonides' Critique of Anthropocentrism and Teleology," Warren

Zev Harvey notes that, although Maimonides advocated a strong anthropocentric teleology in his early *Commentary on the Mishnah*, he expressed anti-teleological and anti-anthropocentric views in a celebrated, but conflicted, discussion in *Guide* 3.13. Here, Maimonides argues that the universe has no purpose, and certainly was not created for the sake of human beings. Moreover, all created beings exist for their own sakes, and not for that of other beings. He claims that Genesis 1 proves this proposition. However, as Harvey points out, three verses pose a problem for him. According to Genesis 1:17–1:18, the heavenly bodies were created "to rule over the day and the night." According to Genesis 1:28, human beings were created "to have dominion over" the fish, birds, and beasts. According to Genesis 1:29–1:30, God gave the plants to human beings and other animals "for food." In his resourceful exegeses of these three passages, Maimonides sets down his most considered views on final causality and on the place of human beings, the other animals, and plants in the universe.

It is well known that Maimonides espouses the generally discredited Neoplatonic view that evil is merely a privation. In his essay "Maimonides and the Problem(s) of Evil," David Shatz shows that there is much more to Maimonides' discussion of theodicy than this. Shatz shows how Maimonides' thesis of equivocity and his view of "good" threaten his ability to even state the problem of evil; assesses whether the thesis that evil is a privation can exonerate God's allowing evil; explains how Maimonides can embrace Rabbi Ammi's statement in the Talmud, "there is no death without sin, no suffering without transgression" despite his naturalistic outlook; and examines Maimonides' view that people's concern with the problem of evil reflects their egocentrism or anthropocentrism. As Shatz presents the case, critically assessing Maimonides' views on theodicy yields philosophical fruit, and we come away seeing the pros and cons of his varied approaches. Shatz also points to psychological dimensions of Maimonides' discussion of the problem of evil. In approaching evil, Maimonides incorporates views about the nature of human beings, the scope of human responsibility, anthropocentrism, and value judgments.

As noted at the outset, the *Guide* is a very "human" work, offering practical guidance throughout, and aiming at the human good. As befits this trajectory, the volume concludes with two essays on law and human perfection. In his essay "The Nature and Purpose of Divine Law," Moshe Halbertal explores two separate yet related questions in Maimonides' thought concerning the nature and purpose of divine law. The first fundamental question relates to Maimonides' conception of the authority of divine law in light of his own approach to prophecy and revelation. Given Maimonides' fierce rejection of any anthropomorphic conception of God and any modeling of divine revelation on human political sovereign structures, what is his alternative conception of the authority of divine law? Put differently: for Maimonides, what makes a law *divine*, if not divine command? The second issue addressed in the essay examines the broader implications of the Maimonidean grounding of the meaning and authority of the divine law in *wisdom* rather than in *will*. The focus here is on Maimonides' interpretation of the content of divine law and its rationale.

Like the very beginning of the *Guide*, so too the end of the *Guide* is much commented on, but as Steven Nadler notes in his essay, "Maimonides on Human Perfection and the Love of God," although the question of what the love of God involves for Maimonides is much debated in the literature, very little clarity has been achieved so far. In fact, it appears that the love of God in the philosophical *Guide* – more specifically, in the final chapters – is not the same thing that we find in the halakhic writings. In Maimonides' halakhic works and in earlier chapters of the *Guide*, the love of God is an affective state that is subsequent to a certain kind of knowledge about God – in particular, the knowledge of God's "actions" achieved through the study of His creation, through natural science; this knowledge and its attendant love is in principle open to many, including the common people. In chapters 51–52 of part III of the *Guide*, by contrast, where Maimonides turns at last to true human perfection, the love of God is a cognitive state – it is identical to the intellectual apprehension of God's nature, that is, the "divine science" that is the ultimate goal of metaphysics and that constitutes the highest human condition. This intellectual knowledge/love is beyond the reach of the masses, and is accessible (at least in principle, if not in fact) to only a very select few, primarily prophets and philosophers. In so addressing issues at the very end of the *Guide*, issues about true human perfection and the goal of human life, Nadler's essay is a fitting conclusion to our volume.

PART I

Form

CHAPTER I

The Structure and Purpose of the Guide

Daniel Frank

"Now I know I have been a fool, and that folly is with me."
(Thomas Hardy, *Jude the Obscure*)

In delineating the causes or reasons for a thing's being, Aristotle notes, "what something is and what it is for are one ..." (Aristotle 1984, 198a25–6). The nature and structure of a thing and its purpose coincide. The nature and structure of a table is what it is for. The nature and structure of the heart is no different than its purpose, to pump blood. And so it is, as I shall argue, with Maimonides' *Guide of the Perplexed* (c. 1190). The structure of the work is intimately related to its purpose and ultimate goal. That there is an overall structure needs to be unpacked, and that the structure, overall and even within its discrete parts, serves a particular end also needs to be clarified. If this programmatic essay succeeds, it will provide a framework for reading the essays that follow. Each essay may be read as offering insight to the specific issue at hand, but *also* may be read as, in its own way, aiming at the ultimate purpose of the work as a whole.

In briefest summary, I argue that Maimonides' *Guide of the Perplexed*, the most important medieval Jewish philosophical work, which set the agenda for Jewish philosophy until Spinoza upended him (or thought he did) some 475 years later, is a work in *practical* philosophy, and serves a practical goal (in Aristotle's sense of 'practical'): the goal of attaining, for its addressee and for any other serious reader, the true human good.[1] The trajectory of the work over its three parts, and in each of its parts, is directed at this. Topics in (what we would describe as) philosophy of language, semantics, metaphysics, epistemology, cosmology, philosophical psychology, philosophy of law, ethics, and political philosophy are indexed to this practical goal, and in so proceeding, Maimonides' *Guide* can be understood as a guide for achieving the human telos, a life of rational

[1] Frank (1992; 1994).

excellence. Perplexity and mental unease give way in the end to the peace of mind and equanimity that attends intellectual insight.

So construed, the *Guide* is no more a 'theoretical' work than is Plato's *Republic* or Spinoza's *Ethics*. No one can deny that embedded in these masterpieces are rich discussions of a theoretical nature: of metaphysics, cosmology, and mind. But all such discussions in these works are not offered for their own sake, even as we today may so pursue them as such by ripping them from their contexts in the work as a whole. Rather, the metaphysics and epistemology support a view of human perfection. For Plato, the best life is grounded in a deep understanding of what is real. For Plato, that is ultimately what metaphysics is *for*. For Spinoza, knowledge and love of God – human perfection – is grounded in an understanding of the workings of nature and its causal interconnections. For Spinoza, that is what science is *for*. The curricular model here is most prominently associated with the Hellenistic schools: meta/physics is done for the sake of tranquility and achieving the human good. For Epicurus, "if our suspicions about heavenly phenomena and about death did not trouble us at all and were never anything to us, and, moreover, if not knowing the limits of pains and desires did not trouble us, then we would have no need of natural science" (*Kuriai Doxai* #11).[2] Likewise for Maimonides, an understanding of the nature of the created order, of the reasons for the Laws, etc., is the means whereby one overcomes perplexity and achieves the human good. The duty to philosophize and to understand the created order is an imperative enjoined on those whose goal in life can be brought about through such practices.[3]

1.1 R. Joseph and His Perplexity

Maimonides' *Guide of the Perplexed* is a sprawling work. It is presented over three not-too-unequal parts: the three-volume Arabic original of S. Munk (Maïmonide, 1856–1866) comes to 365 double-column pages, and the celebrated English translation of Shlomo Pines (Maimonides 1963) rounds off at about 640 pages. One may well wonder what the overall structure and goal of the whole is, if indeed there is one. I think there is, and in this essay I attempt to lay it out.

The *Guide* famously commences with an introduction to its audience – a particular student – but more broadly, to those caught in the grip of a dilemma. Maimonides writes:

---

[2] Diogenes Laertius 10.142. [3] Davidson (1974), Frank (1993).

> The aim of our treatise is not to explain all these [homonymous, metaphorical and ambiguous] terms to the vulgar crowd or to mere beginners in philosophy, or even to those who study nothing but the Law – i.e. the legal and the ritual aspects of our religion (since the whole purpose of this and similar treatises is the true understanding of the Law). Its aim is rather to stimulate the mind of the religious man who has arrived at deep-set belief in the truth of our faith and who is perfect in the religious and moral sense. If such a man has also made a study of the philosophical sciences and grasped their meaning, and feels attracted to rationalism and at home with it, he may be worried about the literal meaning of some scriptural passages as well as the sense of those homonymous, metaphorical, or ambiguous expressions, as he has always understood them, or as they are explained to him. He will thus fall into confusion and be faced by a dilemma: either he follows his reason and rejects those expressions as he understands them: then he will think that he is rejecting the dogmas of our religion. Or else he continues to accept them in the way he has been taught and refuses to be guided by his reason. He thus brusquely turns his back on his own reason, and yet he cannot help feeling that his faith has been gravely impaired. He will continue to hold those fanciful beliefs although they inspire him with uneasiness and disgust, and be continuously sick at heart and utterly bewildered in his mind. (Maimonides 1995, 41)

The *Guide* is not for everyone, but only for those few (religious intellectuals) who wish to maintain allegiance to their traditional faith community and religious beliefs in the face of what seem to be contrary beliefs emanating from the philosophical sciences. Maimonides' *Guide* will act as a guide to alleviate the perplexity, the unease resultant upon attempting to square the explicit meaning of biblical text with what, from the vantage point of philosophical reason, the text *must* intend.

Straightaway, before we continue, I offer a cautionary note: As I have presented it just now, here is the usual gloss for the impetus for the *Guide*: A smart lad has trouble making sense of the Bible from the vantage point of philosophy and science. The Bible offends his intelligence because of its prima facie anthropomorphism and philosophical unintelligibility. He is driven to perplexity thereby, and Maimonides writes the *Guide of the Perplexed* to help him out, to help him to see that the Bible can be rendered intelligible and so inoffensive. Problem solved, case closed. There is much to complain about in this story. One of the main problems is that it is too episodic, focused on a particular intellectual conundrum, that of revelation versus reason, we would say. I think this telling "over-intellectualizes" the issue at hand. The student's unease is not rooted in a conundrum; it is not a puzzle awaiting resolution in any straightforward way. The root cause, the generative source of the perplexity, lies far deeper, and Maimonides needs to address this if the *life* of the perplexed one is ever to be set aright. In due course, I will suggest that the deep source of the perplexity lies at a material, characterological level, and the *Guide* is written to address this source for perplexity. The *Guide* is therefore written for a flawed character who finds himself in a situation in which we would say "his life [or "my life"] makes no sense" or "has gone off the rails." How would we go about setting *this* right? I don't think we resolve it by being given in any straightforward way a "right answer." It is not clear what the right answer would even be. We might seek therapy for the root causes, and I will suggest that Maimonides is a therapist of a sort, and the *Guide* itself is meant to be transformative in a deep way.

So, the *Guide* is written for a 'practical' purpose, to alleviate unease and to advance one toward the good. In his own way, Maimonides is a therapist of sorts, and his cure takes on a peculiar form – biblical exegesis. Odd medicine! Biblical exegesis of one sort or another – midrashic, halakhic, philosophic – has been practiced from rabbinic times. Some exegetical works take the form of a commentary on a particular text. Saadia wrote a commentary on *Job* and Maimonides himself commented on the Mishnah early in his career. While the form of the *Guide* is not a formal line-by-line commentary, it is still reminiscent of all those efforts, from Philo on, to understand the Bible philosophically.[4] Given this, we might note a fine irony, as Maimonides presents his own radical, revisionist views of the nature of divinity, miracles, prophecy, and providence as a form of biblical exegesis. In explicating the Law – the religious tradition – he quite radically revises commonplace conceptions and lays bare the deeply philosophical nature of the tradition. The "true understanding [or science] of the Law," the purpose of the *Guide,* is not so much a delineation of legal practice as it is a foundational study of the religious tradition, rooted in categories that only those of philosophical discernment may appreciate and may in due course be aided by.

In thinking of biblical exegesis *more philosophico* as a therapeutic device, we may find ourselves a bit perplexed. How precisely can this way of proceeding assuage the mental unease that besets a philosophically-

---

[4] In Essay 2 in this volume, Igor De Souza writes, "The *Guide* is manifestly not a commentary." I take the point that the *Guide* is not a *formal* commentary, working through a text line by line, and for a broad audience. Yet, Maimonides does "comment" on biblical texts, for his own philosophical purposes and for a select audience. The manifest purpose of the work is signaled at the very beginning: "This treatise has as its principal object to clarify the meaning of certain terms in the Bible." So, however we wish to categorize the *Guide*, and even if it is sui generis as De Souza suggests, it is a work of biblical exegesis and, as such, is part of the exegetical tradition.

The Structure and Purpose of the *Guide*

inclined member of the religious community? For a start, and as I have hinted at earlier, we need to carefully ponder both the precise character of the perplexed one and the nature of his perplexity. He is not someone who merely lacks a certain "answer" to a question and is perplexed and confused as a result. I may be perplexed and confused about how to get from New York to Boston, but that worry hardly renders me "continuously sick at heart and utterly bewildered in his mind." This latter debilitation arises for one, as Maimonides puts it, "who has arrived at deep-set belief in the truth of our faith and who is perfect in the religious and moral sense." If such a devout one has also studied a bit of secular wisdom, philosophy and science, then – and only then – may the kind of perplexity with which Maimonides is concerned kick in. So the *Guide* is written for *good* people, specifically for a devout young man who is caught in the grip of an existential dilemma. This obvious point is also a substantive one. The *Guide* is written for those whose communal lives are beyond reproach ("perfect in the religious and moral sense"), those upstanding members of the community who have encountered a set of universal norms that seemingly run counter to the norms that have governed their lives so far. This is the audience for whom Maimonides is writing. For such an audience, it is not the lack of a certain "answer," a situation relatively easily remediable, that is the root cause of their undoing.

As the perplexity at hand is grounded in honesty and genuine moral excellence, its dissolution must address a false turn – born of good faith – that arises from a genuine, not a facile, commitment to truth. As Maimonides explicitly states, the perplexity does not arise for the vulgar, the amateur philosopher, the legal pedant, or (of course) the atheist; they may be perplexed, but they are not the audience for whom Maimonides is writing the *Guide*. Again, he is writing for those who are good, but nevertheless bewildered, caught in the grips of a dilemma generated from dual heartfelt commitments. We need to ask ourselves: what causes the bewilderment, what is the material cause of it? What is it about this upright person that causes his life to be in such disarray? What positions him in his dilemmatic state?

Permit me a brief aside to put this point in historical context. Compare the very notion of perplexity as it is found in the present context with that found in the Socratic dialogues of Plato, especially those early dialogues in which we see Socrates reducing his interlocutors to a state of *aporia* (perplexity). *Aporia* is the endpoint, the terminus, of the Socratic elenchus, a healthy conclusion for a presumptuous and arrogant person to be brought to. Euthyphro thinks (imagines) he knows what piety is, and envisions himself an expert in such matters. He doesn't – and he isn't – but precisely because he has the presumption of wisdom, Socrates must, in his own way, disabuse him of it. Now this is not just a matter of showing Euthyphro *that* he is wrong about what he thinks piety is, but that his character, the kind of person he is, stands in the way of learning and wisdom.[5] He is deeply flawed and in need of reform. *Aporia* plays to this notion, the necessity of moral reform. Socrates and Plato intend to create good, virtuous people, and the elenchus, leading to *aporia*, is the vehicle.

How different this is from Maimonides' *Guide*. As we have noted, Maimonides is writing for those who are "perfect in the religious and moral sense." They do not need to be disabused of any conceit of wisdom, but – as we shall see – this does not mean that there is not a type of presumption in play. And just because this is so, the antidote to *their* perplexity cannot be a quick fix, a simple answer. The character for whom Maimonides writes will no more be cured by a quick answer than will Euthyphro be cured by simply being told what piety is. To placate such a person's perplexity is to reveal the deep "philosophicality" of Scripture, *but to do so in a manner that addresses itself to the character of a good man who has led himself astray.* How so? The remedy must be two-pronged. It must reveal that the moral and communal life that the perplexed young man is living can be defended at the bar of philosophy, *and* it must be done in such a way that the material conditions that led him astray in the first place are effectively addressed. The cure must chasten as it edifies. In sum, Maimonides reveals the deep "philosophicality" of Scripture, its metaphysical foundations, while at the very same time providing the kind of moral reform and character development that will forestall future crises.

The foregoing remarks are at an unacceptably high level of generality, so let me elaborate. The *Guide* is an elitist work, written for a select audience. Only this select group, which has acquired the kind of knowledge that appears to be at odds with the Law, is liable to be perplexed. For Maimonides, then, perplexity arises from study and knowledge. But more than this, and as the case of young R. Joseph plainly indicates, perplexity arises from knowledge too hastily gained, or – perhaps more accurately – gained in a haphazard fashion. And this latter is itself due to a moral failing, a flaw in R. Joseph's character. That R. Joseph's (self-induced) perplexity arises from his (youthful) exuberance – a reckless and premature desire that leads him, as Maimonides indicates, to study metaphysics

---

[5] A particularly good passage illustrating this flaw in character and the (presumed) benefit of the elenchus-inducing *aporia* is *Meno* 84a–c.

before he has properly studied God's creation, the natural world – and that the beginning of its resolution awaits elimination of this moral failing is the Maimonidean analogue to Plato's (moral) point that perplexity is mandated by the conceit of wisdom, and that it is a flaw in one's character that is the bar to intellectual progress. For both Plato and Maimonides, perplexity is the result not merely of intellectual error or confusion, but also of moral failing – a shortcoming in character. Euthyphro and, in his own way, R. Joseph are both vain. For his part, R. Joseph thinks he has the capacity, at a stage when in fact he does not, to embark upon a study of metaphysics. Indeed, R. Joseph's "desire to learn did exceed his grasp" (Maimonides 1963, dedicatory epistle: 3).

Although Maimonides asserts that the student for whom the *Guide* is written is "perfect in his religion and character" *(din w'akhlaq/de'ot v'middot)* (Maimonides 1963, introduction: 5), this cannot be quite correct as it stands. If it were, the just-mentioned reasons for R. Joseph's perplexity would be inexplicable. R. Joseph's perplexity is self-induced. Unlike those flawed, conceited characters whom Socrates encounters and brings to perplexity, R. Joseph's perplexity is very much of his own making and, as noted, due to his premature desire to commence upon a study of metaphysics. As a result, the *Guide* is a treatise devoted (necessarily) not only to showing the deep harmony between Judaism and philosophy and thus alleviating the intellectual perplexity that R. Joseph feels, but also to tempering, in ways that we shall soon clarify, the enthusiasm of R. Joseph (and those like him), the young traditional Jew ("for whom the validity of our Law has become established in his soul and has become actual in his belief") (Maimonides 1963, introduction: 5), who, because of his too early (and haphazard) study of "the sciences of the philosophers" (Maimonides 1963, introduction: 5), has become perplexed. Maimonides has R. Joseph in mind in 1.34 when he argues strongly against the teaching of metaphysics to the young:

> It is accordingly indubitable that preparatory moral training should be carried out before beginning with this science [metaphysics], so that man should be in a state of extreme uprightness and perfection ... For this reason the teaching of this science to the young is disapproved of. In fact it is impossible for them to absorb it because of the *effervescence* of their natures and of their minds being occupied with the flame of growth.[6] When, however, this flame that gives rise to perplexity is extinguished, the young achieve tranquility and quiet; and their hearts submit and yield

---

[6] Cf. Plato, *Republic* 539b; *Philebus* 15d–e.

with respect to their temperament. They then may call upon their souls to raise themselves up to this rank, which is that of the apprehension of Him, may He be exalted; I mean thereby the divine science that is designated as the Account of the Chariot. (Maimonides 1963, 1.34: 77) (my emphasis)

The reason here offered why one ought not to teach metaphysics to the young is perfectly illustrated by the case of R. Joseph and his perplexity.[7]

1.2 The Trajectory of the *Guide*

I now change the register, and move to a slightly different, but related, topic. While to some degree Maimonides' etiological project of providing the "true understanding [or science] of the Law" reminds us of the way that Aristotle proceeds in his own *Ethics*, providing his own audience of well-brought-up young men with a kind-of backdrop for or justification of the lives they are living (transporting them from the "that" to the "because," from a state of unreflective activity to one of reasoned action),[8] there is a key difference to be noted between Aristotle's and Maimonides' respective projects. The foundations for Aristotle's ethics are not metaphysical, nor is the project grounded in broad cosmological speculation. By contrast, Maimonides' is, and in nesting the human good and peace of mind (the overcoming of perplexity) in physics and cosmology, we can understand Maimonides' project as being, in its own way, of a piece with the great *Hellenistic* projects of grounding the human good and peace of mind in a broad, foundational understanding of the cosmos. Epicurean atomism, Stoic physics, and Skeptic phenomenalism – 'theoretical' endeavors all – are foundational, and manifestly indexed to achievement of the human good, the kind of peace of mind that attends the overcoming of perplexity and worry.[9] Coming to understand the nature of the cosmos, and grounding one's life on such insight, provides stability; indeed, it renders the agent invulnerable.

For the Stoics in particular, physics underwrites ethics,[10] in the sense that understanding, and taking to heart, cosmic determinism aids the

---

[7] For some further commentary on the step-by-step, paced pedagogical approach required to avoid crippling perplexity, see Daniel Davies' and Charles Manekin's essay, "The Scope of Metaphysics" (Essay 5 in this volume).
[8] Cf. Aristotle (2009), *Nicomachean Ethics* [*NE*] 1.4: 1095b3–8, with Burnyeat (1980, 81) and Lear (1988, 159–160).
[9] See note 2 in Section 1.1 of this essay.
[10] See Diogenes Laertus 7.40 (Long and Sedley 1987, 26B). The very founders of Stoicism – Zeno and Chrysippus – are mentioned in this context.

The Structure and Purpose of the Guide 19

agent in understanding what he can control (and what he cannot), and what is of real and durable value (and what is not). Peace of mind and the calibrating of passionate commitment to reason is the goal. It is not a stretch to see Maimonides as involved in something similar in the *Guide*. The *Guide*, by the very order of its topical presentations, attempts to ground the human good, and attempts to overcome perplexity and unease, by proceeding in a methodical, paced way,[11] taking into account the moral maturity of the student. He is ready to go, ready to be educated, just so long as he proceeds in a paced way, not too quickly, "given the effervescence of his nature." After all, his perplexity is all his own, of his own making, grounded in impetuosity and generated from deep commitments to multiple sources, or perhaps better, from a lack of understanding of the rich "philosophicality" of Scripture.

Let's take a brief look at the how the *Guide* actually proceeds.[12] One of the few attempts to chart its structure and order of presentation is that found in Leo Strauss's introduction to Pines's 1963 translation of the *Guide*. Strauss divided the *Guide* into two major parts: Views and Actions.[13] Perhaps he means nothing more than Theory and Practice, and if so, I am in broad general agreement. But I do not think this is finegrained enough to reveal what I take to be the Hellenistic register I have alluded to previously. I suggest the *Guide* commences in part 1 with logic and language, proceeds to discuss in part 2 issues of physics and cosmology, and mind and matter, and then turns in part 3 to philosophical anthropology, law, politics, and ethics.[14] The overarching point is that the pedagogical project is one that ultimately intends for theory to subserve practice, in Hellenistic fashion. In the Dedicatory Epistle to R. Joseph, the very addressee of the *Guide*, Maimonides notes the importance of proceeding "in an orderly manner." (cf. Maimonides 1963, 1.34: 73–76) The *Guide*, written for R. Joseph in his absence, does this for the practical purpose mentioned, to pace the student, with the goal of overcoming perplexity and thereby achieving peace of mind.

---

[11] The table of contents of this volume may be consulted for a sense of the "orderly" progression of topics; see also note 7 in Section 1.1 of this essay.
[12] See note 11 in this essay.   [13] Strauss (1963, xi–xiii).
[14] With reference to the table of contents of this volume, Essays 5–7 map on to part 1 of the *Guide*, Essays 8–10 map to part 2, and Essays 11–14 map to part 3. The trajectory of the *Guide* is from divine to human, from discussions of the nature of the creator and his creation to discussions of human finitude and human ends. The latter are grounded in the former, and are inexplicable without them. The *Guide* is a work in "practical" philosophy in the sense that all the (prior) 'theoretical' discussions are indexed to the practical end of achieving the *human* telos.

I am emphasizing this once again because it is key to understanding that the worry that besets the person who is perplexed is one that arises from a good-faith effort of an impetuous young man to understand the tradition that gives form to his life. The intellectual conundrum such a person finds himself in requires a certain deflation of the ego, a curbing of his youthful "effervescence," if ever the existential crisis is to be overcome, with the resultant peace of mind and assurance that the tradition, the religio-legal tradition that *is* rabbinic Judaism, is supportive of, amenable to deep philosophical insight. R. Joseph's intellectual impetuosity has led him to an impasse (literally *aporia* – no way out), he despairs of the intelligibility of the tradition, and Maimonides writes to help him, and writes in such an "orderly" way that the (material) conditions of the perplexity are addressed.

1.3 Good, but Not Wise: Job and R. Joseph

I want now to present in some detail a case study of how Maimonides proceeds in the *Guide* to fundamentally address the material, root cause of R. Joseph's perplexity – his impetuosity and presumption (his "effervescence"). Maimonides' goal will be, as I have previously put it, to chasten as he edifies – to offer a moral education as he addresses an intellectual knot. My case study is Maimonides' discussion of Job and his trials in part 3, chapters 22 and 23 of the *Guide*. Maimonides discusses *Job* in the context of divine providence, but as we shall see, the entire discussion has (indirect) reference to R. Joseph and his own trials. So . . .

Consider Job. 'Poor Job,' we say. Why? It is on account of his unmerited suffering. He did nothing to deserve what he got. Implicit in this thought is the idea that one gets, and ought to get, what one deserves. Maimonides does not disagree with the implicit idea, but vigorously denies that Job is blameless in his suffering – indeed, this is Eliphaz's (traditional) view, the view "in keeping with the opinion of our Law," according to Maimonides.[15] We read the trial of Job as an exercise in theodicy, divine justice: How are divine knowledge, power, and goodness compatible with evil and misfortune, for the latter seem to offend against the former? But Maimonides doesn't read the parable of Job that way; he doesn't emphasize the divine wager. For him, as for the young Elihu, *Job* is not so much about God and divine justice, but rather about Job himself and human finitude, human arrogance and presumption, and the insufficiency of moral virtue to secure happiness and beatitude.[16] To be sure,

---

[15] Maimonides (1963, 3.23: 494).   [16] Ibid.

Maimonides takes himself to be illustrating his own view about divine providence – divine knowledge of human affairs – by the story of Job. But the role of God in the story is, for Maimonides, quite secondary. The real 'culprit' in the story, at least for a while, is he who suffers – Job himself. Indeed, I shall argue on Maimonides' behalf that it is Job himself who is the (real) cause of his own undoing (with a sideways glance to R. Joseph and his perplexity). His 'innocence', understood aright, is far from exculpatory. Further, as I shall indicate, Maimonides' discussion of the parable of Job is thrown into sharp relief against the background of Aristotle's own discussion of the nature of moral virtue, and its relative *insufficiency* to secure happiness.

As Maimonides says early in his discussion of Job,

> the most marvelous and extraordinary thing about this story is the fact that knowledge is not attributed in it to Job. He is not said to be a wise or comprehending or an intelligent man. Only moral virtue and righteousness in action are ascribed to him. For if he had been wise, his situation would not have been obscure for him, as will become clear. (Maimonides 1963, 3.22: 487)

For Maimonides, Job is good, but not wise. As a result, he suffers. He suffers on account of his innocence, i.e. lack of wisdom. What sort of wisdom does Job lack? On a grand level, he lacks the kind of wisdom vouchsafed someone like the Stoic sage, knowledge of the rational order of the universe, that everything is in its place and as it ought to be. It is presumably the beginning of an insight such as this that God offers Job from the whirlwind at the end of the tale. But we don't have to abstract to this rather grand level for purposes now. More locally, Job is bereft of the wisdom that would clarify and explain his own predicament. Job follows common sense in imagining that his material possessions, health, wealth, and family are constitutive of happiness and that they are a sure sign of his goodness, and divine favor; this latter we might denominate Job's 'Calvinism.' Further, Job imagines that (his) moral virtue, his piety, guarantees happiness – otherwise, why is he so utterly confused and embittered, imagining that "the righteous man and the wicked are regarded as equal by God"? (Maimonides 1963, 3.23: 491; cf. *Job* 9: 22) In so following common sense, Job shows himself both presumptuous and innocent of any understanding of what brings about true happiness and completely lacking in any sense of the real link between righteousness and its (purported) reward. For Maimonides, Job suffers precisely because he has no (real) understanding of what is truly valuable and because he cannot fathom what is happening to him, and why. Of course, these two are linked and an understanding of the former is key to unlocking the latter. But let us take the two separately for the moment.

Recall Aristotle. In outlining the human good, Aristotle canvasses a variety of candidates for what constitutes human well-being. Pleasure, honor and esteem, and wealth are discussed and rather quickly dismissed from contention, being either too base, too instrumental, or too dependent on an external source to merit serious consideration.[17] Even moral virtue itself is called into question as being the *summum bonum*, for it is compatible "with the greatest sufferings and misfortunes; but a man who was living so no one would call happy, unless he were maintaining a thesis at all costs."[18] (Indeed, this latter comment reminds one immediately of Job, morally virtuous, but subject to misfortune.) Nevertheless, for Aristotle, each of the rejected candidates has a role to play in happiness, even though, by itself, none is sufficient to guarantee it. Each is a necessary condition of happiness, so much so that Aristotle can appeal to common sense to establish the point that happiness requires external goods such as wealth, good birth, physical beauty, etc.[19] Without these, the final goal is impossible to attain and one is rendered an outcast. (We might note in passing that the very external goods that Aristotle deems so necessary are precisely the ones Socrates – poor, ugly, baseborn – lacked, an indication of Aristotle's anti-Socraticism, his anti–anti-conventionalism.)

Aristotle's position drives him to the following dilemma, a conflict between his deepest intuitions: either happiness (like moral virtue) is something in our control and not easily snatched from us,[20] or happiness is, at least in part, outside of our control, dependent on luck and good fortune.[21] Aristotle does not resolve the dilemma. Nor, I think, does he want to, wishing thereby to indicate that happiness and the human condition hover between stability and fragility. On the one hand, happiness (and moral virtue) is attainable and sustainable by our own efforts and consequent upon actions chosen by the agent.[22] On the other hand, as a student of tragedy Aristotle could hardly overlook the extent to which a life can be wrecked from the 'outside,' and through no fault attributable to the agent. King Priam of Troy is his explicit example.[23]

For Aristotle, then, contingency is woven into the fabric of human happiness and the human condition. Indeed, he even suggests that the

---

[17] *NE* 1.5. [18] *NE* 1.5: 1095b31–1096a2. [19] *NE* 1.8: 1099a31–b8.
[20] *NE* 1.5: 1095b25–26. [21] *NE* 1.8: 1099b7–8. [22] *NE* 3.5: 1113b3–14.
[23] *NE* 1.9: 1100a5–9; 1.10: 1101a6–8.

virtue of the virtuous individual shines forth in adversity, in "bearing with resignation many great misfortunes."[24] Again, one is reminded of Job and his misfortunes. But in being so reminded one must signal an important difference here between Aristotle and Maimonides.

In pointing out the importance of external goods in the achievement of happiness, and in the very doing of virtuous deeds, Aristotle imports contingency into the very notion of happiness, and in so doing shows a deep sensitivity to the ultimately tragic condition of humankind. Misfortune can snatch happiness from us. But Aristotle's tragic sense is matched by no parallel in Maimonides. Maimonides does not view the suffering Job, the righteous and morally virtuous man, as a tragic figure. Instead, he views him as a fool,[25] one who, though morally upright, has no idea of what is truly valuable and who is perplexed and utterly uncomprehending of the meaning of his misfortune.

For Maimonides, Job represents common sense in holding material goods to be of real value and, further, in imagining that righteousness and virtue do not go unrewarded and are themselves sufficient for happiness. In holding these beliefs, Job had, according to Maimonides, "no true knowledge and knew the deity only because of his acceptance of authority, just as the multitude adhering to a law know it" (Maimonides 1963, 492). Job is, from Maimonides' point of view, like those who, at a later stage of the *Guide*, countenance traditional authority, "but do not engage in speculation concerning the fundamental principles of religion and make no inquiry whatever regarding the rectification of belief" (Maimonides 1963, 619; cf. Maimonides 1963, 3.23: 492–493). Such individuals merit no praise from Maimonides, and Job and his friends are no exception. So long as one follows and lives in accordance with traditional authority, the analogue to unreflective common sense, one shall be ensnared in contingency, and one's felicity shall be held captive to forces beyond one's control. Note that for Maimonides misfortune is a function of ignorance, perhaps even culpable ignorance, and, contra Aristotle, not an ineliminable part of the world, a function of the human condition. Let me stress this point. For Aristotle, as we have seen, happiness requires external goods and is consequent upon good fortune, with the result that – to a degree – happiness is beyond our control. The human condition is at root tragic. For Maimonides, true human happiness, the insight into which comes through philosophical speculation and "knowledge of the deity,"[26] does not require external goods for its fulfilment. Job's suffering depends very

[24] *NE* 1.10: 1100b30–33.   [25] Maimonides (1963, 487).   [26] Maimonides (1963, 492).

much upon himself, not upon forces outside him. If there is a tragic element inherent in Maimonides' view, it is that not all human beings can be philosophers, and hence must live a life mixed with contingency and suffering. This latter point, however, is not one that Maimonides stresses.[27]

For Maimonides, the antidote to human suffering is knowledge, specifically knowledge of God. We need not worry now about precisely what such knowledge amounts to, save to be clear that such knowledge has the effect of putting everything into perspective, clarifying what is truly of value and what is not. Heretofore, Job took happiness to depend on things such as health, wealth, and offspring – commonly held goods – with the result that when these were taken away, suffering ensued. But with God's pronouncements from the whirlwind, and Job's (gradual) realization that his prior perplexity and suffering were grounded in a profound ignorance of the nature and (relative) value of things and a naïve presumption about reward and punishment, Job commences to understand that not even moral virtue guarantees felicity, only knowledge does. Only knowledge of God can guarantee that one possesses a sense of the relative value of things.

Maimonides is clear that if Job had been wise, "his situation would not have been obscure to him," and that "... when he knew God with a certain knowledge, he admitted that true happiness, which is knowledge of the deity, is guaranteed to all who know Him and that a human being cannot be troubled in it by any of all the misfortunes in question" (Maimonides 1963, 492–493). Clarity and knowledge bring with them invulnerability to fortune. This is a very strong claim. I suspect we think it palpably false. But why? Precisely because we have a view of the self that entails that it is embedded in and hence affected by the material world. But Maimonides doesn't hold this view.[28] Nor, finally, did Aristotle; we can only speculate about what effect this had on his appreciation of the importance of external goods in the achievement of happiness.[29] Both link ultimate felicity with an activity akin to divine activity, a cognitive attainment.[30] It is enough for present purposes to underscore that for both thinkers, the true self is the immortal and divine part of "ourselves," and correlative to this metaphysical claim, we may appreciate their choice of philosophical understanding as the human good. For Maimonides, this

---

[27] Cf. Maimonides (1963, 475).   [28] Maimonides (1963, 635).
[29] *NE* 10.7: 1177b30–1178a8; 10.8: 1178a23–28.
[30] *NE* 10.7-8, esp. 1178b28–32; Maimonides (1963, 635–636).

entails that prophecy is the highest good and the prophet – paradigmatically Moses – the human ideal. Divine providential care is a function of intellectual apprehension of the divine. As Maimonides puts it,

> Providence watches over everyone endowed with intellect proportionately to the measure of his intellect ... Providence always watches over an individual endowed with perfect apprehension, whose intellect never ceases from being occupied with God. On the other hand, an individual endowed with perfect apprehension, whose thought sometimes for a certain time is emptied of God, is watched over by providence only during the time when he thinks of God; providence withdraws from him during the time when he is occupied with something else ... and becomes in consequence of this a target for every evil that may happen to befall him. (Maimonides 1963, 624–625)

Indeed, with God's appearance to Job from the whirlwind, Job's education commences: "I had heard of Thee by the hearing of the ear; but now mine eye seeth Thee; wherefore I abhor myself and repent of dust and ashes" (*Job* 42:5–6). Maimonides understands this latter to mean not merely that Job is humbled by the divine presence, but also that he comes to abhor what he used to desire, material goods, now evaluated as no more than "dust and ashes." Job has begun to see that true human happiness does not depend on material possessions, nor are such possessions a sign, a proof, of divine favor. With this realization, he begins to distance himself from a focus on the material, natural world, a realm of contingency and vulnerability, in which "providence withdraws." In the end, Job will come to realize that even moral virtue, enmeshed as it is with a naïve (conventional) understanding of reward and punishment, cannot be the final good.[31]

In sum, both Aristotle and Maimonides have a keen sense of the precariousness of the human condition. But they draw instructively different conclusions. Aristotle takes the human condition to be ineliminably tragic, admitting of no exit from contingency and the possibility of tragic reversal. Maimonides does not draw this conclusion, because – as we see from Job's misfortunes – Job's suffering is his very own doing, a function of his ignorance, his (culpable) lack of wisdom. For Maimonides, we are more in control of our destiny than Aristotle imagined. For Maimonides,

---

[31] Cf. Spinoza, 2p49, scholium: "... our greatest happiness, or blessedness, consists [in this]: namely, in the knowledge of God alone, by which we are led to do only those things which love and morality advise. *From this we clearly understand how far they stray from the true valuation of virtue, who expect to be honored by God with the greatest rewards for their virtue and best actions, as if in return for the basest slavery*" (tr. Curley; my emphasis).

when we find ourselves *in extremis*, we do well to look inward to discover the source of our misfortune and woe.

So much, then, about Job and his trials. I believe Maimonides' discussion is quite relevant to the trials of the young impetuous R. Joseph, the addressee of the *Guide*. I have presented it in this context as a case study of how Maimonides teaches, via a 'theoretical' discussion about divine providence, the necessity of moral reform, if debilitating perplexity is ever to be overcome. As we recall, Maimonides is writing to address the root cause of R. Joseph's perplexity. In underscoring that Job's own trials are very much of his own making, due to a certain ignorance, perhaps even culpable ignorance, we may discern that, like Job, a certain presumption bedevils R. Joseph. Job is good, but not wise; likewise, R. Joseph, a man "perfect in the religious and moral sense," is caught in the grip of his own trials. Two moral paradigms suffer. Why? There is in both cases a characterological flaw. For Job, there is a misplaced presumption about what is of real value, and his (conventional) commitment to the value of material goods leaves him vulnerable when his fortunes change. For R. Joseph, his impetuous forays into metaphysics, difficult terrain that requires arduous preparation ("in an orderly manner"), lands him in perplexity. Both need to be put in their place, we might say. Both need to be instructed in such a way that the lesson learned addresses a flaw in character. So, Maimonides examples Job and his presumption to counter R. Joseph's "effervescence." In this case, a 'theoretical' discussion about divine providence and the salvific qualities of intellectual excellence embeds within it a cautionary tale about presumption, impetuosity, and youthful exuberance.

Let us begin to take stock. We are now in a better position to understand why, in elucidating the deep "philosophicality" of Scripture in response to a young person in the throes of a mental and spiritual crisis, Maimonides proceeds – and must proceed – in a measured and paced fashion. The very order in which the *Guide* proceeds (logic before physics before ethics and politics) is meant to educate one who, by virtue of studying in a haphazard way, has disabled himself. Embedded in this cursus studiorum is a moral, aretaic message. The young person, the addressee of the *Guide*, has attempted too much too soon, and Maimonides is clear that one must be prepared in the right way before the deep truths of Scripture can take hold. As noted, the perplexed person's perplexity arises from a certain intellectual arrogance and impetuosity. And so Maimonides is writing a tract on moral education as much as laying out a variety of philosophical positions. Or perhaps we can better put it this way: Maimonides embeds aretaic points within his philosophical positions.

A notable commentator on the *Guide* writes: "Maimonides' book is transformative and not simply expository, subsuming throughout a practical aim."[32] As I have argued, the *Guide* has as its goal the overcoming of perplexity and the rational grounding of a life constituted by religious norms. To bring this about Maimonides cannot simply give "answers" to questions, for the perplexity arises from a flaw in the character of an otherwise good person. R. Joseph's eager intellect, his impetuosity, has led him to an impasse. He and those like him have moved too quickly. In addressing and overcoming this, Maimonides embeds aretaic elements within his 'theoretical' discussions. In some detail we have noted this in the case of Maimonides' discussion of Job and his trials. Finally, very briefly now, let me just nod at one other example of Maimonides' way of proceeding. Maimonides' apophatic semantic theory, presented in his celebrated discussion of divine attributes and divine otherness in *Guide* 1.50–1.60, is highlighted, in part I would suggest, to counter R. Joseph's impetuosity, even arrogance, concerning the (unlimited) scope and powers of human knowledge, the very cause of his initial perplexity and estrangement from the tradition. In teaching, via the 'theoretical' discussion of divine attributes, that human knowledge is by necessity limited to divine actions, Maimonides hopes to address R. Joseph's presumptuousness, his naïve epistemic optimism.[33] And this latter desideratum is a practical point, requiring a change in R. Joseph's character. In sum, for Maimonides, the discussion of divine attributes entails a certain (epistemic) *humility* as its desired outcome. Much more needs to be said, and of course has been said, about Maimonides' celebrated discussion here, but I think that a full discussion of the subject requires a hint of how the doctrine of negative predication aligns with a felt need to address the material base of an intellectual conundrum.

Theory subserves practice at all stages in the *Guide*. It does so on account of the very nature of the initial worry, the root cause of the perplexity of the student, and those like him. There is no quick fix. Maimonides knows this and brilliantly 'reforms' as he teaches, addressing a character flaw via the theoretical discussions he presents, and even by the very order of his presentation of topics. I would not shy away from

---

[32] Kellner (1990, 64).
[33] Along these same lines, one may read Maimonides' critique of anthropocentrism and teleology in *Guide* 3.13 as motivated by a desire to curb the presumptuousness of R. Joseph and those like him, who imagine that "all the beings exist for the sake of the existence of man" (Maimonides 1963, 452). Readers of this volume may wish to consult Zev Harvey's Essay 11 on the subject. And, of course, the appendix to part I of Spinoza's *Ethics* comes quickly to mind on this general topic.

understanding Maimonides as like Socrates, who in the very elenchus, the testing and refutation of the interlocutor's stubbornly-held positions, attempts (unsuccessfully, I might add) to bring the interlocutor to an awareness that his character, his life is bankrupt. R. Joseph's life is not bankrupt, but he is, as Maimonides puts it, "continuously sick at heart and utterly bewildered in his mind."

CHAPTER 2

The Guide *as Biblical Commentary*

Igor H. De Souza

2.1 Introduction

Maimonides never wrote a commentary on the Hebrew Bible or on any part thereof. That literary choice is belied by the influential legacy of Maimonides' biblical hermeneutics as developed in the *Guide*.[1] For the *Guide* is a work that is declaredly about Scripture. This claim merits emphasis: The *Guide* is first and foremost an exegetical work. In the general introduction, Maimonides writes that the two primary purposes of the *Guide* are: first, to explain the meaning of certain terms that appear in the Bible; second, to explain the meaning of *meshalim*, or parables that appear in the Bible.[2] However, in terms of form, the expected approach for an exegetical work, in light of Maimonides' intellectual background, would have been to compose a commentary on all or part of the Bible. Jewish biblical commentary was a sophisticated art by Maimonides' time, originating as far back as Saadia Gaon's (882–942) commentary on the book of *Job*, which adapted the genre of formal commentary for Hebrew biblical texts. In such formal commentaries, which harken back to models of ancient Greek and medieval Arabic philosophical commentary, three features stand out. One, there is a clear division between text and commentary, between chunks of text (lemmata) and their interpretation, between author and commentator. Two, the commentator follows the order of the text as a structural principle for the commentary. Three, the commentary is the product of one interpreter and reflects an individual

---

[1] Diamond (2014).
[2] While the Pines translation of the *Guide* renders *mashal* (pl. *meshalim*) as "parable," the term acquires a technical meaning in the *Guide* and in subsequent biblical interpretation, and therefore I leave it untranslated here. In the *Guide*, *mashal* is a discrete biblical passage that has a surface meaning as well as a deeper meaning or *nimshal* (Pines: "internal meaning"). Maimonides gives both narrative allegories (Jacob's dream) and non-narrative symbolic passages (the harlot) as examples of *meshalim*. Maimonides (1963, introduction: 12–13).

reading.³ Often the commentator adds a preface of some sort, whose structure and themes were guided by a number of conventions.⁴ Saadia's commentary features all of these elements, including an extensive introduction. As far as Greek commentaries on the philosophical-scientific canon, it is a matter of some contention whether Maimonides was familiar with commentaries on Aristotle by Alexander of Aphrodisias.⁵ We do know that he was familiar with Galen's commentary on Hippocrates' aphorisms, in Arabic translation, since he himself authored a commentary on Galen's commentary.⁶

Maimonides employed the genre of commentary not only with respect to Galen but also for rabbinical literature, composing a commentary on the entire Mishnah, a founding work of the rabbinical legal canon. Why, then, did Maimonides innovate in the form of the *Guide*, producing a work whose exegetical discourse and form is entirely *sui generis*, and which thus fulfills some of the main tasks of biblical commentary without being one? Why did Maimonides reject the form of commentary to approach Scripture, and what is the significance of this literary choice?

In response to this question, it has been claimed that

> [Maimonides] deliberately departed from the models of scriptural exegesis within the tradition. Had he presented his philosophical interpretation of Scripture in the form of a commentary, one would naturally infer that Scripture is primary, Philosophy is secondary, the first the topic, the second simply an instrument to comprehend it. His decision, instead, to compose his exegesis in a self-contained treatise whose order and structure are independent of the Torah, and which is primarily meant for a much more select audience than the entire community of Israel to whom the Torah was ostensibly given, suggests a very different conception of exegesis and of the relation of revelation to philosophy.⁷

The question of the form of the *Guide*, then, is not of purely literary interest. It speaks to the question of what Maimonides counted as sources of knowledge, touching the core of the Maimonidean project in the *Guide* of elucidating the relationship between revealed texts and speculative, scientific knowledge.

In this essay, I will focus instead on aspects of Maimonides' "very different conception of exegesis." I examine the *Guide* here within the

---

³ On the theory of commentary, see Krauss and Gibson (2002), Assmann and Gladigow (1995), and Most (1999).
⁴ On prefaces, see Mansfeld (1994).
⁵ See Pines (1963, lxiv, lxi), and contrast with Davidson (2018, 8–9).
⁶ Edited by Schliwski (2004).   ⁷ Stern (1997, 215).

framework of the genre of commentary, the exegetical genre that Maimonides self-consciously rejects. Despite his rejection, my method in this essay is to analyze the *Guide* as if it were a commentary. I will draw from studies on various commentary traditions – philosophical, classical, and religious – to generate a fresh set of questions on the relationship between the *Guide* and Hebrew Scripture, diagnosing the ways in which the *Guide* does function as a traditional commentary, and the ways in which it departs from that genre. Rather than analyzing the Maimonidean interpretation of specific passages, I focus on questions of form, methodology, and rhetoric.[8]

2.2 What and Who Are Commentaries for?

Recent scholarship has emphasized the ways in which commentary is not merely a literary genre, but also a broader cultural phenomenon. The aims of commentaries, who writes them and for what purposes, and who reads them, are issues that go beyond textual interpretation, spilling over into questions of sociology of knowledge, canonicity, the transmission of texts and ideas, pedagogical practices, and the formation of intellectual communities.[9] Within the realm of literary criticism, scholars have pointed to the ways in which commentaries constitute texts in their own right, apart from the text on which they comment; for instance, commentaries can be understood as narratives of their own, and the commentator becomes an author.[10] As a genre, commentaries are informed by earlier models and conventions, such that it becomes possible to construct formal histories and theories of commentary as their own texts, apart from the texts on which they comment. This view of commentary sees it not as a mental act, but rather as a social practice.[11]

The concept of commentary as a cultural phenomenon involves a specific set of questions. First, there are conceptual questions: What are commentaries for – what is their purpose? Who writes them, and how do those interpreters authorize themselves as sources of legitimate interpretation? Who reads commentaries, and in what contexts? Why are commentaries typically written on some kinds of texts and not others? What is the relationship between a commentary and the text on which it comments?

---

[8] Among modern scholars, Leo Strauss is the founding figure of a literary approach to the *Guide*. See Strauss (1952; 1963).
[9] For a synthesis of these questions, see Hughes (2003).   [10] See Asper (2013).
[11] See Bruns (1982).

What is the relationship between a commentary and the community in which it originates? I categorize such questions as pertaining to the paraformal or *conceptual* features of the genre of commentary. The questions can be asked of any commentary, but the answers will be particular, that is, context-specific. In contrast, the *formal* features of commentary transcend specific contexts. I point to three such features: a separation between text and commentary (thus excluding, for example texts such as translations, paraphrases, abridgments); the commentator follows the order of the text as the structure for the commentary (thus excluding, for example, a topical treatise); the commentary is the product of an individual reading, even if the author's identity is not known. There is often a preface or opening statement of some sort, giving the reader details about the text to be commented on and about the commentary to follow.

While I will not address all of the foregoing questions, this essay will consider the *Guide* as a commentary, interrogating both its conceptual and formal features. In what ways does it function as such a commentary, and in what ways does it not? What are the conceptual features of the *Guide* as a commentary, and what are its formal features?

It must be emphasized that an examination of commentary as phenomenon does not include an assessment of whether a given commentary is right or wrong, good or bad. The fact that a commentator baldly "misinterprets" a given passage is significant in itself: why is this comment considered a misinterpretation? What makes for a "correct" interpretation? Is that the same as a *valid* interpretation? From the perspective I propose, all interpretations constitute valid topics of inquiry. To illustrate my method, I shall cite one example. Maimonides finds that Scripture contains certain truths that coincide with philosophical (speculative) truths. It is not relevant to the present inquiry whether Scripture in fact contains such truths. Rather, for this instance, the question that detains us is: what reasons led Maimonides to make that exegetical determination?

2.3 The *Guide* as a Conceptual Commentary

The ground conceptual question of commentary relates to its purpose. What is it for? Ancient and medieval commentators, as well as modern scholars, tend to point to explanation or clarification: among the primary functions of commentary is the explanation of some text. The utility of the commentary, then, is contingent on the view that a given text is unclear and stands in need of interpretation. The explanatory function of commentary assumes that clarity is a desirable trait for a text, if not also a moral virtue.[12]

These statements raise four central questions about the exegesis of the *Guide*. First, does the *Guide* assume that Scripture is unclear, and that it requires explanation (by Maimonides)? Second, is biblical unclarity, if it exists, accidental or purposeful? As an exegete, Maimonides assumes that biblical unclarity is purposeful. Why? Third, can the explanation of what is unclear in the Bible be disclosed in the commentary (the *Guide*)? Why or why not? If yes, how? The final, fourth question is: for whom is the biblical text unclear – all readers, or just some? Who needs the exegesis of the *Guide*?

Maimonides states in the preface to the *Guide* that biblical terms and *meshalim* – and these are the only two biblical elements that Maimonides proposes to clarify – are unclear not in themselves, but in relation to certain readers. Uneducated readers misread them in a particular way, imagining that they are monosemic discourses (with one exclusive meaning). Educated and perplexed readers misread them in another way, imagining they are polysemic discourses (with multiple meanings), but unable to determine which meaning is fundamental, and which is ancillary. I shall return to these categories of readers. What should detain us at this point is that Maimonides does not offer an exemplar of any individual among his contemporaries who reads the biblical text correctly, except for himself. This is significant because it indicates Maimonides' sense of exegetical independence vis-à-vis other commentators, and serves to set him apart from the history of Jewish exegesis. It is also significant because it indicates that the biblical text is not intrinsically unclear – it is only unclear to those who cannot read it properly. This rhetorical move allows Maimonides to assert not only independence but also authority. He alone – the *Guide* alone – is the key with which to unlock the secrets of Scripture. No other authorities need be consulted. The *Guide* is sufficient, and it is self-sufficient. It does not offer one reading of Scripture among many valid readings; it offers the *only* valid reading.

Maimonides tempers this bold attitude by stating that the biblical terms and *meshalim* he intends to interpret are "secrets," and their full extent is not known to anyone, not even to himself.[13] He writes a *mashal* to illustrate how little is known of these matters, comparing the acquisition

---

[12] Barnes (1992, 270).
[13] Maimonides (1963, introduction: 7). "Secrets" is a technical term in Maimonides' exegesis, indicating a passage that is deliberately obscure.

of this knowledge to the apprehension of intermittent flashes of light.[14] Nonetheless, the fact remains that Maimonides acknowledges no other valid interpretations of Scripture from the time of the rabbis up to his own day. His examples of authoritative exegetical "sages" all belong to the biblical or rabbinical periods. None of his interpretations, according to Maimonides, "have been set down in any book," at least not in any book originating in the Jewish diaspora.[15]

Maimonides' project for the *Guide* as a whole is directly related to the unclarity of the biblical text as it is, and it assumes that previous explanations of that text have fallen short of the mark. Maimonides' attitude, furthermore, illustrates the ways in which commentary can be simultaneously conservative as well as radical. The *Guide* is conservative in the choice of text to be commented on; the genre of Jewish commentary on the Bible, by Maimonides' period, is nothing new. But Maimonides' independence vis-à-vis that history, and his surreptitious indictment of it as inadequate, demonstrates how a commentary on a canonical and familiar text can also be a site of radical re-thinking and reformation of tradition.[16]

Is the unclarity of the Bible accidental or purposeful? The answer to this question constitutes a second significant piece in the investigation of the *Guide* as a commentary. While accidental obscurity speaks to a deficiency with the text, intentional obscurity grants power to the text. It implies that the text contains riches not yet sufficiently mined or even discovered. A notion of intentional obscurity of this sort, within the context of commentary, has a long history among ancient philosophical commentators on Aristotle. Some among them tended to answer the question "why is Aristotle obscure?" by referring to the need to keep certain truths away from public consumption, and to "exercise the wits" of experts.[17] Intentional textual obscurity is a veil akin, though not identical, to Plato's use of riddles and allegories; it can function to preserve secrets out of reach of those who cannot pierce the obscurity or the deeper meaning of an allegory, while still communicating something.

---

[14] Ibid. (introduction: 7–8).

[15] Ibid. (introduction: 16). These statements raise the question of how Maimonides received his own exegetical knowledge – did he imagine his system was entirely original? Is he conscious of relying on unacknowledged sources and precedents? In his interpretation of the book of *Job*, for instance, Maimonides reports that "these notions came to me in something similar to prophetic revelation." See Maimonides (1963, 3.22: 488), and Heschel (1996).

[16] Hughes (2003, 165).   [17] Barnes (1992, 269); Mansfeld (1994, 26).

In the *Guide*, Maimonides reads Scripture as an intentionally obscure text. Deep truths are encoded within obscure language (for example, in "chapter headings") as well as within "parable and riddle" (*mashal ve-chidah*). The "divine purpose" that Maimonides claims for the *Guide* is an indication to his view of Scripture: both Scripture and its commentary, the *Guide*, conceal "from the vulgar among the people those truths especially requisite for [divine] apprehension."[18] Scripture may be a public text, but it is not a democratic text. It purposefully transmits significant, even vital, truths that only a few individuals might be equipped to identify and comprehend. Some of Maimonides' work as an exegete lies in the explanation of the surface meaning of the text, which has been called the "exoteric" layer in Maimonidean scholarship. This is one of the ways in which the utility of the *Guide* as a commentary becomes prominent. Although the *Guide* is written neither for beginners, nor for the masses, nor for legal experts, Maimonides promises in the preface to the *Guide* that even beginners will derive some benefit from the *Guide*'s explanation of the Bible.[19] But the core of the *Guide* is the explanation of biblical secrets, whose interpretation is connected to the way in which they are phrased (obscurity) or the literary form in which they are presented (as parables and riddles). The content and implications of exegetical secrets have been called the "esoteric" layer of the text in Maimonidean scholarship, and they demand close analysis.[20] The core of Scripture, corresponding to the "gold" of the "apples of gold in settings of silver," is per se not visible unless examined closely and carefully, and with the correct tools.[21]

We can now approach the third question posed earlier. Maimonides considers unclarity to be such a significant component of the biblical text that it can (and should) never be completely eliminated.[22] But fundamental obscurity poses a problem for the explanatory function of commentary. As Barnes remarks, "If Aristotle was right to conceal his thought behind a cloud of ink, how may a commentator step in to dispel the darkness?"[23] For Maimonides, if the author of Scripture is purposefully obscure, by

---

[18] Maimonides (1963, introduction: 7). [19] Ibid. (introduction: 16).
[20] See Klein-Braslavy (2006b).
[21] Maimonides interprets Proverbs 25:11 as the paradigm for the exoteric–esoteric distinction. He offers an alternative paradigm where the exoteric layer has very little value (the price of a cheap candle), in contrast to Proverbs 25:11, where the exoteric layer has a political value and is said to be as "useful as silver." Maimonides (1963, introduction: 11–12).
[22] See Ibid. (introduction: 9). [23] Barnes (1992, 271–272).

what rights should he, the commentator, eliminate that obscurity? Obscurity is part of the "divine purpose."[24]

Maimonides therefore aims to explain Scripture in the *Guide* by reproducing the discourse of Scripture – a discourse that is intentionally obscure, yet also precise in its obscurity. As he writes, the "diction of this Treatise has not been chosen at haphazard, but with great exactness and exceeding precision, and with care to avoid failing to explain any obscure point. And nothing has been mentioned out of place, save with a view to explaining some matter in its proper place."[25] Just as the obscurity of seemingly arbitrary details can be significant in the biblical text, such details in the *Guide* can also be significant. The purported precision of the obscure biblical text and of biblical parables becomes its own method of interpretation. In other words, an esoteric text requires an esoteric explanation.[26]

The unclarity of the biblical text, its secrets and its parables, must not be disclosed to all – to do so is to oppose what Maimonides calls the "divine purpose" mentioned earlier. Disclosing the totality of interpretations in plain language, Maimonides declares, would be "unsuitable for the vulgar among the people."[27] Some commentators on the *Guide* remark that such a task would be, in effect, impossible. An interpreter *must* make use of parables (*meshalim*) to transmit certain notions.[28] But some measure of disclosure is necessary to alleviate the perplexity brought on by erroneous readings of Scripture – a perplexity that does not afflict the majority of readers, but only a few. For such perplexed readers, Maimonides claims that the *Guide* will clarify Scripture not by explanation, but by indication. "Once you know [a given story] is a *mashal*, it will immediately become clearer to you what it is a *mashal* of. My remarking that it is a *mashal* will be like someone's removing a screen from between the eye and a visible thing."[29] The unclarity of the biblical text is preserved, then, through a process of wrestling with its literary form. The individual reader becomes aware, through the *Guide*, that the story of Jacob's ladder, for example, is a *mashal*. Maimonides need not (and must not) explain the meaning of that *mashal*; the utility of the Maimonidean method is in making the reader conscious of the form and of its significance. Against this background, it is not surprising that Maimonides forbids his readers, in the strongest terms,

---

[24] Maimonides (1963, introduction: 7). [25] Ibid. (introduction: 15). [26] Strauss (1952, 56).
[27] Maimonides (1963, introduction: 9); see also Maimonides (1963, 1.34: 72–79).
[28] The necessity of *meshalim* is clear from Maimonides' comparison of *meshalim* to a candle without which a lost pearl cannot be found; Maimonides (1963, introduction: 11).
[29] Ibid. (introduction: 14).

The Guide *as Biblical Commentary*

from writing any commentaries on the *Guide*, and from sharing with others any individual insights about Scripture gained from the *Guide*. Doing so would threaten not only the obscurity of the biblical text, but also that of the *Guide*.[30]

For whom is the biblical text unclear? Who needs the exegesis of the *Guide*? The foregoing remarks may lead the reader to conclude that the *Guide* has little utility for uneducated readers of Scripture. Generally, commentaries aim to expand, not restrict, the audience for the texts on which they comment. This aim is connected to the aspect of explanation: an explanation is something that opens up the text to *more* readers, not fewer. I have mentioned that Maimonides promises, in the preface, that some of the *Guide* will benefit even beginning students; and it is also the case that the *Guide* contains a number of exoteric explanations of biblical terms, which are useful to all readers. The final paragraphs in this section expand upon these points.

Despite the fact that the *Guide* is meant for a particular type of reader, there is a way in which the *Guide* is useful for the masses, and which broadens the audience for both the text (Bible) and the commentary (*Guide*). Maimonides exempts biblical anthropomorphic discourse from his prevailing view of Scripture as an obscure and parabolic text, arguing that unlike biblical *meshalim*, biblical anthropomorphic descriptions of God ought rather to be understood by all Jews (and not merely all readers of Scripture) in a definite, precise manner – that is, non-anthropomorphically. Maimonides elevates his reading of biblical anthropomorphisms, expatiated at length in the *Guide*, to the same status of belief as the doctrines of divine unity and that one should not worship other gods, that is, as foundational to Judaism itself. Maimonides' reading of biblical anthropomorphisms is that they should never be constructed to intimate that God is corporeal in any way (physically or emotionally). This reading of biblical anthropomorphism should be inculcated to all believers, including children, in the same manner that they are inculcated to believe that God is one.[31] The Maimonidean reading of anthropomorphisms points to a central feature of the biblical text as "unclear." It creates a problem where, for at least some readers, there may not be one. This strategy aptly illustrates the ways in which commentaries do not passively identify unclarities present in the text, but actively produce and problematize them.

---

[30] Ibid. (introduction: 15).   [31] Maimonides (1963, 1.35: 79–80).

Therefore, while the notion of divine incorporeality may seem obvious or superfluous to modern readers in general, Maimonides' reading of biblical anthropomorphisms is quite radical. It is radical, first, in light of the texts he comments on; and second, in light of contemporaneous intellectual developments in Islam.[32] With respect to the former, Scripture is liberal in describing God in human terms; there is nothing in Hebrew Scripture that indicates divine incorporeality. For the vast majority of Jewish readers of Scripture in Maimonides' time, there is no unclarity or problem in biblical anthropomorphisms. Not only might they be familiar with biblical anthropomorphism, they might also be familiar with rabbinical descriptions of God, which are heavily anthropomorphized – like the Bible, the rabbis of the Talmud do not declare God to be incorporeal.[33] Maimonides' uneducated readers would also be familiar with the language of Jewish prayer, which borrows from biblical and rabbinical anthropomorphism. With respect to developments in Islam that are contemporaneous with the *Guide*, the radicalness of Maimonides' position comes into sharp focus if his views are contrasted with those of his contemporary Ibn Rushd (Averroes, 1126–1198).

While Ibn Rushd agrees with Maimonides that Scripture (in Ibn Rushd's case, the Qur'an) uses purposefully anthropomorphic terms, the two thinkers depart on the question of their interpretation. For Ibn Rushd, the religious beliefs of the masses reflect the literal meaning of such anthropomorphisms, which is indeed incoherent from a philosophical point of view. But the interpreter must not disclose the true meaning of anthropomorphic expressions to the public at large. It is not the place of the interpreter to disturb the erroneous but widespread interpretation of Scriptural language. To do so would deprive the masses of the grounds of their religious beliefs without offering them something to replace it. Furthermore, to disturb the religious beliefs of the masses might lead to adverse political and social consequences.[34]

For Maimonides, on the other hand, the Jewish community as a whole must be taught that God is incorporeal, ideally through proper methods of exegesis, but also through "tradition" and "simple authority." Maimonides raises his notion of divine incorporeality to the status of religious dogma as

---

[32] For philosophical views of biblical anthropomorphism, see Hamori (2008, 35–64).
[33] The Aramaic translation of the Bible, the *Targum Onqelos*, consistently interprets anthropomorphisms as non-physical. Maimonides relies on that work throughout the *Guide*. See Even-Chen (2018) and Weiss (2000).
[34] See Ibn Rushd (2001). For a comparison between Ibn Rushd and Maimonides regarding exegesis, see Fraenkel (2008).

a result of, or as a reflection of, his interpretation of Scripture. What sets him apart from predecessors and contemporaries is not merely the notion that God is incorporeal and that biblical anthropomorphisms ought to be understood as metaphors (which we find already in Saadia Gaon). Rather, the *Guide* innovates in offering an interpretation of anthropomorphic expressions that invalidates *all* other readings, and this interpretation must be widely disseminated as a matter of religious belief, even for those who cannot read (children, for example). Some of the most poignant passages in the *Guide*, where Maimonides confesses difficulty or uncertainty in intimate and personal language, relate to his effort to reread practically all of biblical and rabbinical literature through the lens of divine incorporeality.[35]

Maimonides' stance toward divine anthropomorphism is a feature of the *Guide* that parallels the ways in which commentary aims at utility for the greatest possible number of readers, broadening the audience for both the text and the commentary. A reader of the *Guide*, whether medieval or modern, would presumably not stop with Maimonides' explanations of target anthropomorphic terms, which take up much space in part 1 of the *Guide*. She would seek to re-read all other anthropomorphisms within the Jewish religious canon according to Maimonides' method. Such a hypothetical reader need not necessarily be well-educated in order to engage in this process of rereading. All that needs to be considered is whether God is being described through a human attribute, physical or psychological, followed by a reinterpretation of the text where the human attribute is then explained by recourse to an incorporeal notion.[36] Thus, setting aside the question of esoteric interpretation of the Bible in the *Guide*, which is meant for Maimonides' ideal readers – the perplexed – much of the *Guide* is also meant to guide readers in exoteric interpretation. This double guidance reflects the statement in the preface: "I know that, among men generally, every beginner will derive benefit from some chapters of this Treatise, though he lacks even an inkling of what is involved in speculation. A perfect man, on the other hand, devoted to Law and, as I have mentioned, perplexed, will benefit from all its chapters."[37] In this way, the *Guide* functions as a commentary in expanding the circle of readers of Scripture. Scripture is not meant only for the masses (as Al-Farabi would

---

[35] See, for example, Maimonides (1963, 1.59: 139–140), where Maimonides expresses discomfort with the language of rabbinical anthropomorphic prayer, but acknowledges its necessity.
[36] For example, incorporeal beings can act; hence divine attributes that reflect human emotional traits can be reread as attributes of action. See Maimonides (1963, 1.55: 118–119).
[37] Ibid., (introduction: 16).

have it) or only for scholars, but rather for both. While the deeper implications of some Scriptural passages are not fit for public discussion, every reader, whether educated or not, can learn to reread Scriptural anthropomorphisms. This broader application of the *Guide* reflects a different orientation from Maimonides' statements that the book was written for a specific kind of individual, the perplexed, a "virtuous man" in the midst of "ten thousand ignoramuses."[38] Maimonides' approach to Scripture and its readers in the *Guide*, then, reveals itself to be somewhat more democratic than it seemed at first sight.

In sum, the foregoing analysis of the *Guide* as a commentary reveals the ways in which Maimonides confirms the authority of Scripture while concurrently problematizing the text. It shows how Maimonides establishes his reading as the only valid reading (in the case of anthropomorphisms), even in the face of contradicting evidence, such as rabbinical texts and rabbinically-instituted prayer. Furthermore, this analysis brings to light the explanatory, utilitarian dimension of the *Guide*, and the ways in which, like a commentary, it seeks to broaden the audience for the text being commented on. To paraphrase the words of a fourteenth-century commentator, the *Guide* drives home the point that the biblical text retains its validity for both scholars and non-scholars.[39]

2.4 The *Guide* as a Formal Commentary

It is clear from the structure of the *Guide* that it is not a formal commentary on Scripture. While it aims to explain Scripture, as well as rabbinical literature to some degree, the sequence of topics and quotations in the *Guide* does not follow the order in which they appear in the Bible. However, the *Guide* does contain some formal elements of the genre of commentary: there is a more or less clear division between text and commentary; it is the product of a single interpreter, reflecting an individual reading; and there is a preface where the commentator explains the text to be commented on as well as the nature of the commentary to follow.[40]

A commentary's structural dependence on the text in question is one of the commentary genre's defining features. The fact that the *Guide* does not follow the Scriptural order of exposition is a self-conscious choice on

---

[38] Ibid.
[39] Moses of Narbonne (1300–1362). See his commentary on the *Guide* in De Souza (2018, 262).
[40] On the aims of prefaces, see further in Hadot (1987).

Maimonides' part. Maimonides explains that choice in the following terms: "You should not ask of me here anything beyond the chapter headings. And even those are not set down in order or arranged in coherent fashion in this Treatise, but rather are scattered and entangled with other subjects that are to be clarified. For my purpose is that truths be glimpsed and then again be concealed."[41] Following the order of the text would provide a "coherent fashion," as well as a familiar framework in which to arrange chapter headings. Within the *Guide* as a whole, Maimonides explains a large number of biblical terms, verses, and passages, some more than once. It is thus possible to rewrite much of the *Guide* as a formal commentary, indexed by its quotations of biblical passages.[42]

Maimonides' choice to consciously depart from the form of commentary is significant in revealing how he viewed Scripture, his own role as an exegete, and how he intended the reader to approach the *Guide*. Following the order of the text enhances a commentary's ease of use. The user of a commentary quickly finds the answer for a question or difficulty regarding a biblical passage because the arrangement is clear. The user does not need to be familiar with the commentary as a whole for the commentary to be useful, even – and especially so – for a beginner. The reader can enter the commentary at any point, and that is how commentaries are generally used in pedagogical settings; they are not works that a reader follows from beginning to end in a continuous process, as one would approach a poem, treatise, or monograph. A difficulty within Proverbs 25:11, for example, does not per se require consulting the commentary on Proverbs 25:10 or Proverbs 25:12.

Contrast this approach with the *Guide*, where Maimonides makes it difficult to simply look up the clarification to any particular textual difficulty in Scripture. Topics are scattered in no obvious order. By design, Maimonides brings up a number of subjects whose connection to the main topic of a given chapter is obscure and raises even more questions. He refuses to give complete explanations of biblical verses, promising the reader only the "chapter headings."[43] His view of the exegete's role is not necessarily as one who clarifies the text. Even though beginners may derive benefit from the *Guide*, Maimonides intends the text not to be for beginners, but for a particular kind of reader, as we have seen, one virtuous

---

[41] Maimonides (1963, introduction: 6–7).
[42] For an attempt to rewrite the *Guide* in this manner, see Samuel (2016).
[43] Maimonides (1963, introduction: 6); see also Maimonides (1963, 1.35: 80–81).

individual amongst ten thousand "ignoramuses." Finally, he plans to write with deliberate obscurity, but not so obscurely as to be completely impenetrable; truths are glimpsed but then concealed.

Thus, the fact that the *Guide* is organized differently from a commentary, even though it shares some of the conceptual goals of a commentary, is deeply significant. The structure of the commentary as something that follows the order of the text makes it immediately useful to readers and students as a pedagogical aid. Not only does the form of commentary clarify difficulties, it also makes it relatively easy to find the answers for those difficulties. By contrast, Maimonides' purpose in structuring the *Guide* the way he did was to make it more *difficult* to find specific answers.

Why should Maimonides make it more difficult to locate an answer to a specific biblical conundrum? Exegesis in the *Guide* is not a pedagogical exercise. It is a process involving the soul. As a fragmented and decentralized discourse, a commentary is useful for precise textual difficulties, but less so for structural arguments. However, the point of the *Guide* is not merely to inform the mind – it is to transform it. Broadly speaking, the *Guide* reevaluates what it means to do exegesis.

What Maimonides proposes in the *Guide* is a continuous process of rereading Scripture that can be best analogized to a road or a path. Reading the *Guide* is a transformative process rather than a learning one. At the end of the *Guide*, the reader is no longer the same person he was at the beginning. By communicating the principles of biblical interpretation in the book's general preface and employing those principles throughout the text along with meaningful examples, the *Guide* not only imparts principles and interpretations, but also trains the reader into a consistent method of reading Scripture. The method is the key for shifting the reader's mind from "perplexed" to one that "becomes perfect" and "finds rest."[44] The method consists of Maimonides providing incomplete explanations, mere "chapter headings," hints, and allusions. "In some matters it will suffice you to gather from my remarks that a given story is a parable [*mashal*], even if we explain nothing more; for once you know it is a parable, it will immediately become clear to you what it is a parable of. My remarking that it is a parable will be like someone's removing a screen from between the eye and a visible thing."[45] It is up to the reader to work out the meaning of the *mashal*; the task of the *Guide* is limited to pointing out that

---

[44] Maimonides (1963, introduction: 17). On Maimonides' view of perfection (*shelemut*), see Maimonides (1963, 3.54: 634–638).
[45] Maimonides (1963, introduction: 14).

something is a *mashal*. Maimonides might remove a screen; it is up to the reader to investigate the object that she sees. The *Guide* conceives of itself as a facilitator, "guidance" rather than a "guide."[46] At the end of the *Guide*, the emphasis is not on intellect, as it is at the outset (1.1), but on wisdom and perfection, and on the "way of life" of the individual who has acquired both.[47]

It has now become clear why Maimonides did not write the exegetical *Guide* to follow the order of the biblical text: the sort of exegetical work the *Guide* aims to accomplish cannot be done by a commentary. Furthermore, while the *Guide* is useful as a commentary in some ways (broadening the text's audience), it is less so in others. It cannot be used as a pedagogical tool to accompany the study of a text. Even though the *Guide* is markedly exegetical, it demands attention to itself in a way that would be difficult to attain were it to follow the order of the biblical text.

I turn now to the ways in which the *Guide* functions as a formal commentary. First, the *Guide* generally indicates to readers the distinction between the texts being commented on (chiefly passages from Scripture and rabbinical literature) and the commentary itself. Second, it reflects Maimonides' individual reading of those texts, rather than the product of a school, group, or editor. Third, the *Guide* contains a rich set of introductions that detail the commentator's perspective on the texts in question, and the purposes of the commentary. They are the general introduction to the book, and the prefaces to each of the three parts. Other opening matter in the *Guide* is also significant. The "Epistle Dedicatory" to the addressee of the *Guide* (Joseph ben Judah, a historical figure), the poem and incipit that precede it, and the poem between the Epistle and the general introduction are not mere literary exercises; they also express exegetical concerns.

The *Guide* signals the distinction between the text being commented on and the commentary itself through the use of the original languages of the texts. While the text of the *Guide* is in Judeo-Arabic (Arabic in Hebrew characters), Maimonides' quotations of Scripture and rabbinical literature always appear in their original languages, Hebrew and Aramaic. Maimonides also quotes extensively from the Aramaic translation of the Hebrew Bible by Onqelos. The effect of quotations in Hebrew and

---

[46] The literal translation of the Judeo-Arabic title and of Ibn Tibbon's Hebrew title is "guidance," conveying the sense of continuous development, rather than a "guide" that is set aside once it becomes obsolete.
[47] Maimonides (1963, 3.54: 638).

Aramaic is that Scripture is in certain ways primary, and its explanation is secondary.[48] This is not merely a linguistic quibble. For what the *Guide* interprets is not the abstract meaning of Hebrew terms, but rather the meaning of terms as they appear in Scripture. In the exegesis of the *Guide*, the grammatical form of a Scriptural Hebrew term is meaningful in itself, along with elements such as other occurrences of the term in Scripture, its Aramaic translation by Onqelos, or occurrences of the term in rabbinical literature. Therefore, a translated term is inadequate for proper Maimonidean interpretation. It is impossible to grasp the full spectrum of Maimonides' exegesis, and even the *Guide* as a whole, without recourse to the Hebrew text of the Bible.[49]

The fact that the Hebrew-Aramaic/Judeo-Arabic distinction is never elided in the text illustrates the extent to which the *Guide* functions as a formal commentary. It is neither a paraphrase nor a translation nor an independent treatise. It is contingent on the text of the Bible, in broad terms, and on the Hebrew text of the Bible, in narrow terms. It is a curious choice to write such an exegetical work in Judeo-Arabic at all, when Hebrew would have been perhaps a more suitable alternative – if only to prevent the reader from having to switch between two different languages. Nonetheless, the choice to maintain both the Hebrew and Judeo-Arabic registers within the text of the *Guide* renders visible the boundaries between text and commentary.

Second, the *Guide* is a formal commentary to the extent that it reflects an individualized reading of the text. The author is front and center, everywhere visible. He frequently traces the interpretation back to himself by employing the first person singular and plural, and his individuality is also emphasized by the use of the imperative to the reader ("Know this"; "Understand this").[50] He confesses, in the preface to part 3, that the knowledge he possesses will die with him unless he communicates it, attesting to his view of its singularity.[51] Maimonides saw himself as an independent thinker and designed the *Guide* as a self-consciously original

---

[48] Thus, even though the *Guide* is not a formal commentary, from a linguistic point of view it does depict scripture as "primary" and philosophy as "secondary." The Hebrew words being commented "enjoy their own intrinsic importance" – an aspect of commentary that Smith (1991, 3) calls the "hagiographic dimension of the commentary literature." On the other hand, Maimonides' Judeo-Arabic explanation derives its importance solely from his own authority.
[49] The English translation by Pines addresses this issue by translating Hebrew quotations in italics.
[50] Occurs frequently; cf. Maimonides (1963, 1.17: 43; 1.18: 45).
[51] Ibid. (introduction to part 3: 415–416).

reading of Scripture. He claimed to be entirely self-taught, and to have received neither divine revelation nor knowledge from a teacher.[52]

Formal commentaries tend to reflect an individualized view of the text. A useful contrast to the *Guide* in this instance is the Talmud. The Talmud can be described as exegetical in part, to the extent that it interprets Scripture and the Mishnah. However, it can be argued that the Talmud is not a commentary. It reflects a multitude of readings, some accepted and some discarded, all preserved, lacking an individual point of view. It can be better described as the product of a school as a whole (or more accurately, the Babylonian and Jerusalem schools).[53]

The Talmud likewise lacks a preface, introduction, or any other type of opening statement. A third feature of formal commentaries is that they tend to include an address from the commentator to the reader. In that address the commentator may enumerate several features of the text to be commented on, the reasons that led him to compose the commentary, as well as the principal features of the commentary – purposes, utility, intended audience, and so on. In classical and medieval philosophical literature, we find a number of models for commentary prefaces; their forms and topics become increasingly standardized from Antiquity to the Middle Ages. The significance of a preface is multifold. It lays out the individuality of the commentator's reading, which is closely tied to the utility of the commentary – if a commentary has nothing new to say, it is not useful (although it may be judged useful for certain purposes but not for others).[54] Furthermore, the preface is a text of literary criticism. It lays out in theoretical terms an author's view of some text, and the most suitable methodologies with which to interpret that text. Finally, it is intertextual, expressing the commentator's view of his own text alongside their view of another text, and how they conceive of the relationship between the two. This last aspect sets the preface to a commentary apart from prefaces to non-commentary works, where the author may have much to say about their own text but nothing about another text.[55]

All of these features can be found in the general preface to the *Guide*, which immediately precedes the preface to part 1. Subsequent parts of the *Guide* have their own prefaces as well. The significance of the prefaces of

---

[52] Ibid. (introduction to part 3: 416).
[53] See further reasons why the Talmud is not a commentary in Assmann and Gladigow (1995, 29–30).
[54] "Utility" was a standard item in prefaces of Neoplatonic commentaries on Aristotle. Mansfeld (1994, 10, 11).
[55] Minnis (1984, 1) points to prologues as "valuable repositories of medieval theory of authorship," containing "a conceptual equipment that is at once historically valid and theoretically adequate."

the *Guide* is that they fulfill all the functions associated with commentary prefaces. In the prefaces, and in particular within the general preface to the *Guide*, Maimonides expounds upon the originality of his interpretation of Scripture as well as the necessity of setting it down in writing. He makes clear why the *Guide* is needed, and details the negative consequences of not writing it. The origin of the *Guide* is defined as a response to a historical relationship – between Maimonides and his former student Joseph ben Judah, which is described in the Epistle Dedicatory – and in its broader appeal to all perplexed readers of Scripture. The general preface describes, furthermore, Maimonides' view of how the Bible should be read, as well as the significance of the Bible within the Jewish religious-literary canon. The preface to the *Guide* is a distillation of the principles of Maimonidean hermeneutics and the relationship between the *Guide* and Scripture.

The introduction to the *Guide* – the general preface, along with the preface to part 1 – is a rich text whose main ideas were absorbed by generations of Maimonidean-inflected biblical commentators.[56] By providing the theoretical basis for the exegesis of the *Guide*, Maimonides provided a detailed manual for Maimonidean biblical interpretation that would be applied to a number of books of the Bible.[57] In the introduction we see, once again, the significance of Maimonides' aim in the *Guide* of transmitting a certain method, one that transforms readers, rather than a method that gives them definitive answers.

For example, in the famous passage in the introduction where Maimonides enumerates the "causes" of contradictions that appear "in any book or compilation" (that is, including sacred texts), he highlights that Scripture contains the third and fourth causes – which are not factual contradictions.[58] When it comes to the seventh cause of contradiction, however, the tone changes. The seventh cause of contradiction, which concerns "very obscure matters," indicates a real contradiction, one that cannot be explained away, and the interpreter must not disclose to general readers that the contradiction even exists in the first place (Maimonides does not explain why). Striking a circumspect key, Maimonides claims that "whether contradictions due to the seventh cause are to be found in the books of the prophets is a matter for speculative study and investigation.

---

[56] See De Souza (2018).
[57] The philosophical school associated with Samuel ibn Tibbon, the authoritative translator of the *Guide* into Hebrew, produced a series of Maimonidean biblical commentaries. See Ravitzky (1977, 22, 29).
[58] See the description of the causes in Maimonides (1963, introduction: 17).

Statements about this should not be a matter of conjecture."[59] These words seem to indicate to readers of the *Guide* that Scripture might contain factual contradictions, implying that Scripture might "lie," in at least some cases.[60] However, this conclusion is contingent on a positive identification of the seventh cause in Scripture. How would we identify it? By turning to the text of the *Guide*. "Divergences that are to be found in this Treatise [the *Guide*] are due to the fifth cause and the seventh."[61] Attentive readers of the *Guide* who can distinguish between the fifth and seventh causes in the text will then be able to transfer their identification skills to Scriptural interpretation, and judge for themselves whether Scripture contains examples of the seventh cause.[62]

2.5 Conclusion

The *Guide* is manifestly not a commentary. Nonetheless, this essay argues that if we approach the *Guide* through the questions inherent in the genre of commentary, we can generate vital insights. The essay considers two different dimensions of commentary – conceptual and formal. An analysis of those dimensions in relation to the *Guide* illuminates the extent to which they can be useful tools to excavate a well-trodden text. Moreover, considering the *Guide* as a commentary brings to the fore its exegetical nature. While the *Guide* has much to say about theology, psychology, and metaphysics, Maimonides' foray into every topic is anchored in biblical exegesis. Maimonides' approach to Scripture challenges our artificial boundaries between exegesis and formal commentary – and it renders the *Guide* an essential chapter in the history of biblical exegesis.

---

[59] Ibid. (introduction: 19).
[60] Joseph Ibn Kaspi (c.1270–c.1340) wrestles at length with this question in his esoteric commentary on the *Guide*. See De Souza (2018, 246–250).
[61] Maimonides (1963, introduction: 20).
[62] For example, Moses of Narbonne offers a list of contradictory biblical passages in his commentary on the *Guide*, hinting that some of the contradictions should be explained by recourse to the seventh cause. See De Souza (2018, 280–283).

PART II
Human Beginnings

CHAPTER 3

Paradise and the Fall

Shira Weiss

In the *Guide of the Perplexed* Maimonides offers innovative readings of biblical terms and narratives through which he reveals his philosophy. Since he does not compose a comprehensive commentary on the Bible, Maimonides includes biblical exegesis throughout his philosophic work by explaining philosophic issues within the biblical text, in an effort to resolve seeming contradictions between philosophy and a literal understanding of the Bible. In the Introduction to the *Guide*, Maimonides presents his dual objective: to explain obscure biblical terms and parables, or verses and passages that have an external (literal, conventional) and an internal (philosophic) meaning.[1] Maimonides maintains that the Bible has an esoteric level of philosophic truth, accessible to the intellectually qualified, which he discusses in his *Guide* for the discernment of those capable of understanding. Influenced by Al-Farabi, Maimonides argues that religion defers to philosophy and the Bible presents educational myths in which images represent philosophical truths for the masses.[2] According to Sara Klein-Braslavy, Maimonides views the Garden of Eden narrative as such a myth reflecting "philosophic anthropology rather than historical narrative."[3] In his discussion of the episode in the Garden of Eden, Maimonides explores the human condition before and after the transgression and fulfills both objectives of his philosophic work by explaining an equivocal term and the figurative meaning of the sin and sinners in the parable – an explanation that is critical for a correct philosophical understanding of the challenging narrative.

Maimonides begins his exposition in *Guide* 1.2 with the premise of the equivocity of the term *elohim*, referring to God, angels, or political rulers. In Genesis 3:5, the serpent encourages Eve to eat from the prohibited tree of knowledge, "for God knows that in the day you eat thereof, then your

---

[1] Maimonides (1963, introduction: 6).   [2] Klein-Braslavy (2006a).
[3] Klein-Braslavy (2006a, 255).

eyes shall be opened and you shall be as *elohim*, knowing good and evil." Maimonides follows Onqelos' interpretation that in the context of the Garden of Eden, the term *elohim* refers not to the divine, but to human rulers. Maimonides uses this reading to respond to an objection regarding Adam's apparent reward of gaining the capacity to discern between good and evil as a result of his disobedience. Maimonides sees the objection as due to an error, based on a misunderstanding of the equivocal term.

In the first chapter of the *Guide*, Maimonides explains that Adam was created in God's image, *tzelem elohim*, as rationally perfected and concerned with theoretical perfection, whose norms are truth and falsehood. "The intellect that God made overflow unto man and that is the latter's ultimate perfection, was that which Adam had been provided with before he disobeyed."[4] For Adam's benefit (to achieve truth and eternal life), and because Adam was formed with intellectual apprehension, God prohibited him from eating the fruit of one particular tree. "Of every tree of the garden you may freely eat; but of the tree of the knowledge of good and evil, you shall not eat of it; for in the day that you eat thereof you shall surely die."[5] Prior to his transgression of the prohibition, Adam, in his intellectually perfected state, would have focused exclusively on theoretical truth, disengaged from material or bodily concerns or engagement in the ethical or political sphere. Adam's prelapsarian theoretical concerns would have directed him to pursue the permitted trees in the garden, which represent the intelligible realm, as opposed to the tree of knowledge of good and evil, which represents the material realm. According to Maimonides, the prohibition on eating from the fruit of the tree of knowledge represents the prioritizing of the theoretical over the material, which leads to true happiness, the ideal life, and human perfection.

> The command not to eat from the Tree of Knowledge of Good and Evil is in essence a command not to actualize the corporeal passions, and turn away from the metaphysical contemplation in which Adam was engaged. Only with the sin of becoming preoccupied with the corporeal world, and the loss of perfection that resulted thereby, did Adam's rational faculty have to become engaged in distinguishing between good and bad actions.[6]

Since Adam did not die on the day he ate from the tree, Marvin Fox interprets God's stated consequence to refer not to human death, but rather to the "killing of the dominance of man's rational soul and supplanting it with the appetitive animal soul."[7]

---

[4] Maimonides (1963, 1.2: 24).   [5] Genesis 2:16–17.   [6] Kreisel (1999, 73).
[7] Fox (1990, 185).

Adam's perfect intellect was created in a body, and he was, therefore, subject to material desires.[8] In an effort to entice Adam and Eve to eat from the forbidden tree, the serpent, described as the most cunning of all beasts, subtly inquires of the woman, "Has God said: You shall not eat of any tree of the garden?"[9] To which Eve responds by distorting God's original command, "Of the fruit of the trees of the garden we may eat; but of the fruit of the tree which is in the midst of the garden, God has said: You shall not eat of it, neither shall you touch it, lest you die."[10] In order to persuade the woman, the serpent retorts with the subtle use of the equivocal term, "You shall not surely die; for God knows that in the day you eat thereof, then your eyes shall be opened, and you shall be as *elohim*, knowing good and evil."[11] Eve desired the fruit of the tree, which was described from her perception as "good for food, and that it was a delight to the eyes, and that the tree was to be desired to make one wise,"[12] and, therefore, succumbed to those desires by eating the fruit and sharing it with Adam in order to gratify their bodily appetites.

According to Maimonides, Adam's sin in eating the fruit represents his transition, led by the imagination and passions, from prioritizing the values of the mind over those of the body to a preoccupation with good and evil, "generally-accepted opinions," instead of truth and falsehood.[13] The distinction and superior status of truth and falsehood over good and evil reflect Aristotle's distinction between demonstrative reasoning (grounded in true premises) and dialectical reasoning (generally-accepted views which are not universal).[14] As a result of their disobedience, Adam and Eve became like *elohim*, as the serpent predicted, an equivocal term that Maimonides interprets in this context as human rulers, who are preoccupied with good and evil and focused only on the social and political – but not intellectual – well-being of their citizens. Such rulers "set standards of

---

[8] Fox (1990, 183).   [9] Genesis 3:1.   [10] Genesis 3:2–3.   [11] Genesis 3:4–5.
[12] Genesis 3:6.   [13] Berman (1980).
[14] But note that, unlike Aristotle, Maimonides does not ascribe good and evil to the practical intellect (there is no reference to practical intellect in the *Guide*), since good and evil, according to Maimonides, are not grounded in reason, but are commonly-accepted notions, grounded in imagination. (See Pines 1990, 45). Avicenna also refers to these value judgments as "generally-accepted opinions" in *Theorems and Axioms*, and argues that individuals of pure intellect know primary intelligibles, but not generally-accepted opinions, the need for which reflects human imperfection. (Avicenna 1892, 58ff.) Generally-accepted opinions are normative in the postlapsarian state, a state of human imperfection. Haim Kreisel distinguishes the practical intellect's concern with "becoming," and the theoretical intellect's concern with "being." He views the narrative in the Garden of Eden as a philosophic allegory representing the state of intellectual perfection and imperfection. Only in an imperfect state, subject to the influence of the imagination, must the rational faculty master and channel corporeal passions (Kreisel 1999, 74).

behavior by way of convention, in response to the drives of human passion and the distractions of the imagination."[15] In *Guide* 2.40, Maimonides explains how human rulers can lead by means of the imaginative faculty, but not through reason, on grounds that the moral and political spheres are concerned only with generally-accepted and situationally-dependent opinions.[16] Maimonides' conception of good is relegated to the sphere of generally-accepted opinions, which are necessary for the preservation of the community. The role of generally-accepted opinions is to regulate human conduct after Adam's sin, once human passions and destructive appetites are unleashed,[17] to control anarchic impulses and to maintain order in society.[18]

According to the figurative interpretation of the parable, Maimonides refers to Plato's association of the male with form (intellect) and female with matter.[19] Humanity is composed of matter (Eve) and form (Adam) which are physically inseparable and necessarily coexist, yet exist in tension since matter inhibits the exclusive focus on the intellectual or theoretical realm.[20] The serpent that entices Eve represents the imagination, which together with matter, threatens the control of reason upon them.[21] In another reference in the *Guide* (2.30) to the Garden of Eden episode, one based on a Midrash,[22] Maimonides introduces an additional character to the narrative and offers an allegorical interpretation. "The Serpent had a rider ... who led Eve astray, and that the rider was Sammael. They apply this name to Satan."[23] Eve's seduction represents matter being carried away by desire. Sammael refers to Satan, which "turns people away from the ways of truth and makes them perish in the ways of error."[24] There, Maimonides cites R. Simeon b. Laqish's equation, "Satan, the evil inclination and the angel of death are one and the same."[25] Klein-Braslavy

---

[15] Fox (1990, 185).
[16] Maimonides associates knowledge of generally-accepted opinions with rulers who receive emanations from the Active Intellect to the imagination, but not to the rational faculty (Cf. *Guide* 2.36).
[17] Pines (1990, 141).   [18] Pines (1990, 188).   [19] *Guide* 1.17.
[20] "Inasmuch as it is clear that this is so, and as according to what has been laid down by divine wisdom it is impossible for matter to exist without form and for any of the forms in question to exist without matter, and as consequently it was necessary that man's very noble form, which, as we have explained, is the 'image of God and His likeness,' should be bound to earthly, turbid, and dark matter, which calls down upon man every imperfection and corruption, He granted it – I mean the human form – power, dominion, rule and control over matter, in order that it subjugate it, quell its impulses, and bring it back to the best and most harmonious state that is possible" (Maimonides 1963, 3.8: 431–432).
[21] Berman (1980, 11).   [22] Midrash Chapters of Rabbi Eliezer XIII.
[23] Maimonides (1963, 2.30: 356).   [24] Ibid. (3.22: 489).
[25] Babylonian Talmud Baba Batra 16a.

suggests that Sammael represents the imagination,[26] as elsewhere in the *Guide* Maimonides associates the imaginative faculty with Satan and suggests that the imagination is the source for human sin and relates the imagination to the evil inclination, since "every deficiency of reason or character is due to the action of the imagination or consequent upon its action."[27] In the Midrash, Sammael rode on the serpent, and *Guide* 1.70 defines the term "ride" to mean "dominate." Accordingly, the imagination (represented by Sammael), as opposed to the intellect, dominates human desire (or the appetitive faculty represented by the serpent) to create irrational desire, which caused the sin in the Garden of Eden. According to Klein-Braslavy, "imagination induces man's body (Eve, matter) to pursue physical desires and thus keeps Adam, the intellect, from contemplating the intelligibles and being a perfect actual intellect."[28] Thus, the prohibition to eat from the tree of knowledge of good and evil "is a ban on the pursuit of sensual and imaginative ends and hence on relative moral judgments,"[29] since moral knowledge (of good and evil) results from the pursuit of imaginary desires.[30]

Following their sin, Adam and Eve became consumed with judging things as good and evil. Therefore, they immediately recognized that they were naked and hid out of shame, though they had been unclothed throughout the entire narrative. Shame became associated with nakedness only after they fell to the lower level of knowledge of good and evil, or generally-accepted, conventional, notions. Maimonides cites Genesis 3:7, "And the eyes of both of them were opened (*pakoah*), and they *knew* that they were naked." He interprets the term, *pakoah,* to mean "uncovering mental vision," not literal sight, and highlights the verb, "knew," as opposed to they "saw" that they were naked. After all, they did not see anything different after the sin than they had before, but their knowledge changed as a result of their disobedience, which rendered their nakedness *bad.*

Maimonides then quotes a supporting verse from *Job*, "He changes his face and You send him forth,"[31] to relate to Adam's deviation from his natural intellectual state in which he was created, and for which he was deserving of the punishment of expulsion. According to the Midrash, Adam could have lived eternally in intellectual perfection and material comfort, but instead chose to follow the guidance of the serpent.[32]

---

[26] Klein-Braslavy (2006a, 263). [27] Maimonides (1963, 2.12: 280).
[28] Klein-Braslavy (2006a, 264). [29] Klein-Braslavy (2006a, 265). [30] Kreisel (1999, 95).
[31] *Job* 14:20. [32] Genesis Rabbah XVI,1; XXI,4.

No longer able to sustain his idyllic state due to his preoccupation with the material, he was banished from the Garden of Eden and left to satisfy his own material needs, forced to expend great effort in nature, which prevented him from focusing on the theoretical. "Because you listened to the voice of your wife and ate of the tree … cursed is the ground for your sake; in toil shall you eat of it all the days of your life … thorns and thistles shall it bring forth to you … by the sweat of your brow …"[33] As a result of the transgression, Adam was subjected to the evils from which his intellect had previously protected him.[34] God expels Adam in order to prevent him from eating from the tree of life, as God proclaims, "Behold, the man is become as one of us, to know good and evil; and now, lest he put forth his hand, and take also of the tree of life, and eat, and live forever."[35] In *Shemonah Perakim*, based on Onqelos' reading, Maimonides interprets the verse to mean,

> Man has become the only being in the world who possesses a characteristic which no other being has in common with him. What is this characteristic? It is that by and of himself man can distinguish between good and evil, and do that which he pleases, with absolutely no restraint. Since, then, this is so, it would have even been possible for him to have stretched out his hand, and, taking of the tree of life, to have eaten of its fruit, and thus live forever. Since it is an essential characteristic of man's makeup that he should of his own free will act morally or immorally, doing just as he chooses, it becomes necessary to teach him the ways of righteousness, to command and exhort him, to punish and reward him according to his deserts.[36]

In his ideal created state, Adam should have eaten from the tree of life, to which God had initially intended the cherubim lead him, in order to live eternally. However, due to his sin, God banished him from the Garden and armed the cherubim with fiery swords to prevent his reentry.[37]

Maimonides concludes his discussion with a quote from Psalms 49:13, "Adam, unable to dwell in dignity, is like the beasts that speak not." Since Adam was not capable of sustaining his intellectually perfected state, he became enslaved to his passions like an animal, which lacks *logos*, the power of reason. Maimonides cites the same verse in his discussion of divine providence in *Guide* 3.18 to describe the deprivation of providence from individuals who are "ignorant and disobedient," relegated to the

---

[33] Genesis 3:17–19.
[34] Josef Stern alludes to Maimonides' view of the supervenience of divine providence upon intellectual development; see *Guide* 3.17–18 and Stern (2009, 209–224).
[35] Genesis 3:22. [36] Maimonides (1966 (1912), 92). [37] Kreisel (1999, 109).

status of all other species of animal.[38] Through his exposition of the Garden of Eden parable, Maimonides reverses the impression of the objector, who conceived of humanity as irrational beasts in the beginning, who disobeyed and advanced to enlightened humans with knowledge of good and evil. Rather, Maimonides argues, humanity began as contemplative and fell as a result of sin to a mortal, animalistic state, succumbing to the power of the imagination and becoming enslaved to an animal nature.

Maimonides offers a final ambiguous commendation, "Praise to the master of the will, the aim and wisdom of whose will cannot be apprehended."[39] Even though humans are created in God's intellectual image and have the potential to engage in communion with the divine, the purpose of God's creation transcends human understanding and reflects divine wisdom and will. Lawrence Berman suggests that the statement refers to the challenge of understanding why God created humanity with a duality of theoretical and material pursuits, with the resultant struggle to develop the theoretical over the material.[40] Thus, the entire story represents the tension between the ideal intellectual life and political life, which, in following out the promptings of the imagination, can lead to corruption.

This reading of the biblical story of the Garden of Eden, with which Maimonides commences the *Guide*, reflects his conception of human perfection, the topic of the final chapter of the *Guide* (3.54). He begins his work with humanity's creation in God's intellectual image[41] and concludes with the ultimate goal of human intellectual perfection. Maimonides identifies perfection of the intellect as the fourth and highest perfection, superior to the perfections of possessions, bodily constitution, and moral virtues; such perfection refers to knowledge of the divine. "The true human perfection consists in the acquisition of the rational virtues. I refer to the conception of intelligibles, which teach true opinions concerning the divine things."[42]

In an earlier chapter of the *Guide* (1.54), Maimonides explains what humans can comprehend about God. Since God's essence cannot be grasped by the human mind, knowledge of the divine must be confined to that of God's actions. "The apprehension of these (divine) actions is an apprehension of His attributes."[43] Human perfection entails knowledge of God, and this knowledge has practical and moral ramifications, as

---

[38] Maimonides (1963, 3.18: 475).   [39] Maimonides (1963, 1.2: 26).   [40] Berman (1980, 12).
[41] *Guide* 1.1.   [42] Maimonides (1963, 3.54: 635).   [43] Maimonides (1963, 1.54: 124).

humanity is called upon to imitate divine ways.[44] *Imitatio Dei* as a result of intellectual perfection is distinguished from the perfection of moral virtues, the penultimate perfection enumerated by Maimonides. "The imitation of the Divine attributes, which, unlike the moral virtues, is not the result of practical reasoning, follows from theoretical, metaphysical considerations. *Imitatio Dei* is, therefore, but the practical consequence of the intellectual love of God and is part and parcel of the ultimate perfection."[45] The distinction between morality prior to and following the attainment of knowledge of God reflects Maimonides' position that theoretical knowledge of God affects practice.[46]

Such an understanding can reconcile Maimonides' seemingly contradictory statements in the final chapter of the *Guide*, which has led to scholarly debate over his true view of human perfection.[47] Despite Maimonides' explicit articulation earlier in the final chapter that intellectual perfection is the "true human perfection," the fourth and highest level, the penultimate paragraph of the *Guide* emphasizes the *vita activa* as opposed to the *vita contemplativa*.

> It is clear that the perfection of man that may truly be gloried in is the one acquired by him who has achieved, in a measure corresponding to his capacity, apprehension of Him ... The way of life of such an individual, after he has achieved this apprehension, will always have in view *lovingkindness, righteousness* and *judgment* [my emphasis], through assimilation to His actions ...[48]

This last statement can be understood to mean that the highest state of perfection entails practical action in *imitatio Dei*, after the achievement of intellectual perfection, since humans are actively involved in moral and political affairs. Perfection of the intellect is prized over other perfections, and sustains and elevates proper prescribed conduct in practical life, informed by an awareness that such actions are in imitation of divine acts. As Maimonides states in an earlier chapter, "For the utmost virtue of man is to become like unto Him ... as far as he is able; which means that we should make our actions like unto His ... 'He is gracious, so be you also gracious; He is merciful, so be you also merciful.'"[49]

---

[44] Frank (1985, 490).   [45] Altmann (1981, 73).   [46] Hartman (1976, 205).
[47] See interpretations by Hermann Cohen (1978), Julius Guttmann (1973), and Steven Schwarzschild (1977), which focus on human perfection in moral terms; Leo Strauss (1941), Lawrence Berman (1961) and Shlomo Pines (1986; Maimonides 1963, cxxii), which focus on human perfection in political terms; and Menachem Kellner (1990), Isadore Twersky (1980) and David Hartman (1976), which focus on human perfection in halakhic terms.
[48] Maimonides (1963, 3.54: 638).   [49] Maimonides (1963, 1.54: 128).

Adam, in his created intellectual state in the image of God, ought to have used his knowledge of divine things to obey God's prohibition of eating from the tree of knowledge of good and evil. Instead, he acted against such awareness and succumbed to the material element in the Garden of Eden. As a result of the transgression, he fell from the ideal intellectually perfected state in which he was formed to a lower level of moral judgment, consumed with judging things as good or bad. From this postlapsarian state, humanity is tasked with the objectives of achieving intellectual perfection according to its capacity, and using such knowledge of God to motivate proper conduct in the material world. Humans are called upon to strive to imitate divine ways of righteousness, loving-kindness and judgment, as they navigate the competing demands of theoretical and material pursuits, in an effort to restore the initial perfection of God's creation. The opening and closing chapters of Maimonides' *Guide of the Perplexed* bookend the entire work, which guides the development of humanity on its journey from the lower forms of material, physical, and moral perfections to true human perfection. Such a perfection is unique to humans, as the only species formed in *tzelem Elohim*, and the only species that can act in *imitatio Dei*. Only so being and so acting can ultimately restore the immortal perdurance with which humans were originally created. Maimonides concludes, "This is in true reality the ultimate end; this is what gives the individual true perfection, a perfection belonging to him alone; and it gives him permanent perdurance; through it man is man."[50]

---

[50] Maimonides (1963, 3.54: 635).

CHAPTER 4

Maimonides on the Nature of Good and Evil

Daniel Rynhold

As is often the case with subjects in the labyrinthine work that is the *Guide of the Perplexed*, Maimonides' discussions of the concepts of good and evil are scattered throughout and often interspersed among other topics. In this essay I will endeavor to untangle some of the questions surrounding his treatment of good and evil – or good and bad – specifically as they relate to ethical action.[1] But even limiting oneself to the ethical realm leaves open multiple avenues. Maimonides has much to say concerning virtue ethics, for example, whether with regard to specific virtues, or more generally with his well-known discussion of the Aristotelian doctrine of the mean. Given that our focus here is the *Guide*, however, where discussion of these issues is more limited than in *Mishneh Torah* and *Shemonah Perakim*, and that detailed scholarly work is readily available in these other areas,[2] we will here devote ourselves to a road less traveled but of great significance to the trajectory of the *Guide* itself.

For if we begin with our ordinary intuitive sense of morality, we notice that Maimonides appears to spend most of the *Guide* limiting the moral concepts of good and evil to a supporting role in the quest for what really matters – the intellectual perfection gained through knowledge of "intelligibles, which teach true opinions concerning the divine things" (Maimonides 1963, 3.54: 635).[3] Indeed, the *Guide* is often read as being

---

I am indebted to David Shatz and Josef Stern for invaluable comments on an earlier draft of this essay. Where I continue to contradict them, I hope they will read esoterically.

[1] Other contexts in which good and evil are discussed, such as with respect to "being" or states of affairs, are left in the background since they are treated elsewhere in this volume, though the argument of this essay ultimately provides reason for seeing Maimonides' ontological and ethical uses of "good" as two sides of the same coin. See note 36 in this essay.

[2] See, for example, Frank (1989 and 1990), Weiss (1991), and Shatz (2005).

[3] Or perhaps knowledge of the limits of our ability to gain such knowledge according to certain scholars, including (famously) Pines (1979). For a sophisticated recent iteration of this skeptical view, see Stern (2013). For the purposes of this essay, we generally need not commit on this, so will just speak of intellectual perfection, which readers can take in either a substantive or skeptical sense.

bookended by the relegation of the realm of moral evaluation to secondary status;[4] in what could be read as an excursion into metaethics *avant la lettre*,[5] moral values appear to be relativized to human concerns as matters of convention or "common opinion" and, as such, are compared unfavorably with the intellectual values of truth and falsity. Yet, while Maimonides is not one to let tradition obstruct his quest for truth, the idea that morality or practice in general is secondary to intellectual endeavor would appear to be difficult to square with his practical Jewish commitments, not to mention contrary indications in both the *Guide* and his other writings.

Though Maimonides would obviously not have been aware of the contemporary language of moral cognitivism or the various nuanced forms of moral realism and anti-realism that dominate contemporary metaethics, one certainly finds some quite direct observations in the *Guide* on whether moral judgements are truth-apt, and whether or not the moral values that are their subject matter pick out objective properties that form part of the – to use John Mackie's felicitous phrase – "fabric of the world."[6] At the very least, we find significant material in the *Guide* on some of the basic epistemological and metaphysical questions around which discussions of moral cognitivism and realism revolve.[7] In this piece, therefore, we will attempt to determine where Maimonides stood on such issues.[8]

4.1 Maimonides the Non-Cognitivist?

One of the most famous discussions of good and evil in the *Guide* appears in only the second chapter, where through his discussion of Adam's sin in the Garden of Eden Maimonides sets out what, at first glance, appear to be both a non-cognitivist and anti-realist view of moral value. He writes:

---

[4] Or almost bookended, since it is in the second chapter of the *Guide* that we first encounter this negative evaluation, and even though Maimonides appears to reinforce his moral "skepticism" in the final chapter, its closing paragraphs are infamous for laying him open to an interpretation whereby ultimate significance is given to the practical, if not moral realm, as we will see.

[5] Or an anticipation of the appendix to part one (and more) of Spinoza's *Ethics*. For detailed analysis of the Maimonides-Spinoza nexus, see, for example, W. Z. Harvey (1979; 1981a), Fraenkel (2006), and Parens (2012).

[6] Mackie (1990, 15).

[7] See, for example, the rational reconstruction of his views on natural law that have a bearing on such issues in Novak (1998), especially chapter 4. W. Z. Harvey (1986) also looks at Maimonides' metaethical and ethical theories.

[8] To approach ethics theoretically rather than practically is, as Daniel Frank correctly observes, "not to do ethics in the 'Classical' way. For Aristotle, ethics is a practical science, and this means that it subserves a practical end, namely, how to live well and, thereby, to achieve the human good." (Frank 2006, 960). While this is indeed the case, our theoretical enterprise will turn out to be closely bound up with Maimonides' normative ethics, as we will see.

> Through the intellect one distinguishes between truth and falsehood, and that was found in [Adam] in its perfection and its integrity. Fine and bad on the other hand, belong to the things generally accepted as known, not to those cognized by the intellect ... Now man in virtue of his intellect knows truth from falsehood; and this holds good for all intelligible things. Accordingly, when man was in his most perfect and excellent state, in accordance with his inborn disposition and possessed of his intellectual cognitions ... he had no faculty that was engaged in any way in the consideration of generally accepted things and he did not apprehend them. (Maimonides 1963, 1.2: 24–25)

Taking a first run at Maimonidean metaethics, this tells us that truth values are applicable to matters of the intellect, while judging what is "fine" or "bad," in contrast, reflects "generally accepted things," statements concerning which are not candidates for intellectual apprehension or truth. Inasmuch as the content of moral judgement is thus not truth-apt for Maimonides, this appears to be a pretty explicit statement of moral non-cognitivism – the view that moral judgements do not express beliefs to which truth values can be assigned, but rather express some non-cognitive attitude or emotional state.[9]

Moreover, this is not an isolated statement in the *Guide*. In his discussion of revelation at Mount Sinai, Maimonides once again classes all but the first two commandments within the class of generally accepted opinions and opposes them to "primary intelligibles" that can be known.

> [T]he existence of the deity and His being one, are knowable by human speculation alone ... As for the other commandments, they belong to the class of generally accepted opinions and those adopted in virtue of tradition, not to the class of the intellecta. (Maimonides 1963, 2.33: 364)

While the "other commandments" cover broader ground than we would nowadays think of as ethical, many have formed the backbone of Western moral codes throughout history, such that once again we might take Maimonides to be reinforcing the idea that ordinary moral judgements are not matters of belief gained through rational human speculation. In addition, moral judgements are ultimately the concern of the "desires of the imagination and the pleasures of his corporeal senses" (Maimonides

---

[9] Maimonides' use in *Guide* 1.2 of the terms "fine" (*al-ḥasan*) and "bad" (*al-qabiḥ*), rather than "good" (*al-kair*) and "evil" (*al-sharr*) naturally raises questions. Yet, as Howard Kreisel has shown, Maimonides often uses differing terminology in this area, so it is unclear that we should make too much of this (Kreisel 1999, 109). For detailed analysis of the antecedents of Maimonides' language here among other related issues, see Pines (1990).

1963, 1.2: 25).[10] Even if communal consensus is formed through the acceptance of tradition, it is prompted by what for Maimonides are affective and physical-imaginative rather than cognitive concerns, and thus is entirely parasitic upon our corporeal nature. It would be "unthinkable" if we were pure intellects living a perfect Adamic existence, a state that is identical to the postmortem existence of those select individuals who will qualify for a place in the Maimonidean version of the World to Come. There, one will "neither experience bodily pleasures, nor ... want them" (Maimonides 1972, 411), but instead "souls [will] enjoy blissful delight in their attainment of knowledge of the truly essential nature of God the Creator" (Maimonides 1972, 412).[11]

The link to Maimonidean eschatology is particularly important. As Maimonides explains in his *Mishneh Torah*, the soul referred to is "not the soul that needs a body, but the form of the soul, that is, the knowledge that it apprehends of the Creator according to its capacity, and that it comprehends regarding abstract concepts and other matters" (Mishneh Torah, "Laws of Repentance," 8.3). The reference here to form testifies to Maimonides' attribution of an objective *telos* to humankind – that of actualizing the intellect – and "admission" to his World to Come is only gained through the actualization of this intellect in its coming to know relevant eternal truths:

> The true perfection which gives human beings "permanent perdurance" is one that consists in the acquisition of the rational virtues – I refer to the conception of intelligibles, which teach the true opinions concerning the divine things." (Maimonides 1963, 3.54: 635)

This means that actions are of the wrong type to enable one to enter the World to Come. Moral actions that fall under the categories of good and bad are simply of a different species from judgements of the intellect that have truth values. As Maimonides later tells us of the ultimate intellectual human perfection, it is one to which "there do not belong either actions or moral qualities ... it consists only of ideas towards which speculation has

---

[10] For the grounding of the concepts of good and evil in the imagination, see W. Z. Harvey (1979, 179–183). More generally, based on the definition given at Maimonides (1963, 3.13: 453) – "'Good' is an expression applied by us to what conforms to our purpose" – Harvey argues that, given that human purposes can, and do, vary, Maimonides ends up with a "relativistic and subjectivistic" (W. Z. Harvey 1986, 131) account of the "good" similar to that given here.

[11] While the *Commentary to the Mishnah* is a much earlier work than the *Guide*, Maimonides' views on the World to Come remain consistent throughout his life, appearing unchanged in the much later (and post-*Guide*) "Letter on Resurrection." Moreover, as Moshe Halbertal among others has noted, Maimonides amended and revised the *Commentary to the Mishnah* throughout his life. See Halbertal (2014, 92–93).

led and that investigation has rendered compulsory" (Maimonides 1963, 3.27: 511). Given this, together with the idea that *judgements* regarding what is good and bad do not fall within the scope of the intellect, and cannot be considered truth-apt, one can understand why Marvin Fox would have stated that "In contemporary philosophic terminology we would say that Maimonides considers all moral statements to be noncognitive" (Fox 1990, 150; see also 181 and 190).

4.2 Maimonides the Weak Cognitivist?

The first cut is not always the deepest, and it is of little surprise that as soon as we take a second run at this, we find that matters turn out to be rather more complicated.

We can begin by noting that relegating ordinary moral conceptions of good and evil to secondary status or even relativizing them to the ultimate intellectual endeavor appears at the very least to be in tension with Maimonides's unwavering commitment to Judaism,[12] a commitment that traditionally entailed privileging the *bios praktikos* over the *bios theôrêtikos*. That Maimonides was committed to the system of Judaic law and thus the morality embodied in the halakhic system, not to mention his being the first to codify it in its entirety, cannot be gainsaid, and thus, as David Shatz has written (while fully acknowledging all of the points we have made), "it would be a colossal mistake to ignore what Maimonides does say about ethics" (Shatz 2005, 169). As Joseph Soloveitchik noted in his lecture course on the *Guide*:

> Did [Maimonides] not realize that the view that theoretical knowledge is the highest ideal and that ethical performance is only of practical value goes against the morality of the prophets? ... It is almost unthinkable that Maimonides, the great student of Halakha who in the *Mishne Torah* placed so much emphasis on the ethical gesture, should have, in the manner of Aristotle, demoted that gesture to mere opinion. (Kaplan 2016, 123)

More importantly, however, there are also philosophically substantive reasons for taking this view. A first barrier to applying the truth predicate to moral judgements for Maimonides is an apparently Aristotelian epistemology whereby moral beliefs cannot be truth-apt since they are not the

---

[12] Some question its "unwavering" nature, at least from a descriptive perspective, with reference to an alleged forced conversion to Islam. See Kraemer (2008a, 116–124) and cf. Davidson (2005, 17–28). Whether his "Epistle on Martyrdom" may provide halakhic mitigation for this is a subject of heated debate. See Soloveitchik (1980), Hartman (1985), and Lorberbaum and Shapira (2008).

conclusions of demonstrative arguments.[13] That is, moral judgements, being the mere consensus of the masses, are not theoretical truths that are determined rationally through a demonstration in which the premises are "true and primitive and immediate and more familiar than and prior to and explanatory of the conclusions" (Aristotle 1994, *Posterior Analytics*, 71b20–22).[14] They neither are, nor are based upon, necessary truths concerning universals that are the subject matter for scientific knowledge or *epistême*.[15]

And yet, while Maimonides withholds the truth predicate from moral judgements, it is far from clear that this renders them simply a matter of human affective responses in a way that parallels contemporary forms of moral non-cognitivism. It is true that moral judgements are grounded in the imaginative faculty and thus *are* ultimately based on affective human responses. As a result they are relative to a *human* hierarchy of values unlike the truth values of pure intellection. As W. Z. Harvey (1979) argues, this involvement of the imagination renders application of the predicates "true" and "false" questionable here, at least from a strictly scientific Aristotelian perspective. But as Harvey also contends, once the imagination supplies us with the notions of "good" and "evil," intellect is then "forced to work within its domain" (W. Z. Harvey 1979, 181) in attempting to find the best means to the "imaginatively supplied" ends.

Along similar lines, Howard Kreisel has argued at length that while there is little question that intellectual perfection is indeed the highest perfection for human beings, and, further, that the intellect is only actualized through the demonstration and subsequent contemplation of theoretical truths, this does not relegate the practical realm to being nonrational and a mere function of the imaginative faculty. Even in the account of Adam's sin – a prime source for the relegation of moral value to secondary status, as we have seen – Maimonides writes that it was "on account of [intellect] that he was addressed by God and given commandments" and that "commandments are not given to beasts and beings devoid of intellect" (Maimonides 1963, 1.2: 24). But why would intellect be a necessary condition for the receipt of a command if commandments are solely the concern of nonrational faculties?

---

[13] A view we will shortly have reason to question, even in Aristotle.
[14] A full account of the nature of a demonstration takes matters rather further than this. For a summary in the context of Maimonides' *Guide*, see Rynhold (2005, 12–18).
[15] Note that this introduces a significant "internalist" element to Maimonides' epistemology, such that his alleged non-cognitivism would be largely determined by the internal reasons that one can – or, in this case, cannot – give for one's moral judgements, a point to which we will have cause to return.

As early as the *Treatise on Logic*, Maimonides assigns moral distinctions, among other things, to what he calls "the rational faculty" (Maimonides 1938, 61) and refers to the "science" of governance as one that imparts "to its masters a knowledge of true happiness, showing them the way to obtain it, and a knowledge of true evil, showing them the way to avoid it" (Maimonides 1938, 64). Similar associations between the rational faculty and political or ethical activity also pepper the *Guide* itself (for example in *Guide* 1.53, 1.72, and 3.8). As Kreisel summarizes the matter: "That knowledge of the 'good' is not knowledge of the 'necessary' does not entail that it is essentially subjective. [It] . . . does not have the same certainty as knowledge of the 'intelligibles', but neither for the most part is it false" (Kreisel 1999, 102). When he argues that Maimonides hesitates to use the term "intellect" – or even the Aristotelian notion of the practical intellect – for practical matters, it is not because ethical and political matters are unrelated to reason. Aristotle himself speaks of "practical truth" (Aristotle 2009, *Nicomachean Ethics*, 1139a 24–31), "precisely to make the point that practice like theory is an exercise of reason, its success a success of reason" (S. Broadie 1991, 221),[16] and Maimonides does likewise, such as when describing the highest form of worship in the *Mishneh Torah* as that in which one "does what is true [*emet*] because it is true, and ultimately good will come of it."[17]

Thus, despite his earlier denial of the truth predicate to moral judgements, we can raise the following question – even if it is only our physical and hence imaginative side that provokes moral judgement, would this simple fact of human embodiment be sufficient basis for moral non-cognitivism? Surely, recognizing that moral judgements reflect our embodied nature does neither a noncognitivist make, nor render our determinations of what is "good" or "evil" simply the relative affective responses of human beings that are, like beauty, entirely in the eyes of the beholder. If this *were* sufficient for moral non-cognitivism, then it would become true by definition.

It seems, then, that we should pay closer attention to Maimonides' account of moral judgements, beginning with his designation of such judgements as *al-mashhūrāt,* or "generally accepted opinions" – a translation of Aristotle's *endoxa*. While Maimonides might well exclude moral value from the realm of pure intellectual cognition, the value of

---

[16] For further discussion of Aristotle's use of "truth" in the practical realm, see S. Broadie (1991, 219ff).

[17] Maimonides, *Mishneh Torah*, "Laws of Repentance" 10.2. See also *Introduction to Perek Helek*: "Since the Torah is truth, the purpose of knowing it is to do it" (Maimonides 1972, 405). Note, however, that for Maimonides the use of truth in this context is not being applied to morality *per se*, but to the Torah. This, as we will discover, might turn out to be an important distinction.

"Aristotelian" *endoxa* should lead us to question whether this amounts to endorsing a view parallel to contemporary non-cognitivism. The precise status of *endoxa* in the Aristotelian worldview is a matter of debate, but Aristotle defines them as the opinions acceptable "to everyone, or to most people, or to the wise – to all of them, or to most, or to the most famous and esteemed" (Aristotle 1997, *Topics*, 100b21–23). So they are judgements maintained by the "esteemed" and not simply human affective responses. Far from yielding non-cognitivism therefore, in the eyes of contemporary theorists this would be a form of weak cognitivism, whereby moral statements are grounded in "generally accepted opinion"; and if "good" is defined as "generally accepted opinion" (within a given population) we may well be able to determine the truth of the statement "X is good." So rather than falling into the non-cognitivist camp, Maimonides appears closer to cognitivists who give a judgement-dependent account of moral qualities, whereby the opinions of the wise – the *endoxa* – determine the application of moral predicates such that the truth of moral judgements is "constitutively tied to facts about human opinion" (Miller 2013, 135). As such, they are truth-apt judgements.[18]

If this is the case, then Maimonides turns out, in contemporary terms, to be marrying weak cognitivism with moral anti-realism. In appealing to human judgement, Maimonides does not appeal to any metaphysically strange mind-independent moral properties as the subjects of moral judgement. In this sense, he turns out to be precisely John Mackie's type of moral skeptic in his denial of "entities or relations of a certain kind, objective values, or requirements" (Mackie 1990, 17). What he does appeal to though, under the guise of "commonly accepted opinion," amounts to more than the mere affective responses of human beings. So though Maimonides may have been reluctant to apply the truth predicate strictly speaking to moral judgements, the view expressed here would nonetheless appear to fall under a weak cognitivist description.[19]

4.3 Maimonides the Strong Cognitivist?

Once more, however, we find further layers to Maimonides' discussion that lead us to question the account given in Section 4.2. For we have so far argued that "generally accepted opinions" have a degree of cognitive

---

[18] I am grateful to Josef Stern for comments that helped me formulate the ideas in this paragraph.
[19] For detailed presentation of the judgement-dependent view, see Wright (1988). Critical discussion can be found in Miller (2013, chapter 7).

standing – albeit a degree below that of demonstrated truths, hence their secondary status. But it turns out that there might be a route to raising their cognitive *bona fides* even higher.

We begin this story at *Guide* 2.40, where Maimonides famously distinguishes between types of systems of law. There are, on the one hand, *nomoi*, which proceed strictly from the imaginative faculty of human lawmakers and are thus "directed exclusively toward the ordering of the city and of its circumstances and the abolition in it of injustice and oppression ... [but] not at all directed toward speculative matters ... to opinions being correct or faulty" (Maimonides 1963, 2.40: 383). On the other hand, we have divine law "that takes pains to inculcate correct opinions with regard to God ... and that desires to make man wise, to give him understanding, and to awaken his attention, so that he should know the whole of that which exists in its true form" (Maimonides 1963, 2.40: 383–384).

While *Guide* 2.40 is interested in the lawgivers rather than the agents, it nonetheless shows us that what is key in determining the status of an act is its goal, and this is reinforced later at the beginning of his discussion of reasons for the commandments, where we find an explicit definition of good action that leads us in an objectivist direction. Maimonides there lists four classes of action – the vain, the futile, the frivolous, and then finally: "The good and excellent action is that accomplished by an agent aiming at a noble end, I mean one that is necessary or useful, and achieves that end" (Maimonides 1963, 3.25: 503). Thus, we are given a definition of a good act that appeals to its *telos*, and as we have already noted, Maimonides posits a "true perfection" or *telos* for human beings – identified in the very first chapter of the *Guide* as the human potential for "intellectual apprehension" (Maimonides 1963, 1.1: 22). It seems, then, that an act that is a means towards one's ultimate perfection is good in an objective sense – and one that hinders this *telos* would presumably be bad. Or, as Kreisel writes, "it is the ultimate purpose or *telos* of the moral order that determines our evaluation of it" (Kreisel 1999, 82). As a result, Maimonides ends up with what Harvey describes as an "intellectualistic teleology [as] a kind of utilitarianism" (W. Z. Harvey 1986, 134), though the more general term "consequentialism" might be more appropriate here.[20]

So can an act be classified as an objectively good act if it achieves this final end? Take the following case: Intellectually imperfect person S performs act x on account of its conventional "goodness." S has acted

---

[20] Since Maimonides identifies pure intellection as the greatest – albeit unfathomable to us corporeal mortals – form of pleasure (see Maimonides 1972, 410–412), however, utilitarianism may indeed be appropriate.

with the intention of achieving straightforward moral perfection – or "welfare of the body" in "Maimonidean" parlance. Over the course of time, though, S achieves his ultimate intellectual perfection. What are we to make of such an act? Is it objectively good?

On the one hand, the act realizes the true "being" or reality of the individual (which also fits well with Maimonides' more general account of good whereby all being is good (Maimonides 1963, 3.10: 440)). So act x would have played a causal role in the ultimate attainment of S's perfection, and the proposition "act x was good" would on this account, be true. On the other hand, both in the case of the lawgivers of 2.40 and the definition at 3.25, Maimonides speaks of the "agent *aiming* at a noble end" (Maimonides 1963, 3.25: 503, emphasis added). It seems, therefore, as if we must add an intentionalist element to our picture. For while one might be able to speak of an *act* as good from a third-person perspective should it achieve the ultimate intellectual end, a good *agent* must be one who is aiming at that end. Should an act just accidentally yield the intellectual end, it would not be the act of a good agent, which requires in addition that the agent *aim* at that end.

This is important because it creates space for elements of the Aristotelian type of virtue ethic that features in Maimonides' thought. For there are now two vectors here to which we must pay attention: one is ontological, to do with the real world effects of an act, and the other is epistemological – in Aristotelian terms, whether the act is a result of *prohairesis*, a rational choice based in virtue, and in this case rationally chosen specifically for the sake of the human intellectual *telos*. Presumably, this would be important to Maimonides, and in addition we would have to differentiate between those who deliberate about what they should be doing so as to achieve social ends, and those who deliberate so as to achieve the ultimate *telos* of intellectual perfection, that is, between:

(1) A morally virtuous agent A who believes, based on generally accepted opinions, that "x is a good act" since it will achieve social and/or political ends – Maimonides' "welfare of the body" which involves "the improvement of their ways of living with one another" (Maimonides 1963, 3.27: 510).
(2) A morally virtuous agent A who believes, based on rational deliberation, that "x is a good act" since it will achieve intellectual ends.

It would appear that "x is a good act" would be objectively true only in cases of type 2 where it is intended and, more importantly, known that the act will realize the human form through the achievement of intellectual perfection. This would give us reason to argue for a cognitivist picture whereby the statement that a specific act is good can indeed be true on grounds that appeal to objective matters of fact rather than subjective matters of opinion, appealing to what for Maimonides would have been real naturalist properties of his Arabic-Aristotelian cosmos. In other words, relative to the science of his day, we seem to have a case for Maimonides as a cognitivist naturalist realist regarding ethics. He appears to believe that moral properties can be identified with natural properties.[21] On this reading then, while granting that Maimonides believes that in the practical sphere one can never get to universal necessary truths that yield *epistême*, from our perspective his view is nonetheless akin to strong cognitivism whereby one can know that "x is a good act" is true.[22]

Regarding judgements of type 1, while the acts in question could turn out in the long run to have played a causal role in the achievement of intellectual perfection, should the agent ultimately develop that perfection, the judgement "x is a good act" could not be considered true for Maimonides in the strong cognitivist sense, given his quasi-intentionalism. Though the application of contemporary categories might be problematic here, one might find room for arguing that moral judgements of type 1 could be considered true from the previously discussed weak-cognitivist perspective. That is, they are judgements that are not merely expressing affects, but they fall short of being "true" in the most robust sense.[23]

And yet, the cognitivist countermove just discussed raises all manner of difficulties. A first question – again leveled by Zev Harvey – is that while any given act, according to Maimonides, can be termed objectively good if it has (and is known to have) the desired intellectual effects, how *is* one to know whether it will indeed have those effects? As Harvey notes: "A final judgment as to whether an act was or was not "right" or "good" cannot thus be made until all its effects (or relevant effects) have transpired" (W. Z. Harvey 1986, 136). What this of course means is that while act

---

[21] This was hardly an unusual view in ancient and medieval times given their teleological cosmologies. Interestingly, though, despite the anachronism given the Aristotelian scientific context, Maimonides would seem to be close in spirit to contemporary reductionists within the naturalist camp such as Peter Railton, rather than the so-called Cornell realists, prominent among whom are Richard Boyd, David Brink, and Nicholas Sturgeon. See Miller (2013, chapters 8 and 9).

[22] Moreover, Arthur Hyman has argued that for Maimonides "dialectical no less than demonstrative arguments have cognitive significance" (Hyman 1989, 51). Kraemer (1989) argues similarly regarding the value of dialectic in Maimonides, albeit to a lesser cognitive degree than Hyman.

[23] This would also render Maimonides "stricter" than Aristotle as regards the application of the truth predicate, if Sarah Broadie is correct that as between theoretic and practical activity "there is no compelling reason to see ... an Aristotelian distinction between strict and deviant senses of 'truth'" (S. Broadie 1991, 223).

tokens can indeed turn out to be objectively correct, working out in advance when that is the case would appear to be a Sisyphean task. Moreover, no act-type can be considered "absolutely right," since on any given occasion, it may not yield the desired outcome.

From here, our problems multiply exponentially. Who is to know whether an act will indeed ultimately yield intellectual perfection, and whose intellectual perfection? If we limit consideration for the moment to one's own perfection, one would need to know all of the effects the act would have, including, presumably, everything that both I and anyone in my environs will be doing in the future such that I can work out how my acts will cohere with theirs in a manner that will not disrupt the causal chain leading up to my perfection. Other than the sheer practical impossibility of doing this, such a view, allowing that it is coherent at all, would seem to require a form of determinism that undercuts Maimonides' exoteric statements on free will at the very least. We would seem to need to know all future occurrences, including those resulting from the free acts of other human beings, such that I could be confident of taking the correct next step in the chain.

What we have discovered, then, is that the entire picture regarding consequentialist calculation – leaving aside the admittedly important question of how precisely to reconcile it with Maimonides' virtue ethics – seems utterly unrealistic. At best, it seems that the only agent who could even come close to potentially calculating whether an act will lead to intellectual perfection would already have to *be* intellectually perfect in order to have deliberated correctly (and to desire such an end). But this, in turn, means that for Maimonides the highest cognitive state regarding ethical action is *not* that which leads the person to intellectual perfection, but that which is consequent upon it. As Shatz puts it:

> [A]lthough there is a certain sort of morality that precedes and is prerequisite for the *vita contemplativa*, there is another sort of morality that is a *consequence* of intellectual perfection and represents an "overflow" or "emanation" from intellectual achievement. This morality ... is quite different from morality as we have considered it so far. (Shatz 2005, 169)[24]

This "consequent" morality consists of acts that *result* from intellectual perfection, not those that are performed either because they are "generally accepted" in a given community or because they *yield* intellectual perfection. It differs in status fundamentally from the "conventional morality"

---

[24] Other versions of this distinction can be found in Kreisel (1999, especially chapter 4 and pages 185–188), Stern (2013, chapter 8), and Kellner (1990), who adds a halakhic twist.

discussed in *Guide* 1.2, and the weak cognitivism we subsequently surveyed that precedes such perfection. It is the "morality" of the intellectually perfected individual or at least of the individual who is already some way down the road in pursuit of that state. And it seems to lead to the following: that only a rationally perfect individual could truly state that "x is a good act," since only such an individual could potentially know which acts lead to – or in their case maintain – rational perfection and act on them for that reason.[25]

4.4 The Ethics of Intellectual Perfection

We have suggested that the only individual who could potentially deliberate correctly in the ethical realm would have to be the apotheosis of intellectual perfection. Yet even for such an individual, it seems to be a superhuman task. If anyone answers to the description "superhuman," though, it is the previously mentioned exemplar of the ultimate perfection described at the end of the *Guide*, who

> has achieved, in a measure corresponding to his capacity, apprehension of Him, may He be exalted, and who knows His providence extending over his creatures as manifested in the act of bringing them into being and their governance as it is. The way of life of such an individual, after he has achieved this apprehension, will always have in view, loving-kindness, righteousness and judgement, through assimilation to His actions, may He be exalted, just as we have explained several times in this Treatise. (Maimonides 1963, 3.54: 638)

Maimonides is here describing a form of practical perfection through a commitment to *imitatio Dei*, whereby God's "moral attributes," at least as evidenced through His actions, are reproduced through our own.[26] And this would appear to be the only type of ethics for which one could give the

---

[25] This would also presumably mean that "trainees" need intellectually advanced teachers to get them to the state where they can truly act ethically themselves, much as Aristotle's virtuous person would have to be trained by a *phronimos* in order to become one.

[26] Hermann Cohen initiated the modern move to a practical – indeed, in Cohen's case, ethical – interpretation of the *Guide*, by appeal to Maimonides' negative theology and the impossibility of comprehending God's nature: "The attributes revealed do not portray God according to the categories of space and time or of substance and power, of number, magnitude, and infinity ... Instead revelation posits those attributes that reveal God solely and exclusively as an ethical being, as a being of ethics, according to the words of scripture: compassionate and gracious, abounding in kindness and faithfulness. This is the focus of Maimonides' doctrine of attributes: he pinpoints and limits the concept of a divine attribute to an ethical attribute, thus identifying the concept of God with the ethical concept of God" (Cohen 2004, 69). Further practical interpretations include the more Farabian political interpretations of Pines (1979) and of Lawrence Berman (1974), and Josef

strong cognitivist account described previously. Yet the acts referred to at the end of the *Guide*, subsequent to our achievement of intellectual perfection, differ from what we would ordinarily term moral acts. In being imitations of divine acts, these acts are *not* the result of ordinary moral dispositions. Just as God's "actions" cannot reflect the virtues qua psychological dispositions that we usually associate with moral action, human "ethical" action as undertaken by intellectually perfect individuals cannot result from "generally accepted opinions" or ordinary moral dispositions if it is to be *imitatio Dei*. Maimonides' describes the unusual state of the very few human exemplars of this perfection as follows:

> And there may be a human individual who, through his apprehension of the true realities and his joy in what he has apprehended, achieves a state in which he talks with people and is occupied with his bodily necessities while his intellect is wholly turned toward [God], may He be exalted, so that in his heart he is always in His presence ... while outwardly he is with people." (Maimonides 1963, 3.51: 623)

These figures, admittedly limited by Maimonides to only four figures from history – Moses and the patriarchs – "were occupied with governing people, increasing their fortune, and endeavoring to acquire property ... they performed these actions with their limbs only, while their intellects were constantly in [God's] presence" (Maimonides 1963, 3.51: 624). These perfect human specimens who act on the basis of perfected intellects do not appear to modern eyes to be acting morally – or, for that matter, to be in the business of making complex practical calculations – in any recognizable sense at all.[27]

If we dig deeper in an attempt to understand the nature of these individuals and their ethical practice, there seem to be two possible interpretations of what "acting on the basis of perfect intellect" could mean for Maimonides:

(1) On the one hand, momentarily setting aside the objections advanced earlier, one could argue for an act-consequentialist account, whereby perfect individuals are able to somehow divine (or intellect) which actions yield or maintain intellectual perfection. Of course, this will also presumably mean that, on occasion, they may perform acts that do not conform to

---

Stern's more recent take (Stern 2013), which though skeptical, still better maintains Maimonides' clear and explicit emphasis on intellectual perfection.

[27] See Rynhold (2009, 202–203) and Stern (2013, 328–330).

the expectations of the general populace, acts that might be seen as "transgressions" from a conventional perspective. Perfect individuals cannot be bound by ordinary moral principles simply because the masses expect them to follow these "absolute" rules. To perform such an act would be objectively the wrong thing to do if these perfect individuals know that perfection demands a different action.[28] It seems, then, as if there would be room to argue that Maimonides takes an act-consequentialist approach to ethics, and one that enables certain extremely rare types to perform acts that can be considered objectively correct, given that they serve their ultimate intellectual state, even if these acts are not in fact those suggested by our ordinary moral principles. On this account, at a metaethical level, the statement that some such act, x, is good, could indeed be known to be true, following the cognitivist realist reading of Maimonides' ethics.

On the other hand, as we have indicated, this interpretation encounters severe obstacles from a practical perspective, given the impossibility of such calculations being made accurately by any human being. It is also unclear how comfortably it can sit with the virtue ethics that we find throughout Maimonides' writings. It does, however, sit well with the idea that from a purely conceptual perspective, as Aristotle openly admits: "We must be content, then, in speaking of such subjects and with such premises to indicate the truth roughly and in outline, and in speaking about things which are only for the most part true, and with premises of the same kind, to reach conclusions that are no better" (Aristotle 2009, *Nicomachean Ethics*, 1094b19–22). But this latter point actually suggests a second (far more likely) interpretation of "acting on the basis of perfect intellect."

(2) By contrast, it could be argued that the Maimonides of the *Guide* understood these limits on ethical knowledge all too well. For Maimonides' instrumentalist account of the commandments (*Guide* 3.25–49)[29] leads to obvious questions regarding what one ought to do if, in a particular situation, one knows that the "right act" as stated by the

---

[28] Lawrence Kaplan (2002) has advanced a reading of Maimonides' introduction to Tractate Avot – better known as the "Eight Chapters" – in support of this idea, whereby "obedience to the Law must give way to the unique urgent need on the part of this unique human being for the attainment of the virtues, since the goal of this individual is the truth, that is to say, the knowledge of God" (Kaplan 2002, 17). Our own discussion would suggest a friendly amendment, whereby it would more likely be the maintenance rather than the attainment of the virtues that is at stake.

[29] Which is later superseded by the succinct account of *Guide* 3.51–52, which aims at the perfection of the solitary individual soul. See Stern (2013, 322–340).

Torah as a general *mitzvah* would *not* serve the desired (intellectually perfect) state. Here, Maimonides famously tells us:

> The Law was not given with a view to things that are rare. For in everything that it wishes to bring about, be it an opinion or a moral habit or a useful work, it is directed only toward the things that occur in the majority of cases and pays no attention to what happens rarely or to the damage occurring to the unique human being because of this way of determination and because of the legal character of the governance ... [G]overnance of the Law ought to be absolute and universal, including everyone, even if it is suitable only for certain individuals and not suitable for others; for if it were made to fit individuals, the whole would be corrupted. (Maimonides 1963, 3.34: 534–535)

Now it might be that this emphasis on "no exceptions" is intended to prevent the perfected act-consequentialist individuals from apparent breaches of the laws, in order to safeguard the Torah from being cheapened in the eyes of the masses should they witness such breaches.[30] But it could be that this is instead Maimonides recognizing human impotence when it comes to calculating the objectively correct act in any given situation – even for the greatest of humanity.[31] Maimonides' response to the issues we have raised is to admit our impotence in this field. But that is why we are given a set of *divine* laws and moral principles. Knowing what set of rules conform to intellectual perfection is delegated to the one "intellect" that could work out the infinite details involved – the infinite divine intellect, which, even taking into account the free decisions of imperfect human beings, can presumably somehow "know" which set of rules will lead to the greatest number of perfect individuals (or, for the masses, to the best possible society necessary for producing and accommodating such individuals). The rules given by God via the intermediation of Moses – who is therefore singled out as the sole individual whose prophecy is unique and cannot be changed – present us with the most perfect system for achieving the ultimate intellectual end. And the ethical principles that it presents are to be understood from a rule-consequentialist perspective.[32]

---

[30] Kreisel (1999, 23) offers a similar argument for the maintenance of Temple sacrifices, even in the absence of the original historical need for them.

[31] Such limits on our knowledge would support a version of Harvey's later contention that "Maimonides' critical epistemology obtains not only in physics as well as in metaphysics, but also on earth as well as in the heavens" (W. Z. Harvey 2008a, 235).

[32] Those who accept the exoteric view whereby Maimonides accepts the possibility of maintaining human free will despite divine foreknowledge will balk at this, but conceptually speaking, one might go so far as to argue that even God could not make the act-consequentialist calculation without

So we end up with a form of (divine) rule-consequentialism, whereby all human beings – including the intellectual elite – are better off maintaining fidelity to the rules even in cases where they might objectively tell us the wrong thing to do, at least according to one who fully understood the instrumental nature of the commandments and the infinite causal effects of our actions. The impossibility of knowing when that is the case, however, given that at the very least it would require exact knowledge of the entirety of one's future life, dictates a conservative approach.[33]

What this leaves us with, however, is the following. In contrast to our first interpretation of "acting on the basis of perfected intellect," this view accepts that *no* human (with the possible exception of Moses and the patriarchs) has the ability to know whether any given act is "objectively good." What these individuals can know, however, is that the system of principles that God has revealed are the most suited for achieving the ultimate end; in light of this knowledge, these individuals willingly submit to these principles, knowing that they will train us in the practical virtues that enable us to act correctly "for the most part," even if we are aware that on occasion these rules may require of us tactical errors in the service of the overall strategic aim.[34] Ultimately, however, these rare individuals know that such moral judgements are not among those that yield truths that actualize their intellects, and thus the pursuit of moral *knowledge* is a fool's errand. They happily delegate the basic practical "calculations" to God and act in accordance with the Torah, which allows them to get on with the important business of contemplating eternal verities that are the realm of genuine truth, safe in the knowledge that their behavioral scheme best serves them and the masses. Such an individual will come closest to that state whereby he is "occupied with his bodily necessities while his intellect is wholly turned toward [God], may He be exalted, so that in his heart he is always in [God's] presence … while outwardly he is with people." (Maimonides 1963, *Guide* 3.51: 623).

---

undermining human free will. This would also further justify the sort of divine rule-consequentialism that we have argued Maimonides presents in *Guide* 3.34.

[33] This gives us a traditionalist reading of Maimonides qua his unwavering commitment to Jewish practice, but for rather untraditional reasons that admit *mitzvot* are objectively correct only from a rule-consequentialist perspective. From an act-consequentialist perspective, it would be wrong to perform them in certain situations.

[34] Which could be justified in line with the (quite rule-consequentialist) idea of "*et la'asot*," that it is time to "act for the Lord" (Psalms 119.126) by transgressing the law in order to ultimately maintain it, an idea that Maimonides himself cites to justify his setting down the "secrets" of the Torah in the *Guide*.

What we see here, then, is that our second interpretation of acting "on the basis of perfected intellect" leads us toward Maimonides' perfect individuals and even explains why they do not appear to be in the business of making any practical calculations at all.[35] For their perfection has led them to understand that the ultimate value is a life of *theoria*. They recognize that, as Aristotle wrote, "in so far as he is a man and lives with a number of people, he chooses to do virtuous acts; he will therefore need such aids to living a human life" (Aristotle 2009, *Nicomachean Ethics*, 1178b5–7). We are physical beings unavoidably "bound to earthy, turbid, and dark matter" for Maimonides (Maimonides 1963, 3.8: 432), who cannot exist as pure intellects. As human beings, even those devoted to the *bios theôrêtikos,* we "must have a life and a life that involves bodily actions and other humans" (Stern 2013, 345). But based on their "perfected intellects" the greatest individuals recognize that they can neither calculate with certainty the actions that will conform to the intellectual *telos*, nor *should* they be focused on such matters, other than in the – admittedly crucial – service of maintaining their commitment to the, at best, asymptotic pursuit of the intellectual ideal. They are able to act in accordance with a law that is tailored as best as any law can be to the ultimate contemplative *telos* – the law given by God in the service of trying to draw one's focus *away* from practical questions and to the *bios theôrêtikos* instead.[36] Whether we see such acts as moral is to some extent a semantic issue, though it appears to better fit a broader conception of the ethical, understood as "any scheme for living that would provide an intelligible answer to Socrates' question [how one ought to live]" (Williams, 1985, 12). That this is, as an objective matter of fact, the best answer to that question for Maimonides seems unquestionable.

---

[35] Weiss argues that Maimonides here significantly downplays the significance of choice in such "virtuous" action (see Weiss 1991, 189). Stern goes rather further in speaking of them leading a life that is barely "imaginable as a human life" and more like a "life of zombies insofar as it is like the 'lives,' of the spheres" (Stern 2013, 329) that populate Aristotelian cosmology.

[36] Maimonides' descriptions of these individuals as divorced in some way from physical concerns is at the foundation of a possible case for the fusing of ethical and ontological discussions of good and evil mentioned in note 1. (I am grateful to David Shatz for alerting me to this.) The correct ethical outlook allows one to transcend all judgements of good and evil relating to worldly states of affairs in Job-like fashion, for "when he knew God with a certain knowledge, he admitted that true happiness, which is the knowledge of the deity, is guaranteed to all who know Him and that a human being cannot be troubled in it by any of all the misfortunes in question" (Maimonides 1963, 3.23: 492–493). Effectively Job, and the perfect individuals of *Guide* 3.51, are not troubled by "evil" since they live a life that enables them to transcend such anthropocentric concerns and understand all being as good. For a somewhat contrary view, however, see Lobel (2011).

4.5 Conclusion

The route has been somewhat labyrinthine, and we have ended up some way from our initial metaethical concerns, so let us return to them as we sum up our conclusions.

We began with the view, primarily based on *Guide* 1.2, that Maimonides denies that the moral realm is a realm of truth. Moral statements, as such, are non-cognitive, since the ordinary moral concepts of good and evil are grounded in the imagination, and what is generally accepted within a community as safeguarding its social welfare. So, if moral cognitivism is the view that *moral* claims simpliciter reflect beliefs that are truth-apt, and we accept a strict Aristotelian view of knowledge as *epistême*, then Maimonides is a non-cognitivist, and there is no realm of moral reality to which these claims could correspond.

We then, however, noted that Maimonides' commonly accepted opinions or *endoxa* appear not to be grounded in the affective realm in a way that would yield contemporary non-cognitivism in any recognizable form. And though it is obvious that moral concerns are *human* (and for Maimonides thus "imaginative") concerns, this hardly renders them simple affective matters. Moreover, Maimonides' own occasional use of the truth predicate for practical matters encouraged a reading of Maimonides as a weak cognitivist who gives a judgement-dependent account of moral truth.

Yet, turning our attention to Maimonides' later teleological account of ethical acts that relates them to an objective human *telos*, one could read him as a moral cognitivist with a realist construal of ethical qualities, though one that does not appeal to metaphysically strange moral properties. He would be appealing to properties of the natural world that ground an intellectualist version of cognitivism that he combines with a form of consequentialism (and that conforms well with his general opposition to nonnatural entities). If an act can be located within this natural intellectualist structure – and in addition the agent *knows* of this structure and acts in order to realize it – we could presumably speak of it as objectively good, and argue that the corresponding judgement as to the goodness of the act was "true," in some significant sense, even if not that of Aristotelian *epistême*.

While this would allow for full-blown cognitivism – there are objective standards according to which we can ascertain the truth of practical statements – our utter inability to make the necessary calculations means that no human could ever actually *know* the objective value of any given act. Such knowledge would be a miraculous achievement – the sort of thing only a god could achieve. But that, we have argued, might be exactly what Maimonides believed. The only agent able to reach knowledge in this sphere would need immediate and certain knowledge of the infinite effects of any given action. That is, the practical realm could only be a realist realm of cognition for God,[37] who reveals a system of rules that are the best possible for the achievement of our ultimate perfection from a rule-consequentialist perspective, and general adherence to the rules will inculcate in humanity the necessary virtues to enable social, political, and, in the best case, intellectual perfection. But even God can only deliver rules that will, in the long run, and for the most part, achieve that perfection, as Maimonides acknowledges at *Guide* 3.34.

Actions are important – even essential – given that we are physical beings. And we can *rationally* commit to divine law as the best approximation we have to a way of inculcating virtues that will issue in the objectively good acts that will maintain our intellectual focus. In the final analysis, however, we can question whether human beings can truly judge that such acts are objectively correct. To Maimonides, though, the limits to our knowledge in the practical sphere – both in principle and in practice – would not be of great concern. Those with the correct ethical perspective understand that the best ethical life should transcend our practical-material natures to the extent that is humanly possible. The life of such an individual would involve following the best law we have – the divine law – as the ideal way to "occupy oneself" so as to not be concerned with practical calculations regarding which actions meet objective standards of value. In the practical realm then, the highest form of knowledge might be beyond us in principle for Maimonides – and a "good" thing too.

---

[37] Whether God would be "bothered" to know such things is another matter.

PART III
The Creator

CHAPTER 5

The Scope of Metaphysics

Daniel Davies and Charles H. Manekin

Maimonides makes extensive use of metaphysics in the *Guide*, but he does not discuss the discipline's nature or many of the basic issues it addresses. Instead, the *Guide's* readers would need to be familiar with the tradition of metaphysical inquiry that Maimonides draws on, which is that of the peripatetic philosophers. Aristotle's *Metaphysics* stands at its head, and Maimonides received it mediated through Greek and Arabic commentaries. Among the major Arabic commentators, Al-Farabi is known as "the second teacher," after Aristotle; the titles are accorded them by Avicenna, who credits Al-Farabi with enabling him to understand the *Metaphysics*. But Al-Farabi states that few understand this book since they approach it with the preconception that metaphysics and theology are equivalent:

> Many people have the preconceived notion that the point and purpose of this book is to discuss the Creator (may He be glorified and exalted!), the intellect, the soul, and other related topics, and that the science of metaphysics and the science of theology are one and the same thing. Consequently, we find that most people who study it are perplexed and misguided by it, since we find that most of the talk in it is devoid of any such aim.[1]

Al-Farabi touches here on a difficulty that continues to be discussed by Aristotle's interpreters today: what is the purpose of metaphysics, and what is the relationship between the various definitions that Aristotle gives to it? Since the word "metaphysics" continues to be used in a variety of ways, Al-Farabi's statement holds true in today's studies on Maimonides as well. The term "metaphysics" is often used to refer to theology or, on occasion, incorporeal beings.[2] As Maimonides instructs readers to peruse the books

---

[1] Al-Farabi's *Aims of Metaphysics* is translated in Bertolacci (2006, 66–72).
[2] For example, Leo Strauss glosses metaphysics as "theology as a philosophic discipline" (Strauss 2004, 538). He also characterizes "divine science" as "the science of the incorporeal beings or of God and the angels" (Strauss 1963, xvi).

of the scientists in order to understand philosophy, it is worth asking what was meant by metaphysics and how it informs the *Guide*.[3] In this essay, we will outline some of the background that stands behind the *Guide*. We will consider Maimonides' own statements about the discipline and its value. Finally, we will briefly touch upon some of the controversies regarding his attitude to metaphysical knowledge and human limitations.

Metaphysics was considered by the Arabic Aristotelian philosophers to be the most exalted of all the sciences. Sciences were divided into practical and speculative, practical dealing with those that lead to action and speculative with matters that end only in thought. Speculative sciences were further divided into three – mathematical, physical, and metaphysical – and distinguished according to their subject matter. Accordingly, mathematical sciences study things inasmuch as they are quantified. They study things that exist in matter but not inasmuch as they are material and subject to motion. Even though mathematical objects, such as shapes for example, only exist in matter, geometry considers them abstracted from matter. Physical sciences study bodily things inasmuch as they are subject to motion, rest, and change. Metaphysics is set apart from other subjects by considering things inasmuch as they are existent, following Aristotle's statement that metaphysics "studies being *qua* being."[4] Metaphysics studies being as a whole, so the object of its study does not necessarily differ from the objects studied by other sciences: each of the other sciences considers existents from a particular perspective. These sciences are particular disciplines, studying a limited aspect of the beings they investigate, while metaphysics is not limited to any particular aspect of being or beings. In this sense, it is the most general of the sciences. It is therefore the "universal science," in that it treats of being as such and is therefore relevant in some way to studying any existing thing. There are concepts – such as unity and multiplicity, act and potency, priority and posteriority, perfection and deficiency – that are used in various sciences, but are not particular to them. These concepts belong to being as such, rather than to being as considered under a particular aspect, and are therefore included in metaphysics.

---

[3] A number of the points made here about the nature of metaphysics were explained in some detail by Alexander Altmann. Altmann's article (Altmann 1987) remains essential reading for anybody interested in Maimonides' understanding of metaphysics and the limits of human cognition, as well as the sources on which he drew.

[4] "Among the sciences, there is one that looks into being inasmuch as it is and speculates on the things that belong to being essentially" (quoted in Averroes 1938, 296).

Given such an account of metaphysics, one might wonder why Al-Farabi's readers might have been confused over the subject matter of metaphysics, and why people think that metaphysics and theology are identical. One simple answer is that Aristotle himself defines metaphysics in different ways, and among these is theology. While he does state that metaphysics investigates "being *qua* being," he also states that it is the study of substance and, on one occasion, that it is concerned with God and the immaterial beings. This raises a question that Al-Farabi attempts to answer by arguing that the same science can be about existence as a whole, about substance, and about God as the cause of all existing things and as the most primary substance. Al-Farabi therefore saw no conflict between the various Aristotelian statements about the nature of metaphysics: it is not limited to theology, but neither is it separate. Ultimately, theology is the most important part of metaphysics and that toward which it builds, but it is the culmination of a lengthy course of study.

Clarifying further, Avicenna distinguished a science's subject from its goal. The subject's existence must be granted by the science in question, as it is that which the science investigates. For example, in geometry, what is investigated is the measurements of continuous quantity abstracted from matter, but the notion of continuous quantity is itself not a measure but a concept. Inasmuch as it is applicable to various things, whatever their matter, it can be said to be itself immaterial. As something immaterial, it is the subject matter of metaphysics rather than of mathematics. Like the other sciences, metaphysics investigates its own subject matter, which it must assume. It cannot assume God's existence, since, in Avicenna's view, God is not shown to exist by any other science. Instead, Avicenna argues that theology is what metaphysics aims at. Maimonides does present physical proofs of God's existence, so he need not have accepted Avicenna's claim that God is not part of the subject of metaphysics.[5] He would nevertheless have recognized that the science is not to be identified

---

[5] The first two of the four enumerated arguments that Maimonides advances for God's existence are physical. See Stern (2001) for an examination of the arguments. Maimonides seems to prevaricate on the matter, as he states that these four proofs demonstrate God's existence but also claims that "it cannot be true that the intellect that moves the highest sphere is the necessary existent, since it has a single notion in common with the other intellects, which is imparting motion to bodies." In the latter claim, he accords with Avicenna, who wished to set the proof of God's existence on purely metaphysical grounds. Avicenna says this in statements gathered by Toby Mayer (2003, 199). Maimonides' conflicting claims are beyond the scope of this essay, but they could perhaps be explained by attending to the diverse aims of the different chapters in which Maimonides makes these claims.

exclusively with theology, even if it is in theological contexts that he makes use of it.

As metaphysics is the most general of the sciences, it is assumed by the others. Concepts that play a key role in physics, for example, are discussed and justified only in metaphysics. So at the beginning of Avicenna's *Physics* of the *Salvation*, following an account of the subject matter of the science, he includes a chapter entitled "On the Principles that the Physicist Accepts and Which Are Demonstrated by the Investigator into Divine Science."[6] Accordingly, because it includes the study of being as a whole, metaphysics also encompasses study into the principles of all the sciences which, after all, enquire into existing things but from particular aspects other than their simply being existents. In view of its generality, Al-Ghazali reverses the order in which he presents the entire disciplines in the *Intentions of the Philosophers*, offering the following explanation:

> Know that their usual custom is to place the physics prior. However, we have chosen to preface this [metaphysics] because it is more important, the disagreements concerning it are greater, and because it is the goal and the aim of the sciences. They only placed it afterwards because of its obscurity and the difficulty in comprehending it before comprehending the physics. (Al-Ghazali 2000, 61)[7]

From this passage, it is clear that the reason metaphysics appears "after the physics" is not only because of its greater eminence, but also because it is easier to grasp natural science first.[8] While metaphysics is prior to the other speculative sciences in nobility and generality, it is posterior in the accepted order of study. There was a broad agreement that students must begin their studies with the exact sciences, move from there to natural science, and finally progress to metaphysics.[9]

In the *Guide*'s opening letter, Maimonides mentions the proper order of study and stresses its importance. The recipient, Joseph ben Judah, had studied the preparatory sciences together with Maimonides, including mathematics, astronomy, and logic, before Maimonides deemed him ready

---

[6] Avicenna (1959, 190–197).
[7] Warren Zev Harvey argues that Maimonides' metaphysics largely follows Avicenna (W. Z. Harvey 2008b, 107–119). Herbert Davidson explains that when Maimonides talks about Aristotle, the doctrines he discusses are Avicenna's. However, when it comes to metaphysics, Davidson argues that Maimonides' arguments could have stemmed from Ghazālī's *Intentions* (Davidson 2005, 103–104).
[8] Avicenna suggests that it would be appropriate to consider metaphysics to be "the science of what is prior to nature," when considered absolutely (Bertolacci 2006, 93).
[9] There was some disagreement over the precise order of elements within those three realms. See Steven Harvey (2006, 676–688).

for exposure to "the secrets of the prophetic books" and allowed him to see "certain flashes" and "certain indications." Only after this, Joseph asks for "additional knowledge" and clarity concerning "certain things pertaining to divine matters." "Divine matters" could be taken to include metaphysics as a whole, but it can also be used to refer specifically to the theological aspects of metaphysics.[10] Either way, we are reminded that there are matters that should not or cannot be taught perspicuously and explicitly. "Know that to begin with this science is very harmful, I mean the divine science. In the same way, it is also harmful to make clear the meaning of the parables of the prophets and to draw attention to the figurative senses of terms used in addressing people, figurative senses of which the books of prophecy are full." (Maimonides 1963, 1.33: 70) But Maimonides does not mention that Joseph had completed his studies in physics before the "secrets of the prophetic books" began to be revealed to him. At this point, it seems, Joseph had learned only the preparatory sciences; the secrets are evidently not limited to metaphysics. This is borne out by Maimonides' practice in the *Guide*. When expounding the secrets, Maimonides includes teachings from both physics and metaphysics.[11] He states that teachers must be wary when instructing pupils in both: "Do not think that only the divine science should be withheld from the multitude. This holds good also for the greater part of natural science" (Maimonides 1963, 1.17: 42).

Maimonides emphasizes the need for a careful program when embarking on the scientific curriculum, in which people are first taught true beliefs and only afterwards authorized to study them in depth. Believing on the basis of imitation (*taqlīd*) is often considered negative. Imitation rubs against the imperative to understand and thereby perfect the intellect, which is necessary for human perfection, but tradition also plays an important positive role here.[12] Maimonides states that everybody must be taught certain doctrinal truths about God: unity, eternity,

---

[10] In Al-Farabi's *Aims of Metaphysics*, the "divine science" is said to belong to metaphysics and also to be "this science in a certain way" (Bertolacci 2006, 70). Avicenna also uses the term to refer at times to metaphysics as a whole and at others to its theological aspects. See Bertolacci (2006, 126–130).
[11] For the different kinds of biblical parables Maimonides identifies, and the relative worth of their "external" meanings, see Kaplan (2018, 67–85). Kaplan explains that ethical matters are sometimes indicated by the "external" meanings of the texts while speculative sciences constitute the "internal" meanings. Note especially his interpretation of the Account of the Beginning, in which he includes a description of the physical world.
[12] For a recent account of the complexity of "imitation," see Ibrahim (2016). For imitation in the *Guide*, see Michaelis (2017). Yehuda Halper examines a passage in the *Mishneh Torah* (Laws Concerning Idolatry 2:2–3) in which Maimonides forbids philosophy to those who have not yet internalized true religious beliefs on the basis of tradition. He argues that Maimonides thereby forbids philosophy altogether and that the *Guide* is intended to save those who have already fallen

incorporeality, impassivity, and dissimilarity to all created beings (Maimonides 1963, 1.35: 80–81). That goes even for those who are incapable of properly understanding the full import of such ideas – and this, Maimonides states, includes the vast majority of people. According to Maimonides, to know that God exists, is one, and is incorporeal, is a commandment incumbent on all Jews – the multitude as well as the intellectual elite – and the forswearance of idolatry is incumbent upon all gentiles. If one believes that God is corporeal, one denies his unity (Maimonides 1963, 1.35: 81); indeed, if one believes that God has attributes superadded to his essence, one lacks a concept of God altogether and "denies the existence of the deity without being aware of it" (Maimonides 1963, 1.60: 145). On the one hand, divine science is not for the uneducated or for those without preparation; on the other hand, some correct theological beliefs are required even for the uneducated multitude. Maimonides is adamant about the need to provide children and the multitude with a measure of knowledge sufficient to establish in their minds "that there is a perfect being who is neither a body nor a force in a body, and that He is the deity, that no sort of deficiency and therefore no affection whatever can attain Him" (Maimonides 1963, 1.35: 80). If they are unable to see the truth of these beliefs for themselves, they should be made to accept them on traditional authority. Nonetheless, even though most people are incapable of grasping such doctrines and, therefore, should not be taught them in detail, the ultimate human goal involves properly understanding them. In cases in which people are able to progress beyond mere imitation, imitation is an initial step that fixes belief in fundamental principles in the minds of those who have not yet begun their development; they should progress gradually in that understanding, lest doubt and confusion shake their beliefs.

Maimonides' elitism is displayed here, and he finds support for it in both the philosophical and rabbinic traditions. The philosophers argued that not everybody is suited to undertake speculative investigation. People are born with varied capacities and, additionally, circumstances prevent

---

prey to its pernicious effect (Halper 2018). Halper's argument relies on equating philosophical study with "freethinking" or "free inquiry." In opposition, if the important positive role of *taqlīd* is taken into account, the two can be differentiated. The passage to which he refers does not forbid the study of philosophy; it forbids questioning the truth of the fundamental principles of the Law. So just as philosophical inquiry is forbidden to those for whom it will lead to doubting those true beliefs, it is mandated for those who require it in order to possess those true beliefs with certainty and understanding. After these foundational doctrines have been properly fixed in the mind of the enquirer, together with a thorough knowledge of the *halakhah*, philosophical thinking is permitted in order to understand them correctly.

many from pursuing scientific study (*Guide* 1.34). Arabic thinkers therefore sometimes presented works in a way that would be deliberately obscure to uneducated readers, in order to make sure that they were not exposed to material that was beyond them and which would confuse them. This had the added advantage of enabling the author to test and train readers as it forced them to work in order to understand the text.[13] By employing methods like dispersing information across different parts of a work, they were able to conceal certain teachings while revealing it only to the worthy.[14] This aspect was particularly important in the *Guide*, as Maimonides' work replaces personal tuition of the now-absent Joseph. Maimonides also warns the readers not to expect more than "chapter headings," and that even they "are not set down in order or arranged in coherent fashion in this treatise" (Maimonides 1963, 1.introduction: 6).

When, in his letter to Joseph, Maimonides speaks of "divine secrets" hidden in the prophetic books, a great deal of biblical scripture is included. However, he states that the primary purpose of the *Guide* is to explain the "account [or: work] of the beginning" and the "account [or: work] of the chariot," the two deepest secrets, generally taken to be the opening passages of Genesis and Ezekiel. In the Commentary on the Mishnah, he explains that the "account of the beginning" stands for "natural science" and the "account of the chariot" for "divine science," which he glosses as "metaphysics."[15] He therefore identifies metaphysics with the rabbinic esoteric wisdom known as "the account of the chariot" (*ma'aseh merkavah*). By identifying the account of the beginning and the account of the chariot with physics and metaphysics, respectively, Maimonides not only legitimized these areas of knowledge from a rabbinic point of view but also subjected them to Jewish legal strictures. Neither subject was to be taught publicly, and the account of the chariot was to be taught only to solitary individuals who are capable of understanding it on their own.

What was so dangerous about metaphysics that merited limiting its instruction? Maimonides hints at an answer in the introduction to the *Guide*'s first part:

> God, may His mention be exalted, wished us to be perfected and the state of our societies to be improved by His laws regarding actions. Now this can come about only after the adoption of intellectual beliefs, the first of which

---

[13] For an outline of some background, see Dimitri Gutas (2014, 256–266).
[14] See, for example, the discussion by Mohammad Ali Amir-Muezzi (1994, 127–128).
[15] Maimonides (1992, Heb. 256, Arab. 398), where the phrase glosses *al-'ilm al-'ilāhī*. See also *Guide* 1.introduction: 6 and 1.34.

being His apprehension, according to our capacity. This, in its turn cannot come about except through divine science, and this divine science cannot become actual except after a study of natural science. (Maimonides 1963, 1. introduction: 8–9)

Human perfection requires the possession of intellectual beliefs that are contained in divine science, chief of which is the apprehension of God. But this claim returns us to the need for a correct programme in which pupils move through a set syllabus in order to train their capacities. Divine science involves many obscure matters and can only be achieved after mastering, to the best of our abilities, natural science. The latter requires knowledge of the propaedeutic sciences, like math and astronomy, and the art of logic, through which one distinguishes demonstration from dialectical and rhetorical arguments. One who begins one's studies with divine science will never be able to digest its doctrines. Maimonides devotes several chapters of the *Guide* to the difficulties of divine science and the harm caused when one begins one's studies with it (*Guide* 1.31–34). He refers both to the doctrines of divine science and to the interpretation of the scriptural passages that indicate these doctrines. One of Maimonides' goals in the *Guide* is to delineate what of divine science can be known with certainty or near certainty and what will be subject to doubt. Not knowing what one can and cannot know with certainty or near certainty leads to intellectual error, and intellectual error for Maimonides spells heresy, idolatry, and spiritual extinction. There are beliefs whose possession can be fatal, and teaching them may be punishable by death (Maimonides 1963, 3.51: 619).

What does Maimonides mean by "divine science"? When explaining the rabbinic prohibition of teaching the account of the chariot, he writes:

> Hear from me what has become evident to me, according to my opinion, from what I examined of the sages' discourse. Natural science and delving into the principles of existence, they call "the account of the beginning." And by "the account of the chariot" they mean divine science, i.e., the discourse on the totality of existence, and on the existence of the Creator, and his knowledge, and his attributes, and the necessary following (*luzūm*) of the existents from him, and the angels, and the soul and the intellect conjoined with man, and the fate after death.[16]

If "totality of existence" means something like existence in general, or absolute existence, then Maimonides may be assuming the Farabian

---

[16] *Commentary on the Mishnah: Hagigah* 2:1.

distinction between general and special metaphysics, i.e., between the investigation of that which is common to all existing beings (existence and unity and their accidents), and the investigation of God and His attributes, the incorporeal intellects (including the human acquired intellect and its fate after death), and how existing things follow or emanate from God.[17] In any event, neither he nor his Arabic Aristotelian predecessors always limit "divine science" to theology, strictly speaking, though the latter is an important part of divine science. Maimonides might be inconsistent in his use of the term, like his predecessors, by applying it sometimes to metaphysics as a whole and sometimes to the particularly theological aspect of metaphysics, whether they are the most exalted parts of metaphysics or its goal.

In the *Mishneh Torah*, Maimonides spells out more. He begins by outlining the two subjects he identifies in the Mishnah. He devotes the first two chapters of the Laws Concerning the Foundations of the Torah to the "principles," or "chapter headings," of subjects whose elucidation constitutes "the account of the chariot." These chapters include information about God's existence, His relationship to the world, how He is to be described, and how He knows the world, as well as information about the existence of the separate incorporeal intellects, their incorporeal nature, relation to each other, scriptural names, intellective activities, and how they know God. By contrast, the principles in the next two chapters – which deal with the existence of the celestial spheres, their number, movements, and divisions into subsidiary spheres, and substance, as well as the existence of the sublunar elements and their number, place, nature, and activity – belong to the account of the beginning (i.e., physical science). Even that part of the human soul that is independent in some sense of the body – what Maimonides calls "the form of the soul," namely, the intellect that cognizes the incorporeal intelligibles like the angels – is mentioned by Maimonides in the chapters that deal with the account of the beginning rather than the account of the chariot.[18] This is certainly not unusual in Arabic philosophy; Avicenna includes the human intellective soul within the scope of physics rather than metaphysics, despite his belief that the human soul is substantial and the human intellect incorporeal.[19] However, Avicenna also includes prophetology and the fate of the human

---

[17] See note 1, this essay.
[18] *Mishneh Torah*, Laws Concerning the Foundations of the Torah, 4:8–9.
[19] Some passages on the soul are translated in Fazlur Rahman (1952).

soul in his metaphysics.[20] In sum, in the pre-*Guide* writings, the scope of divine science, which Maimonides identifies with the rabbinic statements about the account of the chariot, includes truths about God and the incorporeal intellects, but not – at least directly – the celestial bodies and their movements. The distinction between divine science and natural science appears to be based on the entities investigated.

Maimonides does not engage in the *Guide* in classifying the sciences, so the use to which he puts metaphysics is seen only through the lens of the work's overall purpose, which is religious and theological, not through his own definition. Nor can one simply look to explicit references to the term. He rarely uses the Arabic or Hebrew terms for "metaphysics" (*ma ba'da al-tabi'a/ma-she-achar ha-teva*) to describe an area of inquiry or science. The term is used in the *Guide* as part of the phrase "the Book of the Metaphysics," sometimes with an explicit reference to Aristotle. However, not all these references are to Aristotle's *Metaphysics*, at least not in the Arabic versions known to us, and some are reference to concepts that are distinctly Avicennan.[21] So one cannot determine Maimonides' views of the scope of metaphysics merely by examining passages in which he refers to "metaphysics" or to books by the Arabic Aristotelians with the title "Metaphysics." In the Commentary on the Mishnah, there is reference to "first philosophy" (*al-falsafa al-ūlā*), which is another Aristotelian term for metaphysics.[22] Maimonides reports that the nature of human felicity, which involves knowing God as far as possible and, consequently, the soul's endurance, is explained in "first philosophy," which may recall how Avicenna included it in the metaphysics.[23]

While "divine science" is said in the Commentary on the Mishnah to be metaphysics, Maimonides does not offer a formal definition in the *Guide*, nor does he provide a statement of its scope. Perhaps he assumes that the reader will know what the term includes; after all, his purpose is not "to make an epitome of the divine science according to some doctrines" but rather "to elucidate the difficult points of the Law and to make manifest the true realities of its hidden meanings." (Maimonides 1963, 2.2: 253). In the absence of a clear delineation one should be careful about interpreting certain passages. For example, Maimonides writes that the second-century

---

[20] In the *Intentions*, Al-Ghazali attaches these questions to the *Physics*, in a section concerning what the Active Intellect bestows on the human souls. He explains that it is appropriate for natural science because it does not concern the Active Intellect in itself but, rather, its influence on souls. See Al-Ghazali (2000, 211).
[21] Davidson (2005, 93; 102); Freudenthal and Zonta (2012, 223–226).
[22] Maimonides (1964, 205).   [23] Avicenna (1959, 698–718).

Tanna, R. Aqiba, "entered in peace and went out in peace"[24] when he was occupied in the theoretical study of *hadhihī al-'umūr al-'ilāhiya*, which Pines, following Munk, translates as "these metaphysical matters."[25] But later in the *Guide*, when R. Aqiba is quoted as saying, "When you come to the stones of pure marble [in Pardes] do not say, Water, Water ...," Maimonides writes that the Tanna is referring to the substance beyond the firmament and not to sublunar water. Whether Rabbi Aqiba is referring to the substance of the heavenly bodies, or to a phenomenon in the upper atmosphere,[26] it would appear to belong to the account of the beginning, and thus be relevant to *Guide* 2.30, Maimonides' cryptic interpretation of the account of the beginning in Genesis, and not in *Guide* 3.1–7, Maimonides' equally cryptic interpretation of Ezekiel's account of the chariot. It is perhaps for this reason that Samuel ibn Tibbon, in his glossary to his revised translation of the *Guide*, writes that the phrase "divine matters" (*'inyanim elohiyim*) in the *Guide* "alludes to the spheres, the planets, and their accidents."[27]

On the other hand, the phrase "divine matters" can also refer to God and the incorporeal intellects (Maimonides 1963, 3.23: 472; 3.51: 619). Perhaps Maimonides distinguishes between "divine science" and "divine matters," treating the former as coextensive with metaphysics, and the latter as having a wider extension, which includes on occasions the heavens. Considering the celestial bodies "divine" captures their intermediate status: insofar as the spheres and planets are bodies in motion, they are to be investigated by physics, but insofar as their matter and motion are noble, and their rank and distance remote from coarse sublunar matter, they are to be considered as divine matters. In fact, as we shall see in Section 5.1, the study of the heavens can be considered part of divine science insofar as the heavens exercise divine governance. Moreover, in Al-Farabi's scheme, they can be studied as part of metaphysics when they are considered as causes of the existence of sublunar beings, not only as the causes of their motion.[28]

As for the phrase "divine science," Maimonides writes in one passage that apprehension of God is meant by the divine science that is designated as "account of the chariot" (Maimonides 1963, 1.34: 77), and in another

---

[24] *Babylonian Talmud* Chagigah, 14b.
[25] Maimonides (1963, 1.32: 68). Pines provides the literal translation ("divine") in a footnote.
[26] See Klein-Braslavy (1986, 186); Davies (2011, 130).
[27] Maimonides (2000, 74). In Avicenna's *Compendium on the Soul*, "Divine Matters" encompasses the entire discipline of metaphysics. See Bertolacci (2006, 581).
[28] Bertolacci (2006, 97).

that "it is impossible to forget this [divine] science, I mean, the apprehension of the active intellect." (Maimonides 1963, 1.62: 152). In yet another passage he discusses a list of topics that are "mysteries of the Torah ... that ought not to be spoken of except in chapter headings ... and only with an individual such as has been described," which is another way of referring to the topics falling within the scope of divine science (Maimonides 1963, 1.35: 80–81). These include the discussion of divine attributes, creation, governance, providence, prophecy, etc., as well as the concepts and doctrines that such subjects presuppose. Maimonides' doctrine of divine attributes, for example, requires knowledge of, *inter alia*, the distinction between substance and attribute, the concept of unity, the principle that existence is an accident attached to what exists, etc. His arguments against the Kalam theologians, and for and against the philosophers with respect to theological positions, rest on physical and metaphysical principles.

5.1 The Account of the Chariot and Ezekiel's Vision of the Chariot

The phrase "account of the chariot" stems from Ezekiel's visions, in which the prophet describes a rider on top of four beasts steering a chariot. It is an awesome depiction and became the focus of a good deal of speculation. In the introduction to his interpretation, Maimonides writes,

> ...in that which has occurred to me with regard to these matters, I followed conjecture and supposition; no divine revelation has come to me to teach me that the intention in the matter in question was such and such, nor did I receive what I believe in these matters from a teacher. But the texts of the prophetic books and the dicta of the *Sages*, together with the speculative premises that I possess, showed me that things are indubitably so and so. Yet it is possible that they are different and that something else is intended. Now rightly guided reflection and divine aid in this matter have moved me to a position, which I shall describe. (Maimonides 1963, 3.Int: 415)

Note that Maimonides does not write that he understood the intention of Ezekiel's vision solely with the aid of his knowledge of physics and metaphysics. Rather, he writes that the prophetic books, the dicta of the sages, and the speculative (i.e., philosophical) premises taken together showed him the proper interpretation. Although he has no grounds upon which to doubt that interpretation, he allows that he may be mistaken, probably because of the obscurity of the matter and because of Scripture's concealment. But he draws on all three sources – scripture, the dicta of the sages, and reason (i.e., philosophy) – to come up with his interpretation of Ezekiel, and of how the vision portrays the heavenly influence on sublunar reality.[29]

As mentioned in the previous section, Maimonides claimed that the rabbis referred to divine science as "the account of the chariot," but little of Maimonides' interpretation of Ezekiel's visions of the heavenly chariots appears to relate to the subject matter of metaphysics. The beasts dragging the chariot represent the heavenly spheres; the wheels symbolize sublunar matter; and the rider stands for the intelligences. The visions of the chariot have much more to do with cosmology than with metaphysics, a point already made by the medieval commentators.[30] Maimonides is adamant that nowhere in the visions is God Himself portrayed as a likeness (Maimonides 1963, 3.7: 430), but the apprehension of God was seen to be the object of divine science. Cosmology, according to Maimonides, is part of the account of the beginning, not the account of the chariot.[31] Even if Maimonides holds that there is more to the account of the chariot than Ezekiel's visions of the chariot, it still seems odd that Ezekiel's visions have little or nothing to do with metaphysics. Has Maimonides shifted the borders of the account of the chariot to include cosmology? Has he removed Ezekiel's vision of the chariot from the account of the chariot?

Scholars are divided as to why Maimonides limits Ezekiel's vision to cosmology. According to Gad Freudenthal, Maimonides's thought evolved between writing the *Mishneh Torah* and writing the *Guide*. In the former, Ezekiel's vision appeared to be entirely within the scope of metaphysics. The "wheels" (*ofannim*) of the chariot, the cherubs (*keruvim*), and the holy beasts (*chayyot ha-qodesh*) were identified with the angels, i.e., separate intelligences; the holy beasts were considered to be the highest rank of angels, below that of God. By the time of the *Guide*, however, the wheels were taken to indicate the sublunar elements and the cherubs and beasts the celestial spheres.[32] Why did Maimonides change the interpretation?

---

[29] The notion that Maimonides genuinely was influenced by scripture and the dicta of the sages in developing his views on divine science is not uncontroversial. Altmann, for example, claims that "...in [Maimonides'] view, the outline of Aristotelian metaphysics may be legitimately projected upon the basic teachings of the Jewish esoteric tradition" (Altmann 1987, 109). Yet Maimonides does not consider himself to be projecting the outline of Aristotelian metaphysics upon the teachings of the Jewish esoteric tradition so much as uncovering within that tradition certain ideas also taught by the Aristotelian. Where there is fundamental disagreement over metaphysical issues (e.g., creation, prophecy, providence) Maimonides relies on Jewish tradition as he philosophically interprets it.

[30] For a recent analysis of Maimonides' interpretation of the vision, see Davies (2011, 106–132); cf. Kreisel (2015, 209–270), for an account of the history of *ma'aseh merkavah* through thirteenth century Maimonidean philosophy.

[31] *Mishneh Torah, Laws Concerning the Foundations of the Torah* 3; 4:10. Cf. *Guide* 2.30.

[32] Freudenthal (2007, 228–229).

The answer, according to Freudenthal, lies in Maimonides' adoption, after he wrote the *Mishneh Torah*, of a four-globe model of the heavens. According to his model, five planets (Venus, Mars, Mercury, Jupiter, and Saturn) are contained in one globe, and the sun, the moon, and the fixed star in three others, with each globe governing one of the four sublunar elements. There are also four causes of the movements of the sphere and four sorts of general forces deriving from the motion of the spheres that generate and preserve sublunar existents. Maimonides views this as his own original view and interprets Ezekiel's vision of the chariot in its light. In other words, the account of the chariot shifted from metaphysics to cosmology because the four-globe cosmology Maimonides had recently adopted accorded well with the four-wheeled chariot led by the four beasts of the vision. Since the vision also alluded to the separate intellects, the movers of the spheres, it could still be considered within the scope of metaphysics.[33]

Daniel Davies argues that Maimonides' presentation indicates that Ezekiel's cosmological vision of the chariot is not as profound as the rabbis seem to indicate, a reflection of the relatively low rank of prophecy that Ezekiel attained. Rather than metaphysics, the vision portrays the cosmos as a whole, including the heavens and the sublunar world, together with their interrelationships. Much of this is a part of natural science. Furthermore, he argues that Maimonides associated Ezekiel with streams of thought popular in his time but to which he objected, particularly those exemplified by the Brethren of Purity. Building on a number of medieval and modern commentators, Davies argues that Maimonides viewed the four-globe model in which each globe influences a separate element as a mistaken understanding of how the heavenly motions cause those on earth, one of several mistakes to be found in Ezekiel's visions. Ezekiel's vision not only omits much of what is important in the account of the chariot, understood as metaphysics, but it also veers into the direction of Maimonides' *bête noire*, astrology. Since Maimonides cannot openly attribute these errors to the prophet Ezekiel, he can only hint at them to the careful reader, which accounts, in part, for his cryptic explanations.[34] It would also explain why Maimonides thought that the rabbis wanted to conceal Ezekiel's views, as he interprets the teachings of the Law to be opposed to some of them.

Whether Maimonides enthusiastically embraced Ezekiel's vision, or rejected it as flawed, one can read the vision as dealing with an eminently theological – hence metaphysical – topic, i. e., the character of God's

---

[33] Ibid. (229–230). [34] Davies (2011, 146–154).

governance of the world. In several places Maimonides writes that the philosophers, the Torah, and the sages teach that God governs the world through the forces overflowing from the spheres (Maimonides 1963, 1.72: 186–187; 2.5: 261; 2.10). The four-globe theory is introduced in *Guide* 2.10 to offer one of the theories concerning how sublunar existence is generated and preserved, i. e, "the preservation of its species in a permanent way and the preservation of the individuals for a certain period of time":

> This is the meaning of "nature," which is said to be wise, having governance ... What is intended hereby is the divine decree from which these two activities [generation and preservation of sublunar existents] drive through the intermediary of the sphere. (Maimonides 1963, 2.10: 272)

The term translated in this quotation as "the divine decree" is *al-'amr al-ilāhī*, which in the plural is translated by Pines as "divine matters," the term that Samuel Ibn Tibbon says alludes to the spheres, the planets, and their accidents. Ezekiel's visions of the structure of the heavens, insofar as the heavens are the agents of divine governance, belong to metaphysics rather than cosmology. Indeed, it is not surprising that Maimonides begins part three of the *Guide* with his interpretation of Ezekiel's visions since the overarching theme of this part is divine governance, first via nature and second via the law. So even if Maimonides has changed the details of his interpretation of the wheels and the beasts, he continues to use the term "account of the chariot" to refer to divine science. If this interpretation is correct, then he has not opted for the greater importance of cosmology over metaphysics. Rather, he has interpreted Ezekiel's account in light of a theory of how the spheres generate and preserve the world, a topic that belongs to divine science and not only to natural science. It is also possible that he uses the term "account of the chariot" to refer to different things, which would explain why he discusses theological matters after finishing his chapters on Ezekiel with the comment that he will not say anything more about the subject, but will now embark on other subjects instead (Maimonides 1963, 3.7: 430).

The nature of human perfection runs through those subjects, which include the nature of evil, the purpose of creation, and the Law's aim. Since the human goal includes intellectual perfection, it involves learning scientific and philosophical truth, which culminates in knowledge of metaphysics. This assumes that people are capable of obtaining, in varying measures, knowledge concerning divine matters. However, although it is a universal science, there are limitations to metaphysics, as there are to the human intellect. Maimonides qualifies the human goal, to know God, with the phrase "to the extent possible" (Maimonides 1963, 1.54: 123; 3.51: 619). Accordingly, the epistemic worth of such knowledge has been the subject of scholarly dispute, not only in the case of the multitude, but also in the case of the elite. Much ink has been spilled in recent years over whether Maimonides genuinely believes that the intellectual elite, those who have studied philosophy and science in the proper way, are able to possess genuine metaphysical knowledge, i.e., the sort that allows for attachment or conjunction with the active intellect, and the immortality of the acquired intellect. Attempts have been made to see him as a proto-Kantian or within a skeptical tradition on the subject of the possibility of genuine metaphysical knowledge.[35]

The present writers believe that Maimonides' views on the limitations of human knowledge of metaphysics place him squarely within the mainstream Aristotelian tradition. As he puts it,

> Do not think that what we have said with regard to the insufficiency of the human intellect and its having a limit at which it stops is a statement made in order to conform to Law. For it is something that has already been said and truly grasped by the philosophers without their having concern for a particular doctrine or opinion. And it is a true thing that cannot be doubted except by an individual ignorant of what has already been demonstrated. (Maimonides 1963, 1.31: 67)

The philosophers, in this case, the Arabic Aristotelians, teach that the human intellect is limited, and that the failure to appreciate these limits may indeed be the cause of holding false beliefs or beliefs without sufficient warrant. With the exception of the doctrines of creation, prophecy, providence, and divine knowledge of particulars, all of which pertain to what he calls the foundations of the Law, Maimonides sides with the Arabic Aristotelians, as he understands them; at the end of the *Guide* he provides an interpretation of special providence that he believes fulfils the requirements of the philosophers (Maimonides 1963, 3.51: 625). His deviations stem from his desire to preserve a more robust notion of divine justice and omnipotence than he finds within his philosophical predecessors. At least within his self-perception, Maimonides comes down squarely on the side of the philosophers on the question of the divine attributes. His account differs from those of many of his contemporaries only in the

---

[35] For the proto-Kantian interpretation, see Pines (1979) and rejoinders by Altmann (1987) and Davidson (2011, 173–211); for the sceptical reading see Stern (2009; 2013) and rejoinder by Manekin (2012; 2018). What follows draws from Manekin (2018).

extent to which he explicitly permits words to be used properly of God, not in the extent to which God can be known.[36]

Although Maimonides emphasizes the insufficiency of the human intellect in achieving knowledge of some parts of reality, he is deeply indebted to Aristotelian metaphysics. Throughout the *Guide*, he refers to, indeed assumes the truth of, such principles as are taught outright by philosophers, and alluded to by scriptural hints, indications, and parables. They "have been expounded in many books, and the correctness of most of them have been demonstrated" (Maimonides 1963, 2.2: 253). Even though he debates the philosophers over whether the world is causally necessitated from God, he does not take the road of Al-Ghazali and question the adequacy of their concept of causation; on the contrary, he finds nothing wrong with the philosophers' view that God is first cause and first ground of the world (Maimonides 1963, 1.69: 166–171). His argument against the philosophical denial of God's knowledge of particulars rests on his acceptance of the philosophers' premises that God's essence cannot be comprehended, and that his essence is not distinct from his knowledge; his complaint against the philosophers is that they should have concluded from this that God's knowledge is incomprehensible (Maimonides 1963, 3.20: 481). Aside from this comment about God's knowledge, Maimonides' disagreements with the philosophers are, at least in part, theologically motivated.

Despite Maimonides' real debt to Aristotelian metaphysics, he does not *identify* it with divine science: Maimonides' divine science is metaphysics, but not purely Aristotelian, for there are places where the two diverge. For example, his view that God wills the world into existence after absolute nonexistence, a doctrine for which he argues with "proofs approximating a demonstration," is a doctrine that clearly belongs to divine science, yet it runs counter to the metaphysics of the philosophers. So are his doctrines of miracles and prophecy, although they also share much in common. His doctrine of special providence could have been taught by the philosophers, but in fact all doctrines are taught only by Scripture and the Law.[37] Like other doctrines of divine science, they are not taught openly; on the contrary, the discussion of divine attributes, creation, governance, providence, prophecy, etc., are "obscure matters ... truly the mysteries of the Torah and the secrets

---

[36] See Manekin (1990, 117–141) and Davies (2011, 54–105).

[37] In the *Letter on Astrology*, which refers to the *Guide*, Maimonides claims that creation after absolute nonexistence was taught by a group of philosophers. See Maimonides (1995, 483); English translation is in Lerner (2000, 182).

constantly mentioned in the books of the prophets and in the dicta of the sages" (Maimonides 1963, 1.35: 80).

What interests Maimonides is not whether one can possess scientific knowledge of divine matters, but rather what sort of theological beliefs can and cannot be held with certain and near-certain knowledge. According to our view, Maimonides' enemy is doubt, not dogmatism. Although doubts sometimes have pedagogic value in spurring students on to find new answers that will relieve their doubts, doubts are, on the whole, bad because they can lead people astray. Thus, Maimonides warns in the *Mishneh Torah* against speculating on the foundations of religion by those who are easily led astray by doubts and false beliefs:

> For man's intellect is limited, and not all intellects are able to apprehend truth fully; thus, if every man follows his own thoughts, he will destroy his world according to his limited intellect. How? Sometimes he will stray after idolatry and sometimes he will think concerning the Creator's oneness, perhaps it is the case, perhaps it is not [...] *He doesn't know the measures* (middot) *according to which one knows the truth fully, and hence he becomes a heretic* (our italics).[38]

Maimonides distinguishes between those who can apprehend the truth fully and those who cannot; the latter lack the proper measures or procedure according to which one comes to know the truth fully. Receiving a theological doctrine on the basis of *taqlīd* may be necessary for those who are at the beginning of their studies or who are not able to understand on their own, but, even if the tradition is correct, such beliefs are subject to doubt. Speculation concerning the foundations of religion is not just dangerous for the ignorant but also for the educated who engage in it. If they fall into error in the course of speculation or because they follow the authority of others who are have fallen into error, they distance themselves from the truth.

Maimonides writes that certainty and near certainty are attainable in divine matters, and, in Maimonides' parable of the palace, those who have attained "perfection in the natural things and have understood divine science," to the extent that it is possible, are within the habitation of the ruler;" They are the *'ulamā'*, the men of knowledge or science, of which there are varying degrees. (Maimonides 1963, 3.51, 619). But the goal of certain and near-certain knowledge (where certain knowledge is unattainable) can be achieved only through following the proper methods and going about things in the right order. As Maimonides reminds his student in the dedicatory epistle to the *Guide*,

---

[38] *Mishneh Torah, Laws Concerning Idolatry* 2:3.

> Yet I did not cease dissuading you from this and enjoining upon you to approach matters in an orderly manner. My purpose in this was that the truth should be established in your mind according to the proper methods and that certainty should not come to you by accident. (Maimonides 1963, 1. epistle dedicatory, 4)

For Maimonides, then, certain knowledge (i.e., the knowledge that is established in the mind essentially and according to the proper methods) provides the *firm and rooted* experience of the intelligible. That may be why the quest for certainty, even in metaphysics, is such an important part of Maimonides' epistemological project.

CHAPTER 6

His Existence Is Essentiality
Maimonides as Metaphysician

Aaron Segal

6.1 Metaphysical Maimonides

Maimonides famously says some rather radical things about God – radical even by philosophical standards – both about what God is like "in Himself" and about God's relationship with the created universe. Maimonides' most detailed and sustained presentation of these radical ideas is in his discussion of divine attributes in chapters 50–70 of the *Guide*. Indeed, it seems evident that Maimonides' *point* in that section is to make plain these radical ideas. To put matters rather simply and straightforwardly, the radical ideas are these: Strictly speaking, God shares nothing substantive in common with created beings, neither **existence** nor **life** nor **power** nor **knowledge**. Indeed, strictly speaking, God *has no intrinsic nature at all, no attributes at all,* and stands in *no relations whatsoever to the created universe* – save for negative attributes and attributes of action. Even speaking strictly, God *does* have negative attributes and *does* stand in whatever relations to the created universe are entailed by His having attributes of action.

As I say, all this is plainly contained in chapters 50–70 of the *Guide*. But, as is so often the case with Maimonides, if you go ahead and claim that Maimonides' considered view is identical with what he seems to say, you court significant controversy. Due to certain philosophical puzzles and textual tensions to which I will soon turn, a number of scholars have argued that Maimonides' considered view differs from the one he appears to endorse in those chapters. On the one hand, some scholars argue that Maimonides holds a view even *more* radical and austere than what you might naturally understand him to mean, according to which God has no attributes, *period*. That is, strictly speaking, God has neither negative attributes nor attributes of action, either. Austere, indeed – one wonders

I am deeply indebted to Zev Harvey and Josef Stern for providing extensive and invaluable feedback.

if there's anything *there,* there. On the other hand, some scholars argue that Maimonides holds a view less radical and more pedestrian than the impression he gives, according to which: while we don't understand God's nature, we can at least grasp – and even know – *that* God exists and has a nature. And if we can know that it is so, then of course it *is* so. More pedestrian, indeed – one wonders what all the fuss is about.

I don't think either of these positions gets Maimonides right. I think Maimonides means just what he seems to say here. As I have indicated, the scholars who disagree are not without their good reasons. The view Maimonides seems to hold certainly faces a number of challenges and involves us in some serious puzzles. I will turn in Section 6.3 to the task of outlining and addressing these challenges and puzzles, a task that will occupy me for the remainder of the essay. But the truth is, the divide between my reading and the alternative readings revolves around an issue that is in some ways deeper, and prior to, any of those individual challenges. For even my description of the *topic* of these chapters is likely to draw resistance, if not outright criticism, from some quarters.

Notice that as I put it, Maimonides is in these chapters making robustly *metaphysical* claims – claims that are, in the first instance at least, about the nature of *reality*; and, in particular, about the nature of God. If I am right, then Maimonides is not, at least in the first instance, making second-order claims about what we can say, or truly say, about the nature of God. Of course, any claim, even one about extralinguistic reality, has implications for what one can truly say. For if it's the case that p, then 'p' is true. And *maybe* the particular claims Maimonides makes about God have implications for what we can say (about God), *period*. But these implications are just that; *implications* of Maimonides' central contentions about reality itself, all of them downstream of his main point.

But that is not how most scholars seem to approach this section of the *Guide*.[1] Here, for example, is how Arthur Hyman begins a classic paper entitled "Maimonides on Religious Language":

> Moses Maimonides maintained a lively interest in questions of language, particularly language concerning God, throughout his life ... and in his philosophic *Guide of the Perplexed* he devotes most of the first part of the

---

[1] There are exceptions. Buijs, for example, clearly draws the distinction between the metaphysical component of negative theology and the semantic component of negative theology (and between both of them and the epistemic component), and sees the former as explaining or undergirding the latter (Buijs 1988, note 10). See also Feldman (1968), Manekin (1990), and Stern (2013), who are careful to disentangle these different strands.

work to a more rigorous, philosophic discussion of divine attributes and names. (Hyman 1991, 175)

As Hyman goes on to make clear (Hyman 1991, 179–180), the "most of the first part" to which he refers includes not just the explicitly exegetical chapters (1–49) – which deal with the meanings of anthropomorphic and anthropopathic Biblical terms – but also with the continuation that deals with divine attributes in general.

And Hyman is far from alone in seeing this section of the *Guide* as centrally focused on religious *language*, on what we can *say*, or *say truly*, about God – or, more broadly, on how we can correctly represent God, whether in speech or in thought – rather than on God Himself. Thus, in a recent work devoted to Maimonides' life and thought, the discussion of this section of the *Guide*, and of the topic of divine attributes in general, is in a chapter entitled "What we can say about God."[2]

Call my reading of this section 'the metaphysical reading', and the dominant reading 'the linguistic reading'.[3] It might seem that the metaphysical reading and the linguistic reading can agree on all points of substance, and that what divides them is merely a matter of emphasis. But that isn't so. The one affirms what the other denies, and the other affirms what the one denies. For according to the metaphysical reading Maimonides is making certain metaphysical claims about God, claims that no one can make (let alone make truly) if the linguistic reading is right. Moreover, differing emphases can *lead* to asking different questions and reaching very different conclusions. The puzzles that are raised on the metaphysical reading are very different from the puzzles that are raised on the linguistic reading, and call for metaphysical solutions, not linguistic ones. As I will argue, solving the metaphysical puzzle seems to require claims that are less radical than those which would be required to solve the parallel linguistic ones, were there such problems that we had to contend with.

Again, the proponents of the linguistic reading in general are not without their good reasons. For one thing, Maimonides undoubtedly did "maintain a lively interest in questions of language," as Hyman claims. For

---

[2] Rudavsky (2010). See also Ivry (2016), whose discussion of chapters 50–68 in the *Guide* is part and parcel of a larger section entitled "Wrestling with Language."

[3] I don't mean to imply that these readings are exhaustive – neither one captures the emphasis on epistemology found in some readings (e.g., Stern 2013) – and I should make clear that the linguistic reading might in some cases be more aptly named 'the representational reading', since in those cases it sees Maimonides as concerned with representation of God more broadly, not just in external speech.

another thing, chapters 50–70 of the *Guide* do of course follow immediately upon the heels of the explicitly exegetical chapters (1–49), which are explicitly concerned with Biblical terms. For a final thing, a distinction between two senses of 'attribute' – the one, metaphysical sense, in which attributes are on the world-side of the word/world divide, and the other, linguistic sense, in which they are on the word-side of that divide – is hard to draw given the so-called conceptualist theory of universals that Maimonides seems to endorse.[4] If universals are in the mind or of the mind's making, then there would seem to be just one kind of thing, attributes, that play both a linguistic/mental role and a metaphysical role – or at least it would be quite uneconomical to assume otherwise. And if that's the case, then even Maimonides' statements about divine attributes that are prima facie about extralinguistic/extramental reality – about God Himself – are in the end about linguistic/mental reality.

Despite these good reasons, I suggest that when we carefully attend to the details of Maimonides' arguments, there is no escaping the fact that Maimonides is first and foremost making straightforwardly metaphysical claims. We will carefully attend to these details in Section 6.2. But what of the good reasons to accept the linguistic reading? Well, the first two reasons are obviously defeasible. That Maimonides maintained a lively interest in questions of religious language obviously doesn't mean that he was interested *exclusively* in religious language or that he wrote about language everywhere that he wrote anything at all. And that Maimonides placed his discussion of divine attributes immediately after his lexicographical chapters obviously doesn't mean that since the latter is about matters of religious language, so too is the former. There can be abrupt shifts, especially in the *Guide*, especially when a chapter begins, "There are many things in existence that are clear and manifest ... If man had been left as he [naturally] is, he would not have needed a proof of them ..." (Maimonides 1963, 1.51: 112).[5] In any case, the lexicographical chapters don't obviously evince a lively interest in questions of religious language, at least not as such. A very natural way to understand what's going on the lexicographical chapters is just this: In order to defend incorporealism, Maimonides needs to refute the main reason a religious Jew would be a corporealist, viz. the huge number of Biblical terms that seem to have corporeal implications and are applied in the Bible to God. And so,

---

[4] See *Guide* 2.9–10 and 3.18; Wolfson (1966); and Feldman (1968).
[5] See Manekin (1990, 129), who likewise suggests that there is an abrupt shift following the lexicographical chapters (starting in chapter 51 of the *Guide*).

Maimonides explains or explains away these terms. Of course, it's possible that once forced to address the textual evidence against corporealism, Maimonides makes some philosophically interesting claims about polysemy, or language more generally. But the philosophical *purpose* of these chapters is to defend the metaphysical claim that *God is incorporeal*. On this natural way of reading the lexicographical chapters, one can accept *both* the metaphysical reading of the section on divine attributes and that the section is a direct continuation of the lexicographical chapters: it's metaphysics in two stages. Indeed, as Maimonides maintains – and as he emphasizes at the very outset of chapter 51 of the *Guide* – his denial of divine attributes *follows* (at least in part) from the incorporealism that he defended until that point.

What of the third reason to embrace the linguistic reading? If attributes really are linguistic or mental items, then doesn't it just follow that Maimonides' claims about divine attributes are about the language or concepts we use to talk about God, and not about God? Well, no, because as we have already noted, attributes play *two* roles – one linguistic, and the other metaphysical. So, the issue is not whether Maimonides is making claims about linguistic items – surely, he is, since he is making claims about attributes, which are (among other things) linguistic items – it's whether he's making *linguistic claims*, i.e., claims about attributes in their capacity, or *qua* their role, *as linguistic items*. According to the metaphysical reading, he isn't, at least not in the first instance. I shall now turn to the details of Maimonides' discussion, which I think bears this out.

6.2 The Claims and Arguments

While much about chapters 50–70 of the *Guide* is perplexing, there are some claims that Maimonides makes plainly and repeatedly, both within this section and elsewhere, that I will take as starting points. Here are three such claims.

(C1): God shares no attributes in common with creatures

Maimonides reiterates this claims several times (*Guide* 1.35, 1.52, 1.55, 1.56), and he repeatedly highlights the same specific consequences, viz. that strictly speaking, God does not share with any creatures the attributes of **life, power,** and **knowledge** (*Guide* 1.56). Indeed, Maimonides does not shy away from embracing the very radical conclusion that God does not even share with creatures the attribute of **existence** (*Guide* 1.35, 1.52, 1.56). [The attributes **life, power, knowledge,** and **existence,** are the attributes expressed by the predicates "is alive," "is powerful," "is knowledgeable," and "is existent," *when applied to creatures*.] As a linguistic corollary of these assertions, Maimonides famously says that when such terms as "alive," "powerful," "knowledgeable," and "existent," are applied to God, they are "purely equivocal" (*Guide* 1.35, 1.52, 1.56): There is literally nothing at all common to God and a creature in virtue of which it's true to say of both that they are alive, or powerful, or knowledgeable, or even existent.[6] In particular, it's not as though they are both knowledgeable, and God is just much *more* (or even infinitely more) knowledgeable than creatures; and it's not as though they both exist, and God just exists to a much greater *degree* than creatures (*Guide* 1.35, 1.56). No, if there is a creature who is knowledgeable, then (strictly speaking) God isn't knowledgeable (in anything but a purely equivocal sense); and if there is a creature who is existent, then (strictly speaking) God isn't existent (in anything but a purely equivocal sense).

Maimonides presses things one step further. Not only does God share no attributes in common with creatures, God has no attributes, period. Well, not *period*; Maimonides carves out a few exceptions. What's clear is that God has no positive (or "affirmative"), nonactional attributes – whether they be accidental *or* essential. Moreover, God stands in no relations to any creature (*Guide* 1.52); but since everything is either God or a creature, and nothing stands in any nontrivial relations to itself, God stands in no relation to anything whatsoever. Thus, we have:

(C2): (a) God has no positive, nonactional attributes, and (b) God stands in no relations to anything

Maimonides argues at some length for (C2), and it's worth dwelling on at least part of the argument. The argument proceeds by examination of cases. He first considers the two categories of *definitions* and *parts of definitions*, then the category of *accidents*, and then the category of *relations*, and argues regarding each that no attribute belonging to any of these categories can be had by God (*Guide* 1.52). While the issues he raises regarding the first three cases are subtly different from one another, he summarizes the basic difficulty as follows:

> With regard to those three groups of attributes – which are the attributes indicative of the essence or of a part of the essence or of a certain quality subsisting in the essence – it has already been made clear that they are

---

[6] This explication of "purely equivocal term" is drawn from Maimonides' *Treatise on Logic*; I return to this explication in Section 6.5.2.

impossible with reference to Him, may He be exalted, *for all of them are indicative of composition*, and the impossibility of composition in respect to the deity we shall make clear by demonstration. (Maimonides 1963, 1.52: 116) (emphasis mine)

In other words, God is simple not only inasmuch as He lacks any "gross parts," like a left half and a right half, but also in that He lacks any "finer parts," or constituents, which He would have if He had any attribute belonging to one of those three categories.[7] What seems to be in play in this argument is a view about the metaphysical nature of particulars, which now goes by the name of "constituent ontology," according to which a particular is made up of (or composed of, or constituted by) whatever attributes it has.[8]

The third and final claim is a counterpart to the second. It says that what (C2) permitted – i.e., God's possession of negative attributes or attributes of action – is in fact the case. That is, Maimonides doesn't remain neutral on the question of whether God has those sorts of attributes; he asserts that God does (*Guide* 1.52, 1.54, 1.58). Thus, he tells us, "The purpose of all this is to show that the attributes ascribed to Him are attributes of His actions..." (Maimonides 1963, 1.54: 128). And later, "It has thus become clear to you that every attribute that we predicate of Him is an attribute of action, or, if the attribute is intended for the apprehension of His essence and not of His action, it signifies the negation of the privation of the attribute in question" (Maimonides 1963, 1.58: 136). I presume he means to speak of the attributes that are *correctly* ascribed to Him or predicated of Him, and thus that he endorses the following:

(C3): God has both negative attributes and attributes of action

On the face of it, the third claim is not just a counterpart to the second, but a counter*balance* to both of the first two claims. Indeed, on the linguistic reading, the third claim provides a *solution* to the problem, generated by the first two claims, of how we can manage to speak truly and even know something about God. The solution is that we can speak of both what God is not and what God does. But on the metaphysical reading, the third claim stands in prima facie tension with the first two claims, a tension to which I now turn.

---

[7] See Williams (1953) for this way of putting things.
[8] See Russell (1940), Castañeda (1974), Van Cleve (1985), Loux (2006), and Van Inwagen (2011) for foundational discussions of the contrast between a "relational ontology" and a "constituent ontology."

6.3 The Puzzles

The tension between the third claim and the first two is itself multifarious, and is accompanied by still other tensions with other things Maimonides says. Let's begin with the multifarious tension between the third claim and the first two.

(P1): As we noted, and as Maimonides himself notes explicitly, it seems to follow both from (C1) and from (C2) that God does not have **existence**. But anything that exists has **existence**. So, strictly speaking, God does not exist. But if God does not even exist, then it's puzzling, to say the least, how He could manage to have *any* attributes, even if they are negative or actional. (You might think this is the least of Maimonides' problems. Hold your fire, for now.) Here I assume the following principle: of necessity, anything that has any property (or attribute) whatsoever *exists*.[9] How else does it manage to achieve the feat of having a property?

Some would deny this principle, on the grounds that (in their view) there *are* things – things that have being – that don't *exist*.[10] In their view, the principle I just stated is false, while, presumably, the following, weaker principle, is true: of necessity, anything that has any property (or attribute) whatsoever, *is* (that is, it has being). Never mind whether you think their view is coherent or correct, or whether we really need to weaken the principle in this way. The weaker principle also seems to land Maimonides in hot water. For the upshot of both (C1) and (C2) would seem to be that, strictly speaking, God does not have **being** either – indeed, it would seem to be a consequence of those two claims that God has nothing of any "existential import." For if He did, then (a) there would be something that God shares in common with creatures, contra (C1), and (b) there would be some positive nonactional attribute that God has, contra (C2). Or at least so it seems. So, a retreat to the weaker principle does nothing to help.

Some have denied the principle in whatever form.[11] In their view it's possible for something to have properties even in a situation in which it has no being whatsoever. But that this view is held doesn't mean it's plausible. And in any case, their view is consistent with the following, still weaker principle: of necessity, anything that has any property whatsoever, *at least possibly* exists (or has being). But even this principle spells trouble for Maimonides, for according to Maimonides it's not just a *contingent* fact

---

[9] See Plantinga (1983) and Williamson (2002).   [10] See Reicher (2019) for an overview.
[11] See Salmon (1998).

that God doesn't have **existence** (or **being**), of course, it's a matter of *necessity*. We are left with a puzzle.

(P2): The third claim is in tension with the first two in yet another way. (C1), which rules out any sharing of attributes between God and creatures, makes no exceptions. So, it is hard to see how it is consistent with (C3), since some of the attributes that the latter attributes to God are, on the face of it, shared by creatures. Anyone who lacks the privation of foolishness will have the negative attribute, **not being foolish**, which is a negative attribute that God has. Likewise, anyone who heals the sick will have the actional attribute of **healing the sick**, which is an attribute of action that God has; indeed, it's an attribute of God that we're supposed to imitate (*Guide* 1.54, 3.54).

Of course, the natural suggestion to make is that just as (C2) is restricted to positive nonactional attributes, (C1) needs to be so restricted as well. But this raises the question of whether a version of (C1) restricted in that way can be adequately motivated. Once we say creatures can be genuinely like God in certain ways – i.e., with respect to *certain* attributes – then haven't we already given up on a strictly transcendent God? Why then insist that God can't share any positive nonactional attributes with creatures? (Here we are not permitted to appeal to (C2), since I take it that is supposed to be motivated independently of (C1).) Moreover, if (C1) is restricted in that way, then it is logically implied by (C2), making it redundant. But it doesn't *seem* like Maimonides thinks that once he puts forward (C2), he can dispense with (C1) – as if the latter were a just a ladder to be kicked away once he gets to the former – because Maimonides repeatedly *appeals* to (C1), even after he has stated (C2) (*Guide* 1.55, 1.56), and it is a reliance on (C1) that guides the ideal inquirer as he proceeds along the *via negativa* (*Guide* 1.60).[12]

But, in any case, restricting (C1) won't help to address a related tension between (C3) and (C2). (C3) says that God has attributes of action. But then He acts. Presumably He acts, at the very least, on creation. But then He causes something about creation to be the case. One can't well act on X without causing something about X to be the case. So, he stands in some causal *relation* to creation. So, He stands in some relation to something.

---

[12] It is precisely this apparent redundancy that Crescas (1990, 1.3.3: 103) exploits in one of his criticisms of Maimonides: What knowledge is gained, Crescas asks, by negating of God *human* perfections, once we know that God has no positive nonactional attributes at all?

And (C2) says that God stands in no relation to anything. The tension is manifest.[13]

(P3): A final puzzle concerns the relation between (C1) and what Maimonides writes elsewhere. Thus, for example, despite his repeated affirmation that 'knowledge' is purely equivocal in its two applications to creatures and to the divine (*Guide* 1.56, 3.20), in *Guide* 1.68–69 Maimonides seems to concur with "the philosophers" that for God, just as for creatures, knowledge involves an identity between subject, object, and the act of intellection.[14] Likewise, despite his repeated affirmation that 'existence' is purely equivocal in its two applications to creatures and the divine, Maimonides' proofs for God's existence (*Guide* 2.1–2) seem to go by way of principles that involve existence *as such*; it's hard to see how these proofs could be any good, let alone how we could *see* that they're any good, if there is nothing in common between divine existence and creaturely existence.

6.4 Extant Resolutions

These puzzles cry out for resolution. Two prominent resolutions involve qualifications of at least one of the three claims. The first resolution qualifies, or just outright rejects, (C3), making Maimonides even more radical than he appears. The second resolution qualifies (C1) and (C2), making Maimonides more conservative than he appears. I turn all too briefly to these two resolutions.[15]

6.4.1 Go Radical

Josef Stern (2000; 2008; 2013, 204–218) argues that Maimonides doesn't in fact accept (C3) – at least not as *true*, even if it's in some sense *correct* (i.e. it captures a more *proper* way to represent God). Stern's point of

---

[13] See Feldman (1968) and Harvey (1996), who interpret attributes of action in such a way that they say nothing positive at all, not even something relational, about God. I myself don't see how such attributes could be aptly described as attributes *of action* if they fail to entail any relation whatsoever, nor do I see how to reconcile that interpretation with Maimonides' own causal-sounding language when explicating the attributes of action ("It is then clear that the ways ... are the actions *proceeding from God* ..." (Maimonides 1963, 1.54: 124; emphasis mine)).

[14] See Lobel (2002) and Shatz (Essay 12, this volume). I should note that Josef Stern contends that Maimonides doesn't concur in this chapter with "the philosophers," he is rather "arguing with the philosophers according to their conception of the deity" (Stern 2013, 235–240, 236).

[15] I don't mean to imply that the authors whose views I subsequently discuss were proposing these views *as resolutions* to any or all of the puzzles I've listed. I am enlisting their views for my purposes.

departure is Maimonides' argument for (C2), understood *linguistically* (or, more broadly, representationally). As he interprets (at least one of) the arguments for (C2), the central point is that every claim we can make about anything and every thought we can have about anything – including God – has a complex, subject/predicate, syntactical structure. But no claim about *God* with such complex syntactical structure could be true, for God would have to exhibit a corresponding complexity, and God is absolutely simple, not complex. Stern then argues that if this is true, it holds equally of *negative* predications – indeed, even so-called categorial negations of privations – for those too have a complex, subject/predicate, syntactic structure: it matters not what the predicate is. But then no sentence that predicates a negative attribute of God will be true. From which it seems to follow that it's false that God has negative attributes, and so (C3) is false.

Of course, dropping (C3) immediately dissolves the first two puzzles. And both Stern's linguistic reading of the argument for (C2) and the dropping of (C3) have textual basis for them. As to the former, Maimonides says as follows:

> For there is no oneness at all except in believing that there is one simple essence in which there is no complexity ... and you will not find therein any multiplicity either in the thing as it is outside of the mind *or as it is in the mind*. (Maimonides 1963, 1.51: 113) (emphasis mine)[16]

As for the latter, Maimonides seems to hedge in places on whether the predication of negative attributes is ultimately sustainable. As he says:

> The most apt phrase concerning this subject is the dictum occurring in the Psalms, *Silence is praise to Thee*, which interpreted signifies: silence with regard to you is praise ... For of whatever we say intending to magnify and exalt, on the one hand we find that it can have some application to Him, may He be exalted, and on the other we perceive in it some deficiency. (Maimonides 1963, 1.59:139–140)

This seems to suggest, perhaps, that while the predication of negative attributes is better than the predication of positive attributes, it's still a less than ideal concession to human frailty. And it's presumably less than ideal because it's not, strictly speaking, *true*.[17]

---

[16] As Stern points out, "Maimonides' Arabic term for complexity... is the very same term appropriated by Al-Farabi for logical syntax" (Stern 2013, 217).
[17] At least it's not strictly speaking true until and unless it reaches its final station, in absolute silence. Thanks to Zev Harvey here.

But whatever the merits of this interpretation, it encounters difficulties, at least one of them serious. There is, of course, the fact that Maimonides says much *else*, both about God and about what one can say or truly say about God, that implies (C3) (or some other claim that "permits" predicating certain attributes of God). For example, Maimonides says just one chapter earlier:

> Know that the descriptions of God, may He be cherished and exalted, by means of negations is the correct description. (Maimonides 1963, 1.58: 134)

This and other such statements can be handled in a variety of ways. Stern (2013, 210–213) suggests, regarding the statement in *Guide* 1.58, that descriptions by way of negations are "correct" only insofar as they are superior to those that use "indefinite nouns" – descriptions that Al-Farabi had allowed, but that Maimonides held to be inappropriate because of their positive content.

But I don't see how the view being attributed to Maimonides can avoid the more serious problem of *self-defeat*, a problem to which many such sweeping views succumb. For the view says something about God, albeit something negative – to wit, that God isn't something that anyone can say anything about – indeed, it says a whole lot of things about God, albeit all of them negative. And if the view is true, then nothing at all can be said about God. So, if the view is true, then it isn't true. In fact, if the view is true, then there is no such view! So either the view is false or there is no such view. And it's surely uncharitable to Maimonides to see him as writing and saying so much that expresses no view at all, especially since doing so contravenes Maimonides' own admonition, at the beginning of the section on divine attributes, not to be among those who "merely proclaim it [the theological truth] without representing to themselves that it has a meaning" (Maimonides 1963, 1.50: 112).

There is much more to say about this problem – and, indeed, Stern (2013, 240–249) himself has more to say about it – but I myself see no viable solution on the horizon. One of the morals to be drawn from this discussion is that a linguistic interpretation of the "argument from complexity" for (C2) leads us down a dead end. *If* there is an in-principle problem with our saying something of God, then the problem will completely generalize, and swallow itself with it.

6.4.2 Go Conservative

A second resolution lies in a qualification of the first two claims, or at least in what we took to follow from them. The key distinction to draw is between God's *whatness* and God's *thatness*, between *what* God is like and the fact *that* God is. Charles Manekin (1990; 2008b) and Herbert Davidson (1992–1993) point to a number of passages in which Maimonides seems to assert not only *that* God *is*, but that we can completely grasp and prove it with certainty (even if it doesn't amount to a scientific demonstration). What we can't completely grasp is what God is like (*Guide* 1.58, 1.59).

The distinction between whatness and thatness opens the door to either (a) interpreting (C1) and (C2) as restricted to the "attributes of *whatness*" – to those attributes that characterize what the thing is like – and not applying to the attribute of **existence** or (b) keeping (C1) and (C2) as they are and denying that there *is* any attribute of **existence** (a la Kant), even if there are attributes of *whatness*.

This would seem to address at least (P1). Yes, perhaps having negative or actional attributes requires having the attribute of **existence**, or, at the very least it requires that the thing exists, but that's no problem: *that* God *is* is something not only true, but demonstrably so.

Of course, this leaves the other two puzzles unresolved. But worse still, it's not clear that it even resolves the first puzzle. For, as we noted, Maimonides explicitly endorses, as a consequence of (C1), the pure equivocity of the term 'exists'. And that seems to be enough to get the first puzzle off the ground, whether or not there is such an attribute as **existence**. For without any tempering or modification or reinterpretation of the claim of pure equivocity, it would seem to follow from it that nothing of any "existential import" can be said of God – whatever is of existential import, after all, can also be said of creatures (whether it's that they exist, or that they are). And if we do temper or modify or reinterpret the claim of pure equivocity, as I will soon suggest we should, it's not clear that we will *need* to qualify the first two claims or deny that there is any such attribute as **existence**. The proposed resolution is therefore either inadequate or idle.

6.5 New Resolution: Go Maimonidean

I suggest taking Maimonides at his word. None of the three claims needs to be qualified in order to resolve our puzzles. They just need to be better understood. In order to understand them, we need some background on the relationship between predicates and attributes, and to correct what I think is a misunderstanding of Maimonides' doctrine of pure equivocation.

6.5.1 Predicates and Attributes

Following Lewis (1983; 1986), let us distinguish among the realists about attributes (universals) between those who maintain a sparse conception of attributes and those who maintain an abundant conception. The latter hold that for every predicate that can be truly applied to something, there is a genuine attribute (universal), expressed by that predicate, which the thing instantiates. The former deny this, to one degree or another; they hold that there are predicates, whether disjunctive, conjunctive, negative, "grue-like," mere-Cambridge, or what have you, that can be truly applied to a thing without there being any genuine attribute (universal) that the predicate expresses.[18] What makes statements involving such predicates true is the pattern of instantiation of the *genuine* (positive, basic, intrinsic...) attributes. In a word, in their view not every *bit of language that could rightly be said of something* corresponds to some *worldly bit of reality*.[19]

This inegalitarian division among predicates was endorsed by a number of philosophers throughout history, including, it seems to me, Maimonides. Or, taking account of the fact that Maimonides maintains a "conceptualist theory of universals," we can put Maimonides' view this way: While *some* attributes play both a linguistic/mental role and a metaphysical role (of constituting the objects that instantiate them), other attributes play only the former role and not the latter.

Thus, Maimonides assumes that relational predicates, like "*x* is five meters from the Empire State Building," don't correspond to anything *in* the object that satisfies that predicate (*Guide* 1.52). Likewise, while "attributes of affirmation ... indicate a part of the thing the knowledge of which is sought, that part being either a part of its substance or one of its accidents," negative attributes do *not* (Maimonides 1963, 1.58: 135). In contemporary parlance, we would say that (in Maimonides' view) there *are no* negative or actional attributes, just negative and actional predicates. We, along with Maimonides, will sometimes speak as if there are such attributes, but that's because attributes themselves wear two hats, one on the word side (predicates) and one on the world side (universals).

---

[18] "Grue-like" predicates are those relevantly like the predicate "grue," introduced by Goodman (1955) in his presentation of the New Riddle of Induction.

[19] See Armstrong (1978) for a robust contemporary defense, and Loux (2006) for a historical discussion, well-informed by contemporary debates, that focuses on Aristotle.

6.5.2 What Is "Pure Equivocation"?

As we noted in Section 6.2, a number of times in the *Guide* Maimonides tells us that a certain term is purely equivocal, or absolutely homonymous, when used regarding both God and creatures.[20] But nowhere in the *Guide* does he explicitly define the term "purely equivocal." The standard interpretation – indeed, the interpretation that, as far as I can tell, is unanimously accepted by interpreters of Maimonides – can be put as follows:

> (D1) "term F is used purely equivocally in contexts A and B" = $_{df}$ the attribute picked out by F in context A (call it F-ness$_A$) shares nothing in common with the attribute picked out by F in context B (call it F-ness$_B$).

Thus, Michael Schwarz, in the explanatory notes accompanying his translation of the *Guide*, explains that a term is purely equivocal when it "expresses two meanings (or more) that are entirely different from one another" (Maimonides 2002a, introduction, note 8). It is also commonly held to follow from the definiens of (D1) that neither F-ness$_A$ nor F-ness$_B$ can be defined in terms of the other, nor can they be defined in terms of some other attribute. This is what underlies the classical criticism of Maimonides, going back to the medievals, that if every term F we use regarding God is purely equivocal, then we can't infer anything at all from such statements as "God is F," nor can we infer that statement from anything else (Gersonides 1987, 108–111).[21]

But while Maimonides does not explicitly define the "purely equivocal" in the *Guide*, he does so in his *Treatise on Logic*.[22] And quite remarkably, his own definition appears to disagree with what the interpretive consensus has taken him to mean in the *Guide* (and everywhere else). Here is what he says in the *Logic*:

> The absolute homonym is one applied to two things, between which there is nothing in common to account for their common name, like the name *'ain* signifying an eye and a spring of water . . . (Maimonides 1938, 59)

---

[20] ism mushtarik = إِسْم مُشْتَرِك = משתרק = אסם in Arabic; Ibn Tibbon usually translates it as '*shemot mishtatfim*'; Schwartz translates it as '*shemot meshutafim*'; Efros translates it as 'absolute homonym'; Pines (in his translation of the *Guide*) usually translates it as 'purely equivocal' (and sometimes as 'absolutely equivocal'). I will use the terms interchangeably.

[21] See W. Z. Harvey (1988) and Eisenmann (2007) for a defense that points to the *pedagogical* value in using certain terms and not others regarding God.

[22] On the attribution of the *Logic* to Maimonides, see Davidson (2001) and Stroumsa (2009, 127–128).

His Existence Is Essentiality 117

That is, a given eye and a given spring of water share nothing in common in virtue of which it is true of each of them that it is an *ayin*.²³ More generally, a general term F is purely equivocal when used regarding some Gs and some Hs just in the case that there is no single attribute in virtue of which both a given G is F and a given H is F. If we put this in attribute-terms – and the attribute names we used in (D1) – we seem to have the following:

> (D2) "term F is used purely equivocally in contexts A and B" =$_{df}$ for anything x that has F-ness$_A$ and anything y that has F-ness$_B$, there is no single attribute F-ness such that (a) x has F-ness$_A$ (at least partly) in virtue of having F-ness and (b) y has F-ness$_B$ (at least partly) in virtue of having F-ness.

This definition, I contend, aligns precisely with what Maimonides tell us in his own explicit definition. But notice that it disagrees, and disagrees rather badly, with (D1). For (D1) stays at the attribute-level, and (D2) descends to the object-level. In particular, the definiens of (D2) says nowhere that F-ness$_A$ and F-ness$_B$ *themselves* share nothing in common, just that *the things that have the respective attributes* share nothing in common; indeed, more carefully, it makes the even weaker claim that the things that have the respective attributes share nothing in common *in virtue of which they both have F-ness*. As far as the definiens of (D2) says, there might even *be* an attribute of F-ness, and it might even be shared by any two things, one of which has F-ness$_A$ and the other of which has F-ness$_B$. It just won't ever be that in virtue of which the one has F-ness$_A$ and the other has F-ness$_B$; it will be, to use some contemporary jargon, an intrinsically disjunctive attribute.²⁴ In all likelihood, the existence of such disjunctive attributes is ruled out by Maimonides' sparse conception of

---

²³ As others have noted, this category has no counterpart in Aristotle's list at the beginning of his *Categories*, as evidenced by the fact that Aristotle's example of his first category – the "most" homonymous of his categories – is an example that Maimonides uses to illustrate his *third* category, that of the amphibolous term, i.e., "a term applied to two or more objects because of something which they have in common but which does not constitute the essence of each one of them" (Maimonides 1938, 60). There *were* earlier commentators on Aristotle who had a category that corresponded more closely to Maimonides' absolute homonymy – and Aristotle himself elsewhere (Aristotle 1984, *Metaphysics* 1060b33–34) mentions in passing a category of 'homonymy, but according to nothing in common' – but one has to be careful not to assimilate their category to Maimonides' without justification. (See Irwin (1981) for an excellent discussion of Aristotle's own views. Thanks to Josef Stern for pointing me to this article.) In particular, I disagree with Horovitz's identification (cited in Baneth 1935, 34) of Maimonides' absolute homonymy with the chance homonymy of Porphyry (1992, 65; see also Aristotle 2009, *Nicomachean Ethics*, 1096, b26–31; Simplicius 2003, 31; and Al-Farabi 1981, 49–50), since I see no evidence in Maimonides' definition that the shared usage must be by chance (a point whose importance will emerge shortly).
²⁴ See Sider (2011) and McDaniel (2017).

attributes. At the very least, however, the following is clear: A term F in contexts A and B can satisfy (D2) – if any two things that have F-ness$_A$ and F-ness$_B$ (respectively) share nothing in common – but fail to satisfy (D1), because F-ness$_A$ and F-ness$_B$ themselves share something in common.

This can happen in any number of ways, corresponding to those ways in which attributes can share something in common that don't entail or derive from a commonality in their instances. Thus, the cardinality of the set of their instances (perhaps they both have just a finite number of instances), or their formal features (perhaps they are both symmetric relations), or their modal status (perhaps they are both essential to anything that has them), or their logical relations to other attributes – all of these could serve as something that attributes share in common without that requiring that their instances share anything in common (let alone something in common in virtue of which they have the attributes in question).

To take what is (in most cases) a trivial sort of example: An attribute F-ness and its negation, non-F-ness, where they both exist, certainly share something in common, since at the very least the latter can be defined in terms of the former. But it's hard to see how two things – one of which has F-ness and one of which has non-F-ness – could share some attribute *in virtue of which the one has F-ness and the other has non-F-ness*. As we shall see momentarily, this sort of case is far from a triviality, and indeed lies at the heart of Maimonidean theology. (And the general point that (D2) is weaker than (D1) suffices to address Gersonides' objection.)

It's worth emphasizing that pure equivocation, despite its being weaker than traditionally understood, still has teeth. For one thing, (D2) still sets the "purely equivocal" apart from the other five cases of equivocation or homonymy that Maimonides lists in that chapter of the *Logic* (I leave this as an exercise for the reader). For another thing, the definiens of (D2) still has the consequence that it's not the case that F-ness$_A$ is just F-ness to a much greater *degree* than F-ness$_B$, for if the latter were so then (plausibly at least) there would be something, viz. F-ness, at least partly in virtue of which the one thing has F-ness$_A$ and the other has F-ness$_B$. As we've already indicated previously, Maimonides takes note of exactly that consequence of the pure equivocity of "knowledge" and "exists" (when used regarding both God and creatures).

6.5.3 The View

With this background in place, we are ready to lay out the relevant parts of the Maimonidean outlook. Crucially, Maimonides sides with Aristotle

(*Metaphysics* Γ.2, *Metaphysics* Z.1) that "being is said in many ways."²⁵ In particular, for Maimonides, "being" is said in at least *two* ways. But unlike Aristotle – who thinks that "being" is *pros hen equivocal* in its various usages (Aristotle (*Metaphysics* Γ.2, *Metaphysics* Z.1) – Maimonides thinks that "being"/"exists" is *purely* equivocal in its expressions of these two ways. When we say of a creature that it exists, we pick out the attribute of being **utterly contingent**, or what comes to the same thing for Maimonides, **radically dependent**. They are dependent not just in the efficient causal way, but in the formal and teleological ways, ultimately on God (*Guide* 1.69, 2.11–12).²⁶ That's not a further attribute of creatures, that's just what it *is* for them to exist. On the other hand, when we say of God that He exists, we pick out the feature of being **necessarily-existent**, or what comes to the same thing for Maimonides, **absolutely *in*dependent**, not being caused in any of those ways. That's not a further attribute of God, that's just what it *is* for God to exist.

This emerges from a number of passages in the Maimonidean corpus.²⁷ Here, for example is what he says at the beginning of the *Laws of the Foundations of the Law*²⁸:

> All existing things, whether celestial, terrestrial, or belonging to an intermediate class, exist only through His true existence. If it were supposed that He did not exist, it would follow that nothing else could possibly exist. If, however, it were supposed that all other beings were non-existent, He alone would still exist ... *Hence, His true reality is unlike that of any of them* (Mishneh Torah, Laws of the Foundations of the Law 1.1–3) (emphasis mine)

Notice that the difference in dependence/independence is translated into a difference in the *sort of reality* that God and creatures possess.

The identification of divine existence with absolute independence helps illuminate another Maimonidean claim. Maimonides famously holds, apparently following Avicenna, that God's essence just *is* existence, where

---

²⁵ For a contemporary wide-ranging and penetrating development of this view, see McDaniel (2017).
²⁶ See Segal (forthcoming).
²⁷ See also Stern (Essay 10 in this volume) for excellent discussion. While I agree wholeheartedly with Stern that Maimonides identifies divine existence with absolute independence, I disagree with his assertion that we don't understand what that is; I think we understand perfectly well what it is, since it's the (categorial) negation of creaturely existence.
²⁸ Translation taken from Twersky (1972), with a few modifications. (Most importantly, I have translated *amitato* as "His true reality" rather than "His real essence," since the latter translation is ill-suited for the other instances of the term in *Mishneh Torah, Laws of the Foundations of the Law* 1.4, a point implicitly acknowledged by Twersky in his translation of the latter.)

the latter, just in the case of God, is not "superadded" to the former.[29] On the face of it, it's hard to understand what this could mean, in a way that doesn't make it trivial (and in a way that sets God apart from creatures): isn't existence part and parcel of *everything*'s essence? For anything whatsoever, it's part of what it is to be that thing that at the very least it exists, and it's necessarily (and trivially) true that if it exists, then it exists.[30] But none of these facts sets God apart, and each is trivial. I think we can get a better grip on the Maimonidean formula if we pay more careful attention to it. Here is what Maimonides says:

> As for that which has no cause for its existence, there is only God, may He be magnified and glorified, who is like that. For this is the meaning of our saying about Him, may He be exalted, that His existence is necessary. *Accordingly, His existence is identical with His essence and His true reality, and His essence is His existence.* (Maimonides 1963, 1.57: 132) (emphasis mine)

Two points are noteworthy. First, Maimonides identifies God's essence not with existence as such, but with *God's* existence – God's essence just is *God's* existence. Second, Maimonides explicitly calls attention to the symmetric nature of the identity claim. We could put Maimonides' claim equally well this way instead: God's existence just is God's essence. That is, we have here a claim about God's existence, about the *sort of being* that God enjoys. In particular, the claim is that God's way or manner of being is captured by His essence. But His essence just is **being absolutely independent**. So, we have a straightforward and nontrivial way to construe Maimonides' claim that God's essence is existence; it might be more perspicuously put by saying that God's existence – God's way of being – is *essentiality*.[31]

This difference in ways of being trickles down into differences between all the other attributes that God and creatures have. Thus, **knowledge**$_{\text{divine}}$ and **knowledge**$_{\text{creature}}$ are different ways of knowing. The latter is the sort of knowledge we have, in which we depend for having it on the state of the world. The former, on the other hand, is the sort of knowledge God has, in

---

[29] Avicenna *seems* to make this point in his *Metaphysics of the Healing* (Avicenna 2005, viii.4, 343.10–15 and 345.6–347.16). But as Adamson (2013) notes, he elsewhere seems to say that God has no essence at all, and as I read him, he may be better understood as identifying God's essence with His *haecceity*, not His existence.

[30] See Plantinga (1974, 61).

[31] This way of understanding the Maimonidean formula shows just how different Maimonides' view is from Avicenna's, since the latter held that "exists" is univocal, or at least not purely equivocal. (Much closer to Maimonides on this point is al-Shahrastānī, a sharp critic of Avicenna. See Adamson 2013.)

which the state of the world depends on God's knowledge – and in particular His self-knowledge – and not vice versa. This is why, I take it, divine foreknowledge, as opposed to creaturely foreknowledge, doesn't exclude free will (*Guide* 3.20). The same goes for the other attributes.

Note well: it is at this point that it is absolutely critical that Maimonides had in mind (D2), rather than (D1). Maimonides is explicit that "exists," and "knowledge," and so on, are all purely equivocal in their divine and creaturely usages. If (D1) gives the correct meaning of "purely equivocal," then it would follow that **existence$_{divine}$** and **existence$_{creature}$** share nothing in common – and that, in particular, the former couldn't be understood in terms of the latter – contrary to everything I've just attributed to Maimonides. The same applies for **knowledge$_{divine}$** and **knowledge$_{creature}$**.

But if (D2) gives the correct meaning of "purely equivocal," then **existence$_{divine}$** could well be the negation of **existence$_{creature}$** – and the former attribute could just be **absolute independence** and the latter, **radical dependence** – even though "exists" is purely equivocal in its divine and creaturely usages. For the pure equivocality of "exists" implies nothing stronger than that there isn't any single attribute in virtue of which creatures have **radical dependence** and God has **absolute independence**. The only decent candidate for such a single attribute would be generic **being**, equivalent at least to the disjunction **being either radically dependent or absolutely independent**. But, if there were such an attribute, Maimonides would hold that it's an *intrinsically* disjunctive one, always instantiated in virtue of one of the disjuncts, and not vice versa. And indeed, given Maimonides' sparse conception of attributes, there won't be any intrinsically disjunctive attributes, and so there won't be any such attribute as generic **being**, at all. All of that, however, is consistent with **existence$_{divine}$** and **existence$_{creature}$** being defined in exactly the way that I have suggested, and in the former being perfectly well understood.

Note well, a second time: each of the nonactional divine attributes is a specification of a negative attribute. **Being absolutely independent** is the negation of the (relational) attribute of **being dependent**; and, as Maimonides sees it, the latter is (in itself) positive, and the former is (in itself) negative, as it says what God *isn't*. **Knowledge$_{divine}$** is a *specification* of being absolutely independent; it is to not just to *be* in a way that has no cause, but specifically to *know* in a way that has no cause. And so on for the other nonactional divine attributes. And each of the actional attributes – or the relations entailed by having those actional attributes – is a specification of the relation of **radical dependence** that creatures bear to God; it is not just to *be* radically dependent on God, but to be radically dependent *in such-and-such a way* on God.³²

Note well, a third and final time: all the talk of negative and actional *attributes* is a facon-de-parler, for given Maimonides' sparse conception of attributes, there are no such things. (Or, at least there are no such *worldly* things; at most they are *wordy* things.) But we can still truly say of God that He is absolutely independent, that He independently-knows..., and that everything depends on Him for their existence and nature. And all of that is strictly and literally true.

Let's see how all of this allows us to resolve the puzzles.

6.5.4 Puzzles Resolved

Solution to (P1): In developing (P1), we assumed that it was a consequence of each of (C1) and (C2) that God has nothing of any "existential import." But now we can see that this is a consequence of neither of those claims. God has **existence**$_{\text{divine}}$ (aka **necessary-existence**, aka **absolute independence**). This is not shared with any creature, so God's "having" it doesn't violate (C1), and it is a negative attribute, so God's "having" it doesn't violate (C2). But, crucially, it has "existential import," in the sense relevant to whether (C3) could be true. Being absolutely independent is evidently sufficiently robust, ontologically speaking, to allow *other* things to be true of something that is absolutely independent. It is, again, critical that we understand "pure equivocation" in terms of (D2) rather than (D1), so that **existence**$_{\text{divine}}$ really does have "existential import." If we understood "pure equivocation" in terms of (D1), then **existence**$_{\text{divine}}$ *couldn't* have "existential import."

Solution to (P2): There is no need to restrict (C1). God and creatures share absolutely no attributes in common. And not only in the sense that there is no worldly bit (no genuine attribute) that God and creatures share – a fact that is entailed by God having no attributes (in that sense of attribute) *at all*. It's also true in the sense that *whatever* can be truly said of God and *whatever* can be truly said of creatures – and there is plenty of each of those things – none of those things that can be said make for any *similarity* between God and creatures. And that's because each of the

---

³² For a different take on the relationship between attributes of action and negative attributes – one that sees the latter as a "photo negative" of the former – see Harvey (1996). (This is a consequence of his taking attributes of action to be saying nothing positive at all, not even something relational, about God. See note 13, this essay.)

things that can be truly said of God and each of the things that can be truly said of creatures are specifications of their respective *ways of being*. And, Maimonides contends, no two things can be similar in any way if they don't belong to the same genus, let alone if they don't enjoy the same sort of being (*Guide* 1.52).

Moreover, there is no tension between God having actional attributes and His standing in no relations to anything. As Maimonides makes clear, by "relation" he has in mind a proper subset of what we would call relations: only those that entail some similarity between the relata. (This is not an ad hoc restriction. It seems that Maimonides didn't think there *were* any other possible relations.) Perhaps ordinary causal relations are like that – so Maimonides seems to have thought. But the relations entailed by God's possessing actional attributes are not like that. Indeed, since they're all specifications of the relation of **absolute independence**, they're all relations the standing in which entails that the relata *are not at all similar*, because the relata, of necessity, *enjoy different sorts of being*.

Solution to (P3): It should be obvious how I think the final puzzle should be resolved, since it relies on a misunderstanding of "purely equivocal" that I have sought to clarify. There is no incompatibility between the pure equivocality of "knows" and the claim that for God, just as for creatures, knowledge involves an identity between subject, object, and the act of intellection. For the former just requires that there is no shared attribute *in virtue of which* God knows what He knows and creatures know what they know; and that's true, because **knowledge$_{divine}$** and **knowledge$_{creature}$** are specifications of different ways of being. Again, there can be a structural similarity between the two kinds of knowledge, without there being any similarity between the things that possess the two kinds of knowledge, let alone a similarity in virtue of which they both have the kind of knowledge they do. Likewise, there is no incompatibility between the pure equivocality of "exists" and the fact that Maimonides' proofs for God's (necessary-)existence go by way of principles that involve some notion of "existential import." For the former is compatible with **existence$_{divine}$** (aka **necessary-existence**, aka **absolute independence**) having existential import.

6.6 Conclusion

It is uncontroversial that Maimonides had some subtle and interesting views in the philosophy of language, even if he didn't present them systematically.[33] But seeing him as primarily, or even exclusively, interested in matters of religious *language*, as opposed to religious *metaphysics*, has tended to obscure Maimonides' true view about divine attributes – and other matters besides – and mired us in insoluble puzzles. Maimonides was a very fine metaphysician, whose metaphysical views beautifully cohere, if you let them speak for themselves.

---

[33] See Stern (2000).

CHAPTER 7

"Whereof One Cannot Speak"

Silvia Jonas

7.1 Maimonides' Theory of Divine Ineffability

Maimonides is one of the most radical defenders of apophaticism, the view according to which no positive attribute can be truthfully applied to God, and that God is consequently ineffable.[1] His apophatic theology has several important dimensions, and it is in the *Guide for the Perplexed* that he offers the most elaborate account of his views.

The starting point of his theory is a metaphysical one, relating to God's particular form of existence:

> God ... is existent of necessity and ... there is no composition in Him ... We are only able to apprehend the fact that He is and cannot apprehend His quiddity. It is consequently impossible that He should have affirmative attributes. For He has no "That" outside of His "What," and hence an attribute cannot be indicative of one of the two; all the more His "What" is not compound so that an attribute cannot be indicative of its two parts; and all the more, He cannot have accidents so that an attribute cannot be indicative of them. Accordingly He cannot have an affirmative attribute in any respect. (Maimonides 1963, 1.58: 135)

There are two central claims here. The first one is:

(1) God exists necessarily.

Necessary existence is a fundamentally different way of existing than anything else we are acquainted with in this universe; all other concrete things and beings exist merely contingently. Thus, already at this point, an essential difference between God and everything else that exists in God's universe is established.

---

[1] Apophatic views have also been defended, amongst others, by Philo of Alexandria (2013), Gregory of Nyssa (2007), Pseudo-Dionysius (1987), Maximus the Confessor (1985), Ibn al-Arabi (2005), and Meister Eckhart (1981).

The second central claim is that:

(2) God is simple (non-compound).

Maimonides argues that God cannot be compound because that would compromise God's absolute metaphysical and logical priority. For if God were compound, there would have to be some cause holding God's parts together, which is equal to saying that there is a cause that is prior to God. So God cannot be compound:

> A thing composed of two elements has necessarily their composition as the cause of its present existence. Its existence is therefore not necessitated by its own essence; it depends on the existence of its two component parts and their combination. (Maimonides 2002b, 2. introduction, proposition 21: 147)

It follows from (1) that God has no accidents; it follows from (2) that there are no parts of God of which an attribute can be indicative. Hence, neither can God have an affirmative attribute in any respect, nor can we provide any positive description of God:

> When the tongues aspire to magnify Him by means of attributive qualifications, all eloquence turns into weariness and incapacity! (Maimonides 1963, 1.58: 137)

This immediately raises the question how we are to understand religious claims about God, such as claims about God's qualities and characteristics made in the Torah, but also in the remaining parts of the Hebrew Bible, the exegetical commentaries of the Talmud, and of course in the daily prayers all Jews are obligated to say. Maimonides' answer is as follows:

> The terms "knowledge," "power," "will," and "life," as applied to Him, may He be exalted, and to all those possessing knowledge, power, will, and life, are purely equivocal, so that their meaning when they are predicated of Him is in no way like their meaning in other applications. Do not deem that they are used amphibolously. For when terms are used amphibolously they are predicated of two things between which there is a likeness in respect to some notion. (Maimonides 1963, 1.56: 131)

Maimonides thus claims that religious language as applied to God is purely equivocal. As such, it cannot and must not be interpreted literally. However, this does not mean that statements like 'God is powerful' or 'God is all-knowing' are nonsensical. Rather, Maimonides offers two possible ways to interpret such statements.

The first possible interpretation is as disguised negations (*Guide* 1.58). For example, 'God is powerful' should be read as 'It is not the case that God is powerless'; 'God is all-knowing' should be taken to mean 'It is not the case that God is ignorant'; etc. However, unlike in ordinary speech, a double negative applied to God does not indicate a positive. A statement like 'God is powerful' – which, according to Maimonides, is correctly interpreted as 'It is not the case that it is not the case that God is powerful' – does not amount to an affirmation of the statement 'God is powerful.' Rather, it amounts to an affirmation of the fact that God does not possess power in a way that would make God's power comparable to the power possessed by other beings, or that would make God comparable to other powerful beings (Maimonides 1963, 1.58: 136). Maimonides thus draws the radical conclusion that:

> We have no way of describing Him unless it be through negations and not otherwise. (Maimonides 1963, 1.58: 134)

In fact, however, Maimonides does offer a second possible way to interpret apparently positive descriptions of God, namely as descriptions of God's actions:

> Whenever any one of His actions is perceived by us, we ascribe to God that emotion which is the source of the act when performed by ourselves, and call Him by an epithet which is formed from the verb expressing that emotion. We see, e.g., how well He provides for the life of the embryo of living beings; how He endows with certain faculties both the embryo itself and those who have to rear it after its birth, in order that it may be protected from death and destruction, guarded against all harm, and assisted in the performance of all that is required [for its development]. Similar acts, when performed by us, are due to a certain emotion and tenderness called mercy and pity. God is, therefore, said to be merciful; e.g., "Like as a father is merciful to his children, so the Lord is merciful to them that fear Him." (Maimonides 2002b, 1.54: 76)

So the idea is that it is appropriate to say that God is merciful to the extent that the world created by God exhibits merciful characteristics. However, this does not mean that God is indeed merciful, but only that the effects of God's actions in the world resemble the effects of human actions we would call 'merciful.'

To sum up, statements that look like positive descriptions of God are to be understood either as disguised negations, or as descriptions of God's actions in terms appropriate for the description of human actions. This is especially important to keep in mind during the mandatory recital of daily prayers, since any praise of God that takes descriptions of God as literal is a sin bordering on idolatry (*Guide* 1.36).[2]

---

[2] It is important to note that, according to Maimonides, taking positive descriptions of God literally can nevertheless have important societal functions. As Scott and Citron explain (citing Maimonides 1963, 3.28: 315), "false representational beliefs about God's benevolence and justice [can be] of instrumental moral value not to the apophatics who know that they are false, but rather, only to the

Moreover, a believer's spiritual maturity is directly proportional to her increasing understanding of the futility of any attempt to talk about God:

> Every time you establish by proof the negation of a thing in reference to God, you become more perfect, while with every additional positive assertion you follow your imagination and recede from the true knowledge of God. Only by such ways must we approach the knowledge of God. (Maimonides 1963, 1.59: 84)

The important fact to note from the preceding explanations is that, although Maimonides defends a radically apophatic position, it is not the case that he disqualifies prayer or other ways of speaking of God as nonsensical. Rather, he offers interpretations of such talk that are, at least on the face of it, coherent with his apophatic stance.³ Hence, another central claim of Maimonides' theology has become visible:

(3) God is indescribable; it is possible to praise God merely indirectly.

However, even indirect descriptions of God must ultimately be acknowledged as inappropriate. The deeper a believer's understanding of God is, the clearer it will become to her how little can be achieved even by indirect praise of God. Maimonides follows this thought through all the way to the end:

> Whatever we utter with the intention of extolling and of praising Him, contains something that cannot be applied to God, and includes derogatory expressions; it is therefore more becoming to be silent, and to be content with intellectual reflection, as has been recommended by men of the highest culture, in the words "Commune with your own heart upon your bed, and be still" (Ps. iv. 4). (Maimonides 2002b, 1.59: 84f)

From this emerges yet another central claim of Maimonides' theology:

(4) Silence is the most appropriate praise.

So religious language has a place in Maimonides' view, and it even plays a crucial role in a believer's ascent from a basic to a more advanced understanding of her faith, culminating in the insight that the total absence of

---

unsophisticated masses who do not know that they are false (and who are not able to follow the arguments of the apophatics). As [Maimonides] says, some beliefs expressed in the Bible are 'only the means of securing the removal of injustice, or the acquisition of good morals' such as 'the belief that God is angry with those who oppress their fellow-men ... or the belief that God hears the crying of the oppressed and vexed'" (Scott and Citron 2016, p. 43, ft. 24).

³ For a comprehensive discussion of apophatic views of God, cf. Scott and Citron (2016).

words is the most appropriate way of praising God. Now, what does all this imply for our knowledge of God? After all,

> Negation does not give knowledge in any respect of the true reality of the thing with regard to which the particular matter in question has been negated. (Maimonides 1963, 1.59: 139)

Since Maimonides' theological view precludes any description of God or God's attributes, a believer's conviction that she has knowledge of God becomes utterly mysterious. What does she have knowledge of? What is it that she knows? Or more precisely, what exactly constitutes her knowledge of God, if not knowledge of what God is like? Maimonides' answer is not entirely illuminating:

> Since it is a well-known fact that even that knowledge of God which is accessible to man cannot be attained except by negations, and that negations do not convey a true idea of the being to which they refer, all people, both of past and present generations, declared that God cannot be the object of human comprehension, that none but Himself comprehends what He is, and that our knowledge consists in knowing that we are unable truly to comprehend Him. (Maimonides 2002b, 1.59: 84f.)

Maimonides is of course committed to the possibility of knowing God; however, his apophatic convictions preclude any further characterisation of what is involved in having knowledge of God. So Maimonides is forced to resort to the final principle of his apophatic view, which is that

(5) God can be known but not comprehended.

This is a surprising – some might even say paradoxical – conclusion:

> Given his metaphysical and religious principles and repeated recommendation of silence about God, it seems that Maimonides either contradicted himself in allowing positive speech about God or failed to derive the semantic implications of his epistemological thesis, which maintains that, although it is possible to know that God is, we can only know what God is not. (Benor 1995, p. 342)

The question thus is: how can we know something without comprehending it?

7.2 The Puzzle of Incomprehensible Knowledge

We typically assume that knowledge and comprehension go hand in hand: when we know something, we take it to be implied that we comprehend what we know. Why do we assume that?

Comprehending some X is equivalent to understanding the nature or meaning of X. For example, comprehending redness is equivalent to understanding that those apples over there are red, that red and green are complementary colours, that mixing red and blue water colours produces a shade of purple, etc. In other words, comprehending redness means understanding that a number of statements about redness are true. Of course, it would be much too strong a condition on comprehension to say that comprehending X requires us to be aware of *all* true statements about X, not only because the set of all true statements about any X is infinitely large, but also because the way in which we use the concept of comprehension suggests that something less than omniscience about X is sufficient for comprehending X. For example, comprehending the concept of a triangle will probably require understanding that triangles have exactly three sides, that every two sides form an angle, that the length of the sides and the size of the inner angles can vary to a certain extent, etc. However, comprehension of triangles certainly does not require understanding every single geometrical theorem entailed by the properties of triangles. Probably it does not even require being aware of any of its mathematical properties (children grasp the concept without knowing that, for every triangle, the sum of its angles is 180 degrees). It may or may not be an interesting philosophical question how many statements about X one must recognise as true in order to comprehend X (most likely, there will not be a definite answer). What is important to note for the purpose of this paper is that comprehending X means understanding that *some* statement S about X is true. So a person A comprehends X if and only if (i) A holds the belief that S is true, (ii) S is true, and (iii) S is a statement about X.

The belief component is precisely what states of comprehension are thought to share with states of knowledge. Consider the JTB model of knowledge that has become somewhat canonical over the last decades, according to which knowledge consists of justified, true belief (JTB) plus some extra component C (e.g. safety, warranted assertibility, reliability, etc.) that is intended to prevent Gettier cases. On this model, a person A knows X if and only if (i) A holds the belief that S is true, (ii) S is true, (iii) S is a statement about X, and (iv) A came to believe S in a way that is justification-conferring and not vulnerable to Gettier-undermining. So comprehension and knowledge share conditions (i)–(iii), but knowledge also requires condition (iv) to be fulfilled. It is now fairly easy to see why we assume that knowledge and comprehension go hand in hand: both states of comprehension and states of knowledge require conditions (i)–(iii) to be fulfilled, such that, if A knows X, A comprehends X. Note that the converse does not hold, i.e. if A comprehends X, it does not mean that A knows X. In order for A to know X, the additional condition (iv) has to be fulfilled. Hence, it is possible to comprehend X without knowing X, but it is not possible to know X without comprehending X. It is this epistemological principle that explains our puzzlement with Maimonides' view: his principle (5) states precisely the opposite, namely, that it is possible to know God without comprehending God.

The JTB analysis of knowledge raises an additional question about Maimonides' principle (5).[4] Consider the following example. Assume that the statement 'Paula knows the capitals of all member states of the United Nations' is true, and let's assume that the correct way to analyse knowledge is as justified true belief plus some X that prevents Gettier cases. It then follows that Paula's knowledge must consist of her justifiedly holding a number of true beliefs (in a non-Gettiered way). What are those beliefs? Clearly, they are beliefs about the capitals of different sovereign states. For example, Paula's knowledge must involve the beliefs that Paris is the capital of France, that Berlin is the capital of Germany, that Kigali is the capital of Rwanda, and so forth. In fact, if it is true that Paula knows the capitals of *all* UN member states, then Paula must hold a set of 193 true beliefs, each one about a sovereign state and its corresponding capital. Paula's knowledge of the capitals of all member states of the United Nations thus consists in her believing (truly, justifiedly, and in a non-Gettiered way) that Paris is the capital of France, Berlin is the capital of Germany, Kigali is the capital of Rwanda, and so forth. A different way of putting this is to say that Paula comprehends what her knowledge of the capitals of all member states of the United Nations entails: it entails that Paris is the capital of France, that Berlin is the capital of Germany, that Kigali is the capital of Rwanda ... This example clearly demonstrates that, if knowledge is indeed justified true belief plus X, then every state of knowledge must entail either one particular true belief, or an entire set of true beliefs, which the believer came to hold in a non-Gettiered, justification-conferring way.

Let's now turn back to Maimonides' principle (5) and the much less trivial case of knowledge of God. Let's assume that the statement

---

[4] The literature on how we ought to analyse the concept of knowledge is vast, of course, and discussions are far from settled. For the most recent and comprehensive overview, see Ichikawa and Steup (2018). For a view that rejects the possibility of analysing knowledge, see Williamson (2000). However, it does seem appropriate to measure Maimonides' apophatic view against the most common account of knowledge, rather than to assume a theory of knowledge that accommodates Maimonides' needs more conveniently from the start.

'Maimonides knows God' is true, or perhaps, formulated more appropriately, 'Maimonides has knowledge of God.' Let's further assume that the correct way to analyse knowledge is as justified true belief plus some X that prevents Gettier cases. It then follows that Maimonides' state of knowledge must entail one or several true beliefs.[5] But this is exactly what Maimonides denies. On his account, there is not a single true positive proposition about God, and hence, not a single positive proposition that could constitute the content of a true belief about God. In other words, if both Maimonides and the JTB analysis of knowledge are correct, then knowledge of God seems either vacuous or simply impossible.[6]

7.3 Non-propositional Knowledge

It is clear now that Maimonides' apophatic views are impossible to square with a JTB analysis of knowledge. A straightforward way to save Maimonides' position is to reject a JTB analysis. However, as indicated earlier, that would constitute an exceedingly radical attempt at saving Maimonides from self-contradiction. The JTB-account of knowledge may still lack a Gettier-proof formulation, but it is doubtless the most established (if yet incomplete) account of propositional knowledge.

However, as I will argue in the following, it is not necessary to reject the JTB-account of knowledge in order to render Maimonides' position coherent. Rather, the solution lies with the acknowledgement that not all knowledge can be brought into propositional form, or put differently, that not all forms of knowledge involve belief in a proposition. In other words, the JTB-account does not cover all forms of knowledge. Of course, it would be *ad hoc* to defend this claim only to save Maimonides, but as I will argue in the following, there are at least three examples that demonstrate the existence of non-propositional forms of knowledge. Once it is established that the concept of non-propositional knowledge is consistent, the claim that apophatic knowledge of God belongs into the category of non-propositional knowledge starts to look attractive.

---

[5] And, of course, that Maimonides came to hold these beliefs in the right way – for brevity's sake, and since what matters is the implication of *belief* in states of knowledge, I will no longer mention the additional qualifications henceforth but take them to be implied in JTB accounts of knowledge.
[6] See also Benor (1995) for the closely related discussion of how to secure reference without comprehension.

7.3.1 Knowledge-how

The first kind of non-propositional knowledge is knowledge how to do something.[7] Take, for example, knowledge how to write. Writing requires knowledge of how to hold a pen, how to move the pen across a sheet of paper, how to form letters, etc. One can bring those pieces of knowledge into propositional form:

- In order to perform a successful act of writing, one must hold the pen between one's thumb and index finger.
- In order to perform a successful act of writing, the angle between pen and paper may not be smaller than 30 degrees.
- In order to perform a successful act of writing, the pressure exerted by the fingers holding the pen may not exceed 47 newtons.
- ...

Let's assume that it is possible to write down a complete list of propositions about what it takes to write (a 'Writing Manual'), and let's imagine a person who knows the Latin alphabet, knows how to read, knows which letters stand for which sounds, but has never written anything by hand – all her life, she has been writing on computers only. Would this person know how to write a letter by hand after reading (and understanding) the Writing Manual? Intuitively, it is very unlikely that she would. In order to learn how to write, she would need to practice how to hold a pen, how to move it across the paper, etc. Propositional knowledge alone cannot teach her how to write. Also conversely, it is very unlikely that all people who know how to write know all the propositions listed in the Writing Manual. In fact, it is very likely that most competent writers do *not* know all the propositions listed in the Writing Manual. Nevertheless, they know how to write.

The anti-intellectualist explanation of our intuitions about cases like the Writing Manual is that knowledge-how cannot be reduced to knowledge-that, or put differently, that not all knowledge can be reduced to knowledge of *propositions*.

---

[7] The question whether all kinds of knowledge, and specifically, instances of knowledge how, can be reduced to propositional knowledge has been a topic of discussion for decades. The canonical formulation of the intuition that (non-propositional) knowledge-how and (propositional) knowledge-that are two distinct, mutually irreducible forms of knowledge is due to Ryle (1949, p. 29). The view, called 'anti-intellectualism', has been attacked by 'intellectualists' like Stanley (2011) and Stanley and Williamson (2001). For a recent defense of anti-intellectualism, see Jonas (2016).

7.3.2 Phenomenal Knowledge

But this is not the only example of non-propositional knowledge. A further example is phenomenal knowledge, i.e. the kind of knowledge that can be gained exclusively through sense perception. The classic examples intended to demonstrate the existence of such knowledge are due to Nagel (1974) and Jackson (1982).[8]

Nagel asks the rhetorical question what it is like (for a bat) to be a bat, and argues that humans, given their restriction to a human cognitive apparatus, do not have access to a bat's phenomenal knowledge and its corresponding particular perspective on the world, which are accessible only from a bat's point of view. He then argues that the inaccessibility of facts about what it is like to be a non-human organism poses a difficulty for (though not necessarily a refutation of) physicalism:

> If the facts of experience – facts about what it is like for the experiencing organism – are accessible only from one point of view, then it is a mystery how the true character of experiences could be revealed in the physical operation of that organism. (Nagel 1974, p. 442)

Jackson goes even one step further and argues that the existence of phenomenal knowledge refutes physicalism. To see why, he asks his readers to imagine Mary, a neuroscientist who has spent her entire life in a black-and-white environment and who knows every physical fact about colours and colour perception (including facts about the human visible spectrum, the wave lengths associated with specific colours, the functioning of retina receptors, the neural processing of visual input, etc.). Jackson then invites us to imagine that Mary steps out of her black-and-white environment and sees the colour red for the first time. He argues that in this case, Mary's knowledge about colours would be enhanced, i.e. in addition to knowing all the physical facts about red wavelengths, etc., she would learn what it is like to see the colour red. In other words, she would gain phenomenal knowledge of redness, i.e. a kind of knowledge not expressible in physical (or any other) language. Jackson's argument is mainly directed against physicalism, but it serves equally well as a refutation of the view that all knowledge can be reduced to knowledge of propositions.

---

[8] Jackson's argument about Mary has come to be known as the 'Knowledge Argument' and plays a central role both in debates about qualia, and in the debate about physicalism, i.e. the view that all facts about the universe, including facts about our mental lives, are physical facts. Also here it should be noted that debates about the (non-)existence of phenomenal knowledge are far from settled; cf. Stoljar (2017); Tye (2018); Van Gulick (2018). It is worth noting that, according to Lewis, phenomenal knowledge is a variety of knowledge-how; cf. Lewis (1988).

7.3.3 Indexical Knowledge

The final example of non-propositional knowledge I want to mention is indexical knowledge, i.e. the kind of knowledge that enables us to integrate our propositional knowledge in such a way as to be able to identify ourselves and our spatiotemporal location in the world. A canonical example that illustrates this kind of knowledge is discussed by John Perry:

> An amnesiac, Rudolf Lingens, is lost in the Stanford library. He reads a number of things in the library, including a biography of himself, and a detailed account of the library in which he is lost. He believes any Fregean [descriptive] thought you think might help him. He still won't know who he is, and where he is, no matter how much knowledge he piles up, until that moment when he is ready to say, '*This* place is aisle five, floor six, of Main Library, Stanford. *I* am Rudolf Lingens.' (Perry 1977, p. 492)

Perry's example illustrates that, in the scenario he sketches, mere propositional knowledge isn't enough for Rudolf Lingens to figure out who and where he is. Even if Lingens were given an exhaustive list of facts about himself and his environment (assuming, for the sake of argument, that such a list could be compiled), and even if Lingens read, understood, and believed all the propositions listed on that list, he still would not be able to infer the knowledge necessary to realise that he is Rudolf Lingens, and that this is aisle five, floor six, of Main Library, Stanford. David Lewis, discussing this example in the context of his theory of *de se* beliefs, summarises the situation as follows:

> Book learning will help Lingens locate himself in logical space. The more he reads, the more he finds out about the world he lives in, so the fewer worlds are left where he may perhaps be living. The more he reads, the more propositions he believes, and the more he is in a position to self-ascribe properties of inhabiting such-and-such a kind of world. But none of this, by itself, can guarantee that he knows where in the world he is. He needs to locate himself not only in logical space but also in ordinary space. He needs to self-ascribe the property of being in aisle five, floor six, of Main Library, Stanford; and this is not one of the properties that corresponds to a proposition. (Lewis 1979, p. 521)

According to Lewis, Lingens is missing a piece of non-propositional knowledge, i.e. knowledge that cannot be rendered in propositional form and thus, does not involve belief in a proposition.[9]

---

[9] It should be stressed that all three examples of non-propositional knowledge I gave in this section are subjects of intense philosophical debate, including debates about whether the kind of knowledge

7.4 Non-propositional Knowledge and Apophaticism

Let us now turn back to Maimonides and the question how best to make sense of his claim that God can be known but not comprehended. In Section 7.2, I argued that the reason this claim raises eyebrows is that comprehension is often thought to be implied in knowledge. The reason for this is that the belief component involved in states of comprehension is what those states share with states of knowledge, at least if knowledge is modelled on the very firmly established JTB account. In Section 7.3, I questioned the comprehensiveness of the JTB account of knowledge by introducing three kinds of knowledge that do not involve propositional belief. I will now offer some positive reasons to think that knowledge of God, as conceived of by Maimonides, is best thought of as an instance of non-propositional knowledge.

In order to see why knowledge of God, as conceived of by Maimonides, is best thought of as a kind of non-propositional knowledge, it is helpful to point out what the three examples of non-propositional knowledge just discussed have in common. Knowledge-how enables us to perform certain actions we intend to perform – riding bikes, writing letters, singing songs. Phenomenal knowledge as acquired through our senses enables each individual's intrinsically subjective perspective on the world, thereby marking us as conscious beings and distinguishing us from mere information-processing machines. Indexical knowledge helps us to locate ourselves in the world by enabling us to self-ascribe properties and processing information that relates to us as individuals. In other words, all three kinds of non-propositional knowledge are *enabling states* that crucially contribute to our ability to interact as individuals with the external world.[10]

Now consider the role that religious believers ascribe to their knowledge of God – what does knowledge of God add to their lives? Typically, religious believers claim that having knowledge of God has a profound impact on their *perspective* on life. For example, many former atheists who

---

in question is really non-propositional (Stanley and Williamson 2001). However, that instances of knowledge-how involve something over and above propositional knowledge is very widely accepted, just like the intuition driving the Mary-example, i.e. that what we receive through our senses cannot be reduced to propositional knowledge. The case of indexical knowledge has been less widely discussed – a notable exception is Cappelen and Dever (2013) – but also here at least the intuitive force of the Rudolf Lingens example is beyond question, and has also been discussed in the philosophy of mind (Seager 2001).

[10] For a detailed discussion of the possibility of defining knowledge in terms of enabling states, and of what distinguishes knowledge thus defined from mere physical abilities, see Moore (1997, 166–194).

became religious believers at some point report that their knowledge of God caused a profound change in the way they evaluate the different dimensions of life, which often involves a shift in focus from primarily material to primarily emotional, ethical, and spiritual aspects of life. In other words, coming to believe in God entails a re-evaluation of one's entire body of (propositional) knowledge about the world. Importantly, this does not usually involve the acquisition of new propositional knowledge (gaining new propositional knowledge, for example about religious scriptures, may be part of what it means to become religious, but the core element of becoming religious is arguably a shift in one's attitude towards what is already known). Rather, knowledge of God enables us to adopt a particular *attitude* towards the world, a religious attitude that will express itself in the way we see and interact with the world. According to Maimonides, a religious attitude towards the world crucially involves, for example, a continuous effort to increase one's knowledge of the things humans are capable of knowing, but also in refraining from the attempt to gain knowledge of things that are beyond the reach of human intellectual capabilities (*Guide* 3.51). It is this fact, i.e. the fact that knowledge of God is a state that enables the subject to relate to the world in this particular way, that explains why knowledge of God is best understood as a kind of non-propositional knowledge.

At this point, a problem of identification arises for Maimonides: how do we know that the knowledge in question, i.e. the non-propositional knowledge that expresses itself in the described attitude towards the world, amounts to knowledge of *God* (rather than, say, knowledge of the ethically optimal way to relate to the world)? After all, non-propositional knowledge does not involve belief in a proposition, so it is not by coming to believe a proposition *about God* that a believer knows that *God* is the object of her knowledge.

It is not obvious that Maimonides can answer this question in a way that is consistent with his apophatic theology, since any attempt to identify the object of one's knowledge is bound to result in a false statement. However, it is also not clear that this puts Maimonides in a worse position than defenders of 'standard' propositional accounts, according to which knowledge of God involves the true belief that some proposition about God is true. This is because defenders of such accounts face the closely related question of how we can know that that a particular proposition about God is true.

In fact, it is possible to argue that defenders of propositional accounts are in a worse position. This is because any claim that a certain statement

S about God is true immediately cries out for an explanation of how we know that it is true. Defenders of a Maimonidean account, on the other hand, do not affirm any statements about God as true, and hence, do not need to explain their methods of verification – a clear advantage over standard accounts.

7.5 Conclusion: Apophaticism and Objectivity

I have argued that it is the fact that knowledge and comprehension can come apart – given that not all knowledge involves belief in a proposition – that supports Maimonides' initially puzzling principle (5). I have further outlined why thinking of knowledge of God as a kind of non-propositional knowledge, i.e. an enabling state, not only explains why such knowledge must necessarily be ineffable, but also appropriately captures what being a religious believer is crucially about. I would like to conclude with a few words about the consequences of this account for the objectivity of knowledge of God.

Objectivity is an epistemological ideal, something all scholarly enquiry should strive for. It is also a property we ascribe to statements about a given subject matter, as well as the methods we use in order to generate those statements. Only statements that are not influenced by a person's individual perspective, interests, unconscious biases, and normative convictions (to name only a few relevant objectivity-distorting factors) may count as objective.

However, if knowledge of God is indeed non-propositional – i.e. does not involve statements to which we could ascribe the property of objectivity – and if it is furthermore an enabling state of an individual person – i.e. entirely entrenched in a subject's individual perspective – then what consequences does this have for its objectivity? Does it mean that there is nothing about our knowledge of God that can be represented objectively?

In one sense there is, in another there isn't. Just like there is a lot we can say in relation to our phenomenal knowledge of the colour red – for example, that red is Pippa's favourite colour, that red Gummi Bears are the best, that red and green are complementary colours, etc. – there is also a lot we can coherently say in relation to our knowledge of God, for example, under which circumstances we acquired knowledge of God, in what way it shapes our way of living, what we take to be the most important implications of there being a God, etc. We can say all these things without it constituting an attempt to 'eff' the ineffable, i.e. without contradicting ourselves. Moreover, it is even conceivable that there is some objective truth about, say, what the most important implications of there being a God are. So in this sense, the objectivity of knowledge of God is not jeopardised by an account that explains knowledge of God in terms of the concept of non-propositional knowledge.

However, nothing we could say in the way just described would ever suffice to pass our knowledge of God on to another person, thereby bringing that person into a state that enables her to relate to the world in a religious way. Getting into that state, just like learning how to ride a bike, is more a matter of practice than instruction, and no matter how many religious wisdoms we heave upon a person, the reasons a person ends up acquiring knowledge of God are entirely subjective. So in this sense, there is nothing about knowledge of God that can be objectively represented and passed on. But this is not a problem for Maimonides. Rather, it is a natural consequence of his apophatic theology. Maimonides is adamant that, concerning our knowledge of God, what can be achieved by means of language is severely restricted. Language only serves to demonstrate the complete inadequacy of human concepts for grasping the nature of God. What can evoke religious knowledge, however, is religious practice,[11] or more precisely, the 'many kinds of knowledge' (Maimonides 2002b, 3.28: 246) we acquire by acting in accordance with the laws of Halakha:

> The true Law, which as we said is one, and beside which there is no other Law, viz., the Law of our teacher Moses, has for its purpose to give us the twofold perfection. It aims first at the establishment of good mutual relations among men by removing injustice and creating the noblest feelings ... Secondly, it seeks to *train us in faith*, and to impart correct and true opinions *when the intellect is sufficiently developed*. (Maimonides 2002b, 3.27: 246) (my italics)

Living an observant life as a Jew can thus be understood as an ongoing, lifelong attempt to follow the divine commandments in order to reach a state of knowledge that enables us to relate to the world in a religious way.

---

[11] Cf. *Guide* 3.27–28.

PART IV

The Created

CHAPTER 8

Creation and Miracles in the Guide

T. M. Rudavsky

8.1 Introduction

Medieval Jewish philosophers thinking about creation were influenced by Aristotle's model of an eternally existing world, by Kalam arguments for a created universe, and of course by the Biblical account of creation found in Genesis. Aristotle's theory of time reinforces a cosmology supportive of an eternally existing universe, thus obviating the need for a creator.[1] Although Aristotle's eternity thesis is often regarded as the target of medieval philosophers, both Dhanani and Langermann suggest that it was possibly Galen rather than Aristotle who posed an equal if not greater threat.[2] In contrast to Aristotle, both Greek and Islamic atomists denied the continuity of time, and posited the existence of discrete time atoms, thus undermining the very assumption that things "persist" through time. Like Aristotle, Galen was famous for having denied creation and emphasizing a self-contained natural order that eschewed a creator; because Galen was careful to reject atomism, the Islamic Kalam theologians might have gravitated toward atomism as an effort to develop an alternative world-view to the Galenic. Given Galen's staunch anti-atomist views, Langermann suggests that "it is not beyond the realm of the possible that Galen's notion of *minima*, and not just his reports concerning his atomist opponents, had some influence upon the Mutakallimûn."[3]

One way of getting a handle on these issues is to examine Aristotle's paradigm of scientific knowledge, which is couched in the context of his theory of demonstration. Aristotle argues that only demonstration leads to

---

[1] See Rudavsky (2000) for discussion of theories of time.
[2] Dhanani (1994) is interested primarily in the Muʻtazilites of Basra, and he emphasizes the link between Kalam and Epicurean minimal parts. Langermann will argue further that "Epicurean teachings are reported in the master's name in the Galenic corpus" in Langermann (2009), the point being that Galen was an important vehicle for the transmission of Epicurean atomism to Islamicate culture.
[3] Langermann (2009, 287); see also Rudavsky (2018).

scientific knowledge. "By demonstration (*apodeixis*) I mean a syllogism productive of scientific knowledge (*syllogismos epistemonikos*), a syllogism, that is, the grasp of which is *eo ipso* such knowledge."[4] According to Aristotle, demonstration differs from other forms of knowledge on the basis of its premises, which must be true, primary and indemonstrable, immediate, better known than the conclusions following them, and causes of the conclusions.[5] The premises in demonstration answer the question "why" and represent the highest sort of scientific knowledge.

In a similar vein, Aristotelian demonstration reappears throughout Maimonides' corpus as a way of distinguishing between true scientific knowledge and lesser forms of knowing. As Joel Kraemer says, "demonstrative reasoning was Maimonides' ultimate touchstone of truth."[6] There are numerous examples in the *Guide* of what can be demonstrated, e.g. the existence, unity, and incorporeality of God.[7] Maimonides agrees with Aristotle that demonstrative arguments are not subject to disagreement: "For in all things whose true reality is known through demonstration there is no tug of war [disagreement] and no refusal to accept a thing proven" (Maimonides 1963, 1.31: 66). Anticipating Galileo's claim that truth cannot contradict truth, Maimonides characterizes demonstrative argument as the ultimate criterion for scientific and philosophical truth. In cases where demonstration is not possible, Maimonides is careful to maintain that "the two contrary opinions with regard to the matter in question should be posited as hypothesis and it should be seen what doubts attach to each of them: the one to which fewer doubts attach should be believed" (Maimonides 1963, 2.22: 230).

Given the importance of scientific demonstration, how does Maimonides make sense of creation *ex nihilo* and miracles, both of which contravene the natural order and lie outside the purview of demonstrative argument? Creation *ex nihilo* presents particular problems; so too, the theological acceptance of miracles provided Maimonides with a particular challenge: how to reconcile Aristotelian science, which rules out supernatural events, with a tradition that includes many examples of miraculous events. In this essay, I shall suggest the cogency of a naturalistic reading of both creation and miracles. Recognizing how different his audiences were, and realizing his attempts to relate to disparate readerships, we can better appreciate the impact played by naturalism on these two discussions.

---

[4] Aristotle (1984, *Posterior Analytics* 71b17–19).   [5] Aristotle (1984, *Topics* 100a27–29).
[6] Kraemer (2008b, 12).   [7] See *Guide* 1.1; 1.18; 2.1.

8.2 Creation

As noted in the previous section, Maimonides' views on creation are embedded in his attitude toward demonstration. In the introduction to the *Guide*, he warns us that certain parables (such as the Account of the Beginning (*ma'aseh b'reishit*), pertaining to natural science, and the Account of the Chariot (*ma'aseh merkabah*), pertaining to divine science) are intentionally vague and must not be fully explicated. Maimonides is explicit in realizing that inasmuch as most individuals are incapable of ascertaining more than "flashes" of truth, any cure can only be partial (Maimonides 1963, introduction: 7).

Speaking of the Account of the Beginning and the Account of the Chariot, Maimonides tells us that his exposition of these two subjects will be "scattered and entangled with other subjects," in order that "the truths be glimpsed and then again be concealed, so as not to oppose that divine purpose which one cannot possibly oppose and which has concealed from the vulgar among the people those truths especially requisite for his apprehension" (Maimonides 1963, introduction: 7). Maimonides adopts a method of concealment similar to the parables used by the Sages, in which difficult philosophical topics are couched. Just as the Sages used parables and riddles when addressing divine matters, so too Maimonides uses the method of concealment when discussing matters of divine science. By concealing these matters, the "multitude" or the "vulgar" (i.e., philosophically unsophisticated readers) will only understand the text on a superficial level. Maimonides thus introduces an ambiguity into the very reading and understanding of his texts, an ambiguity that has persisted to this day.

Maimonides' discussion of creation is couched in the context of both the Kalam theologians and Aristotle. According to Maimonides, Kalam teaching can be summarized in twelve premises, as follows: premises one, two, three, and eleven pertain to the characteristics of atoms; premises four, five, six, seven, eight and nine pertain to the nature of substance and accidents; and premises ten and twelve pertain to the epistemological implications of atomism. From these premises, the Kalam atomists deduced a number of consequences, the most important (for our purposes) being that the whole world has been created in time on the grounds that each individual must also be created in time. Their position is summarized by Maimonides as follows:

> They say: the world in its entirety is composed of substances and accidents. Now no substance can be exempt from one or several accidents. And all

accidents are produced in time. Accordingly it follows necessarily that the substance that serves as a substratum for them is also produced in time ... Accordingly the world in its entirety is produced in time. (Maimonides 1963, 1.74.4: 217)

Maimonides emphasizes how the Kalam doctrine of atomism, combined with the denial of an infinite, leads ineluctably to postulating the beginning of the world. According to Maimonides, the burden of proof is upon the Mutakallimun to demonstrate that, in contradistinction to Aristotle, the accident "circular movement" is produced in time. The major thrust of Maimonides' rejection of the Kalam arguments, however, is contained in *Guide* 1.71. Maimonides' general contention is that these arguments "are derived from premises that run counter to the nature of existence that is perceived" (Maimonides 1963, 1.71: 182). Maimonides himself will adopt the theoretical position of an eternity theorist and try to argue for creation using Aristotle's own premises, rather than those of Kalam. In this way, he feels, the shaky metaphysical ground of Kalam metaphysics has been obviated.

We turn now to Maimonides' theory of creation, a topic that has received much critical attention in recent years.[8] As we have seen, Maimonides characterizes the doctrine of creation as an extremely challenging as well as volatile topic, precisely the sort of issue deserving of an esoteric presentation. Readers of the *Guide* who turn to chapters 2.13–30, which are devoted to creation, have thus been forewarned by the author to expect a modicum of ambiguity at best, or outright secrecy at worst. In *Guide* 2.13 Maimonides states the three standard views on creation. The main features of these three views, characterized as the Law of Moses (Scriptural), Platonic and Aristotelian, can be summarized as follows:

> 1.1 The Scriptural view: that the universe was brought into existence by God after "having been purely and absolutely nonexistent;" through his will and his volition, God brought into "existence out of nothing all the beings as they are, time itself being one of the created things;" (Maimonides 1963, 2.13: 281)
>
> 1.2 The Platonic view: that inasmuch as even God cannot create matter and form out of absolute nonexistence (since this constitutes an ontological impossibility and so does not impute impotence to God), there "exists a certain matter that is eternal as the deity is eternal ... He is the cause of its existence ... and that He creates in it whatever he wishes." (Maimonides 1963, 2.13: 283)

---

[8] The modern scholarly literature on Maimonides' theory of creation continues to grow. For representative discussions, see Davidson (1979); Davies (2011); W. Z. Harvey (1981b); Klein-Braslavy (1987); Manekin (2005); Pines (1963); Rudavsky (2010); Rudavsky (2018); Seeskin (2005).

1.3 The Aristotelian view: that matter cannot be created from absolute nonexistence, concluding that the heaven is not subject to generation/corruption and that "time and motion are perpetual and everlasting and not subject to generation and passing-away." (Maimonides 1963, 2.13: 284)

Each of these positions carries with it both metaphysical and theological implications. The first [1.1] clearly reflects the first words of Genesis and postulates creation after absolute nonexistence. [1.1] is thus incompatible with the eternity of time, and incorporates four distinct propositions: that God brought the world into existence after absolute nonexistence; that he did so through his will and volition; that he did so not from anything (Arabic: *la min shay*; Hebrew: *lo midavar*); and that time is created. The last position [1.3] can be seen as postulating an eternally beginningless universe; in other words, it contradicts [1.1] in that according to Aristotle the universe was not created. Finally, [1.2] postulates both a creator as well as an eternal material substance out of which the universe is formed. That is, it represents a version of eternal creation, adopting features of both [1.1] and [1.3].

Maimonides specifies several observations concerning the relations among these three characterizations. First, contrary to those who "imagine that our opinion and his [Plato's] opinion are identical," Maimonides is quick to disabuse those who are tempted to posit a connection between [1.1] and [1.2]. The Platonic view, he states, cannot be substituted for Mosaic doctrine, even though there appear to be superficial similarities – most notably the postulation of a creator – between the two. But is the similarity in postulating a creator in both positions really that "superficial"? In fact, it might be argued that this in itself is a crucial point and should not be so quickly discarded.

Secondly, Maimonides' attitude toward the relation between [1.2] and [1.3] is itself ambiguous. Maimonides first contrasts them on the grounds that, whereas the Platonists believed that the entire heaven is subject to generation and passing-away, the Aristotelians believed that only the sublunar sphere is subject to such generation and passing-away. But he then dismisses [1.2] as not worthy of serious consideration on the grounds that "[both] believe in eternity; and there is, in our opinion, no difference between those who believe that heaven must of necessity be generated from and pass away into a thing or the belief of Aristotle who believed that it is not subject to generation and corruption" (Maimonides 1963, 2.13: 285). That is, after dismissing the original grounds for contrast between [1.2] and [1.3], he then argues that if Aristotle can be refuted, so too can Plato's theory be disqualified as a justifiable creation theory. In short,

Maimonides appears to equate the positing of eternal preexistent matter with the positing of an eternally beginningless universe. Having dismissed [1.2] as a weaker version of [1.3], Maimonides argues that the Scriptural account is no more flawed than is the Aristotelian account. Then, pointing to the possibility of [1.1], coupled with its Mosaic (and Abrahamic) sanction, Maimonides argues that the very plausibility of Scripture suggests the nonnecessity of Aristotle.

In chapter 25 of part 2 of the *Guide*, Maimonides lays out several pragmatic reasons as well for supporting the Mosaic view of creation [1.1] over that of Plato [1.2] and Aristotle [1.3]. The most important of these is that [1.3] would destroy belief not only in the Law but in miracles and prophecy as well: Aristotle's view, "the belief according to which the world exists in virtue of necessity, that no nature changes at all, and that the customary course of events cannot be modified with regard to anything," has the effect that it "destroys the Law in its principle, necessarily gives the lie to every miracle, and reduces to inanity all the hopes and threats that the Law has held out" (Maimonides 1963, 2.25: 328). Maimonides is quick to point out, however, that the Platonic view is not nearly as devastating: the opinion of Plato would "not destroy the foundations of the Law and would be followed not by the lie being given to miracles, but by their becoming admissible" (Maimonides 1963, 2.25: 328). Why, then, does Maimonides not accept the authority of Plato? The main reason, he tells us, is that the Platonic view has not been demonstrated: "In view of the fact that it has not been demonstrated, we shall not favor this [Plato's] opinion, nor shall we at all heed that other opinion [Aristotle's], but rather shall take the texts according to their external sense" (Maimonides 1963, 2.25: 329). It might appear, then, that the Scriptural account of creation of the universe out of absolute nonexistence [1.1], is Maimonides' final view. But as we shall soon see, [1.1] represents an exoteric reading.

Given Maimonides' explicit support of [1.1], the view of Scripture, why not simply accept this as Maimonides' "real" view on creation? I am suggesting that Maimonides has given readers ample ammunition to interpret his support of [1.1] as an exoteric ploy and to search for the underlying, or concealed, theory of creation. In other words, Maimonides has introduced many contradictions, false starts, and misleading comparisons between Plato and Aristotle. And as commentators working through these chapters have demonstrated, textual evidence abounds to support either Plato or Aristotle as an alternative expression of Maimonides' esoteric view of creation. Moreover, some recent scholars have suggested an even more radical reading of the *Guide*, namely that Maimondes did not adopt any of the three listed positions with respect to creation. Sara Klein-Braslavy, for example, following the suggestion of Pines, argues that, ultimately, Maimonides upholds a skeptical stance in light of the evidence and does not subscribe to any of the three positions. Inasmuch as Maimonides has clearly questioned the demonstrability of each of these views, she suggests that Maimonides' ultimate position is one of epistemological skepticism: the human intellect is simply unable to resolve the issue.[9]

In earlier chapters, Maimonides has claimed that disagreements in matters of metaphysics occur in cases where demonstrative arguments are not available. So too, when the evidence is conflicting and unsupported by sound Aristotelian demonstration, the only justifiably rational stance (on this reading) is to withhold one's belief until such time as adequate demonstration becomes possible. In fact, Maimonides reminds us that Aristotle did not claim to have a demonstrative proof for the eternity thesis; Aristotle himself considered his proofs in support of eternity to be "mere arguments" as opposed to logical demonstrations (Maimonides 1963, 2.15: 291). Although he is quick to point out that Aristotle "does not affirm categorically that the arguments he put forward in its favor constitute a demonstration" for the eternity thesis, Maimonides clearly disagrees with the Mutakallimun who attempted to demonstrate the impossibility of such a claim. Rather, Maimonides states that "it seems that the premise in question is possible – that is, neither necessary... nor impossible..." (Maimonides 1963, 2.introduction: 241). Aristotle himself, he points out, only considered his theory to be probable and not necessary: "Now to me it seems that he [Aristotle] does not affirm categorically that the arguments he put forward in its favor constitute a demonstration. The premise in question is rather, in his opinion, the most fitting and the most probable" (Maimonides 1963, 2.introduction: 241). It is because he was lacking demonstrative arguments that Aristotle had to "buttress his opinion by means of the fact that the physicists who preceded him had the same belief as he" (Maimonides 1963, 2.15: 290). For Maimonides, Aristotle's proofs for eternity constitute not "a cogent demonstration" but rather dialectical arguments, and so cannot be regarded as indubitable support for the eternity thesis (Maimonides 1963, 2.15: 293).

I shall argue in what follows that Maimonides recognizes that the creation account in Scripture [1.1] is ultimately untenable. I offer two

[9] See Klein-Braslavy (1987).

arguments in support of this contention. First, it is important to point out that Maimonides has offered no demonstrative arguments in favor of [1.1], the view of Scripture. Demonstration cuts both ways: Maimonides has offered his reader no indubitable foundation upon which to accept either [1.1] or [1.3]. Although epistemological skepticism would not be quite as heretical as espousing either [1.2] or [1.3], it nevertheless constitutes a provisional rejection of [1.1], which is tantamount to a rejection of the Mosaic theory found in Scripture. Maimonides is inclined to accept [1.2] on the grounds that it offers the possibility of reconciling theories of creation and eternity. However, he has already intimated that a stringent reading of [1.2] is tantamount to an acceptance of [1.3]. Although [1.3] would greatly reduce the need for a Creator of the universe, and would eliminate the emphasis upon will and volition, it would accord with Maimonides' own views on time and enable him to reconcile a theory of creation with an Aristotelian theory of time. This position, while similar to [1.2], employs aspects of [1.3] as well; it is closest in temperament to a Neoplatonic version of eternal creation.

A second argument is based on a critical passage in *Guide* 2.17, in which Maimonides wishes to show that Aristotle's arguments for eternity are not demonstrative. An exoteric reading of *Guide* 2.17 would have us conclude that [1.1] is preferable to [1.3] because Aristotle has offered no acceptable demonstrations for [1.3]. But commentators have noted that *Guide* 2.17 could in fact be read as *supporting* [1.3]. Maimonides ostensibly would like to show that Aristotle's arguments for eternity rest on a fundamental assumption which can be shown to be false. Maimonides' rejection of this assumption is based on the presumed fact that the nature of the world after it exists "does not resemble in anything the state it was in while in the state of being generated" (Maimonides 1963, 2.17: 296). Just as a grown adult does not resemble a fetus, and so inferring from the nature of the adult the nature of the fetus would be absurd, so too Maimonides argues that inferring anything from the state of the present nature of the world to the initial instance of the world is absurd. One important disanalogy between the world and the fetus, however, is that whereas in the case of a fetus we do have observational evidence of what a fetus actually looks like, with the beginning of the world we have no sensory or observational input. And so, Maimonides' objection to Aristotle's claim turns out to be weak.[10]

Let us summarize our discussion to this point. With respect to creation, Maimonides maintains that "God's bringing the world into existence does

---

[10] For additional considerations supporting my argument, see Rudavsky (2010).

not have a temporal beginning, for time is one of the created things" (Maimonides 1963, 2.13: 282). Maimonides does not want to suggest that time itself is eternal, for "if you affirm as true the existence of time prior to the world, you are necessarily bound to believe in the eternity [of the world]" (Maimonides 1963, 2.13: 282). But neither will he claim that the creation of the world is a temporally specifiable action, for on the Aristotelian definition of time, the world must be beginningless in the sense that it has no temporal beginning. While supporting on an exoteric level the scriptural reading of creation, on an esoteric level Maimonides is suggesting that an Aristotelian theory of time (which he accepts) is more consistent with an eternity model of the universe. But does this mean that Maimonides is supportive of [1.3]? If so, then the radical esotericists are right that Maimonides is a closet Aristotelian with respect to creation.

Maimonides concludes his analysis of the rabbinic comments by dismissing their authority: "To sum up: you should not, in considering these points, take into account the statements made by this or that one" (Maimonides 1963, 2.30: 349). Here Maimonides seems to be suggesting that in considering the issues of time and creation, one ought not be misled by the opinions of sundry rabbis. If this is so, what sense, then, should we make of Maimonides' overt espousal of the scriptural reading of creation [1.1] on the basis of Mosaic authority? At least Plato and Aristotle both have other considerations in their favor. But if the sole basis for [1.1] is authority, then Maimonides has undermined its very plausibility. In fact, these final chapters point to the credibility of Plato's view on creation as a compromise between that of Scripture and Aristotle. Unlike the view of Aristotle, Plato's view [1.2], as Maimonides has reminded us, does not undercut the foundations of Judaism, but is still consistent with an Aristotelian theory of time. [1.1] has no demonstrative underpinnings, and in *Guide* 2.30 Maimonides has undercut rabbinic authority. And so, given that we will never be able to demonstrate creation with absolute certainty, Maimonides is *inclined* to follow the position most consistent with Aristotelian science, but least capable of undermining Jewish belief. This position he identifies with Plato. Maimonides is a skeptic in the sense that he realizes there can be no definitive proof either way, but on this score the scientific views of Aristotle fare no worse than the views found in Scripture.

8.3 Creation and Miracles

We turn now to our final question, namely how to understand the occurrence of miracles within the context of a naturally ordered universe.

The very nature of a miracle suggests the overturning of the natural order, and so miracles raise an important philosophical question: whether it is epistemically and ontologically possible to hold that the natural order of things is preserved while at the same time admitting the possibility of exceptions. To say of an event that it is *natural* means that it obeys fixed laws such that even occasional anomalies or deviations may be accounted for in strictly natural terms. To say that something is *miraculous* means that it contravenes fixed laws in a way that cannot be accounted for in strictly natural terms, but introduces an element of divine will. As Roslyn Weiss has pointed out, any worldview that accommodates miracles is not a world governed by the necessity of natural law: things subject to divine will cannot be natural, nor can they be "just like" natural things.[11] Most Jewish philosophers accept the veracity of miraculous events as providing evidence for God's intervention in the natural order. But to what extent is this intervention even possible? The topic of miracles renders more potent the struggles between Judaism and science.

For a philosopher who recognizes no limits to God's omnipotence, miracles simply reflect another example of God's volitional will intervening in the natural order. God's unbridled power was established already by Al-Ghazali in *The Incoherence of the Philosophers,* his extended diatribe against the philosophers. In this work, Al-Ghazali provided an occasionalist explanation of miracles, arguing in effect that *all* events, insofar as they reflect the continuous recreation of the world, are miracles. It is the philosophers, he avers, that are at a loss to explain causality: "Whoever renders the habitual courses [of nature] a necessary constant makes all these [miracles] impossible."[12] Claiming that the philosophers have nothing but constant conjunction to justify their belief in causality, Al-Ghazali rejects the Aristotelian theory of cause and effect, replacing it with God's continuous recreation: the apparent connection between "effects" and their "causes" is "due to the prior decree of God, who creates them side by side."[13]

While Maimonides' early halakhic writings present a straightforwardly naturalistic view of miracles, his later works, including the *Guide* and *Essay on Resurrection*, appear to reflect a shift from a totally deterministic, naturalistic system to one that at least appears to makes room for miracles. In his *Essay on Resurrection*, for example, Maimonides articulates the following important principle: "I try to reconcile the law and reason, and wherever possible consider all things as of the natural order. Only when

---

[11] See Weiss (2007, 14) for further discussion of the implications of these characterizations.
[12] Al-Ghazali (1997, part II.17 introduction, 166).   [13] Al-Ghazali (1997, part II.17, 171).

something is explicitly identified as a miracle, and reinterpretation of it cannot be accommodated, only then I feel forced to grant that this is a miracle" (Maimonides 1985, 223). On the basis of this statement, it might be argued that Maimonides did not believe in the possibility of miracles.

In contradistinction to the Kalam theologians, Maimonides struggles to provide an account of miracles that accords with an Aristotelian view. Much of Maimonides' discussion centers around the notion of "possibility." According to Aristotle's cosmology, no change can take place in the superlunar sphere. In *Guide* 3.15, Maimonides struggles with the problem of defining the limits of the "possible." Part of his struggle has to do with whether God can perform miracles at will. Clearly an incorporeal deity cannot act in time, since the temporal domain pertains to matter. Furthermore, since creation is perfect (*Guide* 2.13; 2.28–29), no new volition can arise in God leading Him to introduce something new. And so, Maimonides suggests in 2.29 the Sages' view that miracles have been integrated into nature at the time of creation. Miracles are on this view "the product of natural causes rather than suspensions in the laws of nature."[14]

Kreisel notes that while in theory Maimonides affirms the possibility of miracles, he does not interpret them all literally. In agreement with Aristotle's view that no change can take place in the heavens, he interprets all miracles involving celestial bodies figuratively.[15] Even in the sublunar sphere, Maimonides appears to agree with Aristotle: is God unable to introduce even small changes in nature, such as lengthening a fly's wing? "But Aristotle will say that He would not wish it and that it is impossible for Him to will something different from what is; that it would not add to His perfection but would perhaps from a certain point of view be a deficiency" (Maimonides 1963, 2.22: 319).

In Maimonides' early writings, both miracles and natural events take place in accordance with the preordained nature of things. Maimonides embraces in *Commentary on the Mishnah* the rabbinic view that miracles are rare but not supernatural phenomena, and are already embedded into the natural order during the act of Creation. The best known, and most-quoted discussion of miracles, occurs in the context of explaining the splitting of the Red Sea. In the context of explaining what is meant by human volition and its relation to divine volition, Maimonides explains

---

[14] Kreisel (1984, 109). Kreisel provides a detailed analysis of miracles in medieval Jewish thought. See also Ackerman (2009).
[15] Kreisel (1984, 111).

that the splitting of the Red Sea was already written into the natural order, as it were.[16] What we or Scripture are tempted to describe as miraculous turns out to represent the actualization of a nature that was determined at the beginning of creation. There are no actions that are *contrary* to nature, and hence there are no "supernatural" miracles. Concomitant with the disavowal of miracles is the view that events unfold according to a natural, regular order, and there is no room for actions that represent a violation of this order. As put succinctly by Langermann, the author of the *Commentary on the Mishnah* was convinced that natural science could account for all phenomena and rejected miracles on the grounds that the supposedly miraculously events can be explained naturalistically.[17]

Maimonides revisits the issue of miracles in his *Medical Aphorisms,* in the context of a sustained critique of Galen. Both he and Galen are concerned with the limits of God's creative powers. Galen used the example of eyebrow and eyelash hair to support his claim that God has created the best possible state of affairs, and could not have created any other state of affairs: because this is the best possible world, some things are inherently impossible for God. That eyebrow and eyelash hairs do not grow overly long, as does facial hair, reflects God's purpose in providing a teleological order to nature. Galen used this example to drive a wedge between the view of Moses and that of the philosophers, claiming that while according to "the faith of Moses" all things are possible for God, the Greek philosophers claimed that "there are certain things inherently impossible" (Maimonides 1970–1971/1989, 438). Galen [in Maimonides' restatement] argued that "if God had wished a thousand times a thousand that this hair should be so, it would never have been so if He had let it grow from soft skin. Had He not planted the roots of the hair in a hard body, they would not have remained erect and rigid in spite of His command" (Maimonides 1970–1971/1989, 438). Galen's point is that, given the best possible state of affairs (one in which eyebrows can

---

[16] In his commentary on *Avot*, the "Eight Chapters," Maimonides writes: "[we] believe that the Divine Will ordained everything at creation and that all things, at all times, are regulated by the laws of nature and run their natural course in accordance with what Solomon said ... This occasioned the sages to say that all miracles which deviate from the natural course of events, whether they have already occurred or, according to promise, are to take place in the future, were foreordained by the Divine Will during the six days of creation, nature being then so constituted that those miracles which were to happen really did afterward take place. Then when such an occurrence happens at its proper time, it may have been regarded as an absolute innovation, whereas in reality it was not" (Twersky 1972, 382–383).

[17] Langermann (2004, 150).

only grow to the proper length if embedded in hard cartilage), it follows that even God could not have coaxed eyebrows from soft skin.

Maimonides agrees with Galen's claim that, according to Moses, "to God everything is possible," and asserts that, according to Moses, "something can suddenly exist in a manner contrary to the laws of nature, such as the transformation of a staff into a snake, and of dust into lice" (Maimonides 1970–1971/1989, 441). Maimonides attributes to Scripture the view that it is possible for God to change the nature of any creation (Maimonides 1970–1971/1989, 441). This ability depends solely on God's Divine Will. Maimonides defines miracle as "the coming into existence of something which is outside its normal and permanent nature" (Maimonides 1970–1971/1989, 442). He then distinguishes two types of miracles: those that include an instantaneous transformation, like the transformation of a staff into a snake, or water into blood; and those that attribute to an object predicates that it normally doesn't have, like the simultaneous hardness and softness of manna. According to Maimonides, the eternity theorist cannot account for these latter cases, because on the eternity model, God's divine Will cannot exert an influence upon matter: "All this results from the arrangement of matter over which the Lord, blessed be He, can exert no influence" (Maimonides 1970–1971/1989, 443). In fact, as Langermann notes, once again, these miracles do not necessarily violate the natural order: it is "the regularity of natural processes, but not the rules that limit the scope of these processes," that has been violated.[18] And so God *can* make it be the case that the hair of the eyebrows grow beyond a certain length, or that dust be converted to lice, or water to blood, etc., because none of these examples are *contrary* to nature. We can imagine a natural process occurring instantaneously, rather than over a period of time, but acceleration of a natural process is not itself tantamount to a supernatural event. And so, neither the early halakhic works nor the *Medical Aphorisms* present a theory of supernatural miracle that necessarily violates the natural order.

The *Guide* reflects an apparent shift from a totally deterministic, naturalistic order to one that ostensibly makes room for at least the *possibility* of miracles. On the one hand, Maimonides accepts Aristotle's view that God will not change the laws of the universe. This position is articulated already in *Guide* 2.11, in which Maimonides clearly states that God creates directly the first Intelligence, and through successive natural emanations, the Intelligences create the rest of the universe. Maimonides then notes in

[18] Langermann (2004, 160).

Guide 2.13 several "naturally impossible events," among them that God by his free will brought into existence out of nothing all the beings as they are, and that the heaven was generated out of nothing after a state of absolute nonexistence. See also *Guide* 2.28, in which Maimonides suggests that miracles are impossible; the works of the deity are perfect as they are and permanently established as they are, "for there is no possibility of something calling for a change in them" (Maimonides 1970–1971/1989, 443). Since creation is already perfect, no new volition can arise in God leading Him to create something new.[19] On the other hand, several passages in the *Guide* evince evidence for the recognition of the *possibility* of miracles. For example, Maimonides tells us in *Guide* 2.25 that not accepting creation *ex nihilo* would violate one's belief in miracles. He ostensibly upholds the assumption of the temporal creation of the world as the only one that allows for miracles. Note that whereas in *Medical Aphorisms* Maimonides used creation to establish the existence of miracles, in the *Guide* he uses miracles to uphold the veracity of creation.

How, then, does Maimonides reconcile the notion of miracles (the existence of which are intimated in *Guide* 2.19 and 2.25) with the Aristotelian naturalism espoused in *Guide* 2.11, 2.13, and 2.28? One way is by claiming that although miracles are voluntary acts of God, nevertheless they are predetermined at the time of creation, and do not indicate a *change* in God's will or wisdom. A miracle represents a unique occurrence of an event that can still be understood within the causal nexus. On this reading, the *Guide* reinforces the idea already suggested in *Commentary on the Mishnah* and *Medical Aphorisms*, namely, that miracles do not represent the abrogation of the laws of nature. In *Guide* 2.29, Maimonides states (in accordance with the Sages) that when God created the primary parts of the universe (the heavens and first matter), God impressed upon them their various natural properties, which contained the very characteristics that would make them produce anomalies at various times in the future. What we might be tempted to call "miraculous events" are already contained in embryo in nature, and will be revealed to the prophet shortly before they occur. God does not need to initiate the miracle when it occurs, nor does the prophet need to do anything special to bring about a miracle; when God warns the prophet about an impending natural event, that event "is effected according to what was put into its nature when first it received its particular impress" (Maimonides 1963, 2.29: 345). On this reading, a prophet plays much the same role as the

---

[19] For further discussion of this point, see Kreisel (1984).

natural scientist: the prophet must possess the information necessary to predict that a certain anomaly will occur. Thus, for example, part of Moses' prophetic excellence was in knowing that the Red Sea would part at a certain time, enabling the Israelites to cross on dry land. All the other miracles, he tells us, "can be explained in an analogous manner" (Maimonides 1963, 2.29: 346). On this reading, Maimonides accepts both the permanence of natural laws and the possibility of a particular, temporary change, but this temporary change is itself part of natural law.[20]

Clearly, however, there are certain things that even God cannot do. What criteria do we use to determine the limits of God's possibility? In *Guide* 1.73, Maimonides committed himself to the conclusion that the intellectual faculty determines the realm of possibility, and that whatever was imaginable was *ipso facto* possible. But in *Guide* 3.15 he juxtaposes imagination against intellect: "Should this be verified and examined with the help of the imaginative faculty or with the intellect … Is there accordingly something that permits differentiation between the imaginative faculty and the intellect?" (Maimonides 1963, 3.15: 460). If imagination provides the criterion for divine possibility, then God can do anything imaginable; but if the intellectual faculty provides the criterion, then the possible turns out to be only what is logical and rational. There is no way, Maimonides concludes, to determine which of these two tests is operative. Maimonides lists a number of impossible states of affairs that he claims are agreed "according to all men of speculation": these include the coming together of contraries at the same instant and place; the transmutation of substances; that God should bring into existence an entity like Himself, or annihilate Himself, or become a body, or change (Maimonides 1963, 3.15: 460). Reflecting these counter-instances to what God can do, Maimonides lays down a general limiting principle on God's ability to perform miracles: "there are impossible things whose existence cannot be admitted" (Maimonides 1963, 3.15: 461). Hence God cannot produce just any miracle that He pleases: There are limits to what God can do, although, as Maimonides is quick to note, such a limit "signifies neither inability nor deficiency of Power on his part" (Maimonides 1963, 3.15: 461).

Maimonides both naturalizes and subjectivizes many so-called miracles described in Scripture, claiming that the events in question occurred in the agent's mind and not in reality. Take, for example, Jacob's wrestling with God, or Balaam's ass speaking. In both these cases, Maimonides reminds us that the event in question happened in a vision of prophecy and not in

---

[20] See Kasher (1998) for further discussion of this point.

reality, thus undermining the objective status of the event (*Guide* 2.42). Other miraculous accounts are reduced to natural events as well, as in the case of Daniel's surviving in the lion's den (*Guide* 2.6). In the case of the Revelation at Sinai, Maimonides offers the reader several ways to understand the miracle: either as a prophetic vision rooted in intellectual apprehension, or as a prophetic vision that incorporated sight as well, or one that incorporated hearing as well. "Choose whatever opinion you wish," says Maimonides (*Guide* 1.21), signaling that even this event is not necessarily rooted in objective fact. Again, in the case of explaining the extraordinary lifespan of certain individuals, Maimonides gives us the option to explain such an anomaly either naturally or supernaturally: "only that individual who is mentioned lived so long a life, whereas the other men lived lives that had the natural and usual duration. The anomaly in the individual in question may be due either to numerous causes attaching to his nutrition and his regimen or is due to a miracle and follows the laws thereof" (Maimonides 1963, 2.47: 408). In all of these cases, Maimonides is providing his readers with different ways of understanding miracles, depending on their intellectual sophistication: whereas the "vulgar" will cling to the supernatural interpretation that reinforces God's willfully transforming the natural order, those initiated in philosophy and science will recognize that none of these events contravenes the natural order.

The extent to which Maimonides was willing to naturalize miracles in Scripture is reflected in his interpretation of the famous passage in Joshua 10:12, a text discussed throughout the medieval and early modern period. This passage relates that Joshua and his men are worried that there will not be sufficient time to defeat the five Amorite kings, and so Joshua prays to God to extend the day:

> Joshua addressed the Lord; he said in the presence of the Israelites: "Stand still, Oh sun, at Gibeon, Oh moon, in the Valley of Ajalon!" and the sun stood still and the moon halted, while a nation wreaked judgment on its foes ... thus the sun halted in mid-heaven, and did not press on to set, for a whole day. (Joshua 10:12–13)

The miracle described in Joshua 10:12–13 posed a particular problem for rationalists who found it hard to accept such a collapse of celestial order, and tried to attribute the arrest of the sun to natural or seminatural causes. For these philosophers, the underlying question became whether the heavenly bodies could have actually stopped in their tracks, implying a complete suspension of the natural order, or might there not be some natural explanation of the phenomenon.

In his early *Commentary to the Mishnah (Avot)*, Maimonides uses the Joshua proof text to reiterate the principle that nature was created together with the potential for certain changes, some of which appear as miracles, but actually are woven into the fabric of natural events. As an example, Maimonides gives the following case: "On the fourth day, when the sun was created, it was granted the potential to stand still as Joshua commanded it. The same applies with regard to the other miracles" (*Commentary on the Mishnah* Avot 5:6). On this reading, it appears that the sun actually did stand still, but that its standing still was itself an anomalous event prefixed in the natural order. By the time of the *Guide*, however, his explanation has changed.

Maimonides raises Joshua's miracle in the context of his presentation of the ways in which Moses' prophecy differs from other prophecies. In *Guide* 2.35 he suggests that only Moses' miracles were visible to all the people. But how does this compare to the Joshua example, in which all Israel apparently witnessed the stoppage of the sun? Maimonides resolves the discrepancy by claiming that Joshua's miracle did not occur in front of "all Israel" but only in front of some Israelites. Further, he argues that the event in question was temporary. Maimonides focuses on the words "for a whole day" to mean "the longest day that may happen," suggesting that "it is *as if* it said that the day of Gibeon was for them *as* the longest of the days of the summer that may occur there" (Maimonides 1963, 2.35: 368; my emphasis). Maimonides thus undercuts the supernaturalist interpretation of this event, according to which the sun actually stopped in its tracks and the entire celestial order was abrogated (in which case the entire world would have been witness to the event). Rather does he suggest that *perhaps* the "sun stood still" only in the minds of the soldiers, for whom the day "was for them *as* the longest of days;" that is, it was, *in their minds*, the longest day of summer, but not in actuality. Note that in both texts, the miraculous nature of this event has been removed: whereas in *Avot* the event is seen as embedded already in the natural order, in the *Guide* the apparent miracle was not a "real event," but rather a subjective event imagined in the minds of the soldiers.

8.4 Conclusion

I have tried to argue in this essay that both creation and the existence of miracles must be understood against Maimonides' scientific naturalism. In the case of creation, Maimonides' effort has been aimed at showing that the scriptural view of creation is inconsistent with an Aristotelian theory.

Aristotelian cosmology represents the acme of modern science for Maimonides, and presents a coherent alternative to creation ex nihilo as presented in Scripture. And yet, Maimonides is unwilling to support Aristotle altogether. Maimonides realizes that the Aristotelian eternity thesis has not been definitely demonstrated. Thus, while both Platonic and Aristotelian theories of time and matter are important in shaping Maimonides' modes of discourse pertaining to creation, they are interwoven along with Rabbinic material to create an intertextual garment that takes on a life of its own. Maimonides certainly does not give up a creator deity altogether, but Maimonides' God is not the God of Genesis. Maimonides is drawn to an Aristotelian theory of creation, but one tempered by Platonic underpinnings. Because Maimonides recognizes that neither can be demonstrated definitively, he leaves open the door to further inquiry. Given the centrality of demonstrative argument to Maimonides' analysis, it is clear that the doctrine of Scripture does not pass the test of scientific certainty.

So too, in the case of miracles, Maimonides presents a naturalized account. Even his late writings can be construed in a way that present miracles either as natural events or anomalies embedded into the natural order, or as subjective perceptions not grounded in an objective reality. This naturalizing of miracles affects our understanding of creation ex nihilo, which of course exemplifies the most miraculous event of all. Maimonides does not rule out an eternal model of creation. This position does not deny the incorporation of anomalies into the natural order, but it does underscore a rationalist and naturalized understanding of both prophecy and miracle. This position also minimizes the role played by divine will.

CHAPTER 9

The Prophetic Method in the Guide

Dani Rabinowitz

Prophetic Method (**PM**): Know that the true reality and quiddity of prophecy consists in its being an emanation emanating from God, may He be cherished and honored, through the intermediation of the Active Intellect, toward the rational faculty in the first place and thereafter toward the imaginative faculty. (Maimonides 1963, 2.36: 369)

Maimonides' definition of prophecy is a sophisticated hybrid engineered from the materials of Jewish theology and medieval Arabic philosophy. This essay opens with a brief exploration of the theology, epistemology and cognitive psychology shaping PM, which, together, informs Maimonides' view that prophecy is a cognitive feat that will naturally be experienced by certain people as a dream or vision. The remainder of the essay seeks to determine the precise point in which Maimonides' prophet formed the propositional attitude of central importance to epistemologists, namely belief. In so doing, it shall become apparent that in no way can the epistemology of prophecy be reduced to the epistemology of divine testimony, which demonstrates that prophecy, at least in Maimonides' hands, is fallible and that the distinction between Mosaic and non-Mosaic prophecy is problematic.

9.1 Background

9.1.1 Constraints from Jewish Theology

Accounts of prophecy within the Jewish tradition typically respect two overriding theological constraints: (i) that all non-Mosaic prophecy occurs in either a dream or a vision and (ii) that Mosaic prophecy is qualitatively superior to non-Mosaic prophecy.[1] The source for these constraints is Numbers 12. Maimonides adheres to these constraints yet refuses to delve, at least in an explicit fashion, into the nature of Mosaic prophecy. The scope of PM is therefore restricted to the phenomenon of non-Mosaic prophecy.

The epistemic appeal of the Maimonidean model of non-Mosaic prophecy undoubtedly lies in his controversial claim that, contrary to the plain meaning of scripture, at no point in the process does God actually speak to or address the prophet; that is, there is no transfer of propositional content from God to prophet as one finds in testimonial models of prophecy. Maimonides takes seriously the constraint on non-Mosaic prophecy stipulated in Numbers 12:6. During a prophetic experience the prophet does not hear with her ears or see with her eyes since every instance of prophecy occurs in either a dream or a vision when the prophet's senses cease to function (Maimonides 1963, 2.36: 370). Consequently, prophets never actually saw angels or heard God or angels speaking.

9.1.2 Method Individuation

If prophets acquired prophetic knowledge by way of prophecy, then prophecy must count as a belief-forming method given that belief is an ingredient of knowledge.[2] The precise manner in which prophets formed such beliefs and the epistemic character of such beliefs is the focus of this essay.

One helpful aid in this task is recent work in twentieth-century analytic epistemology, which experienced a robust interest in method individuation following the pivot toward externalism in response to Edmund Gettier's (1967) seminal paper. By way of example, a method is a way of forming beliefs which "includes the specific causal process leading to it and the relevant causal background" (Williamson 2009, 307). Methods can be individuated in a variety of ways: internally or externally and in a coarse-grained or fine-grained way.

Much can be said in favor of fine-grained, externally individuated methods since such an approach delivers the correct result in a variety of cases. A way of individuating methods is internal if it respects the constraint that agents who form a belief p and who are internal duplicates share the same method; and external if it does not respect that constraint. Alternatively, if method individuation supervenes solely on brain states, then methods are internally individuated; if two agents can be in the same

---

[1] Saadia Gaon is a notable exception. See Kreisel (2001, 27–93).
[2] Knowing that p entails believing that p.

brain state yet be using different methods, then methods are individuated externally.

A way of individuating methods is coarse-grained if methods are described broadly (e.g., the visual method). On the other hand, a way of individuating methods is fine-grained if methods are described in detail (e.g., the visual method for large objects at close range under favorable lighting conditions). While we typically talk about methods in a coarse-grained way, Williamson favors a fine-grained, external individuation of methods. For example, Williamson (2009, 307; 2009, 325 note 13) thinks that, other things being equal, seeing a daschund and seeing a wolf count as different methods. Consequently, minimal changes in the external environment can result in a difference in the method of belief formation.

From the foregoing it should be apparent that there is no such thing as *the* prophetic method. Rather, for each prophet there will be numerous such methods and the epistemic credentials of each of her beliefs so formed will differ depending on the precise character of the prophetic method underpinning the belief in each belief episode. Therefore, insofar as the epistemologist is concerned, we look at each method sitting behind each instance of prophetic belief since there is no single method producing all these prophetic beliefs, much as there is no one single perceptual method producing all perceptual beliefs.[3]

While it is technically incorrect to speak of the prophetic method simpliciter given fine-grained individuation of methods, I use the generic (and perhaps slightly misleading) definite article *the* prophetic method in this essay for ease of reference. It will prove helpful to think of "the prophetic method" as a placeholder for a set of finely-grained prophetic methods satisfying Maimonides' definition of non-Mosaic prophecy.

9.1.3 *Maimonides' Cognitive Psychology*

Much of the cognitive psychology found in the *Guide* can be traced back to Aristotle's *De Anima* (*On the Soul*), though many of Aristotle's original ideas only reached Maimonides through their various percolations in Alexander of Aphrodisias and the Arabic philosophers. Working from

---

[3] It would not be strictly anachronistic to approach Maimonides on these terms, since the broadly Aristotelian epistemology to which Maimonides subscribed would have been accommodating of such insights, given that, e.g., *scientia* (scientific knowledge) requires demonstration, which is a method of belief formation. See Sections 9.1.4 and 9.2.4.1 for instances of Maimonides and the Arabic Aristotelians being acutely aware of method individuation and the epistemic consequences thereof.

within this tradition, Maimonides recognized that the human soul, which he takes to be the form of the human body, is divided into faculties, two of which are relevant here: the rational faculty and the imagination. While the imagination "retains impressions of things perceptible to the mind, after they have ceased to affect directly, the senses," the rational faculty "divides the composite things and differentiates their parts and makes abstractions of them, represents things to itself in their true reality."[4]

Once the rational faculty begins to abstract from those impressions retained by the imagination, it is called an "Actual Intellect." In line with broadly Aristotelian notions, the motion necessary to move from a state of potentiality to a state of actuality requires an outside force: "everything that passes from potentiality to actuality must have necessarily something that causes it to pass and that is *outside* it. And this cause must belong to the *species* of that which it causes to pass from potentiality to actuality" (Maimonides 1963, 2.4: 257, emphasis added). To explain this motion Aristotle posited the existence of the Active Intellect, a further yet *immanent* intellect. However, by the time this idea, one of the most controversial in Aristotelian scholarship, reached Maimonides, the Active Intellect was considered a *transcendent* intellect. It is at this point that Arabic cognitive psychology and cosmology come together. Aristotle attributed the eternal movement of heavenly bodies to a unique First Cause or Unmoved Mover (Aristotle 1984, *Metaphysics* 1072a). The Arabic neo-Aristotelians, however, adopted a Ptolemaic version thereof according to which God (the Unmoved Mover) brought into existence another intellect, the first intelligence, by an act of "emanation," the term Maimonides uses for action by an incorporeal agent (Maimonides 1963, 2.12: 279). In turn the first intelligence emanates its sphere, the soul of its sphere, and a second intelligence. The second intelligence repeats this process with regard to a third intelligence, and so on, until a tenth intelligence comes into being. It is this tenth intelligence that Maimonides recognizes as the Active Intellect and to which he attributes the emanation of forms in the sublunar world inhabited by humans.

In Maimonidean cognitive psychology, therefore, the actualization of the rational faculty is dependent on emanation originating in the Active Intellect, which in turn draws its powers of emanation from the ninth intelligence, and so forth, until the series terminates in God's constant act of emanation. It is in this sense that the actualization of the mind and the existence of the world are counterfactually dependent upon God; that is, if

[4] Maimonides (1966, 41; 1963, 209).

God ceased to maintain the stream of emanation, the universe would cease to exist. In *Guide* 2.4 Maimonides attributes his cognitive psychology and cosmology to Aristotle[5] and goes so far as to make the bold claim "there is then nothing in what Aristotle for his part has said about this subject [apart from the eternity of the universe] that is not in agreement with the [Jewish] Law" (Maimonides 1963, 2.6: 265).

9.1.4 Maimonides' Epistemology

Despite the likelihood that Maimonides' epistemology, like his metaphysics and ethics, would have been broadly Aristotelian in nature, the precise nature of Aristotle's epistemology is itself a matter of dispute (Taylor 1990). Moreover, by the time Aristotle's epistemology had percolated into Arabic philosophy and from there to Maimonides it had splintered into competing interpretations (Black 2006). It is therefore unlikely that Maimonides deemed it *un*necessary to clarify his stance on the central concepts in epistemology despite his student's familiarity with Arabic philosophy, and, *pace* Stern (2005, 105), Maimonides' silence cannot, therefore, be comfortably attributed to his disavowal of making original contributions to philosophy or physics (Maimonides 1963, 2.2: 253).

Attempts have been made to reconstruct Maimonides' epistemology in the *Guide* from the few definitions of some key epistemic terms found therein, e.g. belief and certainty, and from the various positions Maimonides takes on matters resting on key epistemic distinctions. But, as Charles Manekin writes, "diverging interpretations demonstrate more than anything else the speculative nature of the enterprise" (Manekin 1990, 117–118).

This precarious state of affairs problematizes those passages in the *Guide* containing "knowledge" (עלם) and its cognates. For instance, in some contexts we find Maimonides using the unqualified noun "knowledge" and in other contexts he qualifies it with the property of certainty, as in "certain knowledge" (עלמא יקינא) (Maimonides 1963, 1.50: 111; 2.47: 407; 3.23: 492). It is unclear whether Maimonides intended to indicate with this terminological inconsistency that he considered

---

[5] This point is emphasized by Kafih and Pines in their respective translations of the *Guide* (Maimonides 1977, 174) and (Maimonides 1963, 258). The relevant sections in Aristotle are *Metaphysics* 12.7 and *Physics* 8.6, 258 b26–259a9. Davidson demurs on this point when he writes that Maimonides' cognitive psychology and cosmology derives "from the Arabic Aristotelians, rather than from Aristotle himself" (Davidson 1992, 201; 1992, 206). Either way, the theme of the Maimonidean approach is broadly Aristotelian in nature.

there to be two kinds of knowledge, one characterized by certainty and one lacking such a property.[6]

The absence of a robust Maimonidean epistemology is acutely felt in the context of prophecy since the *epistemic* relation between the Active Intellect and the rational faculty is central to PM. The nature of this relationship was hotly debated by the medieval Arabic philosophers. Two similar yet competing models dominated the day. According to Al-Farabi, the Active Intellect is a source of "light" that "illuminates" the rational faculty in a way that enables the rational faculty to abstract forms from the sensory images stored in the imagination and, with the aid of first intelligibles, to thereby construct a body of propositional knowledge. The Active Intellect plays no role in the latter project.[7] Avicenna, on the other hand, attributed a more robust role to the Active Intellect in that, in addition to providing the rational faculty with the first intelligibles, it also enters into "conjunction" with a rational faculty that has prepared itself to receive emanation from the Active Intellect by beginning the process of abstraction from images stored in the imagination. In the moment of conjunction between the two, the Active Intellect furnishes the rational faculty with the content of human thought.[8]

Maimonides never explicitly endorses either model and various passages in the *Guide* can be read in support of either model. Since Al-Farabi and Avicenna differed on a number of theological points as a result of their competing models, prophecy being one of them, the significance of this interpretative problem ramifies in Maimonidean scholarship in which prophecy is similarly a central theme. Traditionally Maimonides has been interpreted as being an Al-Farabian since (i) in a letter to the translator of the *Guide* Maimonides lauds Al-Farabi as the philosopher he respects most after Aristotle and (ii) Maimonides never mentions Avicenna by name in the *Guide*.[9] Recently some have drawn on passages in the *Guide* where Maimonides refers to the Active Intellect as the "giver of forms" (Maimonides 1963, 2.12: 278) as proof for his being a follower of the

---

[6] This interpretive obstacle deepens when we take into consideration Aristotle's view that there are five kinds of knowledge, some of which are characterized by certainty and others not. See Taylor (1990) for further discussion on this fivefold division. Unfortunately, Maimonides uses the Arabic word עלם ("knowledge") when discussing "knowledge" and "certain knowledge" whereas Aristotle had different names for the different kinds of knowledge. The lack of a clear linguistic distinction makes it near impossible to claim that Maimonides adopted Aristotle's schema.

[7] Al-Farabi (1972; 1985, 200–203).

[8] Avicenna (1949; 2005). For an extensive treatment of the Active Intellect in Arabic philosophy, see Davidson (1992).

[9] See Kreisel (1999) and Pines (1979).

Avicennian model since that is a term Avicenna, unlike Alfarabi, used to refer to the Active Intellect.[10]

While displaying sensitivity to this debate, my explication of PM sets aside this interesting historical question of which philosopher had more influence over Maimonides for a number of reasons – all of which, apart from the first, are related to the conceptual link between method individuation and knowledge. Firstly, advocates of both interpretative schools admit that in all likelihood Maimonides adopted aspects of *both* models in addition to making modifications of his own.[11] This eclectic methodology rules out a rigid reading of Maimonides along the lines of either model. And as Stern (2005, 114) argues, Maimonides was in places a severe critic of Arabic celestial physics and metaphysics, so much so that it makes it unlikely that he adopted either the Al-Farabian or Avicennian model in full.

With respect to method individuation, we find that Al-Farabi and Avicenna displayed a keen appreciation of the relevance of method individuation. Their shared concerns engender further reasons to downplay the debate over who influenced Maimonides most. Firstly, Al-Farabi and Avicenna recognize two distinct phenomena as prophecy. The distinction between the two phenomena rests on a difference in methods. For Al-Farabi, a person who has yet to achieve perfection of his rational faculty can experience "prophecy" while those who have achieved perfection experience "revelation."[12] Avicenna, on the other hand, recognized "intellectual prophecy," which involves the intellect only, and "imaginative prophecy," which involves the imagination only.[13] Maimonides, on the other hand, recognizes only one phenomenon as prophecy and it involves both the rational faculty and the imagination in addition to requiring that both faculties be in a state of perfection.

Secondly, Avicenna attributes prophetic knowledge of the future to the imagination's conjunction with the celestial spheres; that is, conjunction independent of the rational faculty. In PM there is no indication of the imagination acting independently of the rational faculty. Thirdly, a perfect imagination is not required for prophecy in Al-Farabi (Davidson 1992, 59), while it is a necessary condition for prophecy in Maimonides.

---

[10] This point is central to Davidson's interpretation of Maimonides' cognitive psychology (Davidson 1992, 206).
[11] See Davidson (1992, 199 note 374; 1992, 206–207; 2011, 208), Manekin (1990, 119), and Stern (2005, 114).
[12] Al-Farabi (1972). [13] Davidson (1992, 116–121).

In the absence of a robust Maimonidean epistemology and the sketchiness involved in labeling him as either a thoroughbred Al-Farabian or Avicennian, the remainder of this essay is best viewed as a modest effort to 'lift' the prophetic method from the *Guide* and assess the epistemic upshot thereof.

9.2 The Prophetic Method

With some background in place, the following graphic aid will prove helpful for the forthcoming analysis.

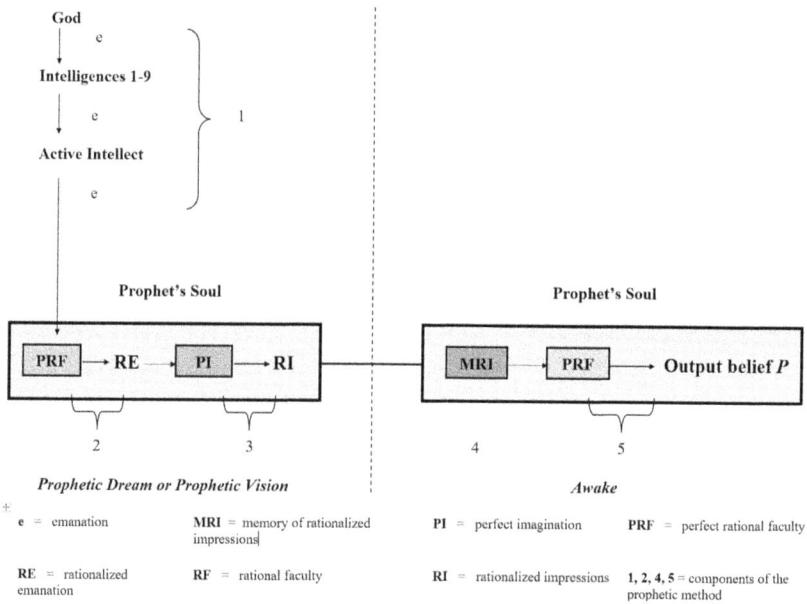

9.2.1 Component 1: Emanation (e)

"Emanation" is the term Maimonides uses for action by an incorporeal agent (Maimonides 1963, 2.12: 279). Though mention of the first nine intelligences is absent from PM, it is assumed that in the Maimonidean model *all* divine emanation resulting in an effect in the sublunar world is channeled through those intelligences before reaching the Active Intellect. This conception of divine action is of particular theological relevance to prophecy. The emanation involved in prophecy is *not* a unique emanation; that is, the emanation of which Maimonides speaks in PM is the same ever-constant emanation originating in God that sustains the existence of the universe. For this reason, one may speak of Maimonides' account of prophecy as prophecy "naturalized" since anyone who fulfills the necessary and jointly sufficient conditions for prophecy will prophesy unless God "intervenes" to deny the prophet.[14] In cases such as these it is considered a "miracle" that the prophet did not prophesy since it is akin to a law of nature that one who satisfies the necessary and jointly sufficient conditions for prophecy will prophesy (Maimonides 1963, 2.32: 361).

9.2.2   Component 2: Rationalized Emanation (RE)

Though not explicit in PM, Maimonides insists that prophecy is an *intellectual* achievement of the highest caliber: "[Prophecy] is the highest degree of man and the ultimate term of perfection that can exist for his species" (Maimonides 1963, 2.36: 369).

Maimonides recognizes that perfection of the rational faculty is a state that comes in degrees; that is, there is some vague quantity of *erudition* that will satisfy the lower boundary or threshold for perfection of the rational faculty. And at the uppermost levels Maimonides recognizes a state in which the prophet is someone who knows "everything concerning all the beings that it is within the capacity of man to know" (Maimonides 1963, 3.27: 511). Thinking of perfection as a property exhibited by degree (i.e., as a threshold, not an endpoint) amounts to far more than a mere quirk on Maimonides' behalf; rather, it functions as a key ingredient. While the emanation radiating from the Active Intellect is constant, the more erudite a person, the larger the quantity of emanation received. Since Maimonides recognizes that the prophets differed in the degree of their intellectual perfection (*Guide* 2.36), he also recognizes higher and lower degrees of prophecy (*Guide* 2.45). Prophets can thus be classified according to their "rank," where Moses is the highest-ranked prophet of them all. Differences in the degree of emanation received, which in Williamson's terms constitute a difference in the causal background to a belief, will be one important parameter along which one can individuate different methods satisfying PM, each resulting in an output belief with a unique epistemic profile.

---

[14] Such conditions include intellectual, moral, and physical perfection (Maimonides 1963, 2.36: 372; 2.32: 360; 2.37: 374).

Closely connected to a perfect rational faculty in the context of prophecy and of central relevance to knowledge of the future is intuition, by which Maimonides means the cognitive aptitude for drawing inferences (Maimonides 1963, 2.38: 376–377).[15] In prophets this aptitude reaches prodigious levels. Given the importance that intuition plays in his prophetic model, the following merits citation:

> [B]y means of his speculation alone, man is unable to grasp the causes [premises] from which what a prophet has come to know necessarily follows ... For the very emanation that affects the imaginative faculty ... is also the emanation that renders perfect the act of the rational faculty, so that its act brings about its knowing things ... and it achieves this apprehension *as if* it had apprehended it by starting from speculative premises ... the rational faculty being affected in a similar way as to apprehend *without having apprehended by way of premises, inference, and reflection* (Maimonides 1963, 2.38: 377) (emphasis added).

The point being stressed in this passage is the twofold epistemic advantage that prophets enjoy over those who are not prophets. Firstly, when emanation hits her perfect rational faculty during a prophetic dream or vision, the prophet's reasoning abilities are not subject to the typical limits associated with reasoning in regular people. When in this state, the prophet does not have to reason toward a conclusion by way of premises, as is the norm. Rather, when aided by her prodigious intuitive faculty, the prophet's rational faculty "hits" the conclusion immediately without having to "bother" with the premises that would lead to that conclusion. It is almost as if she just sees that p is the case.[16] Secondly, those who are not prophets are unable to reconstruct a line of reasoning that would lead to that conclusion. The inferential path to that conclusion is opaque to non-prophets.

For ease of reference, I use the term "the embedded proposition" for the conclusion that the prophet arrives at in Component 2. Component 2 of the prophetic method culminates with an overflow of emanation leaving the prophet's perfect rational faculty. Maimonides does not inform his reader as to the nature of this emanation. However, on the assumption

---

[15] Pines translates the Arabic word *hads* as "divination." In the recent Maimonides literature and in Schwartz's 2002 Hebrew translation, *hads* is translated as "intuition." In keeping with the current trend, I have replaced "divination" in Pines's translation with "intuition."

[16] This is reminiscent of rationalists who define a priori knowledge along the lines of rational insight, where seeing that p is the case is one necessary condition for knowing p a priori, the second necessary condition traditionally being that S came to believe p independent of experience. See BonJour (1998), Plantinga (1993), and Casullo (2003) for discussion of a priori knowledge and justification.

that the prophet "infers" a proposition p while her perfect rational and intuitive faculties are under the influence of an emanation from the Active Intellect (*Guide* 2.38), it seems fair to read Maimonides as saying that when the overflow of emanation leaves the prophet's rational faculty it is appropriately related to the content of p. I call this conditioned overflow of emanation "rationalized emanation."

9.2.3 Component 3: The Perfect Imagination (PI)

Maimonides is conflicted vis-à-vis the imagination. On the one hand, the "imagination is in no way able to hold itself aloof from matter" (Maimonides 1963, 1.73: 209), which is, as we shall see, the source of many errors in human thought, especially those egregious theological errors related to anthropomorphic conceptions of God (Maimonides 1963, 1.73: 209). Yet, a perfect imagination is also a necessary condition for prophecy and is that cognitive faculty charged with the invaluable job of converting the embedded proposition arrived at by the prophet's rational faculty in the prophetic moment into parables or images apprehensible to the lay person.

In Maimonides' cognitive psychology the imagination operates at optimal levels when relieved of its role in the facilitation of perception: "And you know its greatest and noblest action takes place only when the senses rest and do not perform their actions" (Maimonides 1963, 2.36: 370). Unshackled from the responsibility of recording perceptual inputs, the imagination freely indulges in the construction of dreams populated with fanciful combinations of images.

9.2.4 Component 3: Rationalized Impressions (RI)

9.2.4.1 Maimonides on Method Individuation

Evidence for Maimonides' concern with method individuation can be found in his discussion of the different *sources* from which the imagination can receive emanation. Maimonides states that the imagination can receive emanation from two different sources: (i) from the Active Intellect via the rational faculty, as is the case in PM or (ii) direct from the Active Intellect (Maimonides 1963, 2.37: 374). With regard to the latter, the type of person whose imagination receives emanation directly from the Active Intellect is someone who has some kind of deficiency in his rational faculty, so much so that it prevents the imagination from receiving an overflow of what I have termed "rationalized emanation" (Maimonides

1963, 2.37: 374). In this group of people Maimonides includes "dreamers of veridical dreams" (Maimonides 1963, 2.37: 374).

In light of the distinction Maimonides draws between dreams involving *both* a perfect rational faculty *and* a perfect imagination, and dreams involving only an *im*perfect imagination, I venture to suggest that Maimonides was of the opinion that regular dreams/visions and prophetic dreams/visions are the products of two different methods. Support for this claim can be found in *Guide* 2.41, where Maimonides is careful enough to use the expression "*prophetic* vision" as opposed to the terms "vision" or "hallucination." This careful distinction between the two phenomena remains in place in *Guide* 2.42, where we find Maimonides using the term "*prophetic* vision" (Maimonides 1963, 2.42: 388). And in *Guide* 3.25 we find Maimonides using the terms "dream of prophecy" and "vision of prophecy" (Maimonides 1963, 3.25: 501–502). This textual evidence for a difference in the origins of the emanation making for a difference in the method gains further traction when we consider Williamson's "definition" of a method or basis of belief: "the basis of a belief includes the specific causal process leading to it and the relevant causal background" (Williamson 2009, 307).

9.2.4.2 *Parabolic and Non-Parabolic Prophecy*

The imagination's role in Component 3 is perhaps the most delicate aspect of the prophetic method. At this point the imagination must draw on prior sensory impressions to depict in the form of sensory impressions the embedded proposition it receives from the perfect rational faculty. I use the term "rationalized impressions" for the sensory impressions thus generated because these impressions are constructed in response to the rationalized emanation overflowing from the rational faculty.

It proves illustrative to compare the imagination's role in perception to its role in prophecy. With regard to regular perception, the imagination first stores sensory impressions and then passes them along to the rational faculty for the purposes of abstraction, reasoning, etc. In prophecy, however, the process begins with the cogitations of the rational faculty, which is then followed by the imagination's depiction of those thoughts in the form of sensory impressions. Maimonides writes that "the imaginative faculty achieves so great a perfection of action that is sees the thing as if it were outside, and that the thing whose origin is due to it appears to have come to it by way of external sensation" (Maimonides 1963, 2.36: 370). In other words, rationalized impressions seem tantalizingly real to the prophet.

The dominant sensory modalities involved in Component 3 are audio-visual (*Guide* 2.45). A prophet, during a prophetic dream or a prophetic vision, will "hear" someone talking to him. Typically, the agent addressing the prophet will be an unfamiliar man, an angel, or God (*Guide* 2.45). And in those cases in which the prophet only "hears" a voice and "sees" no speaker, the voice "heard" may be that of someone with whom the prophet is familiar, e.g., when Samuel experienced prophecy for the first time he thought Eli was calling him instead of God (Maimonides 1963, 2.44: 395).

At other times the prophet's imagination may generate within the prophetic dream or vision a "scene" in the prophet's "visual field" such that it appears to the prophet as if she is "seeing" objects in the external world. Maimonides calls this scene a "parable" and his use of that term differs from ours in the following significant ways. By "parable," we typically intend an allegorical or an extended metaphorical saying or narrative that conveys a moral lesson. In Maimonides' case, a parable is a scene constructed by the prophet's imagination in response to *two* embedded propositions generated by the rational faculty at Component 2. More precisely, the sentences used to describe the scene depict the embedded propositions. The first proposition is called the parable's "external meaning" while the meaning of the second proposition is called the parable's "internal meaning" (*Maimonides 1963*, 1.introduction: 12). The external meaning is related to the internal meaning insofar as grasping the meaning of the first proposition aids or assists the prophet's audience in grasping the meaning of the second (Maimonides 1963, 1.introduction: 12). It is important to stress that the prophet does not construct the parable when she wakes up. The parable is constructed by the imagination *during* the prophetic dream or vision.

There are thus two overarching types of prophecies – parabolic and non-parabolic.[17] Non-parabolic prophecies have only one meaning, while parabolic prophecies have two meanings – the internal and external. However, parabolic prophecies divide into two further kinds. The first,

---

[17] The precise structure of the Maimonidean parable is a matter of dispute. The traditional view thereof is that the parable has a bipartite semantic structure with the external meaning representing the prophet's exoteric view and the inner meaning her esoteric intentions. Stern (1998; 2009) argues that the parable has a tripartite semantic structure not predicated upon the exoteric-esoteric distinction such that the internal meaning of a parable can sometimes be quite open to view. In my description of the Maimonidean parable I have attempted to navigate a course that effectively incorporates both the traditional view and Stern's view without making the additional theoretical commitments of either.

which I term the "robust" parable, is one in which the "external meaning contains wisdom that is useful in many respects, among which is the welfare of human societies," and the inner meaning "contains wisdom that is useful for beliefs concerned with the truth as it is" (Maimonides 1963, 1.introduction: 12).

The second kind of parable, here referred to as the "lean" parable, is one where the external meaning is "worthless" (i.e., contains no wisdom) and at times may be false, while the inner meaning contains wisdom "concerned with the truth as it is" (Maimonides 1963, 1.introduction: 12). Some anthropomorphic descriptions of God in the external meaning are instances of lean parables that express a false proposition. What Maimonides means by "worthless" is something of a mystery as a false proposition can still be of value, e.g., when one infers a true conclusion from a false premise. Additionally, if the external meaning contains no wisdom yet aids in grasping of the internal meaning, then it should be seen to have some value, however minimal.

The Maimonidean parable can exhibit one of two *design plans*. In the first kind, here called *specific* design, each image in the scene generated by the imagination is of critical relevance to the overall external and internal meanings of that parable (Maimonides 1963, 1.introduction: 12). Therefore, the prophet's description of the scene in words must accurately capture the scene such that the sentences used express the two different propositions depicted by the scene. Maimonides' exemplar of the *specific* parable is Jacob's dream in which "a ladder was set earthward its top reached heavenward; and behold angels of God were ascending and descending on it" (Genesis 28:12). The general idea seems to be that each and every rationalized impression contributes to the external and internal meanings of the parable; that is, when the prophet comes to, the manner in which he *describes* the scene is an intentionally delicate speech act. Without doing too much violence to the original Hebrew, it seems fair to read Maimonides as saying that with respect to Jacob's dream, had Jacob described the scene as one in which he beheld "a ladder on which angels were climbing up and down," that description would have failed to capture the dual meaning of the parable because the image of the earth and the image of the heavens are critical to the expression of that parable.

On the other hand, *general* design occurs when "very many words are to be found, not every one of which adds something to the intended meaning; they [the words] serve to embellish the parable and render it more coherent or to conceal further the intended meaning" (Maimonides 1963,

1.introduction: 12). The idea here seems to be that some impressions are present merely to augment or contribute toward the overall external and internal meanings of the parable. Maimonides' exemplar of the parable in the general mode of design is the book of Proverbs, of which very large sections are a parable, the internal meaning of which is "a warning against the pursuit of bodily pleasures and desires" (Maimonides 1963, 1.introduction: 13). Indeed, Maimonides warns his reader against engaging in excessive interpretation of parables designed using the general mode of design once their overall external and internal meanings have become apparent: "[Y]ou should not inquire into all the details occurring in the parable ... For doing so would lead you into one of two ways: either into turning aside from the parable's intended subject, or into assuming an obligation to interpret things not susceptible of interpretation and that have not been inserted with a view to interpretation" (Maimonides 1963, 1.introduction: 14).

9.2.4.3 Extended and Non-Extended Parabolic Rationalized Impressions
Relatively late in his treatment of prophecy, Maimonides (*Guide* 2.43) adds a final qualification with respect to the rationalized impressions that constitute parabolic prophecies. Sometimes *within* the very prophecy itself an angel will explain the parable to the prophet, as was the case in Zachariah 4 and Daniel 7. It must be remembered that this "explanation" is itself a rationalized impression because any "sight" or "sound" experienced during prophecy constitutes a rationalized impression. Furthermore, as has already been emphasized, prophecy does not involve the perception of God or an angel; rather, it is rational thought expressed or represented in sensory impressions. The angel who explains the meaning thus refers to either the Active Intellect, the prophet's rational faculty, or the prophet's imagination (Maimonides 1963, 2.6: 265, 2.46: 403). In essence, when an extended rationalized emanation occurs, we have a case of a prophet explaining the meaning of the parable to himself, where "meaning" refers to both the internal and external meaning. For those prophetic dreams or visions containing the explanations of their meanings, I use the term "*extended* parables."

In the majority of the cases, however, the meaning of the parable "is known by the prophet *after* he awakens" (Maimonides 1963, 2.43: 392, emphasis added). In these cases, the rationalized impressions are *non*-extended in nature. The extended/non-extended distinction is relevant to the prophet's output beliefs discussed vis-à-vis Component 5.

9.3 Components 4 and 5: Memory and Output Beliefs

For an author as careful as Maimonides, it is surprising that PM gives no indication as to the precise point at which the prophet forms prophetic beliefs. The absence of a definitive Maimonidean epistemology exacerbates the predicament. In this section I argue that regardless of whether a prophecy is parabolic or not, there are a number of reasons to deny that prophets form beliefs *during* prophetic dreams or visions. This section begins with two arguments against belief formation in Component 3 followed by two arguments against belief formation in Component 2. The section concludes with a general argument against belief formation during prophetic dreams and visions. The upshot of these arguments is the inclusion of Component 4 (memory) and Component 5 (interpretation) in the prophetic method.

9.3.1 Contra Belief Formation in Component 3

9.3.1.1 The Coherence Argument

It is generally taken for granted that agents do *not* form beliefs while asleep or hallucinating. Sosa (2005; 2007) substantiates this guiding principle as follows. When we go to sleep we do not lose our knowledge or beliefs. They merely remain latent, as they are much of the time. In particular, when I go to sleep I retain my knowledge of the room's layout, that I am on my bed, my beliefs about what I will do tomorrow, etc. Suppose I then dream of being chased by a lion in the Kruger Park. If it were the case that we form beliefs in dreams, then the result would be that I assent to the obviously contradictory beliefs "that I am in my bed" and "that I am being chased by a lion in the Kruger Park." Similar considerations apply for hallucinations.

For these reasons we may conclude that prophets do *not* form beliefs during a prophetic dream or vision since prophecies involve impressions that are incompatible with the prophet's latent beliefs about his surroundings. Consider the case of Ezekiel's vision of the valley of dry bones (Ezekiel 37). Assuming that the prophets were not irrational enough to affirm an obvious contradiction, it seems problematic, for the reasons outlined by Sosa, to suppose that Ezekiel concurrently believed of himself 'that I am lying down in locale x' and 'that I am in locale y looking at a valley of dry bones.' Similarly, the more natural position would be to deny that Ezekiel actually believed of himself that he was eating a scroll given to him by God (Ezekiel 3:1–3) or that he actually believed that God carried him to Jerusalem in the air by way of a detached arm gripping his hair (Ezekiel 8:1–3), or that Jeremiah believed that he actually saw an almond tree (Jeremiah 1:11), or that Zachariah actually believed he had seen a golden candelabra (Zachariah 4).

9.3.1.2 The Negative Theology Argument

Maimonides vehemently denies that positive or affirmative attributes connected with material constitution can be predicated of God. For example, given Aristotle's definition of time as an accident associated with the motion of physical objects (Maimonides 1963, 2.introduction: 237), Maimonides denies that any durational property may be properly predicated of God. Similar considerations inveigh against spatial properties. Eventually Maimonides concludes that (i) only attributes of action can be predicated of God, for such predicates do not address God's essence or nature; and that such predicates are only attributed homonymously, such that when we say "God is merciful in performing action x," we do not thereby suggest a similarity between human mercy and divine mercy and (ii) negative predications are preferable, where, e.g., the negative predicate "it is not the case that God is present" (following Aristotle's theory of negation in the *Categories*) indicates neither that God is present nor that God is absent; rather it makes the point that the categories of "absence" and "presence" to not attach or pertain to God.

With this core Maimonidean theme in place, there is room to argue that Maimonides would not have considered people as "perfect" as the Old Testament prophets, to actually have believed that which is recorded in their name, for the Old Testament prophecies are replete with anthropomorphic language and extensive reference to God's positive attributes. The prophetic books are written in such language so as to be accessible to the ignorant masses and to guide them thereby toward correct beliefs (*Guide* 1.46).

9.3.2 Contra Belief Formation in Component 2

9.3.2.1 The Extended Parable Argument

Maimonides provides no explanation for the presence of extended rationalized impressions in some cases of *parabolic* prophecies and for their absence in others. That Maimonides mentions Zachariah and Daniel as exemplars of the extended parable phenomenon is revealing, however. In Zachariah's vision, the angel asks the prophet if he *knows* the meaning of the rationalized impressions and the prophet repeatedly answers in the negative. Similarly, Daniel (7:15–16) is described as being *bewildered* by the rationalized impressions in his vision and asks the angel to make the correct interpretation thereof *known* to him. Both prophets are recorded as being stumped by the rationalized impressions that their own imaginations generate in response to the embedded proposition, which is a rather bizarre scenario. The relevant point that needs to be gleaned from this comment is that both prophets did not believe the embedded proposition in Component 2, for otherwise it would make no sense for the prophet to explain the embedded proposition to himself in the dream or vision if he already believes it. Nothing would be gained from extended rationalized impressions if the prophet already believed the embedded proposition.[18]

In response to this line of reasoning, some may contest that extended parabolic prophecies occur when a prophet merely forgets the embedded proposition in the progression from Component 2 to Component 3. As such, there was belief formation in Component 2. This is an unpromising line of reasoning, however, as the prophet is – in Maimonides' view – in possession of both a perfect rational faculty and a perfect imagination. It is therefore unlikely that such an intellectually perfected individual will forget the embedded proposition so quickly. Furthermore, prophecy, for Maimonides, "is the highest degree of man and the ultimate term of perfection" (Maimonides 1963, 2.36: 369). Such lapses of memory seem incompatible with the Maimonidean conception of prophecy.

9.3.2.2 The Non-Extended Parable Argument

The import of the extended/non-extended distinction can be used as a further argument against belief formation in Component 2 of non-extended parabolic prophecies. In *Guide* 2.43 Maimonides writes that vis-à-vis *non*-extended parabolic prophecies, the meaning of the parable is not interpreted to the prophet inside the prophetic dream or vision, but is "*known* by the prophet *after* he awakens" (Maimonides 1963, 2.43: 392, emphasis added). If the prophet did formulate a belief in the embedded proposition in Component 2, then it would have been inaccurate for Maimonides to write that the meaning is known only *after* the prophet wakes up.[19] One natural explanation for the prophet not knowing the

---

[18] The Coherence and Negative Theology Arguments would rule out belief formation in Component 3 of extended parabolic prophecies; that is, forming belief in the meaning of the prophecy once it has been explained by the angel.

[19] The preposition "after" appears in both the Kafih and Schwartz Hebrew translations and in both the Pines and Friedlander English translations. The Judeo-Arabic word for "after" (בעד) appears in the original Judeo-Arabic text of the *Guide*.

meaning of the parable (the embedded proposition) *during* the dream or vision is his not believing the embedded proposition in Component 2 (or 3) of the prophetic method (as knowing p entails believing p).

9.3.3 The General Argument

There is another way to rule out belief formation during prophetic dreams or visions. Maimonides never explains why some parabolic prophecies are extended and others non-extended. I venture to suggest that this distinction can be accounted for by thinking that Maimonides is committed to the position that parabolic prophecies require interpretation on the prophet's part. That is, once the prophet experiences the rationalized impressions of Component 3, she must interpret the internal and external meanings thereof. Sometimes the prophet may, in some subliminal sense, be confident enough that her imperfect rational faculty can achieve this act of interpretation successfully once she wakes up; at other times she may be of the relevant conviction that she can decipher the two meanings only when her rational faculty is in its state of perfection during a prophetic dream or vision. In the latter case, we have the phenomenon of the extended parabolic prophecy; in the former, we have the non-extended parabolic prophecy.

What of non-parabolic prophecy that does not seem to require interpretation? In response to this question, I argue that *all* prophecies require interpretation regardless of whether they are parabolic or not. For example, in a non-parabolic prophecy, the voice chosen to articulate the proposition expressed by "Eliezer will not be my heir" may be part of the meaning of the prophecy. In *Guide* 2.44 Maimonides tells us that the speech involved in prophecies may have a number of different properties. In particular, the voice used may be (i) either familiar or unfamiliar to the prophet and (ii) "loud" or "soft." One might argue that there could be cases in which a variation of these properties is the imagination's way of depicting a segment of the embedded proposition. For instance, suppose the embedded proposition in the case at hand is that which is expressed by "it is a matter of secrecy that Eliezer will not be your heir." As a result, Abraham "hears" a soft voice, resembling a whisper, stating that "Eliezer will not be your heir." The imagination picks up on the association between secrecy and whispering and depicts the first part of the embedded proposition by way of God's whispering "Eliezer will not be your heir." In this scenario it will be up to Abraham to interpret the voice's volume as either relevant or irrelevant to the meaning of the prophecy.

If this is indeed a viable possibility, which it should be given that all non-parabolic prophecies involve a prophet "hearing" a voice, then we may conclude that even easy cases of non-parabolic prophecy require interpretative processing. This also rules out the prophet believing the embedded proposition once the angel explains it to her in extended parabolic prophecy since the properties of the voice in which the angel voices the explanation of the rationalized impressions may itself require interpretation. Alternatively, the angel's explanation may itself be a mixture of parabolic and non-parabolic prophecy, which again requires interpretation.

By way of rough approximation, the mental act of interpretation involves the mapping of an object from one set to the appropriate object in another set, where the "appropriateness" of the mapping is context-dependent. This act involves judgments as to which two objects appropriately map one another. In the Maimonidean scheme, this kind of mental act would most likely be undertaken by the rational faculty. Interpretation of the rationalized impressions of Component 3 would therefore require the involvement of the rational faculty once the imagination has completed the job of depicting the embedded proposition in the form of sensory impressions. But as Maimonides defines the prophet method, PM does not mention the involvement of the rational faculty at a stage following the imagination. We may therefore conclude that if interpretation is required it would have to be undertaken once the prophet wakes up and recalls the rationalized impressions of her prophetic dream or vision. The necessary recall occurs in Component 4 and the act of interpretation culminating in the relevant output belief in Component 5.

My reading of Maimonides on the prophetic method can be summarized as follows. When not distracted by emotions and perceptual inputs, a prophet who is both sufficiently healthy and sufficiently erudite will experience a prophetic dream or prophetic vision, during which time the prophet's rational faculty will receive a quantity of emanation from the Active Intellect proportional to its degree of perfection. While in this heightened state, the rational faculty, with the aid of prodigious intuition, will generate the embedded proposition p, and, if sufficient emanation is present, yield an overflow of rationalized emanation conditioned by the propositional content of p. The prophet's perfect imagination will then receive that rationalized emanation and depict the embedded proposition in the form of rationalized sensory impressions, where the rationalized impressions can be structured in a variety of ways. The prophet will then wake up, recall the rationalized impressions, and will then believe p, all things going well, as a result of interpreting the rationalized impressions to be depicting *p*. When the prophet's perfect rational faculty generates more than one embedded proposition in Component 2, the prophet will likewise believe a conjunction of propositions in Component 5.

9.4 The Epistemology of Prophecy

Insofar as PM is concerned, there are a number of considerations in favor of the view that prophets do *not* form beliefs during a prophetic dream or vision. The upshot of this result is the inclusion of memory in Component 4 and interpretation in Component 5 followed by the output belief. This result is important for at least two reasons. The first is epistemic and the second questions Maimonides' distinction between Mosaic and non-Mosaic prophecy.

Firstly, the absence of belief during Component 2 or Component 3 introduces a range of epistemic concerns that may have been absent had there been belief during the prophetic dream or vision. By including memory and interpretation, PM opens the door to errors since neither of these mental acts is infallible. For instance, truly believing *p* by way of prophecy will hardly result in prophetic knowledge that *p* if the prophet could easily have erred with respect to *p*, an epistemic result supported by both modern externalists and those in the Aristotelian tradition who appreciated that certainty (a necessary condition for Aristotelian *scientia*) is associated with specific methods.[20] Given the sophisticated mechanics of rationalized impressions, there may be instances in which the prophet, much like Daniel, is bewildered by the meaning thereof. The interpretive exercise that followed might easily have been riddled with errors or dangerously close to error. In other cases (e.g., where the prophet's recall of the prophetic dream or vision is hazy), her prophecy will not constitute knowledge despite being true, for even if she recalled the prophecy in its entirety she was dangerously close to not doing so, in which case she would have formed a false belief by way of PM. Spinoza[21] and Charles Touati (1968, 169–187), for example, have identified instances in which prophets formed false beliefs by way of prophecy. Similarly, Maimonides can be read as thinking that Ezekiel and Samuel (Maimonides 1963, 3.3: 422 and

---

[20] An Aristotelian would deny that *scientia* is possible by way of unreliable methods, e.g. lucky guesses. Given that Maimonides recognized prophecy as "the highest degree of man" (Maimonides 1963, 2.36: 369), it is unlikely that he would have attributed to prophets those inferior forms of knowledge recognized by Aristotle, but which lacked certainty.

[21] *Tractatus Theologico-Politicus*, chapter 2.

3.7: 428) and Isaiah and Jonah[22] erred in some of their prophecies, indicating a fallibilist view of prophecy consistent with my interpretation of PM. In both of these instances, false background beliefs acting as inputs during Component 2 of PM resulted in false beliefs acquired by way of prophecy.[23]

Secondly, Maimonides claims that Mosaic prophecy differs from non-Mosaic prophecy only insofar as the latter method involves the imagination whereas the former does not (Maimonides 1963, 2.46: 403). Rationalized impressions and the interpretation thereof are therefore absent from the method underpinning Mosaic prophecy. Nor is memory a constituent element of the method underpinning Mosaic prophecy, as Moses was neither dreaming nor having a vision during the formation of prophetic beliefs. Yet the stark difference in method is problematized by instances in which God is deemed to have "spoken" with Moses and another prophet simultaneously (e.g., Exodus 7:8–9, Numbers 12:4–8). In such cases we have instances of Mosaic prophecy and non-Mosaic prophecy occurring simultaneously and resulting in identical output beliefs. One prophet (Moses) is awake and alert, and the other sleeping or in a convulsive state.[24] Having two prophets arrive at the same belief under such circumstances is questionable, especially when the prophetic methods underpinning such belief(s) differed quite radically despite both methods starting off in the same way, viz. by the impact of the ever-constant emanation on the prophet's rational faculty.[25,26] The situation is analogous to one person believing that "parking is prohibited on this road today" by seeing a sign to that effect and another person simultaneously

---

[22] *Mishneh Torah* (Foundations of the Law 10.4). Isaiah 38:1 prophesied King Hezekiah's imminent death and Jonah 3:4 prophesied the destruction of the city of Nineveh. Neither event occurred as prophesied.

[23] Preaching or acting on the basis of prophecies that do not constitute knowledge would then violate certain epistemic norms that are intuitively compelling, e.g., the knowledge norm of assertion and the knowledge norm of reasons: "[W]here one's choice is p-dependent, it is appropriate to treat the proposition that p as a reason for acting if you know that p" (Hawthorne and Stanley 2008, 581). A prophet would treat his prophetic beliefs as a reason to preach his prophecy and the prophet's audience would treat the prophet's prophetic beliefs as the reason for changing their behavior.

[24] Maimonides tells us that in the grip of a prophetic vision the prophet's senses cease to function, he becomes gripped by fear, and his body convulses (Maimonides 1963, 2.41: 385).

[25] Maimonides could respond by considering such simultaneous prophecy a miracle. But a miracle – for Maimonides at least – is a predetermined exception to a law of nature (Maimonides 1963, 2.29: 345). In other words, to avail himself of this solution, Maimonides would have to consider it predetermined that two such prophets would prophesy at exactly the same moment and arrive at the identical output belief(s). Prophecy would not, on such a model, be consistent with Maimonides' view that prophecy is an intellectual achievement (Maimonides 1963, 2.36: 369).

[26] This problem would similarly arise even if the instances of belief formation by Moses and the other prophet were not strictly simultaneous.

arriving at that very belief as a result of interpreting a series of rationalized impressions crafted in response to a series of deductions from background beliefs experienced during a dream. By reducing the difference between Mosaic and non-Mosaic prophecy to a difference in method, Maimonides undermines the very distinction he aims to secure.

Reading Maimonides through an epistemic lens draws into sharp focus the doxastic lacuna in PM and leads one closer to the conclusion that non-Mosaic prophets arrived at their prophetic beliefs only after they had awoken and correctly interpreted their prophetic dreams or visions. The upshot of this is a fallible, non-testimonial model of non-Mosaic prophecy, which may come as an uncomfortable result for those who look to the biblical prophets as mouthpieces of God.

CHAPTER 10

Maimonides' Modalities

Josef Stern

The modalities – necessity, possibility, and impossibility – are not topics like the existence of God, creation versus eternity, prophecy, divine attributes, or providence whose "secrets" Maimonides investigates in the *Guide*. They belong instead to the philosophical and logical framework within which these topics are explored. But they are no less perplexing. The modal terms often differ in meaning in different contexts, depending on whether the subject is physics or metaphysics, and for the *falasifa* and the *mutakallimun*. Therefore, in order to address any of the central controversies of the *Guide*, we must first sort out these modal notions, distinguishing the different conceptions in different contexts.[1]

In this essay, I distinguish five different interpretations of the modalities in the Maimonidean corpus. I begin with the brief presentation in the *Treatise on the Art of Logic* of the Al-Farabian version of the standard Aristotelian approach.[2] I then turn to two different conceptions that underlie arguments of the *falasifa* for eternity in the *Guide* and then the Avicennean model on which Maimonides' own conception of God is based. In the last section, I show how Maimonides reconstructs the

---

The support of the EURIAS Fellowship Program and of the European Commission (Marie-Skolodowska-Curie Actions-COFUND Programme–FDP7) while I was a Marie Curie Senior Fellow at the Israel Institute for Advanced Studies in 2018–2019 enabled me to begin research on this paper. I want to thank Suf Amichay, Zev Harvey, David Shatz, Reimund Leicht, Mark Steiner, and Riccardo Strobino for comments and criticisms of earlier drafts.

[1] Previous studies of the modalities in the Maimonidean corpus, almost all of which discuss only one or the other model, include Davidson (1987); Fackenheim (1946/1947); Glucker (1959); Ivry (1982); Rabinovitch (1974); Ravitzky (1978–1979); Rosenberg (1978a; 1978b); Steiner (2019a; 2019b).

[2] On Maimonides' authorship of the *Logic*, see Davidson (2001, 118–125); Hasnawy (2004); and Stroumsa (2009, 126–128). Even if it was not written by him, there is every reason to believe that he would have been familiar, and probably agreed, with its basic Aristotelian interpretation.

controversy between the *falasifa* and *mutakallimun* over modality, from which we can glimpse his own stance.³

10.1 The Logic of the Modalities

In the *Logic*, chapter 3, the terms "possible (Arabic: *mumkin*; Hebrew: *efshar*)," "impossible (Arabic: *mumtani*; Hebrew: *nimna'*)," and "necessary (Arabic: *wajib*; Hebrew: *mehuyav*)" are each introduced as a "mode (Arabic: *giha*; Hebrew: *tzad*)" that signifies "the manner of existence of the predicate in the subject" – i.e, whether their respective properties or qualities are related essentially and "inseparably" (Maimonides 1963, 1.5: 115), or accidentally. In *Logic* chapter 4, turning from the explicit terms for the modes to the contents, or "matter," of statements, each is said to express either a necessary (e.g., "Humans are animals") or possible proposition (e.g., "Some humans write"), reducing the impossible (e.g., "Humans are birds") to the necessarily not.⁴ The "truly" possible, Maimonides adds in explication, is the statement that at its time of assertion might or might not be the case. However, as the author recognizes, this will vary with the time of assertion. For example, at the time of Ezra's birth the statement "Ezra writes" is truly possible, but when he is writing it is "absolute or actual," i.e., assertoric or a factual report.⁵ "For a thing can be truly possible only with reference to the future, before one of the alternatives is actualized; when it is actually true, the possibility is removed … it resembles something necessary" (Maimonides 1938, 39).⁶

In these passages Maimonides first characterizes the modalities "intensionally," in terms of the essential or accidental relation between the subject and predicate, but his account of the truly possible shows that he is also conceiving of them extensionally, quantifying over instants of time. On this "temporal-frequency," or "statistical," Aristotelian model of

---

³ Maimonides' conceptions of the modalities can only be analyzed in the context of specific controversies in the *Guide*, e.g., creation versus eternity. However, I say nothing, exoteric or esoteric, about the controversies themselves.
⁴ See Maimonides (1938, 23); the term "matter" is Al-Farabi's, as noted by Efros.
⁵ The choice of Ezra, the great biblical scribe, was that of the Hebrew translator of the *Logic*. As Brague notes in his French translation (Maïmonide 1996, 45, note 34), the example in the Arab original is the celebrated Muslim scribe Abu Ishaq Ibrahim al-Harrani as-Sabi (925–994). Cf. Efros' comment in Maimonides (1938, 13). (I am indebted here to Zev Harvey.)
⁶ On the phrase "truly possible," see Zimmermann (1981, 181–182). The passage deserves further examination. It is not entirely clear how much to read into the author's reference to the future; some of Maimonides' remarks suggest that the "truly possible" is the epistemic "might" rather than a metaphysical modality. Cf. Al-Farabi on indefinite truths in Zimmermann (1981, 163, 181, and 244ff). Rosenberg (1978b) reads these sentences as elliptically context-dependent.

modality, the necessary is that which is true at all times, eternally, and undergoes no change, while the impossible is what is true at no time – hence, necessarily not true. For Aristotle, the possible was the contradictory only of impossibility, hence, simply what is true (at least) at some time, but not excluding all times (hence, the necessary).[7] Here Maimonides, following Al-Farabi, takes the (truly) possible to be opposed to all that is necessary, both the necessarily true *and* the necessarily not, namely, the impossible. As Maimonides writes, the possible is what might or might not be the case, true at some time but not another, neither necessary nor impossible.[8] But if the possible is what might be true and what might not be, it also excludes past and present tense sentences whose "reality (*haqiqa*)" is determined, which could no longer be otherwise, and for which, therefore, "possibility is removed."[9] Hence, although they are not "truly" necessary (true at all times), assertoric, factual, or actually true statements "resemble the necessary."[10]

Closely associated with the temporal/statistical model, and possibly even integral to it, is the so-called Principle of Plenitude (PoP): the idea that all genuine possibilities are realized at some moment in infinite time or, in negative terms, that no genuine possibilities go forever unactualized.[11] Maimonides does not explicitly mention the PoP in either the *Logic* or

---

[7] On the temporal-statistical model, see Becker (1952), Hintikka (1973), and Knuuttila (1993). For an example, see Maimonides' characterization of the necessary as "the existent not subject to generation and corruption" in the first half of the third of the philosophers' proofs in Maimonides 1963, 2.1: 247.

[8] Contemporary scholars label Aristotle's conception of possibility (opposed only to the impossible) "one-sided" and Al-Farabi's (opposed both to the necessary and impossible) "two-sided." One might also call the former "possible" and the latter "contingent."

[9] Aristotle (1984, *De Interpretatione* 19a2); cf. Al-Farabi on *De Interpretatione* 23a15–16 in Zimmermann (1981, 180) and on the third sense of necessity discussed on page 247 (Zimmerman 1981). On the assertoric, see Rosenberg (1978a, 61–63).

[10] See Zimmermann (1981, 166–187) on *De Interpretatione* 12–13; Wisnovsky (2003, 213–217); Rosenberg (1978a, 58–68). Note that Aristotle and Al-Farabi are both concerned to distinguish contradictories from contraries, which is not Maimonides' concern. Thanks throughout this paragraph to Reimund Leicht.

[11] On the principle of plenitude, see Lovejoy (1936); Hintikka (1973); Knuuttila (1993) and, on Maimonides, Manekin (1988). Other examples of the PoP are Maimonides (1931, 3.25: 367), where God's "primary intention [is to] bring into existence everything whose existence is possible, existence being indubitably a good" and Maimonides (1963, 3.26: 509) where Maimonides appeals to "the nature of the possible, for it is certain that one of the possibilities will come to pass." For an interesting example that is ambiguous depending on its translation, see *Guide* 3.25. 505 (Arabic): *lakinahu ta'ala la yaridu ila mumkinan wa-laisa kullu mumkinin illa ma taqtadi hikmatuhu annahu yakuna kadha*. As Manekin (2008a, 217–218) observes, Pines and Munk (Maïmonide 1856–1866, 3:200) translate this as "He... wills only what is possible, and not everything that is possible, but only which is required by His wisdom to be such," denying the PoP, while Schwarz (Maimonides 2002a, 510) translates it as "He ... wills only what is possible. There is nothing possible except what His wisdom required to be such," affirming the PoP.

the *Guide*. However, one passage in which he makes use of it occurs in the first half of the philosophers' third proof for the existence of God (Maimonides 1963, 2.1: 247). The proof opens by distinguishing three options for all empirically observable existents, assuming the temporal model of modality: (i) none are subject to generation and corruption, (ii) all are, or (iii) some are and some aren't; i.e., either (i) all are eternal, (ii) none are, or (iii) some are and some aren't. Focusing now only on (ii) for present purposes, Maimonides argues that if everything is subject to generation and corruption, then "all the existents and every one of them have a possibility of undergoing corruption." And here the PoP comes on stage: "Now it is indubitable ... that what is possible with regard to a species must necessarily come about," i.e., every possibility must be actualized at some time. Hence, "all existents will necessarily undergo corruption," and if they all do at a moment in infinite time (and time being infinite in both directions, this must already have occurred in the infinite past), it would be impossible for anything to exist now "for there would remain no one who would bring anything into existence." But it is self-evident that there are existents: "In fact we ourselves are existent" (Maimonides 1963, 2.1: 247). Hence, this option must be rejected.[12]

10.2 *Guide* 2.14: Possibility as Potentiality, Necessity as Actuality

According to the fourth "method" of the Aristotelian *falasifa* to demonstrate the eternity of the world, we begin by supposing to the contrary that the world was originated – before which it must have been either necessary, impossible, or possible.[13] But it could never have been *originated* if it was either necessary or impossible. Therefore, its origination must have been "preceded in time" by its possibility. But a possibility is not a substance that exists. Therefore, there must have existed a preexisting substratum "in virtue of which it is said of [the world] that it is possible." This, Maimonides quickly concludes, "is a very powerful method" (Maimonides 1963, 2.14: 287) for establishing eternity.

This is at most a sketch that calls for explication. Both the reference to a "preceding possibility" and the constraint that possibility requires a

---

[12] This argument faces the prima facie objection that even if "all existents and every one of them" cease to exist at some time, it does not follow that there is a single time at which they all cease to exist. If, however, in addition to the possibility that each thing will cease to exist at some (but not necessarily the same) time, there exists also the possibility that at one time the totality of corruptible existents will cease to exist, a second appeal to PoP will save the validity of the proof.

[13] Aristotle (1984, *Physics* 192a26–34); Aristotle (1984, *On Generation* 317b16–17).

substratum indicate that the philosophers' notion of possibility in this argument is that of a potency or potentiality.[14] The substratum for potentiality is matter but, because matter never exists without form, that substratum must be "part" of a composite material substance.[15] Whether this preexisting composite substance is the actualized world – which is as much as to say that the world is eternal – or another existent that contains the preexistent potentiality of the originated world is not clear. In either case, the same question will arise for this prior existent whether – before it was originated – it was necessary, possible, or impossible and – following the same reasoning – it will have to have been possible, leading to an actual infinity of possible existents, itself an impossibility for an Aristotelian. Hence, the preexistent substratum or subject for the possibility of the world cannot itself be originated but must be eternal. Origination entails eternity.

Maimonides follows his exposition of this argument with a rejoinder by "an intelligent man from among the later *mutakallimun* [who] thought that he had solved this difficulty," i.e., refuted it, claiming that "possibility resides in the agent and not in the thing that is the object of action" (Maimonides 1963, 2.14: 287). Maimonides himself responds to this objection that "there are two possibilities" (Maimonides 1963, 2.14: 287): one corresponding to the thing originated (as just noted) and a second corresponding to the originating agent (as the *mutakallim* claims): before an agent originates something, it must be possible for her to so act. Thus Maimonides understands the *mutakallim's* "possibility residing in the agent," like that residing "in the originated thing," as a potentiality. Since both are required for origination and motion, the argument for eternity from the possibility "in the originated thing" stands.[16]

Herbert Davidson has proposed that the source of this argument for eternity from a preceding possibility is Avicenna. In that case, it is possible if not likely that the "later *mutakallim*" is Al-Ghazali, who critiques this

---

[14] As Davidson (1987, 17) notes, the two terms in Arabic for "possibility" (*imkan*) and "potentiality" (*quwa*) translate the same Greek term. Maimonides does not generally distinguish the two; see Stern (2013, 100–102). For an important discussion of potentialities as a subset of possibilities which, in the order of actualization, need only one more "step" to be realized, see Frede (1994). On remote and proximate potentialities illustrated by the writing/scribing image of the *Logic*, see Maimonides (1938/1966, 54) and Maimonides (1963, 3.51: 625) where, using the same image, he alludes to the distinction between first and second potentialities/actualities.

[15] See the 22nd and 24th of the philosophers' premises in Maimonides (1963, 2.introduction: 238–239).

[16] For a similar response to Al-Ghazali by Averroes, see Van den Bergh (1954, 59).

Avicennean argument in his *Incoherence of the Philosophers*.[17] But Al-Ghazali's "possibility residing in the agent" is entirely different from a potentiality. The philosophers' notion not only presupposes an analogue of the PoP – that every genuine potentiality will be actualized at some time in the infinite span of time – but, more generally, it assumes that to determine what is possible one must take into consideration the actual facts of nature as revealed by physics. It conceives of possibility *cum* potentiality as a feature of actual existent substances in the world. Furthermore, as on the statistical model, when a potentiality is actualized, it becomes necessary and is no longer possible. This notion of possibility, like the first one, is two-sided, opposed both to the impossible and to the necessary.

In contrast, what Al-Ghazali means by "possibility residing in the agent" is that

> possibility ... reverts to a judgment of the mind. Anything whose existence the mind supposes, [nothing] preventing ... supposing [its existence], we call "possible," and if prevented we call "impossible"; and if it is unable to suppose its nonexistence, we name it "necessary." For these are rational propositions that do not require an existent ... (Al-Ghazali 1997, 42)

That is, possibility is an object of an agent's mental judgment, a function of what a mind can rationally suppose, not a potentiality whose substratum is the matter of an existent actualized in the physical world. Rather, Al-Ghazali's possibilities are synchronic mentally supposable alternatives among which an agent picks and, because Al-Ghazali's paradigmatic agent is the omnipotent deity whose will is completely unconstrained by any external reason or cause, all possibilities are equal.[18] The only constraint, as we shall see, is internal logical

---

[17] Davidson (1987, 16–17) identifies the Avicennean source as *Al-Shifa': Ilahiyat* 4, ch. 2; cf. Avicenna (2005, 140–142). However, given the possible reference to Al-Ghazali as the *mutakallim*, it is at least as probable that Maimonides' source is Al-Ghazali (1997, 39–46). Maimonides' fourth argument from possibility does not correspond exactly to Al-Ghazali's third argument, but also incorporates elements of his fourth proof that argues for the eternity of matter rather than of a substance. For excellent discussion of the Al-Ghazali passages (and Averroes' response in Van den Bergh 1954), see Kukkonen (2000a; 2000b); Dutton (2001); Griffel (2009, 160–171). On the contested question whether Maimonides knew Al-Ghazali's writings, was influenced by him, or alluded to him, see Pines (1963, cxxvii); Lazarus-Yafeh (1997, 163–193); Ivry (2005, 68–75); Stroumsa (2009, 25); Griffel (2019, 413–427); and, for a dissenting opinion, Langermann (2019) and Stern (2020).

[18] In this and the previous sentence, I use "pick" and "choose" in conformity with the distinction drawn in Ullmann-Margalit and Morgenbesser (1977).

or conceptual consistency. We will return to this mentalistic, or conceptual, conception of possibility in later sections, but for now I want to emphasize two main differences between the models of modality advocated by the *falasifa* and the Al-Ghazalian *mutakallim*. (1) The *falasifa's* conception is temporal and diachronic; the *kalam* model, anticipating John Duns Scotus, treats a possibility as one among multiple synchronic alternative states of affairs. (2) The *falasifa's* modalities are situated in the external physical or natural world; those of the *mutakallim* are in the mind of an agent. More generally, the *falasifa* begin by investigating what exists to determine the possible; actuality constrains possibility. For the *kalam*, possibility and necessity are rational notions that "do not require an existent" and depend only on what the mind can consistently and coherently suppose or conceptualize.[19]

It should be clear by now that, if what the *mutakallim* means by "possibility resid[ing] in the agent" is a mental judgment, Maimonides' response concerning *potentiality* misses the mark.[20] However, Maimonides' own objection to the philosophers' conception of possibility as potentiality may also undermine his response to the *mutakallim*. Maimonides' objection is that the principle that "possibility must of necessity precede everything that is generated ... is only necessary in regard to this being that is stabilized ... In the course of its very origination, no such principle need obtain" (Maimonides 1963, 2.17: 297). Like Hume's objection that the justification of induction presupposes the uniformity of nature, which itself is justified only by past inductions, Maimonides objects that the *falasifa's* principle – that all change (including origination) requires a preceding possibility, or potentiality – cannot be used in an argument for eternity because, made into a precondition for origination, it presupposes that the very principle is preoriginated – or eternal – rather than holding only after the world has reached a stable state.[21] Thus, Maimonides turns the philosophers' world-situated conception of possibility as potentiality against their own argument for eternity.

---

[19] Here the *mutakallim* or Al-Ghazali seems to be influenced by Avicenna's notion of "the possible in itself," which is determined by the essence or whatness of a thing considered "in itself" independently of its existence. See Section 10.4, this essay.

[20] This misunderstanding is surprising because elsewhere Maimonides acknowledges that the *mutakallimun* think of possibility from "the mental point of view" (Maimonides 1963, 1.74: 220).

[21] Cf. Manekin (2005, 44–45).

10.3 Necessitation versus Purposeful Particularization: *Guide* 2.19-22

In *Metaphysics* 5.5, Aristotle distinguishes five senses in which things are said to be necessary (Aristotle 1984, *Metaphysics* 1015a20–1015b15). In this section I explore Maimonides' use of the first two and the fifth senses. The third sense – compulsion – does not concern us and I address the fourth sense – the invariable – in Section 10.4. The first two senses are both instances of hypothetical necessity: that which is necessary on the hypothesis that a specific end is to be sought. In the first sense, the hypothetical end is existence or survival, in the second, a good or well-being. Nowadays we refer to these as necessary conditions, but for Aristotle and the medievals they are truly necessary, though on the assumption or hypothesis of a chosen end. We will return to hypothetical necessity in a moment.

Aristotle's fifth sense is

> Demonstration [which] is a necessary thing, because the conclusion cannot be otherwise, if there has been demonstration in the full sense; and the causes of this necessity are the first premises, i.e., the fact that the proposition from which the deduction proceeds cannot be otherwise. (Aristotle 1984, Metaphysics 1015b7–9)[22]

The Arabic *falasifa* understood Aristotle to mean that the conclusion of a demonstration is necessary, not because *the act of inferring* the conclusion from the premises compels us to assent to it (which could occur even if the premises are not themselves necessary), but because the necessity *possessed* by the premises *produces,* or perhaps transfers, the same modal status in the conclusion.[23] I shall refer to this fifth sense of demonstrative necessity as "necessitation."

Necessitation plays a crucial role in Maimonides' critique of the Aristotelian proofs for the eternity of the world. According to a well-known Aristotelian thesis, the world is eternal if and only if it is necessary.[24] Therefore, in *Guide* 2.19–22 Maimonides turns to criticisms of the necessity of the world. In particular, he attacks the Aristotelian claim that the existence and circular motion of the spheres is scientifically demonstrated and thereby necessitated. If Maimonides can show that they are not

---

[22] On the Arabic translation of this passage, see Wisnovsky (2003, 201–205).
[23] Wisnovsky (2003, 203); Strobino (forthcoming). On the necessity of premises, see Section 10.1 in this essay.
[24] See, e.g., Aristotle (1984, *On the Heavens* 282a22–27); Aristotle (1984, *Metaphysics* 1026b27–28).

necessitated, it follows that they are also not eternal. What is striking about his critique is its repeated demand that a necessitating demonstration furnish a cause for its conclusion.[25] Indeed Maimonides states that "by the term 'necessity' [the Aristotelian] merely means to signify causality" (Maimonides 1963, 2.21: 316), recalling that for Aristotle a cause is a principle that *explains* its effect, an answer to a why-question. In the *Posterior Analytics* 1.2, Aristotle requires, among other conditions for a demonstration of a proposition *P*, that its premises be necessary and explanatory, i.e., they must contain the cause of *P* as the so-called middle term. Among his late Ancient and medieval commentators, it then became a live controversy whether a syllogism that does not contain the cause counts as a demonstration. But here we are focusing not on demonstration simpliciter but on demonstrations "in the full sense" (Maimonides 1963, 2.21: 316), i.e., necessitating demonstrations, and for this class of demonstrations, Maimonides' requirement for a cause "explanatory of the conclusion" (Aristotle 1994, *Posterior Analytics* 71b20–23) is explicit. This causal dimension of necessitation locates it centrally in a model of scientific knowledge and understanding, and such a demonstration demands that we actually be in a position to give the explanatory cause. Indeed we manifest our understanding of a proposition *P* by producing a causal demonstration of its necessity.[26]

Now, for the sublunar sphere Maimonides allows that Aristotle did succeed in showing that phenomena "follow an order conforming to what exists, an order whose causes are clear"; hence, sublunar motion "derives of necessity from the motion and powers of the sphere" (Maimonides 1963, 2.19: 307). However, for celestial phenomena Maimonides objects that the Aristotelian eternalists/necessitarians have utterly failed until now to accomplish this task and are unlikely ever to succeed. Despite Aristotle's "wish to assign causes ... so that these things would be ordered for us in a natural order that is due to necessity, ... [he] has assigned no clear cause ... it does not follow an order for which necessity can be claimed" (Maimonides 1963, 2.19: 306–307). Instead, Maimonides proposes that

---

[25] See, e.g., the repeated requests for causes in Maimonides (1963, 2.19: 304, 306–307, 310–311; 2.20: 312–313; 2.21: 316).

[26] On the connection between demonstration, explanation, and scientific knowledge or understanding (*episteme*, *'ilm*), see Aristotle (1984, *Metaphysics* 1013a24–1013b31); Aristotle (1984, *Physics* 194b18–195b30); cf. also Maimonides (1963, 2.12: 77ff.; 2.48: 409–412). For its implications for Maimonides' skepticism about metaphysics, see Stern (2013, 117–119; 159–168) and, for an opposing view, Manekin (2012; 2018).

the sphere was "particularized" by a divine agent who created the world for a "purpose."

To explain what Maimonides means here by "particularization" (*takhsis*) and "purpose" (*qasd*) and how his account differs from Aristotelian necessitation, let me situate his position in the complicated dialectic of *Guide* 2.19–22 over origination versus eternity. Of four opinions, Maimonides absolutely rejects the first that the world originated spontaneously or as the random outcome of chance.[27] Likewise, he rejects the second, *kalam* view that an omnipotent, absolutely free deity at each moment occasionalistically "particularizes," "makes," "creates," "brings into existence," or "purposes" the world – "all these terms ... signify one notion" (Maimonides 1963, 1.74: 218) – picking accidents for atoms from among equally possible synchronic alternatives "according to His will whatever it be" (Maimonides 1963, 2.19: 306; see also 303) – because it "abolishes the nature of that which exists" (Maimonides 1963, 2.19: 303). Nonetheless, while denying the *kalam* position, Maimonides makes the remarkable announcement that he will adopt its vocabulary "particularization" and "purpose" to express his own view, though "without having to take upon myself what the Mutakallimun have undertaken." Instead he will "establish particularization ... by means of philosophic premises derived from the nature of that which exists." Yet, and in the same breath, Maimonides also dismisses the philosophers' view that the world is necessitated. He will show

> that all things exist in virtue of a purpose and not of necessity, and that He who purposed them may change them and conceive another purpose, though not absolutely any purpose whatever. (Maimonides 1963, 2.19: 303)

This is perplexing. Despite his unequivocal censure of the *kalam*, Maimonides says that they share the same desired aim: "There is no doubt that they wished what I wish" (Maimonides 1963, 2.19: 303). And while he rejects the philosophers' necessitating causes, his own "purposes" are prima facie no different from final ends or causes. Indeed he concludes: "There is no doubt that all of these things are *necessary* according to the *purpose* of one who purposes" (Maimonides 1963, 2.19: 310; my emphasis). How, then, does Maimonides' view differ from those of the *kalam* and *falsafa*?

---

[27] Maimonides (1963, 2.19: 308–311; 2.20: 312–313).

Let's begin with Maimonides' best case of necessitation in the sublunar sphere: the primary qualities (hot, cold, wet, dry) causally necessitate that and thereby explain why a material substance is, say, rough or smooth. The latter "necessarily derives" from the former (Maimonides 1963, 2.21: 316). Turning then to the heavens, the philosophers' purported analogue to the sublunar case is that "the first intellect necessarily proceeds from God, and the second [intellect] from the first ... and the spheres necessarily proceed from the intellects" (Maimonides 1963, 2.21: 316). This necessitating procession, Maimonides says, is meant to be explained by a number of "universally agreed upon" propositions: for example, (i) that only simple things proceed from simple things; (ii) that from compounds composed of n simple things, n things will proceed; and (iii) that effects "conform" to their causes, so a quality (but not a quantity) proceeds from a quality, matter proceeds from matter but not from form (Maimonides 1963, 2.22: 317f.).

Given these principles defining the necessitating relation, Maimonides objects that the heavenly phenomena in reality "do not conform to [Aristotle's] conception of necessity" (Maimonides 1963, 2.22: 318). Among his examples, here are two: (1) A sphere, which is composite and material (even if its matter is not sublunar matter), can proceed from an intellect that is both simple and purely intelligible, violating (i) and (iii). (2) In the sublunar sphere we explain the different directions of the rectilinear motion of bodies by the natural places of their constituent elements where they seek to come to rest. But we cannot explain the different directions and velocities of the motions of the spheres by their respective places relative to one another (Maimonides 1963, 2.19: 306–307, 310). A sphere whose velocity ought to be slower because it is further away from the first cause is in fact faster, and to explain the spheres' directions and velocities by appeal to their respective separate intellects is a pseudo-explanation because it employs spatial terms for immaterial intellects (violating (iii)) (Maimonides 1963, 2.19: 311). Therefore, because these purported causes do not scientifically explain their effects, the effects are not necessitated and, hence, not eternal.

Why, then, if he denies that necessitating – including final – causes explain the existence and motion of heavenly bodies, does Maimonides think that the purpose of the particularizer will do any better? I want to propose that Maimonides' idea is a hybrid of the philosophers' and *mutakallimun's* views. Recall his perplexing statement that "things are necessary according to the purpose of one who purposes." What kind of necessity is this and what is a purpose if not a final end? First, I propose that by "necessity" Maimonides means here *hypothetical necessity*; i.e., x is necessary or necessitated on the hypothesis that a given purpose P is to be sought by an act or object y, such that without x, P for whose sake y exists or is performed, cannot be achieved.[28] So bricks and mortar (x) are hypothetically necessary for the security or protection (P) for whose sake a wall (y) exists or is built. To this extent, Maimonides' purposes are like the philosophers' final causes but they also differ in two ways. The philosophers' final (indeed all) causes must be known, and one must have the "capacity to assign them" in order to provide explanations that yield necessitating demonstrations (Maimonides 1963, 2.19: 308).[29] Purposes do not have this epistemic constraint. On the contrary, it is precisely *because* we do not know and cannot "assign" a final cause for the spheres and their motions although we have grounds to believe that they "certainly have a cause and ground and are not … by chance," that Maimonides invokes his talk of purpose to baptize our epistemic situation: "All this has been produced for an object that we do not know and is not an aimless and fortuitous act" (Maimonides 1963, 2.19: 310).[30]

The second way necessitation and purposeful particularization differ concerns their models of modality.[31] Necessitation is a matter of demonstrating that a conclusion could not be otherwise from premises that could not be otherwise. "The effect necessarily proceeds from its cause without being able to be separated from it or to change unless its cause or one of its modes also changes" (Maimonides 1963, 2.21: 315). In contrast, when we are dealing with "the purpose of One … who chose freely and willed that all things should be as they are … He who purposed them may change them and conceive another purpose, though not absolutely any purpose whatever" (Maimonides 1963, 2.19: 303). Here Maimonides is thinking

---

[28] On hypothetical necessity, see also Aristotle (1984, *Physics* 199b33–200a14) and Aristotle (1984, *Parts of Animals* 642a1–13).

[29] Or the philosopher must at least have the evidence (say, of observable regularities) to be in a position to know *that* such an end or cause exists, even if he does know what it is. Cf. Avicenna on *tajriba* in his *Burhan* 1, 9 and in Black (2013).

[30] Indeed, the human intellect does not know two things: (i) why a specific purpose was particularized or willed and (ii) how the hypothetically necessary conditions achieve the hypothesized end. Note that Maimonides' claim that humans do not know the final cause or purpose is not due to accidental ignorance, or suspicion of teleology, but to a principled skeptical argument about human knowledge of metaphysics: see Section 10.5, this essay; Stern (2013, 168–177; 278–289); and Stern (manuscript).

[31] There is a third difference between the two views (which I ignore here) concerning whether the world is originated after nonexistence or is eternal. Maimonides insightfully distinguishes this question from the question of causal necessitation versus purposeful particularization (Maimonides 1963, 2.19: 312).

of selecting a purpose, the hypothesis, on the model of the Al-Ghazalian idea of an agent/particularizer/purposer – terms whose meanings we said earlier Maimonides identifies – making a mental judgment to will one among a set of possibilities. When an agent deliberates how to act, he has before him a set of synchronic alternatives, each laying out a possible state of affairs with a purpose and what is necessary to achieve it, among which he wills or desires – or "particularizes" – one rather than another. So, once the agent has willed a given purpose, necessity (or a set of necessities) kicks in and determines what must occur to achieve that purpose. However, the agent could have willed another purpose, which would have triggered a different set of necessities. So, instead of willing a wall's purpose to be that it provide security and protection, a purpose that necessitates bricks and mortar, the agent could have willed its purpose to be privacy, for which any opaque material would suffice, and if he had willed the purpose to be decorative, the wall could consist in plants and flowers. However, Maimonides departs from this Al-Ghazalian model in insisting that the alternative possibilities are not absolutely equal. Rather, Divine "wisdom, which cannot be grasped, required" (Maimonides 1963, 2.22: 319) one rather than another.[32] In sum, the basic model at the stage of hypothesizing the end, or purpose, is a mental judgment choosing among synchronic possibilities, and once a purpose is chosen, necessitation determines how that purpose, or end, is achieved. Maimonides' adoption of the terms "purposeful particularization" attempts both to synthesize the philosophers' and *mutakallimun's* models of modality and to baptize our lack of knowledge of the wisdom lying behind the particularized purpose.

10.4 Avicenna and the Possible/Necessary of Existence and in Virtue of Itself/through a Cause

The nineteenth, twentieth, and twenty-first of the philosophers' premises in the introduction to part 2 of the *Guide* introduce another pair of opposing modal notions: (i) the necessarily existent being in itself (*wajib al-wujud*, for short: the NEI), identified with the deity and (ii) (all other) beings that are possible of existence in themselves and necessary of existence through a cause (PEI-and-NEC). This distinction is central to the

---

[32] On the relation between divine will and wisdom, see Maimonides (1963, 2.18: 302; 2.25: 306). Maimonides does not explain how God "knows" the (infinite?) number of synchronic alternative possibilities among which He chooses a purpose, although this is a striking formal analogue to Molinist middle knowledge. I am indebted in this paragraph to discussion with Suf Amichay.

philosophers' third proof of the existence of God and Maimonides' own constructive dilemma proof (Maimonides 1963, 2.1: 247–280; 2.2: 252).[33] Furthermore, he explicitly identifies God with the NEI (Maimonides 1963, 1.57: 132) whom he distinguishes from the first intellect or prime mover (Maimonides 1963, 2.4: 258–259).[34] The NEI also underlies Maimonides' conception of divine unity as absolute simplicity, which in turn lies behind his argument that no divine attributive statements are true (Maimonides 1963, 1.58: 135–137, 1.59: 139, 1.60: 146–147).[35]

The source of these ideas of necessity and possibility *of* existence and of the distinction between "in itself" and "through a cause" is Aristotle's fourth and most basic sense of "necessary" in *Metaphysics* 5.5. The necessary is that which cannot be other than it is (Aristotle 1984, *Metaphysics* 1015a35–36). Aristotle also distinguishes between things that "owe their necessity to something other than themselves" and those that "are the source of necessity in other things", and concludes that "the necessary in the primary and strict sense is the simple" (Aristotle 1984, *Metaphysics* 1015b10–11), implying that "eternal and unmovable things," i.e., necessary and unchanging beings, are simple. By contrast, it follows that the possible is what could be otherwise, that undergoes change, is contingent, and is composite.

Aristotle's late Ancient and Arabic commentators all developed this fourth sense of necessity and possibility, though in different directions. Maimonides' own proximate source was Avicenna, who was influenced by the *kalam* as well as Aristotle.[36] Unlike Al-Farabi (and later Averroes), who took the necessary to be the eternal and the possible to be (two-sided) temporally possible beings subject to corruption and generation (entailing that nothing can be both necessary and possible), Avicenna sought a stronger distinction that would distinguish the creator deity from all creat*ed* beings, including the eternal spheres, stars, separate intellects, and the divine attributes, and not only from contingent sublunar substances that go in and out of existence. But in different works, he distinguishes the NEI from the PEI-and-NEC along different dimensions:

---

[33] The philosophers' third proof, however, employs the Al-Farabi–Averroes conception of the NEI in its first half, and Avicenna's only in the second half; see Stern (2001).
[34] As Adamson (2013) shows, the NEI is not yet the deity in the classical theistic sense, although one can demonstrate that the NEI possesses the additional attributes that the classical concept demands.
[35] See Stern (2013, 198–218).
[36] Wisnovsky (2003, 197–217; 227–243). For reasons of space, I cannot do justice to Avicenna's rich conception.

e.g., whether the thing is caused or uncaused or something conceivable or not (to not exist) without entailing an absurdity or something that must exist or might not considered in itself by grasping what it is.[37]

For Maimonides, what it means for the deity to be the NEI as opposed to the PEI-and-NEC is to be absolutely uncaused. For all other beings, nothing in their essence or what-ness determines their existence; hence, existence is either an accident "superadded to [their] quiddity" (Maimonides 1963, 1.57: 132) or, if the being is eternal, an affirmative attribute. In either case, the being is composite, containing an essence and existence-attribute, and requires a cause to explain that it is *one* being. In contrast, if God is necessary, meaning absolutely uncaused, His existence cannot be distinct from His essence in any way that would render Him composite and, in turn, require a cause. He must be absolutely one and simple, indivisible and incomposite (Maimonides 1963, 1.57: 132; 1.58: 135; 1.60: 146). For the same reason – the principle that "every composite requires a composer" – Maimonides also denies that the absolutely uncaused NEI can be identified with the first intellect (or prime mover) because the latter is composed of two notions, one that it shares with all other intellects and one that distinguishes it from them, requiring a cause to explain why it nonetheless exists as one intellect (Maimonides 1963, 2.4: 258–259).[38]

However, Maimonides' conception of God as the NEI goes further than Avicenna, transforming his metaphysical claim into a semantic thesis. First, Maimonides states that the predicate "exists" is purely equivocal in its applications to God and creatures and, since our understanding is limited to that of creatures, it follows that its entirely equivocal application to God is not at all understood by us (Maimonides 1963, 1.56: 131). Therefore, God's necessary existence should not be understood to mean that it is necessary that God *exists* (in the creaturely sense). Second, by saying that "necessarily (exists)" means uncaused (existence), Maimonides transforms the affirmative "necessarily" into a negative attribute or, more precisely, the categorial negation of a privation. To be caused (to exist), and thus (for one's existence) to be only possible in itself and dependent on something else, is a privation.[39] The negation of that privation, in turn, is not a simple sentential negation but rather categorial: it denies that God

---

[37] Wisnovsky (2003, 245–263). Note that the last two distinctions are reminiscent of the *kalam* idea that modality is the object of a mental judgment or supposition.
[38] On the composition principle, see Davidson (1987, 146–153) and Wisnovsky (2003, 248–250).
[39] On possibility or potentiality as a privation and imperfection, see Avicenna (2005, 142).

falls under the category of things that are either caused or not caused, for the reason that causation is a relation and God possesses no relational attributes, either because relations are reciprocal (correlations) or accidents (Maimonides 1963, 1.52: 116–118). Hence, the full significance of saying that God necessarily exists means that His existence is uncaused, is that His existence is neither caused nor not-caused, nor does He cause or not-cause, and in any case we have no understanding of the existence-predicate applied to God.

What, then, is left of the content of the claim that God is the NEI? On the one hand, Maimonides tells us that "these subtle notions that very clearly elude the minds cannot be considered through the instrumentality of the customary words," on the other, that they "give the gist of the notion" and "give the mind the correct direction toward the true reality" (Maimonides 1963, 1.57: 133). What Maimonides is suggesting is that what we do understand is that *we*, i.e., all beings other than God, are no more than possible of existence in ourselves. Insofar as we grasp what we are, our essence – say, rational animality – we know that that content does not determine that we exist. Because we nonetheless do exist, we must be so necessitated by some other cause and, ultimately (on pain of an absurdity), by something that itself is *not* a PEI-and-NEC, namely, the NEI – although we have no understanding of what this NEI is. Like the unknown final ends of the purposeful particularizer that we nonetheless know exist, our contingent existence necessitates *that* there be such a thing although we have no knowledge of *what* it is.

What emerges from Maimonides' adaptation of the Avicennean modal conception of God as the NEI is an original understanding of contingency. Maimonidean contingency is not a matter of what might be and might not be, two-sided possibility, being subject to generation and corruption, being non-eternal or true at some time but not another. Maimonidean contingency, being a PEI-and-NEC, is radical dependence on the NEI, without which one would not be. This characterization of contingency emerges clearly in three passages: *Mishneh Torah*, "Laws of the Foundations of the Law" 1.1; Maimonides (1963, 1.69: 169; 1.71: 191). For reasons of space, I quote only the second:

> ... [T]here subsists the very same relation between the deity and the totality of the remote principles of existence. For the universe exists by virtue of the existence of the Creator and the latter continually endows it with permanence in virtue of the thing that is spoken of as overflow ... Accordingly, if the nonexistence of the Creator were supposed, all that exists would likewise be nonexistent; and the essence of its remote causes, of its ultimate

effects, and of that which is between these, would be abolished ... Such is the relation of the deity to the world. (Maimonides 1963, 1.69: 168–169)

Note that in this passage (as in all three), the possibility that were God not to exist, nothing else would exist is presented as the object of a supposition or conception – a mental judgment, like that of the *kalam* and Avicenna. However, there is a difference. Avicenna focuses on suppositions about the NEI and whether It exists considered "in itself" or "by its essence." For Maimonides, this focus is misplaced since we know or understand nothing about the NEI. Instead, Maimonides' suppositions and judgments concern PEI's, creatures, and their radical existential dependence on an uncaused cause that itself is completely independent of everything else. However, like Avicenna, who introduced the NEI/PEI distinction in order to capture the ontological difference between creator and creatures (including the eternal spheres and divine attributes), so too for Maimonides the mark of createdness is not beginningness, but rather creatures' radical contingency on the NEI, as suggested by his use of the term "Creator" twice in our quoted passage to refer to that on which creatures' existence is contingent. This Avicennean conception of the modalities and the distinctions between necessary and possible of existence and in itself versus through a cause, in turn, had a lasting influence on medieval Jewish philosophers in and beyond the Maimonidean tradition.[40]

10.5 The *Falasifa* versus the *Mutakallimun* on Possibility and Necessity

Probably the best-known passage on modality in the *Guide* is Maimonides' critique of the *kalam* principle of admissibility (*al-tajwiz*) found in his exposition of the *mutakallimun's* premises in *Guide* 1.73 (Tenth Premise), a subject to which he returns in *Guide* 3.15. Most previous discussions of this passage have concentrated on its relation to the particularization argument for creation, its opposition between the intellect and imagination, and on the question of whether the views it reports are actually found in *kalam* texts.[41] There has been little discussion of its conceptions of the modalities. In light of the models we have reviewed, I want to show how Maimonides reconfigures the interlocutors' positions – and thereby glimpse his own stance toward the controversy over the modalities.

---

[40] See Ravitzky (1978–1979).
[41] See Fackenheim (1946/1947); Rabinovitch (1974); Glucker (1959); Rosenberg (1975; 1978b); Steiner (2019a; 2019b); Schwarz (1991/1992–1993).

Although Al-Ghazali is not mentioned by name, the kalam view is very close to his position. As we saw in Section 10.2, he rejected the Aristotelian conception of possibility as a feature of the world – in terms of potentiality, existence, and time – and proposed the idea that it is the object of a mental judgment (or supposition) of a free agent willing one among a set of synchronic alternatives. What is new in *Guide* 1.73 is, first, Maimonides' explicit modeling of a possibility as a mental representation or conception (*tasawwur*) and, second, his recasting of the debate between the *falasifa* and *mutakallimun*, not as a disagreement over *where* the modalities are found – in the world or in the mind – but as a controversy over which of the *faculties* of the mind – the intellect or the imagination – should determine whether a given object, representation, or conception is a genuine possibility, i.e., over the criterion by which to evaluate the possible and the necessary.[42]

Scholars who argue that Maimonides' exposition of the *kalam* is a misrepresentation of its views emphasize that extant *kalam* texts, and in particular Al-Ghazali, never mention the imagination but instead refer to the intellect.[43] True, but that misses Maimonides' point. In defining the principle of "admissibility" as the proposition that "everything that may be *imagined* is an admissible notion for the *intellect*" (Maimonides 1963, 1.73: 206; my emphasis),[44] Maimonides is telling his reader that, for a philosopher (like himself) who distinguishes between the two, the *kalam* may, as Al-Farabi says, "constantly have [the term 'intellect'] on their tongues," but in practice what they employ is not the intellect but the imagination or, "what is commonly accepted on first sight by all people" (Al-Farabi 2007, 70). Indeed the principle of admissibility, as stated, is an oxymoron. Not only are the *mutakallimun* wrong, they also don't know what the intellect is and how it differs from the imagination.[45] They describe their possibilities as admissible "from the point of the intellect" or "intellectually admissible," but "without paying attention to the correspondence or lack of correspondence of that which exists to their assumptions" (Maimonides 1963, 1.73: 206) – the correspondence that is the

---

[42] On the important notion in Arabic logic and epistemology, *tasawwur* (conception), and its difference from *tasdiq* (assent), see Wolfson (1973), Sabra (1980), Black (1990) and now Strobino (forthcoming).

[43] Schwarz (1991/1992–1993).

[44] *Tajwiz*, the term translated here as "admissible," can also be translated as "permissible" and "possible," and indeed Maimonides uses "admissible" and "possible" interchangeably in the paragraph.

[45] For a similar polemical objection, see Maimonides' description of "the learned man" in Maimonides (1963, 1.2: 23–24).

philosopher's very criterion for the intellectually possible.[46] As Maimonides emphasizes: "That which exists is my [i.e., the philosophers'] witness and by means of it we discern the necessary, the possible, and the impossible" (Maimonides 1963, 1.73: 211).[47] Thus, from Maimonides' *philosopher's* perspective, the *mutakallimun's* practice demonstrates that they consider something impossible only "because it cannot be imagined" and possible if it can be.

Maimonides' aim is not, however, only polemical. First, he points to a crucial ambiguity in the mental judgment model: which mental faculty – the intellect or the imagination – makes the judgment. Here I cannot work through Maimonides' rich description of their respective acts, but both are depicted as representational faculties, and possibilities (or admissibilities) are now individuated by what is mentally represent*able*.[48] Hence, the dispute between the *falasifa* and *mutakallimun* is now over representations. Using mathematical examples, Maimonides shows that the intellect's and imagination's respective sets of possibilities are not co-extensive: there are imaginative possibilities that are intellectually impossible and intellectual possibilities that are unimaginable.[49] Both the *kalam* and philosophy, he says, require that representations be logically consistent or conceptually compatible, excluding representations consisting of jointly contradictory and even contrary features or propositions.[50] But the real issue Maimonides wants to highlight is whether, in addition to consistency, the modalities are constrained by what exists, regardless of whether possibilities are "in" the world or "in" the mind.

Exactly what Maimonides means by "That which exists" in *Guide* 1.73 is not entirely clear. Is it the PoP – that every genuine possibility must be fulfilled at some moment in infinite time? Or that every possibility must be a specific feature that exists, e.g., an actualizable potentiality or capacity? Or that the determination of modalities must take into account what science reveals to *really* exist – say, the qualities of the elements, their

---

[46] On the relation between possibility, existence, and representation as interpreted in Ibn Tibbon's, Pines', and Munk's different translations of Maimonides' opening description of Premise 10 (Maimonides 1963, 1.73: 194), see Ivry (1982, 67–70).

[47] The intellect/imagination opposition also carries a rich ethical valence linked to the form/matter and soul/body distinctions: the intellect is good, the imagination evil, strengthening Maimonides' polemic. See Stern (2013, 356–360).

[48] This description of the imagination should be compared with that of chapter 1 of "Eight Chapters" in Maimonides (1975, 63). In the course of knowing things the intellect "represents them to itself in their true reality."

[49] See Steiner (2019a; 2019b).

[50] On Maimonides' idea in *Guide* 3.15 that even God has no power over the impossible, see Avicenna (2005, 139).

natural places and directions, or the dependence of forms on matter? If it is the latter, Maimonides himself recognizes that the *mutakallim* has a ready response which we might paraphrase as follows: "What you, the philosopher, privileges as 'that which exists' is really no more than one of a set of equal alternative possibilities that the deity has repeatedly particularized, or willed, for no reason, and thereby made into a custom which you mistake for a nature or law. Hence, you cannot constrain what is possible by what exists which was, after all, arbitrarily picked" (Compare Maimonides 1963, 1.73: 211). And at yet other times Maimonides contrasts "existents and intellectually cognized *things*" with "imaginations and vain fantasies ... imagining any impossible *thing* whatever that occurs to the imagination" (Maimonides 1963, 1.74: 220; my emphasis).[51] Because Maimonides' imagination does not just retain sensible forms but also composes them into "invented and false" things, "there can be no critical examination in the imagination" (Maimonides 1963, 1.73: 209–211). However, this still leaves us with a question: "With regard to particular mental representations," i.e., purported possibilities, is there "something that would enable us to distinguish the things cognized intellectually from those imagined" (Maimonides 1963, 1.73: 211)?

In *Guide* 1.73, Maimonides leaves this question open, but in *Guide* 3.15 he returns to it. Can anyone

> ... assert with regard to any notion whatever that he conceives: This is possible; whereas someone else says: No, this is impossible because of the nature of the matter ... By what can one differentiate between that which is imagined and that which is cognized by the intellect? ... Is there accordingly something that permits differentiation between the imaginative faculty and the intellect? And is that thing something altogether outside both the intellect and the imagination, or is it by the intellect itself that one distinguishes between that which is cognized by the intellect and that which is imagined? All these are points for investigation which may lead very far ... (Maimonides 1963, 3.15: 459–461)[52]

Here Maimonides adapts the classic skeptical objection to a criterion of truth to question the existence of a criterion to distinguish among the kinds of possibilities, or representations. How can we justifiably know that

---

[51] In *Guide* 1.74, Maimonides seems to limit the method of particularization to alternative possible accidents of *existent things*. That is, it makes no sense to say that the particularizer wills something to exist rather than not to exist because, on the alternative of nonexistence, what is *it* that is willed not to exist?

[52] The first to notice this puzzle about *Guide* 1.73 and 3.15 was Fackenheim (1946/1947: 324, note 61), but he left its resolution open.

a given representation represents what the intellect, and not the imagination, judges possible? For that we need a criterion. Earlier, however, Maimonides has told us that "there is no belief except after a representation" (Maimonides 1963, 1.50: 111), and the same holds for judgments or other acts of assent (*tasdiq*). Hence, to judge whether a given representation R satisfies a criterion C will require a representation R* that R satisfies C. Is R* itself intellectual or imaginative? Again, this judgment requires a criterion – obviously leading us into an unending regress of judgments and criteria. Maimonides' response: "All these are points for investigation which may lead very far" (Maimonides 1963, 3.15: 461). That is, he commits himself to no claim about a criterion to judge the intellectual versus the imaginative modal status of a representation, thereby withholding assent or suspending judgment and leaving the question to unending inquiry, the original meaning of *skepsis*.

10.6 Summing up

We have reviewed five models of the modalities that figure in Maimonides' writings: (i) the temporal or statistical model, extensionalizing possibilities as times; (ii) as potentiality versus actuality; (iii) necessity as demonstrative causal necessitation; (iv) as synchronic internally consistent alternatives that are the object of an agent's mental judgment; and (v) as mental representations or conceptions, either intellectual or imaginative. Some of these are presented as the positions of particular protagonists, the *falasifa* or *mutakallimun*. Hence, one should not identify Maimonides' own view with either – and one should especially resist the temptation to identify it with the philosophers' – and Maimonides indeed raises objections to both schools. On the other hand, he also acknowledges more than a grain of truth in each, and in one case appears to fashion a hybrid out of the two views. But one theme clearly emerges. The philosophers' conceptions of the modalities, whether temporal or as potentiality/actuality or in terms of necessitation, all work well for the sublunar world or physics. Where problems arise is as we move from physics to metaphysics (or pre-physics). To give one example, "preceding possibilities" (aka potentialities) are crucial to the explanation of sublunar change, but if the world is originated, then those very possibilities/potentialities are part of what was originated, and cannot then be extrapolated to what must be the case before or in the process of origination. Similar problems arise for the temporal-statistical conception, inasmuch as time is a measure of (originated) motion, and for causal necessitation because we can furnish causes including final ends only in the sublunar realm, but not for God or the spheres. Metaphysics is where human knowledge stops, where we cannot determine what is genuinely intellectual – hence, scientifically known – as opposed to the imagined or the fantasized, what a bodily faculty judges. At that point, Maimonides' skepticism steps on stage.

I will conclude with an analogy. Maimonides' stance toward the controversy over the modalities recalls his stance toward the twelfth-century Andalusian crisis over the sciences of the heavens: the dispute between Aristotelian cosmology and Ptolemaic astronomy. Unlike most prominent Andalusian philosophers and scientists who took one or the other side, and attempted to construct or revise theories that vindicated either Aristotle or Ptolemy, Maimonides enlisted the ongoing controversy as grist for his skeptical mill: the interminable dispute marks for him the "true perplexity," which brings one to suspend judgment without committing oneself to either theory. Instead he uses the controversy itself to support his view of the limitations of human knowledge of the superlunar world and metaphysics. The same skeptical attitude marks his stance toward the debate over the modalities in metaphysics.

PART V

Human Finitude

CHAPTER 11

Maimonides' Critique of Anthropocentrism and Teleology

Warren Zev Harvey

One of the most provocative chapters in Maimonides' *Guide of the Perplexed* is part 3, chapter 13.[1] In this chapter, Maimonides criticizes anthropocentrism and teleology. He argues, *inter alia*, that it is pointless to seek the *telos* of the universe; that the universe was not created for the sake of humans; and that all beings were intended for their own sakes, not for the sake of something else. These views were rejected by many later philosophers, like Thomas Aquinas, Levi Gersonides, Moses Narboni, Hasdai Crescas, Isaac Arama, Saul Morteira, and Gottfried Wilhelm Leibniz.[2] Narboni wrote: "I am very perplexed by the Master! ... [His words] contradict all the sciences. For the goal of all the sciences is to know the final end ... This is no less than the abolition of the nature of the intellect!"[3] Crescas wrote: "[It cannot be] what appears from the literal sense of the Master's words. Heaven forfend that it should be attributed to God what would be a grave defect in any intelligent being," namely, acting with no purpose![4] Arguably "[the most] systematic effort to rebut Maimonides' discussion [in *Guide* 3.13]" was that of Saul Levi Morteira, Spinoza's teacher.[5] Spinoza, however, was not convinced by him. Indeed, he was the first major philosopher to embrace wholeheartedly Maimonides' criticisms of anthropocentrism and teleology. Maimonides' discussion in *Guide* 3.13, formatively influenced Spinoza's celebrated assault on final causality in his appendix to part 1 of *Ethics*.[6]

---

[1] Maimonides (1963, 448–456; 1931, 323–329). Quotations from the *Guide* will be from the Pines translation, but sometimes modified.
[2] See W. Z. Harvey (1981a, 162–164), Melamed (2020).   [3] Narboni (1852, 51b).
[4] Crescas (2018, II, 6, 5, 241; 1990, 271–272). Translation modified.
[5] Saperstein (2005) concludes: "I have not found any other text containing such a systematic effort to rebut Maimonides' discussion in the *Guide* [3.13]" (Saperstein 2005, p. 229). He suggests that Spinoza's critique of anthropocentrism should be seen not only as an adaptation of Maimonides, but also as a rejection of Morteira (Saperstein 2005, p. 227).
[6] See W. Z. Harvey (1981a, 162–164; 2017, 43–55).

Although Maimonides was critical of anthropocentrism and teleology in *Guide* 3.13, he had not always held such views. In his early *Commentary on the Mishnah*, which he completed at the age of thirty in 1168, he defended anthropocentrism and teleology. His views there are downright Panglossian: all sublunar things exist only for the sake of humans, e.g., sheep and cattle for food, donkeys to carry things, horses for transportation, vipers for medicine, and bloodroot for compresses.[7]

The *Guide of the Perplexed* was completed in 1191, some twenty-three years after the *Commentary on the Mishnah*. Over the years between the two works, Maimonides' thinking on anthropocentrism and teleology underwent a radical transformation. In our following discussion of *Guide* 3.13 we shall see that it is riddled with different sorts of contradiction. At times one gets the impression that Maimonides is trying to be a loyal Aristotelian, but at others one gets the impression that he is trying to overturn Aristotelianism.[8] Some of these contradictions may be explained as being what Maimonides calls contradictions due to the fifth and seventh causes – that is, contradictions required for pedagogical reasons or for concealing esoteric doctrines. However, some may be due to what Maimonides calls the second cause, namely, change of opinion; that is, the chapter may retain material written at different times and reflecting different stages in the metamorphosis of Maimonides' thinking on these subjects.[9]

In what follows, we shall undertake a close reading of *Guide* 3.13. Hopefully, it will help us to distinguish between the different kinds of contradictions in his discussion, and to clarify his views on anthropocentrism and teleology.

11.1 Preamble

Maimonides begins his discussion in *Guide* 3.13 with a "preamble" (*tamhīd*) – that is, a basic introduction that paves the way for an advanced

---

[7] Maimonides (1975, 119–131, esp. 121–122; 1992, 352–356, esp. 353).
[8] See W. Z. Harvey (2017, 53, note 64). Cf. Diesendruck (1928); Brunner (1928); Wolfson (1934, vol. 1, 422–440); Pines (1963); Goldman (1977/1996); Schwartz (2005); Hadad (2011, 21–105); Parens (2012); Wirmer (2018); and Melamed (2020). Some scholars think that Maimonides' position in *Guide* 3.13 is Aristotelian; others, that it is anti-Aristotelian. Some argue that he shows in it how the views of Aristotle and the Law on teleology are in agreement; others, that he shows how they are contradictory; of those who think he shows they are contradictory, some say he sides with Aristotle and others say he sides with the Law.
[9] On the Seven Causes of Contradictions, see Maimonides (1963, 17–20; 1931, 323–324).

Maimonides' Critique of Anthropocentrism and Teleology 211

exposition.[10] Similarly, in *Guide* 1.72 he presents a "preamble" on the structure of the universe (*al-wujūd*), which serves as a basic introduction to his exposition of the premises of the kalam in *Guide* 1.73–76.[11] Again, in *Guide* 2.12, which discusses the divine "overflow," he begins with a "preamble" or basic introduction on the principles of efficient causality, which are said to be valid whether the world is eternal or created.[12] Like the preambles in *Guide* 1.72 and *Guide* 2.12, the preamble in *Guide* 3.13 sets down preliminary propositions about the universe (*al-wujūd*) that are true according to "all schools," "universally admitted," and "clear."[13]

The preamble begins with the observation that "the minds of perfect individuals" (*adhhān al-kāmilīn*) have been perplexed concerning the final end of the universe.[14] Maimonides does not refer here to a perplexity caused by a true *aporia* in natural science, like the disjunction between the corruptibility and incorruptibility of the celestial sphere (*Guide* 1.71; 2.2) or the contradiction between Ptolemaic astronomy and Aristotelian physics (*Guide* 2.24). Rather, he refers to a perplexity arising from unscientific imaginings. Elsewhere he speaks of "the minds of the multitude" (*adhhān al-jamhūr*) in the sense of "the imaginations of the multitude."[15] Here in the preamble he evidently refers to the imaginings of perfect individuals. The fallacy of trying to discover a final end for the universe has ensnared *even* perfect individuals.

Maimonides asserts bluntly that the question of what is the final end of the universe is "abolished," that is, pointless, according to "all schools," that is, according to both Aristotle and the Law of Moses. He explains that we speak about "final causes" only when we refer to the actions of an intelligent agent who acts with intention; e.g., a carpenter makes a throne for the intended purpose of being sat upon. Such actions, Maimonides continues, are produced in time after their nonexistence. The Necessary Existent – God – has no final cause, since He is not the action of an intelligent agent and was not produced in time after His nonexistence.

---

[10] Maimonides 1963, 448–449 (beginning with "Often the minds" and ending with "what has not been produced in time"); Maimonides 1931, 323–324.
[11] Maimonides 1963, 184–194 (beginning with "Know that this whole being" and ending with "and know thou it"); Maimonides 1931, 127–134. Pines translates "*al-tamhīd*" as "simplifying presentation" (Maimonides 1963, 194).
[12] Maimonides 1963, 277 (beginning with "It is clear" and ending with "if the agent is not a body"); Maimonides 1931, 193. Pines translates "*al-tamhīd*" as "preliminary remarks" (Maimonides 1963, 277).
[13] Maimonides 1963, 448; Maimonides 1931, 323.
[14] Maimonides 1963, 448; Maimonides 1931, 323.
[15] Maimonides 1963, 1.26: 57; 1931, 38. Cf., e.g., 1.33, 34, 49, 50, 51, 65, 68 (Maimonides 1963, pp. 71, 73, 109, 111, 114, 158, 163–164; 1931, pp. 48, 49, 73, 75, 76, 108, 112–113).

Similarly, anything that is not the action of an intelligent agent and not produced in time has no final cause.[16]

11.2 Aristotle on Teleology I

According to Aristotle, Maimonides reports, the universe and all natural species in it are pre-eternal. Since it was not produced in time after nonexistence, the universe has no final end. Similarly, since they were not produced in time after nonexistence, the various species of "animals or plants" have no final end. It is true, Maimonides notes, that in physics one seeks a "final end" for every natural being, but that "final end" (*al-ghāya*) is different from the "*ultimate* final end" (*al-ghāya al-akhīra*) under discussion.

Indeed, Maimonides continues, Aristotle held that the final cause was the noblest of the four causes (Aristotle 1984, *Physics* 2.3, 195a; *Parts of Animals* 1.1, 639b; *Metaphysics* 5.2, 1013b), although it is often difficult to discern. His principle was "nature does nothing in vain" (Aristotle 1984, *De Anima*, 3.9, 432b, et al.), that is, "every natural action has a certain final end." Moreover, he held that plants were made for the sake of animals (Aristotle 1984, *On Plants* 1.2, 817b; *Politics* 1.8, 1256b). He also held that animal limbs were made for particular ends, e.g., teeth for chewing (Aristotle 1984, *Physics* 2.8, 198b; *Parts of Animals* 1.5, 645b).[17]

The contradiction is overt, almost droll. According to Aristotle, the various species of animals and plants have no final end, *but* plants were made for the sake of animals. According to Aristotle, there can be no final causes in natural things, *but* every natural action has a final end. How are these contradictions to be explained? Perhaps Maimonides is contrasting what Aristotle, in accordance with his philosophic principles, *should say* with what Aristotle in fact *does say*. Is Maimonides propounding a strict or pristine Aristotelianism against Aristotle's own inconsistent Aristotelianism?

---

[16] Maimonides (1963, 3.13: 448–449; 1931, 323–324). Cf. Maimonides (1963, 1.69: 169–170; 1931, 117). The Arabic "*suqūt*," translated as "abolished" or "pointless," means literally "fall" or collapse." Munk translates: "c'est une question oiseuse" (Maïmonide 1856–1866, vol. 3, 82–83). On Necessary Existence and final causality, see Wisnovsky (2002, 108–110).

[17] Maimonides (1963, 449); Maimonides (1931, 324). According to Aristotle (1984, *On Plants*, 1.2, 817b), "the plant was created for the sake of the animal, but the animal was not created for the sake of the plant"; according to Aristotle (1984, *Politics* 1.8, 1256b), "plants exist for the sake of animals and the other animals for the good of man." It is generally held that an Arabic translation of the *Politics* was not available in Maimonides' day.

11.3 Digression: An Aristotelian Proof for Creation

At this point in his discussion, Maimonides allows himself a theological digression. The discovery of final causes in natural things, he observes, led Aristotle to speak of an "intellectual" or "divine" principle in the world (Aristotle 1984, *Metaphysics* 12.7, 1072b). Aristotle was forced to posit such a principle since the existence of final causes necessitates by definition the existence of an intelligent agent who acts with intention. The existence of final causes in nature, concludes Maimonides, is indeed "one of the strongest proofs" for the creation of the world after nonexistence.[18] Philosophers who hold the eternity of the universe should not speak about final causality in nature, but if they do, they provide a strong proof *against* the eternity of the universe. The fact that Aristotle was compelled to posit final causes in nature may mean that the study of nature, that is, natural science, contradicts the theory of the eternity of the universe.

A similar point was made by Maimonides in *Guide* 2.10. Nature, which is the principle of preservation, is said to be "wise," but this wisdom is in truth that of the Divine Order (*al-amr al-ilāhī*).[19] The term "Divine Order" played a crucial role in Judah Ha-Levi's anti-Aristotelian dialogue, *The Kuzari*. At *Kuzari* 1.69–79, it is explained that nature is not wise in itself, but the existence in nature of "wisdom directed toward an end" points to the wisdom of the Divine Order.[20] Maimonides repeats this idea in *Guide* 3.19, stating that according to both the Law and philosophy, purposefulness in the universe cannot be attributed to nature, which is not endowed with an intellect, but rather it must be attributed to an "intellectual principle" or "intellectual being."[21]

11.4 Aristotle on Teleology II

Resuming his presentation of the Aristotelian approach to teleology, Maimonides states that, according to Aristotle, the final cause is identical in species with the formal and efficient causes: a human being (formal cause) was fathered by a human being (efficient cause) with the purpose of being a human being (final cause). However, notes Maimonides, this identity of the three causes applies only with regard to the "first" or "'proximate' final end" (*al-ghāya al-aula*), not the "ultimate final end"

---

[18] Maimonides (1963, 449; 1931, 324).
[19] Maimonides (1963, 271–272; 1931, 189).
[20] Ha-Levi (1905, 55–57; 1997, 18–21).
[21] Maimonides (1963, 479; 1931, 346).

(*al-ghāya al-akhīra*).²² Here one may wonder how to understand Maimonides' dictum in *Guide* 1.69, according to which God is the formal, efficient, and final cause of the universe. The reference there to the final cause is explicitly to "the ultimate final end."²³

Maimonides goes on to explain that, according to the Aristotelian natural scientists, the ultimate final end is "indispensable." All natural species, they say, have an ultimate final end, although it is often difficult to discern it, and the ultimate final end of the universe is all the more difficult to discern.²⁴ This view of the Aristotelian natural scientists contradicts Aristotle's view, as presented previously, according to which the universe and the natural species in it have no ultimate final end since they were not produced in time after nonexistence. Is this a contradiction between Aristotle and the Aristotelian natural scientists? It may also be recalled that the proviso regarding the difficulty of discerning final causality was stated originally with regard to the first final ends, not the ultimate ones.

According to Aristotle, Maimonides now explains, the ultimate final end of a natural species consists in the perpetuity of generation and corruption, which ensures its eternal preservation despite the necessary corruption of its material individuals. "The ultimate final end," reports Maimonides, "is bringing about perfection"; and the most perfect species that can be formed out of the sublunar corruptible matter is the human being. Thus, in a certain sense, all things in the sublunar world exist for the sake of the human being. The first final end of every individual of every natural species is to realize the form of its species. The ultimate final end of the species is its eternal preservation. Maimonides now concludes his presentation of Aristotle's view: "according to the doctrine of eternity, the question of the ultimate final end of the universe does not arise."²⁵

Maimonides' final summary of Aristotle's view does not follow from his complicated presentation, but from his simple opening premises. Since the universe was not produced in time after nonexistence, it has no final end.

One might sum up Maimonides' presentation of Aristotle more precisely: According to Aristotle, the universe and all the natural species in it have no final ends, since they are pre-eternal, and only beings produced by an intelligent agent after nonexistence have final ends. However, it is also true, according to the Aristotelian view, that the universe and all the natural species in it do have final ends, but these are difficult to discern.

---

[22] Maimonides (1963, 449–450; 1931, 324).
[23] Maimonides (1963, 168–170; 1931, 116–117).
[24] Maimonides (1963, 450; 1931, 324–325).
[25] Maimonides (1963, 450; 1931, 325).

The plants, for example, exist for the sake of the animals. Animal parts, such as teeth, clearly exist for the sake of a particular purpose, such as chewing food. Nature does nothing in vain! Generally speaking, the first final end of every individual is to realize the form of its species, and the ultimate end of the species is its eternal preservation. Put differently, the ultimate end of everything is perfection. Since the human being is the most perfect being produced from corruptible matter, it might be said that the human being is the final end of the world of generation and corruption.

It might be said that Maimonides' presentation of Aristotle's view on teleology in *Guide* 3.13 is a sort of convoluted commentary on Aristotle's remarks in *Physics* (Aristotle 1984, *Physics* 2.8, 198a–b). Here, Aristotle asks whether, as the rain does not fall for the sake of making the corn grow, but rather it falls of necessity, and incidentally the corn grows, so incisors are not designed to cut food and molars to grind it, but rather our teeth just happen to be useful for those tasks. Aristotle defends the teleological position, arguing that the evidence in its favor is too great to be attributed to chance. Maimonides seems to be arguing to Aristotle: If you maintain the doctrine of eternity, you must say that it rains and incidentally the corn grows, and our teeth just happen to be useful for chewing; but if you defend teleology, then you must presuppose the universe was created by an intelligent agent, i.e., you must hold the doctrine of the creation after nonexistence.

It is instructive to compare Maimonides' position with that of Averroes and Aquinas. In his *Long Commentary* on Aristotle's *Physics, ad loc.*, Averroes attributes the non-teleological understanding of rain and teeth to "anyone who denies final cause and denies providence."[26] Thus, Averroes, like Maimonides, seems to hold that the belief in final ends requires the belief in an intelligent agent, namely, God. In his *Commentary* on Aristotle's *Physics, ad loc.*, Aquinas cites Averroes' *Long Commentary* favorably as teaching that the doctrine of final causes "is important with reference to the problem of providence."[27] As opposed to Averroes, Aquinas, and Aristotle himself, Maimonides argues – albeit ambiguously – that the Aristotelian view is the non-teleological one.

11.5 The Law on Teleology

Having presented Aristotle's opinion on teleology, Maimonides now presents the opinion of the Law of Moses. It is, he says, a mistake to think that

[26] See S. Harvey (2004, 97–103, esp. 98–99). [27] Ibid. (103, note 63).

belief in the creation of the universe after nonexistence requires one to seek the final end of the universe. It is true, he admits, that some biblical verses (e.g., Isaiah 40:22; 45:18; Jeremiah 33), according to their external meaning (*ẓāhir*), seem to teach that the universe exists for the sake of human beings. However, such interpretations are indefensible. To say that something exists for the sake of a final end, Maimonides reasons, is to say that it is a necessary condition for it; but all the other beings in the heavens and on earth are manifestly not necessary conditions for the existence of the human being, and God could have created human beings without them. Thus, the human being is not the final end of the universe. Furthermore, Maimonides asks, if we presume that God created the universe for the sake of human beings so that they would worship Him, what could He have gained by it? Even if the entire universe worshipped God, it would not add to His perfection; and if the entire universe ceased to exist, it would not detract from it. If one says that the worship of God perfects the human being, the question arises: what is the purpose of the perfect human being? The only answer to this question is that it is God's *will* or *wisdom*. Maimonides cites the Concluding Prayer recited on the Day of Atonement: "Who can say to You, *What are You doing?!* And if he is righteous, what boon is this to You?" (cf. Ecclesiastes 8:4). Maimonides explains that this prayer means that there is no final end of the universe other than God's will alone. The human being has no final end except to be a human being. As for all the other beings, they too do not exist for the sake of anything else other than themselves.[28]

Maimonides concludes unequivocally:

> To my mind, the correct view according to the beliefs of the Law [as well as according to (Aristotelian) philosophy] is as follows:... All the other beings do not exist for the sake of the existence of the human being ... All the other beings too have been intended for their own sakes and not for the sake of something else ... Thus, according to our view...that the world has been produced in time [after non-existence], the quest for the final end of all the species of beings collapses.[29]

As soon as he enunciates this unequivocal anti-teleological dictum, Maimonides immediately modifies it. Everything exists for its own sake, *but* "whenever the existence of something was impossible unless it was preceded by some other thing, [God] first brought that other thing into

---

[28] Maimonides (1963, 450–452; 1931, 325–326). On Ecclesiastes 8:4, cf. Maimonides (1963, 3.25: 505; 1931, 367). See Hadad (2011, 30–32) on internal and external final causes.
[29] Maimonides (1963, 452; 1931, 326).

existence – as in the case of the [five] senses, which precede reason."[30] This evidently means that Maimonides agrees with Aristotle that, for example, teeth exist for the sake of chewing. In *Guide* 3.25 he returns to this idea, and argues that the nutritional and sensorial faculties exist for the sake of the preservation of the animal.[31] In *Guide* 3.19 he affirms that the eye did not come to be by chance, but was created for the purpose of seeing.[32]

11.6 Biblical Proof Texts

Maimonides now cites biblical proof texts in support of the opinion that the human being is not the final end of the universe, and all natural species exist for their own sakes, not for the sake of something else.

He begins with Proverbs 16:4: "The Lord hath made everything *lamma'anehu*." This verse, he says, can be translated in two ways, and both disconfirm anthropocentrism. The first way: The Lord hath made everything for *its* own sake (with the suffix of *lamma'anehu* referring to the object). Alternatively: The Lord hath made everything for *His* sake, i.e., for His essence (with the suffix of *lamma'anehu* referring to the subject). Thus, everything was created for itself or for the divine Glory – but *not* for human beings.[33]

Next, Maimonides presents a striking textual argument from chapter 1 of Genesis. He asserts that if one examines this chapter, which concerns the Six Days of Creation, one finds that it is *never* said in it that any created being was created for the sake of another being. Each was created for its own sake alone. This is a strong anti-teleological claim. In defense of this claim, Maimonides cites a dictum that appears seven times in the chapter: "And God saw that it was *good*" (Genesis 1:4, 10, 12, 18, 21, 25, 31). "Good," according to Maimonides, means conforming to a purpose. When God says that the created world is "good," He means one of two things: it either conforms to *its* purpose or it conforms to *His* purpose.[34] The parallel between Maimonides' two interpretations of this divine dictum and his two interpretations of Proverbs 16:4 is obvious. God created everything for *its* or *His* sake, and every created thing conformed to *its* or *His* purpose. All the interpretations are anti-anthropocentric – that is, they all deny that things were created for the sake of human beings.

---

[30] Maimonides (1963, 452; 1931, 326).   [31] Maimonides (1963, 503–505; 1931, 366–367).
[32] Maimonides (1963, 478–479; 1931, 346). Cf. Maimonides (1963, 3.25: 504; 1931, 367).
[33] Maimonides (1963, 452–453; 1931, 327).   [34] Maimonides (1963, 453–454; 1931, 327).

Moreover, they all deny that some created things were created for the sake of others.

Having stated categorically that the Scriptural account of Creation *never* says that a created being was created for the sake of another created being, Maimonides turns to confront three problematic texts. These three texts seem to say that some created beings were created for the sake of others. First, according to Genesis 1:17–18, the heavenly bodies were created "to give light upon the earth and to rule over the day and the night." Second, according to Genesis 1:28, human beings were created "to have dominion over" the fish, birds, and beasts. Third, according to Genesis 1:29–30, God gave the plants to human beings and to other animals "for food."[35]

As for Genesis 1:17–18, Maimonides explains that it does *not* mean that the heavenly bodies were created *in order* to give light upon earth, but merely provides "information about their nature ... [and] utility." The verse is descriptive. It does not say that the sun, moon, and stars were created *in order* to give us light, but that in point of fact they do so. No teleology is mentioned in the verse.[36]

As for Genesis 1:28, Maimonides – as we would expect – interprets it similarly. Human beings were *not* created *for the purpose* of having dominion over the fish, birds, and beasts, but it is a fact that they dominate them. The verse gives "information." It does not speak of teleology.[37]

As for Genesis 1:29–30, Maimonides' interpretation is surprising and disappointing. According to a simple reading of these verses, God gave the plants to human beings and the other animals "for food." We should expect Maimonides to interpret this text in the same way he interpreted Genesis 1:17–18 and 1:28. He should say: Just as God did not create the heavenly bodies in order to give us light and did not create the human being in order to dominate the other animals, so too he did not create the vegetables in order to be food for animals. Rather, the verses merely give information: plants are eaten by animals. No teleology is implied. That's what we should have expected.

However, Maimonides does *not* interpret the text in this expected way. Instead, he writes: "As for the statement that [the plants] were given to human beings and the other animals [for food], Aristotle and others have said this explicitly, and it is manifest that the plants were brought into existence only *for the sake* of the animals, for these need to be

---

[35] Maimonides (1963, 454; 1931, 327).   [36] Maimonides (1963, 454; 1931, 327).
[37] Maimonides (1963, 454; 1931, 327). By rejecting the view that God created the human being to dominate the other animals, Maimonides may perhaps be seen as denying speciesism.

nourished."[38] Maimonides thus flatly contradicts his own anti-teleological exegesis of the Creation story! He had assured us that it is *never* stated in chapter 1 of Genesis that one being was created for the sake of another – but here he says that verses 29 and 30 teach that the plants were created for the sake of human beings and the other animals! This is an embarrassing contradiction. It is as if in the middle of his argument, Maimonides forgot what he was supposed to be proving.

Two explanations immediately suggest themselves as to why Maimonides chose not to interpret Genesis 1:29–30 in a non-teleological way. One is that he bowed to the authority of Aristotle, who is cited here as holding that plants exist for the sake of animals. A second explanation is found in the rule posited earlier in the chapter: everything exists for its own sake, *but* "whenever the existence of something was impossible unless it was preceded by some other thing, [God] first brought that other thing into existence – as in the case of the senses, which precede reason"; and nutrition (as noted in 3.25) is a necessary condition for the preservation of an animal. Whatever one thinks of these two explanations, they are relevant to the context.

Maimonides, however, gives a *third* explanation, which is irrelevant to the context. His explanation involves the Neoplatonic ontological principle that the superior does not serve the inferior. He tells us now that Genesis 1:17–18 needed to be reinterpreted, since according to its external sense the superior heavenly bodies serve the inferior earthlings, which contradicts the principle, but Genesis 1:29–30 has no need of such reinterpretation, since according to its external sense the inferior plants exist for the sake of the superior animals, which confirms the principle.[39] However, according to his explicit words in the previous paragraph, he did *not* reinterpret Genesis 1:17–18 because it seemed to contradict the principle that the superior does not serve the inferior, but because it seemed to bear witness that one being was created for the sake of another! He began arguing that Scripture does not teach teleology, but all of a sudden – and right in the middle of his exegesis – he somehow found himself arguing that Scripture does not teach that the superior serves the inferior!

To illustrate the principle that the superior does not serve the inferior, Maimonides relates a parable. A citizen may think the final end of the king is to protect his house at night from robbers. While the king does do that,

---

[38] Maimonides (1963, 454; 1931, 327. On Aristotle's opinion, see note 17, this essay.
[39] Maimonides (1963, 454; 1931, 327–328).

it is not the final end of his royal activities. God or the Active Intellect may be understood to be the king and the human being may be understood to be the citizen (cf. the parables in 1.46, 3.51 and 52).⁴⁰ The parable may also be understood to refer to Genesis 1:17–18: the human being is the king and the other animals represent the citizen. The parable is not anti-teleological, but rather anti-anthropocentric.

A hermeneutical rule is now set down by Maimonides: texts whose external sense (ẓāhir) suggests that something superior serves something inferior (e.g., Genesis 1:17–18) must be interpreted so as not to suggest it. A different hermeneutical rule had been presumed earlier in the chapter: texts whose external sense (ẓāhir) suggests final causality (e.g., Isaiah 40:22; 45:18; and Jeremiah 33:25) must be interpreted so as not to suggest it.⁴¹

How are we to understand Maimonides' abrupt shift from criticizing teleology to defending Neoplatonic ontology? Although the *Guide* is well-known for its riddles and conundrums, this shift seems too crude to be intentional. I imagine that in an early version of the discussion, Maimonides interpreted Genesis 1:17–18, 1:28, and 1:29–30 in connection with the principle that the superior does not serve the inferior; but at a later date – having developed his new critical approach to teleology – he decided to revise his interpretations and to turn them into part of his exegetical argument against final causality based on Genesis 1:1–31. The revision was not carried out thoroughly, and the exegetical argument against final causality was aborted in the middle. While Maimonides' critique of teleology belongs to the latest stage of his philosophic development, the affirmation of the principle that the superior does not serve the inferior is found already in his earliest writings.⁴² For Maimonides, the principle that the superior does not serve the inferior is associated with anti-anthropocentrism. However, the anti-anthropocentrism associated with Maimonides' critique of teleology is much more extreme.

After expounding the principle that the superior does not serve the inferior, Maimonides reverts momentarily to his critique of teleology, and writes: "[A]ll that exists [al-wujūd] was intended by His will. We shall seek for it ... no final end whatever. Just as we do not seek for the final end of His existence, so we do not seek for the final end of his will."⁴³

---

⁴⁰ Maimonides (1963, 454; 1931, 328). On king parables in the *Guide*, see Stern (2013, 168–181).
⁴¹ Maimonides (1963, 451, 454; 1931, 325, 328).
⁴² See Maimonides (1975, 121; 1992, 353). It is also found elsewhere in the *Guide*, e.g., Maimonides (1963, 2.11: 275; 1931, 191–192).
⁴³ Maimonides (1963, 454–455; 1931, 328).

Having pronounced these two short anti-teleological sentences, Maimonides returns to the principle that the superior does not serve the inferior. He proceeds to cite biblical verses (Isaiah 40:15; Job 4:18–19; 15:15–16) to prove that the heavenly bodies and the separate intellects do not exist for the sake of the human being. The human being, he asserts, is the most perfect being created out of corruptible matter, but he is "contemptible" in comparison with the heavenly bodies and the separate intellects.[44]

The final paragraph of the chapter alludes to the perplexity mentioned at the chapter's very beginning:

> When a person understands ... every being according to what it is, he becomes calm and his thoughts are not troubled by seeking a final end for what has no final end, or by seeking a final end for what has no final end except its own essence, which depends on the divine will, or if you prefer, the divine wisdom.[45]

In the preface to the *Guide*, Maimonides writes: "I claim to liberate that virtuous one from that into which he has sunk, and I shall guide him in his perplexity until he becomes perfect and he finds rest."[46] The critique of teleology is therapeutic, liberating. It turns perplexity into ataraxy.

11.7 Conclusion

I have tried to present in a simple way Maimonides' dizzying, conflicted, and audacious discussion of teleology and anthropocentrism in *Guide* 3.13. Maimonides argues in this chapter that, according to the respective principles of both Aristotle and the Law, the search for a final end of the universe is futile, and, moreover, all things exist for their own sakes and not for that of human beings or anything else. Although this is, according to Maimonides, what followers of Aristotle and the Law *should* maintain according to their principles, he knows very well they do not. The teachings of both Aristotle and the Law, as reported in this chapter, are in fact utterly teleological. According to both, the universe has an ultimate final end, all natural species in it have final ends, and plants exist for the sake of animals. In exposing the chasm between what followers of Aristotle and the Law should maintain according to their principles and what they actually do maintain, Maimonides was not, I think, merely interested in

---

[44] Maimonides (1963, 455–456; 1931, 328–329).
[45] Maimonides (1963, 456; 1931, 329). See Stern (2013, 184–186).
[46] Maimonides (1963, 16–17; 1931, 11).

drawing our attention to a curious or disconcerting fact. As an Aristotelian, he was presumably interested in correcting Aristotle, and as a Jew he was definitely interested in reinterpreting the Law. Explicit examples of such reinterpretation can be found in Maimonides' exegeses of Genesis 1:17–18; 1:28; Isaiah 40:22; 45:18; and Jeremiah 33:25 in this chapter.

Maimonides did not, however, deny final causality entirely. He held that the *first* final end of every individual is to realize the form of its species, and the *ultimate* final end of the species is its eternal preservation. He held, in other words, that the final end of everything is its own perfection. He also held that animal limbs have intended purposes: for example, teeth for chewing and eyes for seeing.[47] This presence of purpose in the universe is, in his view, a strong proof of the Creator.

---

[47] Cf. Pines (1963, lxxi, note 29): "[T]he general sense [of *Guide* 3.13] seems to suggest that within the domain of the investigations of the natural sciences teleological explanations may ... be valid only insofar as they concern the relation between the various parts of a living organism. ... The notion that one species of living being may exist for the sake of another species was emphatically not in line with the tendency of Maimonides' thought."

CHAPTER 12

Maimonides and the Problem(s) of Evil

David Shatz

One of the distinctive features of Maimonides' approach to the problem of evil is that he treats the problem not only from a metaphysical viewpoint, but from a psychological one as well. He blends philosophical, biblical, talmudic, and midrashic insight with psychological acumen, just as he does in his writings and communications to beleaguered communities and individuals.[1] In the area of theodicy, then, he tackles two sorts of issue: (1) How God could allow any evil; how, in particular, God could allow the righteous to suffer and the wicked to prosper and (2) How human beings should experience and cope with suffering and death, and behave in its presence. For example, they need to ask themselves whether their personal situations affect how they assess the amount of evil in the world, whether what they regard as evils are truly evils or instead just contrary to their interests, whether they are blaming God for evils they caused out of their own free will, and what they can do to better their condition. Maimonides sometimes commutes between the psychological and philosophical dimensions of the problem.[2]

As with other topics, Maimonides' discussions of evil are diffuse and variegated. Many different tropes and suggestions show their face in the *Guide*, some of which can be explored independently of others, which

---

I thank Warren Zev Harvey, Daniel Rynhold, Aaron Segal, and Josef Stern for their very helpful comments on an earlier draft and extensive email correspondence.

[1] I think especially of his communications on topics like persecution, conversion, and astrology, which reflect sensitivity to the individuals who sought him out and not only allegiance to formal Halakhah. See the three letters collected in *Crisis and Leadership* (Maimonides 1985) along with such missives as his *Letter on Astrology* and his responsum to Ovadayah the proselyte. See also Halbertal (2014, 7–91).

[2] Benor 1985 goes further, arguing that Maimonides is not seeking a solution to the theoretical problem of evil, but rather, at least in part, the sources of human judgments about evil. Philosophy plays the role of therapy. For Harvey 2005, Maimonides'"problem of evil" is how to make people act in conformity with reason. My arguments will point to a qualified version of the Benor-Harvey approach. (See also Halbertal 2014, 330.) That Maimonides blends philosophy and psychology was also stressed by Moshe Sokol in a lecture delivered on May 16, 2018, at Congregation Rinat Israel in Teaneck, New Jersey, and I thank him for conversation about that point.

perforce makes a presentation fragmented. Predictably, the texts in the *Guide* will contain inconsistencies (intended or not) and lead the reader to confusion and ... perplexity. So in what follows, rather than squeeze Maimonides' views on providence and evil into a Procrustean bed, I will assess seriatum several core philosophical and psychological ideas in Maimonides' treatment of suffering and theory of providence. I will raise questions both about the intrinsic merits of Maimonides' arguments and about the coherence and consistency of the chapters under discussion.

12.1 What Is Maimonides' Problem with Evil?

Maimonides endorses the Neoplatonic view that evil is a privation, one necessarily associated with matter. He broaches this idea in *Guide* 3.10–11, and is perhaps alluding to it later in the first of two chapters on *Job* (*Guide* 3:22).[3] But what problem is he trying to solve by asserting that evil is a privation or by other theodicies? Put another way: We have the answer(s). What is the question?

The *standard* problem of evil – of the sort put forth by Epicurus, David Hume, and others – can be constituted as a *reductio ad absurdum*:

(1) God is omniscient, omnipotent, and omnibenevolent. (Premise for *reductio*.)
(2) An omnipotent, omniscient and omnibenevolent being would not allow evil.
(3) But there is evil.
(4) Therefore God (as described in (1)) does not exist.

Much has been said about the problems with this argument.[4] But put those aside. For Maimonides, the argument ought to be almost a nonstarter, and ought to obviate constructing a theodicy. Why? Because clearly the argument operates with the notion that an omniscient being would know about any situation that, if left untreated, would create evil, and that an omnipotent being would have the power to prevent any evil. But

---

[3] Raffel (1987, 53) calls attention to a "curious claim" at the end of *Guide* 3.22: "As I see it now, I have analyzed the story of *Job* up to its ultimate end and conclusion" (Maimonides 1963, 490). The claim is curious because the discussion of *Job* continues for one more chapter. Raffel suggests why the claim is in fact proper.
[4] The philosophical consensus today is that premise 2 is false. An omnipotent, omniscient, and omnibenevolent being would not allow *unjustified* evil, but might allow *justified* evil. But if (2) is corrected to apply only to unjustified evil, (3) would have to establish that there is *unjustified* evil, and it is not clear how that can be achieved.

Maimonides interprets "God is omniscient" and "God is omnipotent" in line with negative theology (*Guide* 1.58). We cannot say anything affirmative about God, Indeed the categories of knowledge/ignorance and power/powerlessness do not apply to Him at all, just as (in his analogy) a wall cannot be properly characterized as sighted or blind. So we cannot affirm premise 2, or, if we do, our allegiance to it vanishes swiftly. Indeed, one of the reasons Gersonides objects to Maimonides' negative theology (Gersonides 1987, 107–115) is that, if we accept the extreme equivocity in Maimonides' understanding of God's attributes of essence, we cannot draw *any* valid inferences from "God is x," or, for that matter, deduce "God is x" from any premises.

Maimonides himself uses equivocity as a resolution to the problem of reconciling divine foreknowledge with human free will (*Guide* 3.20). But more to the point, he apparently applies equivocity to the problem of evil by referring to equivocity with respect to providence. Maimonides invokes Isaiah 55:8: "For My thoughts are not your thoughts, neither are your ways My ways, saith the Lord. For as the heavens are higher than the earth, so are My ways higher than your ways, and My thoughts than your thoughts." Thus, he writes, our knowledge "has only its name in common with His knowledge" (Maimonides 1963, 3.20: 483). He continues:

> It is accordingly true that the meaning of knowledge, the meaning of purpose, and the meaning of providence, when ascribed to us, are different from the meanings of these terms when ascribed to Him. When, therefore, the two providences or knowledges or purposes are taken to have one and the same meaning, the above mentioned difficulties and doubts arise. When, on the other hand, it is known that everything that is ascribed to us is different from everything ascribed to Him, truth becomes manifest ... . "Neither are your ways My ways." (Maimonides 1963, 3.20: 484)

So even if God knows particulars qua particulars and knows future contingents, this creates no problem for human free will, for His knowledge is different from ours, not just in its methods for acquiring truth, but in its very nature. Although it is not absolutely clear that Maimonides is addressing evil, God's attributes will not generate trouble in a putative problem of evil, and no theodicy is needed.[5] If Maimonides can barely

---

[5] Arguably, Maimonides' appeal to equivocity does not solve the foreknowledge-free will problem after all. For whatever "*God knows*" means, this much would seem to be true: If God knows that *p*, then *p*; and that is enough to generate the argument against human free will and force one to find a solution other than equivocity. Further, if God doesn't know that Reuven is scaling Mount Everest in a sense that entails that Reuven scales Mount Everest, isn't He inferior to us in that regard? To rebut the

construct the standard problem of evil because he uses negative theology to interpret *omniscient* and *omnipotent*, what problem(s) *is* the privation thesis and other theodic suggestions[6] meant to solve? In *Guide* 3.16 he constructs a challenge that is like the traditional objection from evil. To wit: Because of "what at first sight" is a "lack of order in the circumstances of the human individuals and the fact that among the Adamites some excellent individuals are in a sorry and grievous plight whereas some wicked individuals are in good and pleasurable circumstances,"[7] we must say that either:

(i) God sets things in perfect order, or
(ii) He is incapable of establishing order and has no power over things, or
(iii) He knows about the disorder and has the power to establish order, "but neglects to do it in consequence of His disdain and contempt or in consequence of His jealousy," just as we might find in the case of a human being who possesses an "ill-nature" and "wickedness" and "jealousy." (Maimonides 1963, 3.16: 461–462)

Maimonides scales down this argument to an attack on omniscience, which of course will invite the response: the term *know* is equivocal.[8] But let us explore a different construction of the problem, built on possibility (iii), namely, might a challenge be constructed as an attack on divine goodness? Certainly Maimonides invokes divine goodness enough times to make this a possible crux of an objection from evil (e.g., Maimonides 1963, 3.10: 440, 3.12: 441, 3.12: 447); and seemingly such an attack would necessitate a theodic response like the privation thesis. So let us

---

objection, Maimonides may hold that the type of knowledge God has and/or the objects of His knowledge are superior to the type and objects of knowledge we have, and the two types are incompatible. (I thank Aaron Segal and Zev Harvey for, independently, suggesting this rejoinder.)
  There are inconsistencies in the *Guide* with regard to whether we can describe God's knowledge, whether He knows particulars, and if so, whether He knows them qua particulars. See Broadie 1989; Davies (2011, 85–105); Rudavsky (2010, 150); Ivry (2016, 180–82).

[6] Maimonides at times seems to be advocating a "greater good" theodicy.

[7] And again three chapters later: "the prophets have already mentioned that the ignorant infer that the deity has no knowledge of our actions merely from the fact that they see wicked people living in prosperity and abundance" (Maimonides 1963, 3.19: 477). They think God "lacks apprehension" because "the circumstances of the human individual, which by their nature are contingent, are not well ordered" (Maimonides 1963, 3.19: 479).

[8] To be more precise, as Josef Stern has pointed out, the objector's argument is characterized as one concerning "disorder," not evil, where disorder refers to a lack of fit between people's conduct and their life circumstances – in other words, a lack of justice; and disorder contradicts providence. This alleged disorder is a type of evil, however, and the problems are similar enough that I believe it is justified to proceed further.

explore the hypothesis that, for Maimonides, one problem of evil is to reconcile God's *goodness*, taken in isolation from His other attributes, with the existence of evil.

But evil cannot be shown to be a problem for belief in God's goodness, unless we assume something Maimonides cannot, namely, that God is omnipotent and omniscient in the ordinary meanings of the terms. For without this assumption, if one asks, "All God's actions are good according to theism, so how can there be evil in the world?" the answer could be: "God is not omniscient or omnipotent in the ordinary sense. Consequently, even if He is good in the ordinary sense, He may not know about everything or have the power to change anything, in the ordinary sense. No human categories apply to Him." Once again, the standard problem of evil is almost a nonstarter.

Another important question in formulating this good-centered version of the problem of evil is what God's goodness means for Maimonides. *Good* appears neither on the list of thirteen attributes of action in *Guide* 1.54 nor among the negative attributes in *Guide* 1.58. Yet Scripture many times describes God as good. "Thank the Lord because He is good, His lovingkindness is forever" (Psalms 136:1) and "Taste and see that the Lord is good" (Psalms 34:9). So, in Scripture *tov* is an attribute of God. But in which category would this attribute fall – action or essence? Might it be the case that it falls into neither, or that Maimonides does not consider *good* an attribute of God?[9]

If *good* is understood as an attribute of essence, we cannot know anything about what God's being good implies, so there is no problem of evil. Perhaps *good* is instead an attribute of action. Admittedly, it is not on Maimonides' list of attributes of action in *Guide* 1.54, but that is because *Guide* 1.54 is built around the list of the specific thirteen attributes Moses comes to know in Exodus 34, and the list in Exodus 34 seems not to be exclusive: "Scripture has restricted itself to mentioning only those 'thirteen characteristics', although [Moses] apprehended 'all His goodness' [*kol tuvi, all My goodness*] – I mean to say all His actions" (Exodus 33:19; cf. Maimonides 1963, 1.54: 124–125). So, despite its absence from Exodus 34,[10] goodness may still be an attribute of action.

---

[9] See the valuable discussion in Lobel (2011) of numerous issues surrounding Maimonides' conception of good. She emphasizes that for Maimonides God *is* the good (and goodness).

[10] In fact, might "good" be an umbrella term that encompasses mercy, lovingkindness, graciousness and the other attributes of action? This was suggested by Daniel Rynhold. I will set aside the point that "all My goodness" may refer to all created beings, since existence itself is a good.

If *good* is an attribute of action, it would mean: God performs actions such that, if a human being performed those actions, we would call that human being "good."[11] *Good* may seem to differ from most other attributes of action, because the thirteen attributes that were revealed to Moses in Exodus 34 are either psychological attributes – "aptitudes of the soul" – when ascribed to human beings (compassionate, merciful, full of lovingkindness) or are *explicitly* descriptions of actions (He extends *chesed*). However, even if we don't regard *good* as a psychological trait, this would not preclude *good*'s being analyzable in terms of actions (and ultimately, natural processes). And if we agree that God produces goodness, and indeed that existence is good (Maimonides 1963, 3.10: 440), does this not make *good* ripe for an analysis in terms of action?

Some other texts are relevant to this discussion. Notwithstanding Maimonides' use of negative theology when he discusses evil (*Guide* 3.20), in some passages he appears to understand certain attributes in their ordinary sense when examining the problem of evil. Thus, in *Guide* 3.16 (Maimonides 1963, 461–464), he doesn't say that *powerful* is equivocal, though in *Guide* 1.58 he included it as an attribute of essence, and hence to be understood by means of negative theology. In *Guide* 3.12 (Maimonides 1963, 446) he appears to regard God as omnipotent (and powerful) in the ordinary sense. The passage from *Guide* 3.20 (Maimonides 1963, 483–484), by contrast, answers using negative theology. So Maimonides' discussion leaves us with numerous questions besides those considered so far.

And there are more. Consider *Guide* 1.2. Maimonides there famously analyzes the Bible's statement that Adam and Eve became "knowers of good and evil" (*yode'ei tov va-ra*; Pines translates it as "the fine and the

---

[11] For Maimonides, divine actions are natural processes (see especially *Guide* 2.48, the examples in *Guide* 1.54 (Maimonides 1963, 125–127), and the opening of *Guide* 3.32), albeit God is the First Cause. So ultimately, if *good* is an attribute of action, "God is good" means: natural processes are such that if they were human actions, they would be described as good.

I thank Warren Zev Harvey and Josef Stern for valuable discussions of how good is to be understood vis-à-vis God (along with other questions). Stern argued (in correspondence) that good is not an attribute of God, because if it were, then why not say that "Tzelem Elohim" (being in God's image), which in *Guide* 1:1 is understood to refer to intellect, would instead refer to being *good*, which is difficult because of Maimonides' gloss on the Garden of Eden episode in *Guide* 1.2. In my discussion I am considering possibilities for considering goodness as a divine attribute, because if "good" is not an attribute of God, the verses I cited from Psalms generate an objection to Maimonides' view.

bad").[12] He explains that unlike knowledge of "the true and the false" (metaphysical and scientific truths), judgments of what is good and what is evil reflect (mere) social conventions. Now, Rambam's analysis of the Eden story has led interpreters, often in conjunction with the definition of "good" as "conforms to a purpose" (cf. Maimonides 1963, 3.13: 453), to characterize his view of good and evil as relative, or as subjective, or as both. These terms may be inaccurate or simplistic as characterizations of Maimonides' view of "good," but this should not obscure the key point – that he denigrates the status of judgments of good and evil; they are products of imagination, not intellect. If so, the problem of evil seems to dissipate. So do we really need a theodicy?[13]

Moreover, if knowing good is a lower state than knowing of the true and the false, how should we evaluate the assertion that whatever God produces is good? Nonetheless, Maimonides himself maintains that certain things are of genuine value – notably knowledge of the intelligibles, and all that proceeds from God. Apparently some truths about good and evil (e.g. those about human perfection and the goal humans should pursue) are subject to demonstration, while others are not. The intellect can determine values; good and bad are not *in every case* products of imagination (*Guide* 3.8). This may reinstate the problem of evil. There will still be many judgments of good and evil that are products of imagination, but the problem of evil will focus on evils that the intellect regards as evil.

What is the upshot? (a) For Maimonides the problem of evil is not the standard one; he can dispense with the standard problem handily – for if we do not know what God's omniscience and omnipotence are, why is there a problem of evil?; (b) although Maimonides at points constructs the problem of evil as primarily an attack on omniscience, one problem he seems to incur is reconciling God's *goodness* with the ostensible fact that evil exists. But this reconciliation is needed only if God is understood to be omnipotent and omniscient in the ordinary sense of the term – which He is not, for Maimonides. Maimonides' negative theology once again preempts the problem of evil; (c) *good*, if conceived as an attribute of God, is

---

[12] On Maimonides' various evaluative terms, see Kreisel (1999, 108–113); Maimonides (2002a, 33, note 15); and Rynhold (Essay 4 in this volume). (In *Guide* 1.2 Maimonides is speaking primarily of good and bad actions, not good and bad states of affairs, events, or things; and the chapter is speaking of communities' judgments, not individuals'.) Authors who argue that there is more to Maimonides' view of good than *Guide* 1.2 include Stern 2013; Harvey 1986; Klein-Braslavy 1987; Kreisel (1999, 93–124); Lobel 2011; Rynhold (Essay 4, this volume).

[13] Benor 1985 answers in the negative, so for him, Maimonides is not posing a philosophical problem at all, but instead a psychological one.

best construed as an attribute of action; and (d) Maimonides' account of good and evil in *Guide* 1.2 prima facie dissolves the problem of evil, but other ("intellectualist") aspects in his account may restore it.

12.2 Matter and the Inexorability of Evil

Maimonides' thesis that evil is merely a privation, an absence of good (a position adopted also by Augustine), is often regarded as the least satisfying part of his account of evil. Are the screaming and writhing and bleeding and death of victims of an explosion or a mass shooting mere privations?

There are further problems with using "evil is a privation" as a solution to the problem of evil. Presumably, "evil is a privation" is meant to get God off the hook. But if the thesis gets God off the hook, and absolves Him of responsibility, why doesn't it also absolve human beings of producing evil? After all, evil is just a privation.

The answer to this last challenge is that it rests on a simplistic understanding of Maimonides. It distorts the concepts of matter and privation, and ignores some remarks Maimonides makes about causation.

Throughout the *Guide*, matter – conceived of as the body and its impulses (appetites and desires) – is the archvillain.[14] It presents ontological, epistemological, and psychological barriers. "All passing-away and corruption or deficiency," including human illness and death, "are due solely to matter" (Maimonides 1963, 3.8: 431). On the epistemological level, matter "is a strong veil preventing the apprehension of that which is separate from matter as it truly is . . . ." (Maimonides 1963, 3.9: 437; cf. Maimonides 1963, 1.49: 109). An individual's intellectual achievement depends on the particular matter with which that person is endowed and the distribution of the elements (Maimonides 1963, 2.36: 369–370). Some people's composition is such that "to make an effort for their benefit is pure ignorance" (Maimonides 1963, 1.34: 77). Matter prevents not only apprehension of truth, however, but also the *concentration* on the truth that one has apprehended (Stern 2013; Shatz 2009). Intellect's foil – imagination – is a *corporeal* faculty.

Matter (as the body) also produces sin and vice, to wit: "All man's acts of disobedience and sins" (Maimonides 1963, 3.8: 431), and "all the hindrances keeping man from his ultimate perfection" (Maimonides

---

[14] In contrast to matter conceived as body, there is nothing evil about matter when it is the locus of potentiality or the elements or substratum. My thanks to Josef Stern for stressing this distinction. On Maimonides' various understandings of matter, see Stern (2013, 97–131).

1963, Introduction: 13). Concomitantly, commandments and prohibitions "are only intended to quell the impulses of matter" (Maimonides 1963, 3.8: 433). Matter (and being embodied) is the object of shame for humans (Maimonides 1963, 3.8: 432–434; 3.52). Maimonides' asceticism in the *Guide*[15] goes hand in hand with this denigration of matter.

Yet, matter's evil character does not make Maimonides deny the goodness of creation. Contrary to Al-Razi, he maintains that there is more good than evil in creation; nor does he deny that some people have the "divine gift" (Maimonides 1963, 3.8: 433) of excellent and suitable matter. He also argues that matter has redeeming value: "Divine wisdom has made it obligatory that there should be no coming-to-be except through passing-away. Were it not for the passing-away of the individuals, the coming-to-be relating to the species would not continue (Maimonides 1963, 3.10: 440; 3.12: 443). For Maimonides, existence is itself a good (Maimonides 1963, 3.10: 440):[16] "His being the absolute good and regarding all that proceeds from Him being indubitably an absolute good" (Maimonides 1963, 3.12: 442, 447). For all that, matter still wreaks its havoc.

Note also that "the nature and the true reality of matter is that it never ceases to be joined to privation," which in turn means that "no form remains constantly in it, for it perpetually puts off one form and puts on another" (Maimonides 1963, 3.8: 430–431). As Josef Stern puts it, "Matter never rests; each form actualized only generates a new privation..." (Stern 2013, 116; see also Maimonides 1963, 1.17: 43 and 1.28: 61). Drawing on his parabolic reading of verses in Proverbs 6:26–7:21, Maimonides depicts matter as a married harlot, who "never ceases to seek for another man to substitute for her husband, and she deceives and draws him on in every way until he obtains from her what her husband used to obtain" (Maimonides 1963, 3.8: 431).

Let's return to our question: Why does God get off the hook because evil is a privation, while a human being cannot rightly claim, "I didn't do anything, evil is just a privation"? The answer is: God cannot alter the nature of matter as He created it, while human beings can alter their intellectual level and achievement. Regarding the former, Maimonides devotes an entire chapter (Maimonides 1963, 3.15: 459–461) to the question of what an omnipotent being must be able to do. Can He do the logically impossible? Can He transform "a substance into an accident

---

[15] Kreisel (1999, 175–182).
[16] See Lobel 2011 for a development of this Maimonidean contention. It is not always clear whether he is referring to being as a totality or to each individual existent.

and an accident into substance" (Maimonides 1963, 3.15: 459–460)? Can He annihilate Himself? While Maimonides acknowledges that it is difficult to draw a line between intellect and imagination so as to perfectly distinguish, in every instance, the impossible from the possible (Maimonides 1963, 3.15: 460), he believes that God cannot perform the logically impossible. Because matter is *necessarily* associated with privation and evil, God cannot be faulted for matter's evil; God is not responsible. By contrast, human beings can be faulted for the privation of knowledge. Why? Because "these great evils that come about between the human beings who inflict them upon one another ... are all of them likewise consequent upon privation. For all of them derive from ignorance, I mean from a privation of knowledge" (Maimonides 1963, 3.11: 440).[17]

The distinction between matter (whose evil nature cannot be changed by God) and human choice is less firm than might appear. Matter (body) is a cause of bad behavior, and recall (Maimonides 1963, 1.34: 77) that matter constrains what a person can achieve, which should diminish responsibility. More fundamentally, though, one might ask why human beings had to be composed of matter.[18] "Whatever he may think," writes Alfred Ivry, Maimonides fails to "absolve God of responsibility for evil in the universe, or for any of the privations that matter forces upon form" (Ivry 2016, 174). Even granting that "it is impossible for matter to exist without form and for any of the forms in question to exist without matter" (Maimonides 1963, 3.8: 432–433), Maimonides needs to explain *why* form has to be accompanied by matter. Maimonides in fact affirms the existence of beings, specifically God and the separate intellects, who are not made of matter.[19]

Several scholars suggest that the answer to the challenge, "why did God create matter?" is an application of the "static" version of the Principle of Plenitude. For the universe to be good, all sorts of beings must exist – pure

---

[17] Warren Zev Harvey, Daniel Rynhold, and Aaron Segal all suggested to me something along the lines sketched in this paragraph. I am not sure that *Guide* 3.11 says everything that I have packed into it, but the reading fits Maimonidean themes about free will. Human beings are responsible for not attaining knowledge. In *Guide* 3.11 Maimonides speaks about free will not as the ability to conform one's will to the truths and values one accepts, but rather to the knowledge of truths and values.

In *Guide* 3.13 (Maimonides 1963, 449), Maimonides states that according to Aristotle – who believes in the eternity of the universe – all things derive from "natural necessity" and "it is not permitted to ask," among other questions, "why matter is as it is." But cf. *Guide* 2.25, where it is the believer in creation who need not supply an answer to certain other questions that Aristotle must answer.

[18] See Nadler (2009, 630); Rudavsky (2010, 140).

[19] But regarding separate intellects, cf. Stern (2013, 250–305).

intellects, human beings (intellect plus matter), and entities like rocks (matter without intellects).[20] Since existence is a good, God produces as much good (as many things, or types of thing) as possible: "The entire purpose consists in bringing into existence the way you see it everything whose existence is possible" (Maimonides 1963, 3.25: 504; see also 3.25: 506). Humans occupy a specific niche on a hierarchy; the niche must remain. Those who realize the impact of matter want to be angels/pure form, but (one explanation) they ignore the value of having diverse types of entities in the world, or (another explanation) they indulge a fantasy of the imagination, namely, that it is possible *for them*, embodied humans, to be immaterial intellects. But another candidate for an explanation of why Maimonides holds that matter must exist is the idea quoted earlier, namely: "Were it not for the passing-away of the individuals, the coming-to-be relating to the species would not continue" (Maimonides 1963, 3.12: 443; see also 3.10: 440; 1.72: 188–190; 1.28: 61). The two explanations are connected, however: the first (using the Principle of Plenitude) explains *why* generating a "coming-to-be" is good.[21] Maimonides would be providing a "greater good" theodicy, and *may* be saying that evil doesn't truly exist. So he is not without replies to the challenge that God should not have created matter. Indeed, he is proffering just such a reply when he argues that matter is necessary for generating new existents.

Maimonides "exonerates" God in another way: he creates a causal and intentional distance between God and evil. Given that God is the *ultimate* cause of things, and "works" through natural causes, causal distance is present whenever any event or phenomenon is said to be caused by God. But Maimonides goes beyond this, saying that "the act of an agent can in no way be connected to privation," and that an agent produces the privation only by accident. Further, "God does not have a primary intention to produce evil" (Maimonides 1963, 3.10: 440). Once again, we wonder why humans cannot avail themselves of the same defense. Consider people who ruin their health by doing foolish things, but didn't intend to produce that evil of bad health. Are they as off the hook as God is? And what if someone creates a monster? Have they created a good by bringing a being into existence? What if someone produces a privation "by

---

[20] Thus Benor (1985, 8); Kreisel (1997, 469); Lobel (2011, 5; 9; 38) and Reines (1972, 201–205). The principle is explored by Lovejoy (1936, 52). A different version of the Principle of Plenitude, endorsed in *Guide* 2.1 (Maimonides 1963, 247) and *Guide* 3.25 (Maimonides 1963, 506; 509), is that over an infinite period of time all possibilities must be realized; cf. Manekin (1988); Stern (Essay 10, this volume).

[21] Daniel Rynhold suggested this connection in correspondence.

accident" – as collateral damage? These problems challenge us to distinguish humans from God with respect to a justification for creating evils. But the very framing of the problem this way overlooks an important issue: equivocity. Does Maimonides, the champion of equivocal theological predication, imagine that "intention" applied to God means the same as when applied to humans? Assuming not, the asymmetry problem may disappear. But how to analyze "intention" as applied to God is obviously an impressive challenge.[22]

A risk in critiquing details of a thinker's approach is that the critic will miss the forest for the trees. Warren Zev Harvey describes the forest – the significance of Maimonides' approach to evil – by defending Maimonides against a charge leveled by Gershom Scholem: that (in Harvey's paraphrase) the formula "evil is a privation" is a failure to acknowledge the reality of evil and is an evasion of a pressing problem. The Kabbalists acknowledged – even celebrated – the reality of evil. Hence, for Scholem, "whereas the Kabbalists had something important to say to suffering human beings, philosophy did not" (Harvey 2005, 195).

Harvey argues that Scholem's assessment is wrong. In Kabbalah, evil is due to the *sitra achra*, the "other side" – an external power. But for Maimonides, evil results from human ignorance. Irrational human beings produce evils; rational individuals do not. Now, if Satan, the *sitra achra*, causes evil, doesn't that diminish human responsibility? And doesn't it leave human beings without knowledge of how to correct their conduct?

> [The Maimonideans] were concerned about human *responsibility*....They insisted that the source of the evils that human beings inflict upon another is not in some external Satan, but inside the human beings themselves. Since the source of evils is human, we humans can prevent them. We are *responsible*. One can prevent evils by acting in accordance with reason. (Harvey 2005, 199)

For Maimonides, Harvey suggests, the "problem of evil," is not a metaphysical one, but a psychological and political problem, viz. how to get people to behave rightly and remove the privation.[23]

In line with this approach, note that Maimonides sets out three sources of suffering: (a) matter; (b) the evils that people inflict upon others; (c) the

---

[22] Indeed, in correspondence, Josef Stern proposed a solution to this problem of asymmetry based on a reading of *Guide* 3.10 that undercuts thinking of God as if He were a human agent in need of exoneration. But for purposes of this essay, I will rest content with putting the asymmetry problem out there, together with the obvious question of what Maimonides' language about "intention" means.
[23] Cf. Benor (1985, 7–8).

evils that people inflict upon themselves, often by desiring luxuries and by failure to care for their health. This last category, he says, is often the largest; and clearly the solution is for people to change in thought and deed (which is also true of (b)).

We shall now turn to a related feature of Maimonides' concept of responsibility – its naturalism.

12.3 Naturalistic Justice

Maimonides is generally characterized as a naturalist. On this account, he denies that God directly intervenes in nature and instead believes that events are explicable entirely by natural laws. Maimonides' naturalism would at first appear to negate the traditional doctrine of *sakhar va-onesh* (reward and punishment). This ostensible denial of divine retribution feeds a widespread perception: that Maimonides did not believe in what was later called *hashgahah peratit* (individual providence), but believed only in general providence (the general teleology in nature, including the specific laws that operate and the way human beings are equipped for exploration of nature). But the perception that he denied individual providence and retributivism in particular is mistaken. Let me explain.

Maimonides famously identifies five theories of providence: those of Epicurus, Aristotle, the Asharites, the Mutazilites, and, finally, a fifth view. This last, as Charles Raffel emphasizes, subdivides into three: "our opinion, I mean the opinion of our Law"; "the view of some of our latter-day scholars"; and "my view" (Raffel 1987, 37–51). "Our opinion" is that human beings have free will and "all the calamities that befall men and all of the good things that come to men, be it a single individual or a group, are all of them determined according to the deserts of the men concerned through equitable judgment in which there is no injustice whatever" (Maimonides 1963, 3.17: 469). The view of "some of our latter-day scholars" (Maimonides 1963, 3.17: 469), which Maimonides rejects, endorses the doctrine of "sufferings of love" (*Berakhot* 5a), i.e. sometimes people undergo misfortune for the sake of increasing their reward.[24] "My view" turns out to be a variant, or a fleshing out, of the retributivist-sounding "our opinion." "My view" is that "providence is consequent upon the intellect." (Maimonides 1963, 3.17: 469–474)

Strangely, whereas the Babylonian Talmud explicitly rejects, at least in part, the statement of Rabbi Ammi that "there is no death without sin, no

---

[24] This view was earlier attributed to the Mutazilites.

suffering without transgression," Maimonides affirms this principle and gives it centrality.[25] How we can make sense of Maimonides adopting a retributivist principle, given his naturalist commitments? The answer is that Maimonides accepts Rabbi Ammi's retributivist principle, but alters the usual understanding of it. "Sin" and "transgression" in the first instance seem to refer to what we would call behavioral infractions, but for Maimonides there are intellectual infractions – errors, cognitive failures, ignorance – many of which cause behavioral infractions or result from them. The ultimate effect of these infractions – and at times their ultimate cause – is intellectual error, cognitive failure. Thus, "providence is consequent upon [and "graded" according to] the intellect" (*Guide* 3.17; 3.18). In a celebrated example, he argues that although a ship's sinking can be explained without reference to human choice and desert (it is merely a natural occurrence, assuming no human error), a person's boarding the ship could be explained as an act of justice. Each person who perished, or stayed home, received his just deserts (Maimonides 1963, 3.17: 472). The "rule" of divine justice "cannot be attained by our intellects," but we may say that each individual's choice to board reflected poor *practical* reasoning (see Raffel 1987, 56–71).

Thus, on the one hand, Maimonides sounds highly conservative in accepting a retributivist outlook, even while some rabbinic views reject it as a picture of this world;[26] on the other hand, there are two features that break with tradition. First, intellectual achievement is the criterion for virtuous and sinful conduct. Second, the connection between good conduct and reward so construed, and between sin and punishment so construed, is natural – that is, not dependent on divine intervention.

A showcase example of how sin in the form of intellectual error can produce evil via a natural process arises in a letter about astrology that Maimonides wrote in response to some French rabbis, in which Maimonides roundly rejected and derogated astrology on both scientific and religious grounds.[27] Why was the Temple destroyed and the Jews exiled? Because the Jews had astrology direct their lives and "did not learn the art of war and the conquest of lands." Note: It's not that God zapped

---

[25] The Babylonian Talmud's rejection of Rabbi Ammi may be limited; see Shatz (2009, 266–267, n. 48, and the sources cited there). My hunch, however, is that Maimonides straight-out ignored the rejection. The Midrash (*Va-Yiqra Rabbah* 37:1, *Qohelet Rabbah* 5:4) cites R. Ammi but does not reject him, and perhaps that is Maimonides' warrant for accepting R. Ammi.

[26] See *Moed Qatan* 28a, *Kiddushin* 40a, discussed in Shatz (2009, 272–274 and accompanying notes).

[27] See Marx (1926). Maimonides does not tell us what proofs he refers to; on this question, see Freudenthal (1993) and Langermann (1991a). See most recently E. Harvey (2019).

the Jews because they committed the sin of astrology, expelling them from the Temple and their land. Rather, living life according to (prohibited) nonsensical practices and ignoring rational strategies for the art of war and the conquest of lands naturally led to the people's loss of their land and temple.[28] Another example of natural retribution is "Laws of Character Traits" (*Mishneh Torah Hilkhot De'ot*) 4:20. There, having presented an array of medical prescriptions, Maimonides self-assuredly "guarantees," with certain qualifications, that anyone who follows the prescriptions will never fall ill until old age.

Thus, Maimonides sought to develop Rabbi Ammi's retributivist approach within a naturalistic framework. But the obvious question is, how can intellectual achievement be protective if God does not intervene in nature to provide rewards for the intellectually accomplished?

Maimonides presents us with three models to explain the connection.[29] The first, just mentioned, is scientific: people with knowledge of how the world operates will protect themselves from harm. The obvious question, though, arises: don't great scientists die from accidents, cancers, and heart attacks, even if they have been vigilant about guarding their health? This problem is acknowledged by not only his commentators, but Maimonides himself when he writes, "the wronged man has no device against them [his attackers]" (Maimonides 1963, 3.12: 444). It is good to bear in mind that people cannot know all the consequences of their actions.

Certainly scientific knowledge often keeps people safe. However, Maimonides has other possibilities in mind when he speaks about "providence is according to the intellect." We turn to a second model, which Raffel (1987) calls "psychic immunity," which could be brought about by what I call "the axiological shift."

The Stoic philosopher Epictetus wrote, "What upsets people is not things themselves but their judgments about the things .... So when we are thwarted or upset, let us never blame someone else but rather ourselves, that is, our own judgments" (Epictetus 1983, [section 5]). Emotions reflect judgments; if the person would change the judgment, the emotion would change from, say, grief, to the desirable state of *apatheia*. Accordingly, Epictetus presents strategies for attaining *apatheia*. In the case of a loved one who has died, Epictetus offers a redescription of external reality, a redescription that prevents distress – "She was given back." Distress may be prevented also by an *axiological shift*, a change in

---

[28] See also *Mishneh Torah, Laws of Idolatry* 11:16.   [29] See Raffel (1987); also Reines (1972).

one's value system. If a small child is distraught over a broken toy, parents might teach the child that toys are not important.

In sharp relief to the Stoics, Maimonides thinks that human beings can have a significant effect on their external circumstances (W. Z. Harvey 2005; Benor 1985, 12–13). He is, in fact, an activist in the critical areas of medicine and politics. Yet he shares with the Stoics the idea that a shift in perception can create affective changes. Maimonides wants not merely a shift in perception, categorization, and evaluation, but a shift toward a *correct* perception, categorization, and evaluation. An axiological shift is the key to Job's ending up untroubled: Job's reaction, "The Lord has given, the Lord has taken away" (*Job* 1:21) encapsulates a correct attitude.

> But when he knew God with a certain knowledge, he admitted that true happiness, which is the knowledge of the Deity, is guaranteed to all who know Him and that a human being cannot be troubled in it by any of all the misfortunes in question. While he had known God only through the traditional stories and not by way of speculation, Job had imagined that the things thought to be happiness, such as health, wealth, and children, are the ultimate goal. For this reason he fell into such perplexity and said such things as he did. (Maimonides 1963, 3.23: 492–493)

Job's shift in perception results from a shift in the method of belief-formation: from reliance on traditional stories to the use of "speculation."

Not to be neglected, however, is the sheer fact that Job is *overwhelmed*. He realizes his insignificance in the scheme of things. Maimonides proposes a shift not only in values, but in theology. In consonance with God's revelation to Job, he believes that the root error is imagining "that His knowledge is like our knowledge and His providence and His governance are like our purpose and our providence and our governance." Once one realizes this error, "every misfortune will be borne lightly by him" (Maimonides 1963, 3.23: 497). Maimonides states that Job's shift to negative theology and the gulf between God and humans led him to tranquility. Thus providence is consequent upon the intellect – in this case, theoretical reason (not *phronesis*) leads the sufferer to an axiological and theological shift that is correct and brings psychic immunity.

The two ideas mentioned so far – that scientific knowledge protects a person and that a shift in values and theology provides psychic immunity – invite troubling objections. Both models imply that, in addition to nonhuman animals, children and adults lacking certain capacities do not enjoy providence. To which Maimonides could reply *in hakhi nammi* ("just so") i.e. indeed, they do not. Another problem as regards the axiological shift, though, is that the losses Job has suffered are of such a type that it is macabre to argue that what he has lost – health, children – is not of real significance. Are these not important? Maimonides himself elsewhere grants that good health is conducive to intellectual achievement. His assessment of matter in the *Guide* seems less commonsensical than his recognition in his legal writings of how health, wealth, and political security facilitate intellectual achievement. That is precisely why God promises these goods for those who observe the commandments. Having received those goods, agents will be in a setting in which they can better perform the commandments.[30]

Thus, the axiological-shift theodicy cannot be a *comprehensive* one; it can apply only when the apparent evils are truly goods, and goods like health and children are properly appreciated *as* goods. Maimonides would view this reply as question-begging, but at some point a critic is entitled to use his or her value judgments to assess a theory. Worse, if material goods are not important and (various) spiritual ones are, then just as we should devalue suffering in our own case, why should we not do so in the case of *other* sufferers? Yet neglect of others' suffering is contrary to ethics and Halakhah (including Maimonidean Halakhah). Additionally, Judaism generally bids human beings to enjoy God's material world. The axiological shift moves us toward asceticism.[31] Now, Maimonides is perfectly entitled to embrace asceticism, and does so in the *Guide*,[32] but if we are looking for a convincing response to evil, a stance that justifies asceticism would have only a limited audience.[33] There is little question that shifting perception or axiology in the way Maimonides suggests is likely to calm someone who has suffered loss. But it would do so at the cost of taking away one's humanity.[34]

Thus far we have seen two models of naturalistic providence: scientific knowledge that protects one from physical evil, and philosophical knowledge of true value that provides one with psychic immunity. But a passage on providence in *Guide* 3.51 creates great difficulties for naturalistic readings of Maimonides, and may demand a third model.

---

[30] See *Mishneh Torah, Laws of Repentance*, chapter 9. Both the realization of the messianic age and the occurrence of prophecy depend on material conditions (see, respectively, *Mishneh Torah, Laws of Kings* 11–12 and *Laws of the Foundations of the Torah* 7; see also Maimonides 1963, 2.32: 362). However, human choices can shape their material conditions (*Guide* 3.11).

[31] This was pointed out to me by Daniel Rynhold.   [32] See Kreisel (1999, 175–182).

[33] This paragraph borrows from Shatz (2013).

[34] See Nussbaum (2018, 359–401). Stern (2013, 347–349) deals with the ideal of the impassive leader in Maimonides (1963, 1.54: 126–128).

The chapter begins with Maimonides asserting that "the chapter contains nothing new ... it is only a kind of conclusion." He contradicts this statement later in the chapter, when he writes: "An extraordinary speculation has occurred to me just now"! To wit: even a person who has achieved intellectual comprehension will enjoy providence only when occupied completely with God. If his thought is "free from distraction," then "that individual cannot be afflicted with evil of any kind. For he is with God and God is with him." If he is distracted, however, "he becomes in consequence of this a target for every evil that may happen to befall him" (Maimonides 1963, 3.51: 625). Maimonides affirms complete protection for such an individual, to the point where (quoting Psalms 91:7–8) if you pass a battlefield, "even if one thousand were killed to your left and ten thousand to your right, no evil at all would befall you" (Maimonides 1963, 3.51: 626–627).

In 1199 Samuel ibn Tibbon wrote to Maimonides for clarification of this passage. Taken on its face, the passage posits a supernatural act by God that protects the righteous person even when armies flank him on both sides and all those around him fall. How else could an individual survive in those circumstances? Yet what happens to the naturalism of the earlier treatment? No reply by Maimonides to Ibn Tibbon has been discovered.

Some options for handling the problem are:

(a) Maimonides is truly doing an about-face. He is embracing a supernaturalist metaphysics for certain people and circumstances.

(b) His portrayal is an esotericist move, meant to *mislead* people into thinking he is doing what (a) describes.

(c) He is maintaining, as he did earlier, that because the person has achieved intellectual perfection, he will know how to guard himself and perhaps escape even in extreme circumstances; and/or that the person attains psychological immunity (which is Ibn Tibbon's favored interpretation).

(d) Since such protection seems unlikely in the battle scenario that the Psalmist depicts, there is some other naturalistic process he has in mind. For example, the commentator Moses Narboni suggested that, when Maimonides claims, "no evil at all will befall you" if you are free of distraction, we must, as it were, italicize the word "you." The individual who has attained the highest degree of knowledge and concentrates on what he knows receives the overflow, transcends his body, and possibly attains partial conjunction with the Active Intellect. His body may be destroyed, but he survives.

A notable feature of all three models – scientific knowledge as protective, psychic immunity, and transcending the body – is that they circle back to the notion of matter.[35] Matter interferes with scientific knowledge; it inhibits the intellectual and axiological shift; and it impedes concentration on God.

12.4 Egocentrism and Anthropocentrism (*Guide* 3.12)

The most psychologically-oriented portion of Maimonides' discussion of theodicy appears in *Guide* 3.12. In it he identifies reasons why the problem of evil arises for people, why it is so formidable to them.

Maimonides begins the chapter by attacking the position of Al-Razi, who thinks that there is more evil than good. Now, as Steven Nadler correctly remarks (Nadler 2009, 630), the problem of evil isn't a numbers game, played to determine whether quantitatively there are more good things than bad things.[36] So, Maimonides' rejection of Al-Razi falls very short of a theodicy.[37] Moreover, even if there is more good than evil – and for Maimonides, it appears that there is *far* more (see Maimonides 1963, 1.54: 127) – this does not turn back a demand to explain why *any* evil exists. For Maimonides, though, in truth there is not even a contest of numbers, for "all that proceeds from Him [is] indubitably an absolute good" (Maimonides 1963, 3.12: 442). And that is his proffered refutation of Al-Razi. He replies using not an empirical argument, but rather an evaluative assertion anchored in theology – all that proceeds from God is good.

Maimonides' problem in *Guide* 3.12 is why people don't accept this assertion. Why do people think there is so much evil? Maimonides says it is because:

> This ignoramus and those like him among the multitude consider that which exists only with reference to a human individual. Every ignoramus imagines that all that exists exists with a view to his individual self. And if anything happens to him that is contrary to what he wishes, he makes the trenchant judgment that all that exists is an evil. (Maimonides 1963, 3.12: 442)

---

[35] I thank Aaron Segal for this point.
[36] I assume that a weighting of the various evils and goods would be called for.
[37] The empirical question of whether evil outnumbers (or outweighs) good is not irrelevant to theodicy. Philosophers often maintain that even if we can explain why there is evil, we must in particular explain why there is so much of it, including "horrendous evils." Arguing that there is more good than evil and that people's perceptions are skewed by certain factors is relevant to assessing this "there's so much" form of the problem of evil.

People are egocentric: they think there is more evil than good because they generalize from their own case. They do not take into that existence itself is a good and, it should be added, even if we view things from their self-interested standpoint, their suffering results from laws of nature that serve valuable human interests.

Maimonides does not expressly differentiate between egocentrism and anthropocentrism, but there is a difference, and the chapter depicts both. The problem of egocentrism is about the effect of one's *own* personal suffering upon one's judgment of the quantity of evil in the universe. A person thinks that everything exists for him or her in particular. The problem of anthropocentrism, though, is not just about misjudging the quantity (better: weight) of evil in the universe, but about misjudging *the significance of human suffering* – no matter whose – in the larger context of the universe. An anthropocentrist imagines that the universe exists for the sake of *human beings*, not him or her alone. In rebuttal, Maimonides says that people are not concerned with the condition of angels, spheres, other species, minerals, and plants (Maimonides 1963, 3.12: 442). They fail to see that humans are but a small part of the universe and, compared to the intellects and spheres, are "very, very contemptible" (Maimonides 1963, 3.13: 455). The Bible compares humans to worms, maggots, vanity, and a drop in a bucket (Maimonides 1963, 3.12: 442). "Man is merely the most noble thing among the things that are subject to generation ... the noblest thing that is composed of elements" (Maimonides 1963, 3.12: 443), For all that, a person's matter is a great boon to him, a "divine gift" (Maimonides 1963, 3.8: 433); and, "withal his existence is a great good" (Maimonides 1963, 3.12: 443).

Maimonides' basic psychological insight here is right: when I think that God should have made my life materially better, or made the lives of humanity better, I am focusing, respectively, on myself or on my species. A shift in focus and the use of intellect rather than imagination will change one's state of mind. Maimonides makes another cogent point when he reiterates his contention that human beings bring evils upon themselves by living poorly. Failure to grasp this fact makes people evade responsibility and seek the causes of evil elsewhere. "We suffer because of evils that we have produced ourselves of our own free will; but we attribute them to God ... [as Solomon explains:] 'The foolishness of man perverteth his way; and his heart fretteth against the Lord' [Proverbs 19:3]" (Maimonides 1963, 3.12: 443).

Maimonides' argumentation can be challenged in several ways. First, it is difficult to square the denigration of human beings' significance with the importance that Judaism (including Maimonides' *Mishneh Torah*!) assigns to alleviating suffering. Perhaps this imperative exists in order to promote social order, but why is social order so valuable? Second, while from *Guide* 3.12 it appears that Maimonides could hardly endorse the "fine-tuning argument" used in our day to argue for the existence of God, he also often highlights how nature is set up in a way that serves human needs (recognizing them *as* needs, rather than mere desires) and the pursuit of intellectual perfection.[38] Given this affirmation of teleology, human beings' expectations of what God should do for them seem justified. Third, Maimonides' psychological claim that people don't care about evils undergone by nonhuman beings doesn't ring true. People are in fact troubled by the suffering or death of other species detailed in evolutionary theory, by the picture of "nature red in tooth and claw." In modern times, the suffering of nonhuman animals indeed forms part of the problem of evil (see Van Inwagen 2006, lecture 7, 113–134), so much so that in contemporary analytic philosophy, an example of a fawn suffering in the forest has become the virtually iconic example of evil (see Rowe 1979 and Oppy 2013). Further, destruction of the environment, whether natural or human, is acknowledged to be an evil. In sum, we humans are troubled by the state of the earth, and both its human and nonhuman inhabitants.[39]

Finally, fourth, how does the charge of anthropocentrism affect theodicy? Why does the existence of anthropocentric, psychological forces that lead people to wonder why there is evil entail that – in truth – evil does not pose a logical problem? And while we don't know the purpose of the universe – indeed, it has no final end – is the suffering of beings troubling *only* if the world was created for their sake? Maimonides is likely here providing a therapeutic answer, a correction of perspective that will reduce one's turmoil. But the theodicy problems remain, which might be why Maimonides concludes *Guide* 3.12 by pointing to the good that God has bestowed on humans, an ending that brings us back from psychology to theodicy. After all, from the perspective of his anti-anthropocentric remarks, why should it matter whether God has benefited humans?[40]

---

[38] The fine-tuning argument maintains that the universe is intelligently designed to produce human beings, based on the empirical claim that the slightest changes in the laws of nature and initial conditions of the universe (as well as subsequent conditions) would have resulted in a world devoid of human life as we know it.

[39] Maimonides thinks the world is good for nonhuman animals too, even though humans use them for food (as Zev Harvey has noted), so he should acknowledge the problem posed by their suffering.

[40] On anthropocentrism, see W. Z. Harvey (Essay 11 in this volume). In the introduction to his *Commentary on the Mishnah*, Maimonides adopts a remarkably anthropocentric theory.

12.5 Conclusion

The *Guide*'s treatment of suffering and providence presents a mélange of penetrating ideas that serve both philosophical and psychological purposes. The philosophical, theodic pieces are hard to assemble due to Maimonides' theory of attributes and analysis of good and evil. His accounts of how the appeal to matter exonerates God and his claim that providence is consequent upon the intellect are *prima facie* difficult. But his discussions also reveal psychological claims about human beings, especially their egocentrism, anthropocentrism, and evasion of personal responsibility. Here one finds more consistency and more immediate cogency, but not much impact on the philosophical problems. By handling the problem of evil from both psychological and philosophical perspectives, Maimonides stimulates his readers to reflect on the problem that perceived evils pose to their psyches, no less than on the morass of challenges that evils pose for belief in God and His providence.

PART VI
Human Ends

CHAPTER 13

The Nature and Purpose of Divine Law
Moshe Halbertal

13.1 The Source and Goal of the Law

In one of the most illuminating chapters in the third part of *The Guide of the Perplexed* concerning the meaning of Divine Law, Maimonides sharply polemicizes against a certain common approach to God's commandments. Maimonides' harsh words can serve as an initial key to explore the high religious stakes that are embedded in this controversy:

> There is a group of human beings who consider it a grievous thing that reasons should be given for any law [of the Torah]; what would please them most is that the intellect would not find a meaning for the commandments and prohibitions. What compels them to feel this is a sickness that they find in their souls. A sickness to which they are unable to give utterance and for which they cannot furnish a satisfactory account. For they think that if those laws [of the Torah] were useful in this existence and had been given to us for this or that reason, it would be as if they are derived from the reflection and understanding of some intelligent being. If, however, there is a thing for which the intellect could not find any meaning at all and that does not lead to something useful, it indubitably derives from God; for the reflection of man would not lead to such a thing. (Maimonides 1963, 3.31: 523–524)

This approach to Divine Law that Maimonides diagnoses as rooted in sickness of the soul has its source in a deep religious impulse and sensibility. Such an outlook assumes that providing humanly useful reasons for the commandments empties them of their religious meaning. Divine Law, if it has its source in a God who transcends humanity, must be inscrutable. Even more so, the religious meaning of fulfilling God's commandments ought to be manifested in the surrender of the human will to the divine will. Worship is constituted as obedience, and such an obedience in principle cannot be in the service of human aims. It is not only the case that humans are incapable of approaching God's mind and understanding His commands, but rather, the ascription of reasons to God's commandments runs against their very purpose. The only reason for obeying a commandment is that God commanded it, and any attempt to harness such commandments to foster human aims would taint and undermine their purity as religiously motivated acts. This view is considered by Maimonides as that of sick souls since it constitutes an arbitrary God who commands with no reason, and it posits a human worshiper engaged in meaningless obedience.[1] Maimonides provides a radical and thoroughly anthropocentric alternative to the meaning and end of Divine Law. Divine Law has a reason, it aims at human flourishing and it guides humans to achieve their ultimate perfection.

Maimonides' affirmation that reason, and not arbitrary will, grants divinity to law ties the question of the meaning of the commandments to a larger metaphysical concern that is central to the *Guide*. Maimonides has formulated this larger metaphysical question in terms of *wisdom* versus *will*:

> Just as there is disagreement among the men of speculation among the adherents of Law whether His works, may He be exalted, are consequent upon *wisdom* or upon *the will* alone without being intended toward any end at all, there is also the same disagreement among them regarding our Laws, which He has given to us. Thus there are people who do not seek for them any cause at all, saying that all Laws are consequent of the *will* alone. (Maimonides 1963, 3.26: 506)

Countering the view that emphasizes sovereign will both in nature and the law, Maimonides poses a radical alternative, claiming that in the same manner that God is manifested in the wisdom and goodness that is revealed in the natural order, so it is the case with the laws of Torah: "Marvel exceedingly in the wisdom of His commandments, may He be exalted, just as you should marvel at the wisdom manifested in the things He had made. It says: *The Rock, His work is perfect, for all His ways are judgment*. It says that just as the things made by Him are consummately perfect, so are His commandments consummately just" (Maimonides 1963, 3.49: 605). Maimonides' opposition to the view that Divine Law is a medium of God's pure sovereign will is thus a continuation of his rejection of the cosmos as an expression of God's will and sheer power.[2]

---

[1] On the particular location of the chapter within Maimonides' reasons for the commandments, see Stern (1998, 36–39). For an analysis of this chapter in the *Guide*, see Lorberbaum (2014).

[2] The view that it is pure will that defines both the created world and the law was embraced by the Asha'rite trend within the Kalam. On Maimonides' attitude toward the Kalam, see Pines (1963, cxxiv–cxxxi).

The Nature and Purpose of Divine Law 249

In Maimonides' view, the miraculous breaking of the causal order is not where revelation of the divine is located, but rather God's revelation is manifested in the wisdom exhibited in nature's immanent causal structure. Nature and Divine Law are both expressions of the same principle – of God's wisdom and benevolence.[3]

The analogy between nature and law runs deeper in Maimonides' thought, since the need for law and the capacity to generate it are rooted in the natural condition of humanity. Law's necessity, according to Maimonides, emerges from two fundamental features of the human condition that stand in tension – a tension that can be resolved only through the institution of law. On the one hand, humans are in need of communal living; they are social animals. On the other hand, the differences between individuals within the human species are radical: "Thus you may find in an individual cruelty that reaches a point at which he kills the youngest of his sons in his great anger, whereas another individual is full of pity at the killing of a bug or any other insect, his soul being too tender for this" (Maimonides 1963, 2.40: 382). Law resolves the tension that is inherent in the human condition by cultivating good virtues and establishing rules that impose unity that governs such radical diversity. The creation of law is natural as well, since within the variety of human diverse capacities there also exists among the few a tendency and skill to lead and legislate. For this reason, though law seems like a thoroughly social institution created or revealed to humans, it is grounded within the natural: "Therefore I say that the Law, although it is not natural, enters into what it is natural. It is part of the wisdom of the deity with regard to the permanence of this species of which He has willed the existence that He put it into its nature that individuals belonging to it should have the faculty of ruling" (Maimonides 1963, 2.40: 382).

The need for a well-ordered society and the capacity to create such order is rooted in human nature, and the Divine Law shares this function with other legal systems. The Torah's first goal is therefore to create a just and stable society. Laws of the Torah related to the social order – dealing with such matters as torts, loans, bailment, theft, assault, and inheritance – are among the commandments meant to establish just relations between individuals. In addition, there are commandments that aim at fostering valuable character traits, thereby further ensuring a sound social order. This group includes commandments forbidding hatred, envy, and

---

[3] For a comprehensive study of the analogy between Torah and Nature in Maimonides' thought, see Hadad (2011).

vengeance on the one hand, and on the other, those requiring sharing and charity and promoting mercy. The forbidding of the slaughter of an animal and its offspring on the same day is meant to prevent the development of cruelty, as is the obligation to send away the mother bird before taking the nestlings.[4] Prohibitions on improper sexual relations are meant to promote control of desire. Close relatives are forbidden to each other because they are regularly in proximity to each other.[5] The limitations on sexuality advance the purpose of the law, which is to promote sound character.

This social aim is shared by legal systems in general; the feature that makes a legal system distinctly a Divine Law is that such law aims at human perfection, not only at social order:

> Accordingly if you find a Law the whole end of which and the whole purpose of the chief thereof ... are directed exclusively toward the ordering of the city and of its circumstances and the abolition in it of injustice and oppression; and if in that Law attention is not at all directed toward speculative matters, no heed is given to the perfecting of the rational faculty, and no regard is accorded to opinions being correct or faulty ... you must know that Law is a nomos ... If, on the other hand, you find a Law all of whose ordinances are due to attention being paid as stated before, to the soundness of the circumstances pertaining to the body and also to the soundness of belief – a Law that takes pains to inculcate correct opinions with regard to God, may He be exalted in the first place, and with regard to the angels, and that desires to make man wise, to give him understanding, and awaken his attention, so that he should know the whole of that which exists in its true form – you must know that this guidance comes from Him, may He be exalted, and that this Law is divine. (Maimonides 1963, 2.40: 383–384)

What differentiates Divine Law from ordinary nomos is not that its *source* is in the sovereign will of God, but rather in its unique *goal*. Divine Law is a law that leads humans to their highest perfection as creatures able to distinguish truth from falsehood. It aims to make humans wise – "so [they] should know the whole of that which exists in its true form." Such a goal is achieved in the Torah through its prohibitions against idolatry, which free humans from the dominance of the imagination. Idolatry gains strength because humans lack the knowledge to distinguish between the possible and the impossible, and the Torah therefore forbids not only actions directly associated with idolatry, but also all activity for which there is no rational basis.[6] The commandments to love God and to affirm His unity

---

[4] *Guide* 3.48.   [5] *Guide* 3.49. On the control of the passions, see *Guide* 3.33.   [6] *Guide* 3.37.

direct one to true knowledge of God and reality.⁷ This layer of commandments, which aims at uprooting false beliefs and fostering true ones, constitutes the Torah as Divine Law above and beyond legal systems that aim merely at ordering society. Establishing social order is a necessary condition for achieving the higher and nobler goal of achieving ultimate human perfection. In its service to human perfection, the Torah as Divine Law is connected to nature in complementing nature. Such completion is achieved through Divine Law by creating the social and personal conditions that foster humans' ability to realize their natural telos and perfection as creatures that are capable of knowing what truly exists.⁸ Maimonides devotes chapters 26–49 of the third part of the *Guide* to explaining the reasons for the commandments, and these chapters are the most meticulous and systematic attempt devoted to this subject in the history of Jewish thought.⁹ They are devoted as well to indicating in detail that the Torah is Divine Law, whose aim is human perfection.¹⁰

Understanding the nature of Divine Law by reference to its *goal* is a surprising substitute for a much more straightforward answer to the question. This alternative answer would take the following form: what distinguishes Divine Law from other legal system is its *source*, not its *goal*.¹¹ On this account, Divine Law originates in God's direct revelation and command, other systems of law are humanly manufactured. Such an alternative view of Divine Law is on the face of it somewhat suspect, since it seems to leave open a question as to the criterion that can be used to distinguish between genuine and false claims to revelation. This question was addressed in the following manner: The validation of Torah as revealed by God rests on the feature of the foundational revelation at Sinai as a public event witnessed by the whole people of Israel. Such an argument was introduced by Judah Ha-Levi in his *Kuzari*, but even more important, it has been articulated by Maimonides himself in his great legal code, *Mishneh Torah*.¹² In the chapter dedicated to the claim that miracles performed by a prophet are not the source of trust in the prophet,

---

⁷ *Guide* 3.28.
⁸ See Maimonides' principled formulation of the goal of Torah as the natural perfection of humans: "His ultimate perfection is to become rational in actu, I mean to have an intellect in actu; this would consist in his knowing everything concerning all the beings that it is within the capacity of man to know in according with his ultimate perfection" (Maimonides 1963, 3.27: 511).
⁹ On the broader analysis of these chapters and their structure, see Ben-Sasson (1960); Galston (1978); Hyman (1979–1980); Nehorai (1983).
¹⁰ See Stern (1998, 37–38).
¹¹ On this feature of Divine Law as constituted by its goal, see W. Z. Harvey (1994, 47–54).
¹² *Kuzari* 1.88; 1.109.

Maimonides extends this claim to apply to Moses as well. The belief in Moses' prophecy didn't stem from the grand spectacles he performed, such as splitting the sea and drawing manna from heaven, but rather in the public nature of God's revelation to Moses at Sinai:

> What is the source of their belief in him [in Moses]? The theophany at Mount Sinai, where our eyes saw, and not a stranger's; our ears heard, and not another. There was fire, thunder, and lightning. He entered the thick clouds; the Voice spoke to him and we heard, 'Moses, Moses, go tell them the following: ...' ... Thus, those to whom he was sent bear witness to the truth of his prophecy; it was not necessary to perform a wonder for them, for he and they were like two witnesses who observed the same event together. (*Mishneh Torah, Laws of Foundations of the Torah* 8:1–2)[13]

The giving of the Torah was a public affair, taking place before all of Israel; all were present to see the vision and hear the sounds. Moses' credibility is not grounded in the miracles he worked, for miracle stories abound in all traditions and all religions. It follows, rather, from the participation of the entire nation in the giving of the Torah.

This account grounds the Divine Law in its *source* in revelation, evidenced by a foundational public, historic event. Such an account is very different than defining Divine Law in terms of its *goal*, which actually establishes such law as a genus, a category that might include a variety of legal systems such as Islamic law that could be understood as aiming, as well, at eradicating false beliefs and inculcating monotheism. Why does Maimonides differentiate Divine Law in relation to its *goal* rather than its *source* in his crucial statement in the *Guide*? The answer to this question relates to Maimonides' philosophical concept of revelation.

In Maimonides' view, the notion of revelation of the Law as a direct speech from a sovereign God expressing his will to a prophet or a people is thoroughly anthropomorphic. It is based on a human analogy of sovereigns commanding their subjects. Speech cannot be attributed to God and, needless to say, use of a particular language. The chapter in the *Guide* which is devoted to the attribution of speech to God, which is abundant in the Torah, begins with the following decisive declaration: "I do not consider that – after having attained this degree and having gained the

---

[13] See as well Maimonides' Epistle to Yemen: "This event is analogous to the situation of two witnesses who observed a certain act simultaneously. Each of them saw what his fellow saw, and each of them is sure of the truth of his fellow's statement as well as of his own, and does not require proof or demonstration ... Similarly, we of the Jewish faith are convinced of the truth of the prophecy of Moses, not simply because of his wonders, but because we, like him, witnessed the theophany on Mount Sinai" (Hartman 1985, 112–113).

true knowledge that He, may He be exalted, exists not by virtue of existence and is one not by virtue of a oneness – you require that the denial of the attribute of speech with reference to Him be explained to you" (Maimonides 1963, 1.65: 158). The attributions of speech to God have to be understood not in their literal direct meaning:

> Now in all cases in which the words *saying* and *speaking* are applied to God, they are used in one of the two latter meanings. I mean to say that they are used to denote either will and volition or a notion that has been grasped by the understanding having come from God, in which case it is indifferent whether it has become known by means of a created voice through one of the ways of prophecy. (Maimonides 1963, 1.65: 158–159)

Speaking and *saying* are equivocal terms, and when applied to God they express a wish of God or a thought that is understood as coming from God.[14] In this bold chapter, the whole idea of direct revelation is rejected, hence the notion of Divine Law as a command uttered to humans by a sovereign God turns out to be utterly meaningless. It is no wonder, therefore, that when defining the distinction between Divine Law and every other nomos, Maimonides doesn't appeal to its direct origin but rather to its content and aim. A validation of Divine Law in actual public hearing of God's voice might be important to anchor the authority of the law, and therefore Maimonides uses it in the *Mishneh Torah*, but as far as this supports a true philosophical account, it cannot be taken at face value.[15]

The meaning of Divine Law cannot, therefore, be separated from the larger question of the nature of prophecy and revelation. Following Al-Farabi, Maimonides distinguished the prophet's perfection from that of the political leader and that of the philosopher.[16] Great political leaders and founders of political communities are graced with perfection in their imaginative faculty. They create captivating images and symbols, spin foundational and organizing tales, and enact laws. Some enjoy the capacity to envision events and see the future, as if it were before their eyes. The philosophers, in contrast to the leaders, are endowed with the perfection of their intellect. They are equipped to deal with abstractions and can think

---

[14] God's will in Maimonides' view is mediated through a natural chain of causes in which God is the ultimate source, while the Torah tends to omit these mediating causes. On this, see *Guide* 2.48 and Stern (1998, 19).

[15] The idea of public revelation as such is problematic given the fact that the attainment of prophecy in Maimonides' view depends upon an excellence that only rare individuals can achieve. Maimonides reinterprets the public revelation at Sinai at *Guide* 2.33.

[16] On Al-Farabi's influence on Maimonides' concept of prophecy, see Pines (1963, xc–xcii).

critically in a way that allows them to distinguish between truth and falsehood. But because they lack imaginative force, they differ from political leaders in that they are unable to translate their insights into popular language. They lack the ability to forge symbols and images that will convey their intellectual achievements in ways that will move people to action. By contrast, prophets possess both perfections: the perfected intellectual power of the philosopher and the perfected imaginative power of the political leader. They are equipped to form images and lead the community, and because they also possess intellectual perfection, prophets do not simply mold the social order as do ordinary political leaders; they also draw the community as a whole to true and appropriate views of the world.[17] It is for that reason that Maimonides, in the chapter that defines Divine Law, makes the claim that a legal system that is directed solely to social order originates in a political leader who is endowed only with the power of the imagination, while a legal system that directs the community to intellectual perfection has its source in a prophet and prophecy.

According to Maimonides, the attainment of prophetic revelation is a natural process. There is no volitional intentional calling by God to a person. Prophecy reaches the imagination through the inspiration of the intellect, ultimately through the (separate) Active Intellect.[18] This concept of prophecy is far removed from the traditional understanding, in which the sovereign God exercises His will to address and issue a command to His messenger. According to Maimonides, when the prophets report hearing God speaking to them or seeing an angel calling them, they are not reporting an actual external event, for neither God nor an angel appear or speak. The prophet *dreamt* that the event was occurring: "Know again that in the case of everyone about whom exists a scriptural text that an angel talked to him or that speech came to him from God, this did not occur in any other way than in a dream or in a vision of prophecy" (Maimonides 1963, 2.41: 386). If we extend this naturalistic view of prophecy to the prophecy of Moses, the following picture emerges: The revelation to Moses consisted of his attainment of truth through his understanding of God's ways in the world, and inspired by that understanding, Moses generated the Law, which we can say was "revealed" to

---

[17] *Guide* 2.37.
[18] See Maimonides' formulation: "Know that the true reality and quiddity of prophecy consists in its being an overflow from God, may He be cherished and honored, through the intermediation of the Active Intellect, toward the rational faculty in the first place and thereafter toward the imaginative faculty" (Maimonides 1963, 2.36: 369).

him.[19] Given Maimonides' understanding of revelation, Divine Law could not be grounded in a direct volitional sovereign command by God, but rather its divinity is constituted by its goal and telos.

The definition of Divine Law as constituted by its goal opens the door to the idea that it is a genus that includes other legal systems such as Islam.[20] By contrast, in the *source*-grounded version of Divine Law, the answer to such a "pluralistic" challenge has been that it is *only* within the Jewish tradition that the foundational moment of the revelation of the Law was publicly witnessed by all, while the revelation of the Quran was a discreet affair reported by an individual, which can be doubted. However, in the *goal*-grounded version of Divine Law that was introduced in the *Guide*, another strategy must be adopted to ascertain the exclusivity of Torah as Divine Law. In the chapter that precedes Maimonides' definition of Divine Law, he provides another intriguing argument for the exclusivity of Torah.[21] According to Maimonides, the examination of Moses' Torah shows that it is perfectly balanced. Imperfection appears in many forms, but perfection has only one form. If at some point in the future a prophet of Moses' stature should appear and enact a Divine Law, that law would be identical to the Torah of Moses:

> We likewise believe that things will always be this way. As it says: *It is not in heaven, and so on; for us and for our children forever*. And that is as it ought to be; for when a thing is as perfect as it is possible within its species, it is impossible that within that species there should be found another thing that does not fall short of that perfection either because of excess or deficiency. (Maimonides 1963, 2.39: 380)

The perfect Law presents a well-balanced regimen for achieving social order and intellectual perfection, and at the end of the chapter Maimonides declares: "Only that Law is called by us Divine Law, whereas the other political regimens – such as the nomoi of the Greeks and the ravings of the Sabians and of others – are due, as I have explained several times, to the actions of groups of rulers who were not prophets" (Maimonides 1963, 2.39: 381). As we shall see, such a defense of the exclusivity of Divine Law stands in tension with Maimonides' own

---

[19] For a comprehensive and naturalistic account of Moses' prophecy, see Reines (1969–1970); see as well Bland (1982) and Kreisel (1999, 12–13, 79–81).
[20] Joel Kraemer suggested that this was Maimonides' intention in the chapter, and that he viewed Islam as based on Divine Law, though its founder imitated such law; see Kraemer (1986, 195–196).
[21] On the tension between chapters 39 and 40 of the *Guide*, see Pines (1963, xc).

explanation of some of the commandments as deriving from a particular historical context.[22]

13.2 Creation and the Law

As can be expected from a complex multilayered text such as the *Guide*, such a central matter that stands at the heart of the question of the foundation and authority of Divine Law is not left without ambiguity. The *goal*-oriented definition of Divine Law and its support in the naturalistic explanation of prophecy and revelation, seems to undermine the very authority of the law as grounded in the expression of the direct affirmation of God's will. The absence of God's volitional engagement in giving the law is deeply troubling in this version. In his long discussion of the central metaphysical question of the *Guide* – whether the world was created in time or whether it is eternal – Maimonides devoted much effort in showing that the philosophers failed to prove the eternity of the world. Creation is possible according to Maimonides, and given this, he adopted the view of creation in time in order to defend the authority and possibility of revelation and Law:

> Know that with a belief in the creation of the world in time, all the miracles become possible and the Law becomes possible, and all the questions that may be asked on this subject vanish. Thus it might be said: Why did God give this law to this particular nation, and why did He not legislate to the others? Why did He legislate at this particular time, and why did He not legislate before or after? ... The answer to all these questions would be that it would be said: He wanted it this way; or His wisdom required it this way. And just as He brought the world into existence, having the form it has, when He wanted to, without our knowing His will with regard to this ... (Maimonides 1963, 2.25: 329)

This important passage makes it clear that what is at stake in the question of whether the world was created in time or is eternal is not merely the cosmological question concerning the origin of the world. The creation/eternity debate reflects a far deeper theological question. It centers on the question of whether we can ascribe to God a will manifested in creation in time, or that ascription of a will to God is flawed and the world is not the result of God's volitional intended act, but rather is eternally caused from

---

[22] Maimonides' concept of Divine Law is influenced by Al-Farabi, though Al-Farabi uses the term "excellent" law rather than "divine." In his description of such a law Al-Farabi does not mention the exclusivity of such a law; see Walzer (1985, 248–253). On Al-Farabi's political theory and his conception of the excellent city, see Galston (1990, 146–179).

God's very being. In turn, we learn as well from this section of the *Guide* that the question of whether a will can be ascribed to God – or not – becomes crucial not only for its own sake, but also gains immense importance because the whole authority and possibility of the Law depends on it. If God has no will, how can we ascribe to Him the giving of the Torah to a particular people in a particular time in history? Such an event must assume an intended decision on the part of God. Judaism as a religion based on revealed Law can be defended only if creation is affirmed, and when it is affirmed, God's volitional act in giving the Law at a certain time and to a certain people becomes possible and defensible.

This affirmation of the foundation of the Law grounded in a willed act of God – which counters the view of revelation as a naturalistic event absent any will of God – is further supported by Maimonides' repeated claim that his theory of prophecy does not apply to Moses. Unlike other prophets, Moses encounters not an angel but God Himself. And while other prophets prophesy in a wakeful vision and dream, Moses prophesies directly, not in a vision or a dream. For that same reason, Moses' prophecy is not tied to the imaginative faculty, as is that of other prophets, but is derived directly from the intellect itself. In effect, Maimonides determines that the natural explanation that underlies his view of prophecy in general simply does not apply to the case of Moses. Moses' prophecy is comparable to that of other prophets homonymously; in essence, however, they differ entirely: "I will let you know that everything I say on prophecy in the chapters of this Treatise refers only to the form of prophecy of all the prophets who were before Moses or who will come after him ... For to my mind the term *prophet* used with reference to Moses and to others is amphibolous" (Maimonides 1963, 2.35: 367).

"Conservative" readers of the *Guide* argue that, by distinguishing Moses from the other prophets not only in rank but also in substance, Maimonides was defending the authoritativeness of the Torah and of revelation. Just as the world was created through a miraculous act of divine will, so was the (unique) Torah given to Moses. The divine will is active only at the original foundational moment; and so, too, with respect to revelation: the divine will appears in the giving of the Torah, in which the absolute standing of the Divine Law is established as the basis for Judaism overall, and forever. By contrast, "radical" readers of the *Guide* introduce the following counterclaim: If this is the case – that the Torah was founded on a willed act of God – why did Maimonides define the nature of Divine Law in terms of its goal and aim? These philosophical readers of the *Guide* interpret Maimonides' defense of creation in time as aimed at establishing the necessary belief that is needed for the unphilosophical majority of people to abide by the law and revelation. Maimonides' true position, such readers claim, is that the world is eternal and that no willed action can be ascribed to God. In line with this view, Maimonides provides a coherent account of prophecy and revelation that is thoroughly naturalistic. As the most perfect of all prophets, Moses generated the law from his knowledge of God's ways in the world. The claim that Moses' prophecy is not included in the naturalistic account of prophecy, and that it is sui generis and mysterious, is likewise a necessary (exoteric) defense of the authority of law. As the radical readers claim, juxtaposed to such statements of Moses' unique revelation, Maimonides provided a thoroughly naturalistic interpretation of Divine Law and Mosaic revelation, fully consonant with the radical philosophical reading of the *Guide*. The great debate among Maimonides' readers regarding his view on creation versus eternity has, therefore, deep echoes in the question of what is Divine Law and where its source of authority lies.[23]

We are faced, then, with the following two parallel pairs constructed side by side in the *Guide*: On the one hand, *creation* of the world and Divine Law as defined by its *source*, and on the other hand, *eternity* of the world and Divine Law as defined by its *goal*. However we adjudicate between these two options of reading the *Guide* (and I doubt there is any way of doing it), there is one feature that the two views share: The commandments of the Torah have reasons and they aim at establishing perfection of both the social order and true beliefs and knowledge. In his view of creation, Maimonides distinguished his position from streams of Islamic thought within the Kalam movement that maintained that since the time of the world's creation, God's willful actions have continued, for no causal nature exists independent of God's ongoing will. Nature, as such, has no existence outside of God's ongoing will. For Maimonides, even if we assume that the world was created in time, we would not on that account have a reason to deny the reality of the causal order. God created the world through an act of will, but He instituted with it an autonomous causal order.[24] The same goes for the Law. The Law was founded on a primary act of will, and its contents express wisdom and reason; its religious meaning is not derived from ongoing submission to God's will. In the same manner that the world, after being founded on an act of will,

---

[23] For a comprehensive account of the "radical" and "conservative" readings of the *Guide* from the beginning of its reception, see Ravitzky (1990).
[24] *Guide* 3.25.

exhibits God's wisdom in its causal structure, so too does the Torah exhibit divine wisdom.

13.3 Idolatry and the Law

Maimonides' monumental attempt to provide systematic reasons for the commandments faces a major difficulty with respect to Torah laws that traditionally have been categorized as *hukkim* (decrees). These laws, such as the prohibition to eat meat and milk simultaneously, or the prohibition of wearing clothes that are made of a mixture of wool and linen, or the prohibition on shaving the hair on the sides of the head, all seem to have no clear reason. They are considered God's inscrutable decrees.[25] Maimonides argues that to understand the rationale behind such laws one has to gain an historical understanding of idolatrous practices at the time of the giving of the Torah. Understanding such practices makes it clear that, in what seem to be decrees with no clear rationale, the Torah actually intended to uproot idolatry by prohibiting common pagan ritualistic practices. Since pagan priests wore clothes made of a mixture of wool and linen and cut the hair on the sides of the head, the Torah prohibited such practices. Maimonides did not rely on mere speculation on these matters; he made a concentrated effort to become fully acquainted with authentic ancient pagan literature:

> I also have read in all matters concerning all of idolatry, so that it seems to me that there does not remain in the world a composition on this subject, having been translated into Arabic from other languages, but that I have read it and have understood its subject matter and have plumbed the depth of its thought. From those books it became clear to me what the reason is for all the commandments that everyone comes to think of as having no reason at all other than the decree of Scripture. I already have a great composition on this subject into the Arabic language [namely the *Guide*] with lucid proofs for every single commandment.[26]

Among these pagan texts were those associated with the Sabians. That group was active in Mesopotamia, and Maimonides had access to some of its writings, such as *The Order of Nabatean Worship*, which might have been a forgery. His study of those works provided the basis for his

---

[25] On the concept of *hukkim* in rabbinic literature, see Urbach (1975, 376–383, 850–851, note 40.). On the broader distinction between *Mishpatim* and *Hukkim* in rabbinic and medieval thought, see Heinemann (1966, vol. I).
[26] *Letter on Astrology*, in Twersky (1972, 465–466).

understanding of the history of idolatry, which he took as the key to understanding those commandments meant to eradicate idolatry:

> I shall now return to my purpose and say that the meaning of many of the laws became clear to me and their causes became known to me through my study of the doctrines, opinions, practices, and cult of Sabians, as you will hear when I explain the reasons for the commandments that are considered to be without a cause. (Maimonides 1963, 3.29: 518)[27]

The historicizing of the Law, situating it in its place and time, takes a bolder turn with a further argument that Maimonides introduced. The battle against idolatry did not include only practices that counter idolatrous behavior, but also included *adopting* idolatrous behaviors, and modifying and channeling them. The main expression of such a strategy is Maimonides' explanation of the biblical sacrificial cult. Worship through animal sacrifice is grounded in a corporeal view of a god, which presumably needs to be fed regularly by his worshipers. Such a cultic practice is utterly foreign to Maimonides' concept of God, and it must be prohibited. Given the fact that it was deeply rooted as a mode of worship, the Torah could not eradicate it in one fell swoop, but rather channeled it to appropriate aims. The Torah allowed sacrifices only in one centralized Temple, thereby dramatically reducing the practice's prevalence. Even more so, as a way of combating idolatry, no image of God was present in that Temple, affirming His transcendence beyond material form and shape. Given the prevalence of animal sacrifice, completely abolishing it at the time when the Torah was revealed would have been impossible. Such total and immediate eradication would have been as unrealistic as an attempt by a legislator to eliminate prayer in Maimonides' own time:

> At that time, this would have been similar to the appearance of a prophet in these times who, calling upon the people to worship God, would say: 'God has given you a Law forbidding you to pray to Him, to fast, to call upon Him for help in misfortune. Your worship should consist solely in meditation without any works at all.' (Maimonides 1963, 3.32: 526)

Like sacrifice, prayer is also modeled on an anthropomorphic image of God, a God that can be appealed to and propitiated to change His plans and decrees. Prohibiting animal sacrifice in biblical times would have been as futile as prohibiting prayer in Maimonides' time.

---

[27] For Maimonides' comparative approach and his Sabian sources, see Stroumsa (2009, 84–124).

The Nature and Purpose of Divine Law 261

The Torah's sensitivity to the psychological and social context of the concrete historical community to which it was given is analogous to God's ways in the natural order:

> Similarly the deity made wily and gracious arrangement with regard to all the individuals of the living beings that suck. For when born, such individuals are extremely soft and cannot feed on dry food. Accordingly breasts were prepared for them so that they should produce milk with a view to their receiving humid food, which is similar to the composition of their bodies, until their limbs gradually and little by little become dry and solid. Many things in our Law are due to something similar to this very governance on the part of Him who governs, may He be glorified and exalted. For a sudden transition from one opposite to another is impossible. And therefore man, according to his nature, is not capable of abandoning suddenly all to which he was accustomed. (Maimonides 1963, 3.32: 525–526)

Nature makes it possible for an infant to survive without solid food, which it is not yet able to ingest, and the Divine Law similarly employs a pedagogic approach that takes account of the historical and spiritual conditions of the time. It does not set out to express eternal, context-independent truth; rather, it attempts to set out a system of rules meant to help human beings in the actual circumstances in which they find themselves.

In situating Divine Law within historical context, the Law's immutability is put into question. If, as Maimonides himself declared, humanity had moved from its need for sacrificial worship to prayer and supplication, the detailed sacrificial laws would have been nullified. Nevertheless, in his legal code *Mishneh Torah* Maimonides provides a full canonical formulation of laws of sacrifice, treating this set of laws as eternally binding without taking consideration of his own claim that they were grounded in response to a particular time. Continuing animal sacrifice is not only redundant and void, it might create a regression from what seemed to be a genuine advancement in the proper worship of God. Maimonides provides an answer to this question in his treatment of the reasons for the commandments that prohibits adding and distracting from the Law, an answer that reveals a great deal about his conception of Divine Law:

> Inasmuch as God, may He be exalted, knew that the commandments of this Law will need in every time and place – as far as some of them are concerned – to be added or subtracted from according to the diversity of places, happenings, and conjectures of circumstances, He forbade adding to them or subtracting from them saying: *Thou shalt not add thereto, nor*

diminish from it. For this might have led to the corruption of the rules of the Law and to the belief that the latter did not come from God. (Maimonides 1963, 3.41: 562–563)

In principle, Divine Law should be changed according to circumstances and times, and insisting on its immutability would be misguided. In spite of this, the Torah forbids changing the Law because such changes might undermine the popular belief in the Law's divine origins. People (wrongly) think that if the Law is not eternal, it cannot be ascribed to God, and taking account of this worry, the Torah prohibits changes in the Law. Such a prohibition is a political condition for anchoring a belief in the divinity and immutability of the Law, and for establishing the authority of the Law and its divine origin.[28] It is no wonder, then, that when he provides reasons for the commandments in his *Mishneh Torah*, Maimonides generally avoids explicit historical explanations.[29] Such explanations, though they reveal the wisdom of the Law and its similarity to nature, might undermine the authority of the Law, which is of utter importance in a legal code. The need for flexibility of the Law is compensated for by the Torah, which provides an opportunity for a provisional change in the Law authorized by the Great Court or by a prophet. Such changes would not undermine the authority of the Law because they are considered as provisional and tentative.

The question of what Divine Law is should therefore be addressed from two perspectives – the philosophical and the social – and each perspective does not yield the same understanding of the Law. From the philosophical perspective, Divine Law is historically situated and dynamic; from the social perspective, Divine Law is eternal and immutable. This dual conception is constituted by a divide between a true belief and a necessary belief. The radical readers of the *Guide*, however, would add to this yet another double perspective. From the philosophical perspective, Divine Law is generated naturally and is defined by its *goal*; from the social and political perspective, Divine Law is grounded in God's will as presented to Moses the prophet and lawgiver, a view that shares nothing with the naturalistic account of prophecy.

---

[28] On the need for necessary beliefs for the masses and the Torah's effort to anchor them, see *Guide* 3.28. On the social and political conditions that are needed to ground the divinity of the law, see Levinger (1989, 55–56); Halbertal (1990, 479); Lorberbaum (2009–2010, 276–279).

[29] On the difference between reasons of the commandments in the *Mishneh Torah* and the *Guide*, see Twersky (1980, 430–447).

13.4 Divine Names and the Occult

In the chapter of the *Guide* devoted to the explanation of the subtle metaphysical meaning of the names of God, Maimonides attacks the view that ascribes occult powers to such names:

> When wicked and ignorant people found these texts, they had great scope for lying statements in that they would put together any letters they liked and would say: This is a name that has efficacy and the power to operate if it is written down or uttered in a particular way. Thereupon these lies invented by the first wicked and ignorant man were written down, and these writings transmitted to good, pious, and foolish men who lack the scales by means of which they can know the true from false ... To sum it up: *A fool believes everything.* (Proverbs 14:15; Maimonides 1963, 1.62: 152)

Maimonides' denunciation aims at a long and widespread esoteric tradition that produced amulets and incantations based on a belief in the potent and occult powers of divine names. In Maimonides' view, God's esoteric names convey a deep metaphysical meaning, but they utterly lack any causal efficacy. Endowing them with such power is grounded in a complete ignorance of natural causality, which opens the possibility of accepting everything fanciful.[30] Maimonides extends this approach to divine names to all ritual objects and ritual performances; they are all devoid of any causal efficacy. In the law concerning *Mezuzah* in *Mishneh Torah*, Maimonides attacks the practice of writing such names on the Mezuzah and ascribing protective powers to the Mezuzah:

> Those, however, who write the names of angels, other sacred names, verses, or forms, on the inside [of a *mezuzah*] are among those who do not have a portion in the world to come. Not only do these fools nullify the mitzvah, but furthermore, they make from a great mitzvah [which reflects] the unity of the name of the Holy One, blessed be He, the love of Him, and the service of Him, a talisman for their own benefit. They, in their foolish conception, think that this will help them regarding the vanities of the world. (Mishneh Torah, Laws of Tefilin, Mezuzah and Sefer Torah 5:4)

The denunciation of treating Mezuzah as an amulet is grounded not only in the ignorance concerning causality that it reflects. In Maimonides' view,

---

[30] On Maimonides' critique of the uses of divine names, see Ravitzky (2002).

such an instrumentalization of a commandment and its performance to effect material benefits undermines its religious meaning. The biblical passage that is located inside the Mezuzah – the Shema – declares God's unity and the commandment to love Him unconditionally. It aims at fostering true belief and a proper religious attitude, rather than providing material benefits. At the end of *Laws of Mezuzah*, Maimonides radically reinterprets the traditions that ascribe protective powers and efficacy to the Mezuzah:

> A person must show great care in [the observance of the mitzvah of] *mezuzah*, because it is an obligation which is constantly incumbent upon everyone. [Through its observance,] whenever a person enters or leaves [the house], he will encounter the unity of the name of the Holy One, blessed be He, and remember his love for Him. Thus, he will awake from his sleep and his obsession with the vanities of time, and recognize that there is nothing which lasts for eternity except the knowledge of the Creator of the world. This will motivate him to regain full awareness and follow the paths of the upright. Whoever wears *tefillin* on his head and arm, wears *tzitzit* on his garment, and has a *mezuzah* on his entrance, can be assured that he will not sin, because he has many who will remind him. These are the angels, who will prevent him from sinning, as states: "The angel of God stands around those who fear and protect them." (Psalms 34:8; Mishneh Torah, Laws of Mezuzah 6:13)

The protection that the Mezuzah and other commandments provide is not from material loss and dangers, but rather from sin and from false beliefs. The focus of Divine Law is human behavior and consciousness.

In his comprehensive treatment of the goal of Divine Law, Maimonides puts at the center human flourishing and development. The Divine Law achieves its ends by shaping the human world and advancing humans in their perfection. It has no direct relevance on anything outside the human realm. In this anthropocentric view of the goal of Divine Law, Maimonides rejected a deep countercurrent that perceives worship as surrender and overcoming. Maimonides' anthropocentric emphasis, which rejects the occult power of ascribing efficacy to Divine Law, constituted as well an alternative to other prominent medieval perceptions of the Divine Law that ascribed to it effectiveness far and beyond human reality. This counterview, which Maimonides was acquainted with, had been articulated by Abraham Ibn Ezra and Judah Ha-Levi. Both thinkers viewed the commandments as a causal mechanism to drawing God's power and presence. The Temple, for example, is perceived by Ibn Ezra as a "talisman" due to its stellar cosmic structure. Through its proper external form, meticulously ordered by the Divine Law, it draws down divine powers into the world.³¹ In emphasizing the causal impact of the commandments, Ha-Levi makes the analogy between the commandments and proper doses of medicine administered by an expert that have a curing effect, even if the patient has no clue as to how they actually work.³² The Divine Law, according to this view, has an unknown occult feature that differentiates it from any other legal system. These sorts of magical and astrological interpretations developed against the background of scientific attitudes grounded in the tradition of astral magic, according to which terrestrial structures paralleled the heavenly order of constellations and stars and drew on their spiritual powers, acting through them. Maimonides associates these positions with false views of the natural world, which formed the pseudo-scientific background of Sabian idolatry.³³

In Maimonides' own view, however, the efficacy of the commandments is limited to influencing human consciousness and the social order, and they have no magical or causal effect on the natural order. In putting at the center of Divine Law the aim of attaining human perfection, Maimonides naturalizes Divine Law in two senses. The first sense is expressed in the way Maimonides "demythologizes" the Divine Law by depriving the law of any occult efficacy on the causal order.³⁴ Needless to say, Maimonides would have utterly rejected the kabbalists' understanding of the Law as having an effect beyond the natural world, extending its impact on preserving the fragile balance and unity within the Godhead. The second sense of Maimonides' naturalizing of Divine Law is expressed in the fact that the human perfection that is aimed at by Divine Law is the perfection ascribed to humans by their natural telos – the perfection of their intellect, which differentiates them qua humans from the rest of organic biological creatures. Among the great questions that are left open within the complex legacy of the *Guide* is whether the naturalization project extends as well to the understanding of the founding moment of Divine Law in revelation.

---

[31] For Ibn Ezra's conception of the Temple as an isomorphic structure devised to draw divine powers, see Schwartz (1999, 73n38, 76).

[32] *Kuzari* 1.79.

[33] "In conformity with these opinions, the Sabians set up statues for the planets, golden statues for the sun and silver ones for the moon, and distributed the minerals and climes between the planets, saying that one particular planet was the deity of one particular clime. And they built temples, set up the statues within them and thought that the forces of the planets overflowed towards these statues" (Maimonides 1963, 3.29: 516).

[34] Maimonides' attempt to empty Law of any causal efficacy is expressed particularly in his rejection of attributing to impurity any semidemonic quality. Impurity is strictly instrumental in restricting entry to the Temple, which in turn would lead to regarding the Temple with awe; see *Guide* 3.47.

CHAPTER 14

Maimonides on Human Perfection and the Love of God

Steven Nadler

14.1 Introduction

Writing in 1191 to his student Joseph ben Judah, to whom Maimonides addressed the *Guide of the Perplexed*, the great rabbi/philosopher complains about how little time he has for study, given the incessant demands of his day job:

> I tell you that I have become known as a physician among the mighty, such as the chief judge, the emirs, and the house of al-Fadil and the other princes of the land, those who lack nothing. But as for the masses, I am beyond their reach, and they have no way to approach me. And this causes me to spend the entire day in Cairo, tending to the sick, and when I get back to Fustat, all I can do for the rest of the day and into the night is to examine the medical texts that I need to consult ... As a result, I do not have a moment to study Torah except on the Sabbath, and as for other sciences, I do not have a moment to study any of them, and this harms me greatly.[1]

In this passage, we see Maimonides wrestling with a certain tension in his life: on the one hand, a devotion to his time-consuming obligations as a physician, to healing the sick among the wealthy and the poor; on the other hand, his personal desire for the opportunity to engage in the study of Torah and other religious and philosophical texts. He is torn between two competing values: the life of practical activity and the life of contemplation.

This same tension that Maimonides experienced existentially in his daily routine also finds expression in his philosophical writings, particularly when he turns to the *summum bonum* of human life. On the one hand, he insists in the final chapter of the *Guide* that "the true human perfection ... consists in the acquisition of the rational virtues – I refer

My thanks to Daniel Frank, Zev Harvey, Menachem Kellner, and Charles Manekin for their helpful comments on earlier drafts of this essay.
[1] Quoted in Halbertal (2014, 63–64).

to the conception of intelligibles, which teach true opinions concerning the divine things." He insists that this intellectual knowledge "is in true reality the ultimate end; this is what gives the individual true perfection, a perfection belonging to him alone" (Maimonides 1963, 3.54: 635). Maimonides notes that the person who has reached perfection of the intellect and "apprehended the true realities" achieves a state in which his mind is singularly focused on these higher truths while, with his body, he only goes through the motions as he interacts with the world around him; he "talks with people and is occupied with his bodily necessities while his intellect is wholly turned towards God" (Maimonides 1963, 3.51: 623). Such "excellent men begrudge the times in which they are turned away from Him by other occupations" (Maimonides 1963, 3.51: 622).

On the other hand, in those same final chapters Maimonides suggests that this occupation, even obsession with the intelligibles, and in particular the apprehension of God, is not the ultimate human end; the activity of pure contemplation and the perfection of the intellect does not by itself constitute true human perfection. Rather, the final goal is subsequent to such contemplation, namely, putting what has been studied into action. The person who apprehends God and his ways through contemplation is now compelled to engage in practical activity that is an imitation of what has been learned of God's nature and actions. Maimonides says that "those actions that ought to be known and imitated are loving-kindness, justice, and righteousness." He says that God has made it clear that "it is My purpose that there should come from you loving-kindness, righteousness, and judgment in the earth," that we should assimilate God's attributes – we should be gracious and merciful and "walk in His ways" in our own actions, and "this should be our way of life" (Maimonides 1963, 3.54: 637). Thus, Maimonides concludes, "the utmost virtue of man is to become like unto Him, may He be exalted, as far as he is able; which means that we should make our actions like unto His" (Maimonides 1963, 1.54: 128; see also *Mishneh Torah, Hilkhot De'ot* 1.5–6).

This prima facie tension in Maimonides' thought has long been the focus of exegetical disagreement: Does human perfection for Maimonides consist in *theoria* or *praxis*? Is the highest good to be found in the life of contemplation itself or in the life of action informed by such intellectual knowledge? Of course, a similar question arises within the ethical texts of Aristotle, Maimonides's mentor on moral matters: is true happiness and the good life for a human being found in the exercise of the moral virtues or the intellectual virtues, in the practical life or the contemplative life?

To be sure, Maimonides' discussion of human perfection leaves no doubt as to where the ordinary moral virtues stand. He is as clear as can be – for example, in *Guide* 1.34 – that they do not themselves form a part of our ultimate good. Human perfection arrives in discrete stages for Maimonides. It begins with "the perfection of possessions," a purely relational condition in which an individual possesses the basic necessities for life, even for a comfortable life. These include shelter, food, wealth, friends, and so forth. The second "species" of perfection is an intrinsic one and has "a greater connection than the first with the individual's self, being the perfection of the bodily constitution and shape" (Maimonides 1963, 3.54: 634). An individual should enjoy a harmonious temperament, his body should be "well-proportioned" and strong, and he should be generally physically healthy. The third and "greater" species of perfection concerns not the individual's body but his "self." This is where the moral virtues come in, whereby "preparatory moral training should be carried out ... so that man should be in a state of extreme uprightness and perfection" (Maimonides 1963, 1.34: 77). This species of perfection "consists in the individual's moral habits having attained their ultimate excellence." Maimonides notes, further, that most of the commandments of the Torah "serve no other end than the attainment of this species of perfection" (Maimonides 1963, 3.54: 634–635).

Maimonides insists, however, that the moral virtues, while they "subsist in the individual's self," are of only instrumental or social value. "For all moral habits are concerned with what occurs between a human individual and someone else" (Maimonides 1963, 3.54:634–635). Generosity, courage, and the other virtues that, on Maimonides' account, are Aristotelian means between extremes – and that he discusses in his ethical writings (such as the *Shemonah Perakim* ["Eight Chapters"], which forms the introduction to his commentary on *Pirkei Avot* in his *Commentary on the Mishnah*) – are of no use (and thus of no value) for a person who is not engaged in interpersonal activity. "For if you suppose a human individual is alone, acting on no one, you will find that all his moral virtues are in vain and without employment and unneeded, and that they do not perfect the individual in anything." Maimonides concludes that "this species of perfection is ... a preparation for something else and not an end in itself" (Maimonides 1963, 3.54: 635).

But what precisely are the moral virtues a preparation for? Ethical perfection is only a necessary (but not sufficient) condition for some higher perfection – most proximately, rational virtue or the perfection of the intellect in metaphysical knowledge, such as that found among philosophers and prophets. But do the moral virtues set us up for purely intellectual perfection alone – an intellectual perfection that, as Josef Stern has recently argued, is, according to Maimonides, impossible for embodied human beings to attain?[2] Or is our ultimate goal to put that intellectual perfection to work in a life of action that is a kind of *imitatio Dei*? It does seem fairly clear from the final chapters of the *Guide* – and this will be my working assumption in this essay – that for Maimonides the true human perfection is indeed intellectual perfection, and that acts of loving-kindness, justice as judgment, and righteousness that constitute the *imitatio Dei* are consequences or byproducts of this perfection. Nonetheless, it is just this question that has generated much scholarly debate.[3]

The general and exceedingly complex topic of Maimonides on human perfection is beyond the scope this essay. Rather, I focus on a particular sub-issue within that broader set of problems. However one reads Maimonides' account of the ultimate human perfection, there is one element that unmistakably and undeniably belongs to it: the love of God. All parties agree that the person who achieves intellectual perfection and who is thereby motivated to engage in divinely-inspired actions of loving-kindness, justice, and righteousness also experiences the love of God.

But what exactly is this love of God that is a part of human perfection? Is it an affective and emotional condition or an intellectual one? How does it relate to the knowledge that, as Maimonides insists, is its foundation? Is it human perfection itself, or merely an epiphenomenal or emergent state of mind that crowns human perfection, a kind of amorous icing on the cake? Is it available – at least in principle – to many, including the common people, or is it reserved for a special (philosophical) elite? The issue is complicated by the fact that the love of God appears in both Maimonides' halakhic (or legal) writings, such as the *Commentary on the Mishnah* and the *Mishneh Torah*, on the one hand, and, on the other hand, his philosophical masterpiece, the *Guide of the Perplexed*.

---

[2] Stern (2013). For a contrasting view, see Lasker (2006).
[3] Scholars who read Maimonides as claiming that human perfection consists in intellectual perfection include Altmann (1981), Kreisel (1987), Blumenthal (1977), and Stern (2013). Those who opt for what Menachem Kellner calls "practical perfection" include Hartman (1976, especially 187–214) and Kellner (1990). Pines (1979) argues that true human perfection is practical, political or moral, not because it follows intellectual perfection but because the latter is impossible. Stern agrees with Pines that for Maimonides intellectual perfection is not humanly realizable, but he insists that it remains the human ideal. (See also Manekin 2005, 90–92.)

Like the topic of human perfection itself, the question of what the love of God involves for Maimonides is much debated in the literature, and so far very little clarity has been achieved. Most scholars seem to claim, on both philosophical and linguistic grounds, that the love of God amounts to the same thing in both the halakhic writings and in the *Guide* (although such a conclusion will have to account for the fact that the *Guide* is directed at a more select audience than the halakhic writings, and it seems at times to propose for that audience a very different normative model of human goodness).[4] On the other hand, it could be argued that the love of God in the philosophical *Guide* – more specifically, in the final chapters – may not be the same thing that we find in the halakhic writings, or even earlier in the *Guide*.

14.2 Predecessors

The Torah commands all Jews to "love the Lord your God with all your heart and with all your soul and with all your might" (Deuteronomy 6:5), a commandment that finds expression in the *Shema*, the most important prayer in Jewish liturgy.

The love of God is also a prominent feature of medieval Jewish, Muslim, and Christian philosophy.[5] Consider just a couple of pre-Maimonidean examples from the Jewish philosophical tradition, in both its Hebrew and Arabic versions.[6] In the eleventh century, Bahya Ibn Pakuda devotes the final chapter of his work *The Book of Direction to the Duties of the Heart* to "the true love of God." He distinguishes among three different varieties of such love. The first two are self-interested, and are based on the hope for divine reward and the hope for divine forgiveness, respectively. But the highest species of love of God, he says, is a "pure" love for "His own sake, His own honor, and to celebrate His greatness."[7] Bahya insists, moreover, that such love must be preceded by a fear of God – indeed, he suggests that fear and reverence are a part of the love of God and a necessary condition for it.[8]

---

[4] There certainly is some overlap between the intended audiences of the *Mishneh Torah* and the *Guide*, and Maimonides often refers readers of his later "popular" works (such as the "Letter on Resurrection") back to the *Guide*. My thanks to Charles Manekin for reminding me of this point.

[5] For a discussion of both the love of God and the intellectual love of God in and before Spinoza, see Wolfson (1934, 274–325).

[6] For an overview of the love of God in medieval Jewish philosophy generally, see Vajda (1957); and in medieval Judeo-Arabic thought, see S. Harvey (1997).

[7] Ibn Pakuda (1973, 429).   [8] Ibid., 427.

By contrast, the tenth-century rationalist Saadia ben Joseph (Saadia Gaon) insists in his *Book of Beliefs and Opinions* that the love of God is a consequence of knowledge of God. "When a person has achieved the knowledge of [God] by means of rational speculation," he writes, "his soul becomes filled with completely sincere love for God, a love which is beyond all doubt."[9] Likewise, the twelfth-century polymath Abraham Ibn Ezra insists that the love of God is intimately connected with knowledge of God; specifically, a knowledge of God's actions as they exhibit kindness, justice, and equity. "The root of all the commandments is that one is to love God with all one's soul and cleave to Him. But this cannot be completed if one does not recognize the acts of God above and below and know His ways."[10] As we will see, knowledge of God's actions plays an important role in one of Maimonides' conceptions of the love of God.[11]

14.3 Love of God in the *Mishneh Torah*

Maimonides first broaches the topic of the love of God in his halakhic writings, particularly the *Commentary on the Mishnah,* the *Sefer ha-Mitzvot (Book of Commandments)*, and the *Mishneh Torah*. I will concentrate here primarily on the more direct and extensive discussion in the *Mishneh Torah*.

In the first section of the first book (*Sefer ha-Madda*) of the *Mishneh Torah*, the *Hilkhot Yesodei ha-Torah* (*Laws of the Foundations of the Torah*), Maimonides notes that it is a commandment "to love and fear this glorious and awesome God." The term for love that Maimonides uses here is *ahavah*. This love arises when one contemplates the world and appreciates it as the product of God's creative activity.

> What is the path to love and fear of Him? When a person contemplates His wondrous and great deeds and creations and sees His infinite wisdom that surpasses all comparison, he will immediate love, praise, and glorify Him. (*Hilkhot Yesodei Ha-Torah* 2.2)

---

[9] *Book of Beliefs and Opinions* 2.13; Saadia (1948, 132). [10] Ibn Ezra (1976, 203 (*Shemot* 31:18)).
[11] It is at least worth noting, in the Christian tradition, St. Thomas Aquinas, who offers a tripartite division of the love of God. In contrast with the "natural love" of the divine, which exists in all created things, animate or otherwise; and with the "sensitive love" of God, which belongs to all animate beings, God is also the object of an *amor intellectualis*. This supreme love is reserved for rational beings alone, and it is grounded in knowledge and not feeling. See *Summa Theologiae*, Prima Secundae, Q. 26, art. 1, and Q. 27, art. 2; Secunda Secundae, Q. 26, art. 3. Wolfson (1934, 305) suggests that Thomas's distinction was the source for a similar distinction in Judah Abravanel (Leo Hebraeus).

In the *Mishneh Torah*, a massive compendium of rabbinic law composed for a broad, literate audience, the love of God is closely associated with knowledge. And the object of knowledge is, in a sense, God. However, the knowledge of God that leads to love of God is not a direct and intimate apprehension of the nature of God. In fact, Maimonides emphasizes to his reader that there is no question here of conceiving "the true nature of the Creator as He [truly] is" (*Hilkhot Yesodei Ha-Torah* 2.8). The problem, he says, is the limitations in our intellectual capacities.[12] Still, we can come to a knowledge of God's actions (*ma'asim*) and, through them, have at least a relational conception of God's wisdom. By God's "actions," Maimonides means God's creation and governance of the cosmos, as this is manifest in what we would now call the laws of nature and the phenomena they cover.

> When a person meditates on these matters and recognizes all the creations, the angels, the spheres, man, and the like, and sees the wisdom of the Holy One, blessed be He, in all these creations, he will add to his love for God [*ahavah le-makom*]. His soul will thirst and his flesh will long with love for God, blessed be He. (*Hilkhot Yesodei Ha-Torah* 4.12)

What such a person achieves at this level is essentially a command of natural science – a knowledge of the workings of the cosmos, including the nature and motions of the celestial spheres and the heavenly bodies they carry in their orbits and the sublunar hylomorphic substances that these spheres govern.[13] This is what Maimonides calls *Ma'aseh Bereshit*, the Story of Creation, as opposed to *Ma'aseh Merkaveh*, the Story of [Ezekiel's] Chariot, or the divine science. (The latter, he says, "should never be expounded upon, even to a single individual, unless he is wise and capable of understanding" [*Mishneh Torah* 4.11]). Through careful observation of the structure of things, from the arrangement of the stars to the organization of living bodies, and study of their lawlike behavior, one is led to think about God as the intelligent agent behind nature, and on that basis to draw certain conclusions about Him. Cosmological knowledge generates an appreciation and admiration of the Creator insofar as nature is taken to express His character – His wisdom, power, purposes, and will. Consequently, that knowledge brings about a love for God.

---

[12] By contrast, the *Guide of the Perplexed* seems, at least initially, to insist on the *in-principle* unknowability of God – and not just on the insufficiency of our intellects – because God's simple nature allows for no positive predications; see, for example, *Guide* 1.58.

[13] It also includes, apparently, some metaphysics, insofar as knowledge of the "angels" (the separate intellects) is metaphysical knowledge.

In *Hilkhot Teshuvah* (*Laws of Repentance*), the final section of *Sefer ha-Madda*, Maimonides expounds on the character of this love of God that arises from the contemplation of nature. He says that "a person should love God with a very great and exceeding love until his soul is bound up in the love of God. Thus, he will always be consumed with this love as if he is lovesick" (*Mishneh Torah, Hilkhot Teshuvah* 10.3). What this "lovesickness" means is that such a person's thoughts "are never diverted" from the object of his love. It is an all-consuming love, one that occupies a person's faculties even while they are engaged in the most mundane of activities. Indeed, one is willing to leave behind "all things in the world" for the sake of this love.[14]

Once again, the love of God is a consequence of, and proportional to, the knowledge that one has acquired.

> One can only love God through the knowledge with which one knows Him. The nature of one's love depends on the nature of one's knowledge. If small, then small; if great, then great. Therefore, it is necessary for a person to seclude himself in order to understand and conceive wisdom and concepts that make his Creator known to him according to the potential which man possesses to understand and comprehend as we explained in *Hilkhot Yesodei ha-Torah*. (*Mishneh Torah, Hilkhot Teshuvah* 10.6)

The nature and extent of one's love depends upon the nature and extent of one's knowledge. The deeper one's understanding of the cosmos, the more one knows about terrestrial and celestial beings and their relations, the more one will love their creator and governor, God. However, the knowledge of God that generates this love remains a relational knowledge: a conception of God derived from contemplation of the world around us and the grander cosmos. Nature and its lawlike regularities, as constitutive of God's "actions," are an expression of – and thus evidence for – God's wisdom and providence, as well as God's justice and equity. In this schema, we cannot know God's true essence; nor do we know anything

---

[14] I should note that, as several scholars have pointed out, there is some ambiguity as to whether, for Maimonides, the love of God in the halakhic writings arises from the knowledge of nature alone, or from a knowledge of Torah and its commandments as well. In the *Sefer ha-Mitzvot* (*Mitzvot Aseh*, or "Positive Commandments"), for example, Maimonides says that "we are commanded to love God ... that is to say, to dwell upon and contemplate His commandments, His injunctions, and His works, so that we may obtain a conception of Him" (Commandment 3). Kreisel (1999, 228–231) believes that Maimonides' view changes between the *Sefer ha-Mitzvot* and the *Mishneh Torah*, with the latter representing his considered view: "In the *Laws of the Principles of the Torah*, Maimonides wishes to stress in no uncertain terms that one fulfills the commandment to love God by means of the apprehension of the sciences, and in no other manner" (Kreisel 1999, 228). For a discussion of this issue, see Lamm (1992–1993).

directly (i.e., non-inferentially) and in positive terms about the nature of God; but we can know God's ways as these are evident in the phenomena of creation, and on this basis make certain qualified attributions of Him.

Moreover, this level of knowledge is – at least in principle – broadly accessible. There is no indication in these texts that the love of God and the knowledge that is its prerequisite is available only to a small and elite cohort, namely, those who have the ability and opportunity to truly perfect their intellects. Indeed, Maimonides notes that even among "children, women, and most of the common people," their knowledge can grow and their wisdom increase, until "they apprehend Him and know Him and worship Him out of love" (*Mishneh Torah, Hilkhot Teshuvah* 10.5).[15]

In sum, what we can say about the love of God in the *Mishneh Torah* (and, I would suggest, other halakhic writings) are three things:

First, the love of God – and the term consistently and exclusively used for "love" is *ahavah* – is, as with Saadia and Ibn Ezra, grounded in the study of the cosmos, in *natural science*. It is through the appreciation of God's creation that we see that God is worthy of love. For the knowing person, the works of the universe are the "door" or "opening" (*petah*) to the love of God. (*Hilkhot Yesodei Ha-Torah* 2.2)

Second, the knowledge of God that mediates between this appreciation of the cosmos and the love of God is only an indirect and *relational* knowledge of God. It is a conception of God's greatness and love-worthiness based solely and inferentially on an acquaintance with God's wondrous works; the content of this knowledge is limited to what can be surmised about God from this examination of, and in relation to, what God does.

Third, this love of God is *consequent* to or a result of knowledge; it is not itself identical to knowledge. The love of God in these texts, while intimately and invariably related to a cognitive or intellectual state – the knowledge of God is necessarily followed by love – is itself an affective state, not a cognitive or intellectual one.[16] As Maimonides says, "we have thus made it clear to you that through this act of contemplation you will attain a conception of God and reach that stage of joy in which *love of Him will follow* of necessity." (*Sefer ha-Mitzvot, Mitzvot Aseh*, Positive Commandment 3) (emphasis added)

---

[15] Still, Maimonides does concede that there are "many people who have received from their first natural disposition a complexion of temperament with which perfection is in no way compatible," and refers as well to those whose "defective natural disposition" renders them incapable of really knowing much about God, aside from the basic truths that God is incorporeal, that "God is one, that He is eternal, and that none but Him should be worshipped" (Maimonides 1963, 1.34: 77; 1.35: 81).

[16] On this point, Kellner (2005) agrees. He notes that in the *Mishneh Torah*, "love of God is an immediate consequence of knowing God; he does not reduce one to the other" (Kellner 2005, 291).

14.4 Love of God in the *Guide*

Let us turn now to the concluding chapters of Maimonides' *Guide of the Perplexed*, a philosophical treatise that is aimed at a different audience than that of the halakhic writings. For the most part, however, scholars do not recognize any significant difference between the two works in their conceptions of the love of God. They tend to regard the love of God in the *Guide* as either continuous with the account in the *Mishneh Torah* or, at best, an "expansion or deepening" of it. Thus, one scholar claims that "a study of Maimonides' approach to love of God in the *Mishneh Torah* and the *Guide* reveals an overall consistency in the views he presents. The fact that the former composition was intended for a general audience and the latter for an elite group did not lead him to formulate his views differently on this issue."[17] On the other hand, there are some texts in the *Guide* that suggest that something significant has changed in the nature of the love of God.

Maimonides insists in the *Guide* that one of the two primary goals at which the Law (or Torah) aims is the perfection of the soul.[18] Such spiritual perfection consists in the intellect being rational *in actu*, being an actual knowing intellect. Maimonides defines this as "knowing everything concerning all the beings that it is within the capacity of man to know in accordance with his ultimate perfection" (Maimonides 1963, 3.27: 511). The Law contributes to this goal by communicating "correct opinions" about the Creator and His creation, albeit in a traditional manner, culminating in the understanding of both natural things and God.

In the *Guide*, as in the *Mishneh Torah*, Maimonides is concerned to rule out, in principle, any knowledge of God's essence (*Guide* 1.52). Moreover, in much of the *Guide* he appears also to be ruling out *any* metaphysical knowledge of God, particularly in the form of positive absolute predications. For example, in *Guide* 1.58, he argues that even propositions about God that, at least in linguistic form, involve a positive predication in fact represent only negative claims; to say that "God is powerful" or "God is knowing" is "only to signify that He is neither powerless nor ignorant"

---

[17] Kreisel (1999, 264). See also Hartmann (1976, 257 note 13); Seeskin (2000, 158–159); and Kellner (2005). Lasker (2006) suggests that the love of God in the *Guide* supplements the account in the *Mishneh Torah* by describing a second level of such love. Vajda, similarly, claims that in the last chapters of the *Guide* "les thèmes de l'amour et de la crainte de Dieu sont récapitulés, mais aussi élargis et approfondis" (Vajda 1957, 134).

[18] The other goal comprises bodily health, social and political well-being, and moral character, all of which provide the necessary conditions for the pursuit of intellectual knowing.

(Maimonides 1963, 1.58: 136). Some commentators take Maimonides at his word here and thus conclude either that such knowledge of God cannot constitute our ultimate perfection, or that it *is* our ultimate perfection and therefore such perfection is not achievable.[19]

Let me note here, in a preliminary way, that I do not see that, from the in-principle unknowability of God's inner essence, it necessarily follows that nothing positive can be known about the nature of God more broadly understood; in fact, it seems that knowledge of God's *essence* aside, the ultimate human perfection may indeed consist in a perfection of the intellect that involves metaphysical knowledge of God.

Be that as it may for now, Maimonides does say in these early chapters of the *Guide* – just as he claimed in the halakhic writings – that it is at least possible for human beings to acquire a knowledge of God's ways or actions insofar as His governance of the world is manifest in the order of nature. Indeed, it is only this level of knowledge of God of which most (but not all) people are capable. Moreover, these chapters from the *Guide* add some detail to the way in which one is supposed to arrive at an inferential, relational knowledge of God.

> The apprehension of these [God's] actions is an apprehension of His attributes, with respect to which He is known ... Whenever one of His actions is apprehended, the attribute from which this actions proceeds is predicated of Him, may He be exalted, and the name deriving from that action is applied to Him ... It is not that He possesses moral qualities, but that He performs actions resembling the actions that in us proceed from moral qualities. (Maimonides 1963, 1.54: 124)

Human beings typically perform actions of type φ from some state of character or motive α. Whenever God is regarded as the agent of an action that has φ-like qualities – evident either in the course of nature or in Torah – a character-state or motive similar to α is projected onto Him (but only in a metaphorical sense). For example, when God is said to be "merciful" just as parents are merciful to their children,

> [i]t is not that He, may He be exalted, is affected and has compassion, but rather an action proceeds from Him that is similar to that which proceeds from a father in respect to his child and that [in the father] is attached to compassion, pity and an absolute passion. (Maimonides 1963, 1.54: 124–125) (translation modified for clarity)

---

[19] The former position is defended in Pines (1979); the latter position is defended in Stern (2013).

Even though Moses was promised by God that he may "know all His attributes," God nonetheless "made it clear to him that these are His actions, and taught him that His essence cannot be grasped as it really is" (Maimonides 1963, 1.53: 123).

14.5 Intellectual Perfection in the *Guide*

Is such relational knowledge of God all there is to the story? Toward the end of the *Guide*, Maimonides points to another, higher, level of knowledge of God available (at least in principle) to an elite – a level of intellectual achievement that would surpass the true beliefs about God that are communicated by the Law and the apprehension of God's "actions" derived from the study of nature. To be sure, Maimonides begins *Guide* 3.51 with the disclaimer that "this chapter that we bring now does not include additional matter over and above what is comprised in the other chapters of this Treatise." At the same time, he says that while these final chapters are "only a kind of a conclusion," they also "explain the worship as practiced by one who has apprehended the true realities peculiar only to Him after he has obtained an apprehension of what He is" (Maimonides 1963, 3.51: 618). At the very least, this higher knowledge of God brings a profound deepening in the love of God for the possessor of such knowledge.

To see how this is so, it is helpful to begin with Maimonides' parable of the palace (Maimonides 1963, 3.51: 618–620). He asks us to imagine a ruler in his palace in a city, with some citizens outside the city altogether, and some in the city but with their backs turned to the palace. The former citizens represent those who have no beliefs about God or the Law whatsoever, while the latter represent those who may have opinions about such matters but, because these opinions are based on the imagination or unguided speculation, they are certainly unjustified and most likely false. Then there are citizens *in* the city who seek out the ruler's palace and are eager to stand before him, but they have not yet found it. These, Maimonides says, "are the multitude of the adherents of the Law who merely observe the commandments" (Maimonides 1963, 3.51: 619). Another group of citizens have come up to the palace walls and walk around it. These represent individuals have gone beyond just observing the commandments and have true opinions on the basis of "traditional authority"; they are devoted to the study of the Law and divine worship, but they do not engage in speculation as to the fundamental principles of religion, the foundations of the Law.

There are some, however, who have made their way into the palace itself. They represent those who have pursued speculation to such a degree that they are on their way to a deeper understanding of God and of the commandments. Within this last category, Maimonides distinguishes two classes. Most of those who have succeeded in entering the palace remain within its antechambers. These, he says, "have understood the natural things." Maimonides is apparently referring here to those who know God only through His actions, through the study of nature, as we have seen described in the *Mishneh Torah* and the earlier chapters of the *Guide*.

A more select group, however, have gone further, beyond the antechamber: "If you have achieved perfection in the natural things and have understood divine science you have entered in the ruler's place into the inner court and are with him in one habitation." This, he continues, "is the rank of the men of science." They have turned "wholly toward God and ... renounce what is other than He" (Maimonides 1963, 3.51: 619–620). Such individuals "are present in the ruler's council," a rank that includes most prophets.

A step yet above these, however, is the individual who is addressing the ruler not as a member of his council, but one on one. This is the individual who, "because of the greatness of his apprehension and his renouncing everything that is other than God ... has attained such a degree that it is said of him, *And he was there with the Lord*, putting questions and receiving answers, speaking and being spoken to, in that holy place" (Maimonides 1963, 3.51: 620). Clearly, such a person has gone beyond those who know something about God in a purely relational manner and who have only beliefs about God's actions through an examination of His works. This person is enjoying a more direct apprehension of God.[20] "This," Maimonides says, "is the worship peculiar to those who have apprehended the true realities; the more they think of Him and of being with Him, the more their worship increases" (Maimonides 1963, 3.51: 620).

What this parable indicates is that Maimonides recognizes a level of knowledge of God that goes beyond that described in the halakhic writings and in parts one and two of the *Guide*. An individual who reaches this highest level of intellectual perfection is not just empirically "examining the beings" that God has created and governs. His knowledge of God is

---

[20] Maimonides suggests in the next chapter (*Guide* 3.52) that the ruler (or "king") in the palace parable is not to be identified with God Himself, but rather with "the intellect that overflows toward us." Still, this intellectual overflow, to which the perfected individual "clings", represents a cognitive bond or connection with God; thus, to be present before the "ruler" in the palace still represents epistemic access to God.

not just relational and indirect, derived inferentially from an apprehension of God's actions. Rather, he grasps what Maimonides calls "the true reality of the divine science" (Maimonides 1963, 3.52: 621). That is, he has moved beyond natural science to metaphysics. He has reached, Maimonides says, "the apprehension of His being as He, may He be exalted, is in truth" (Maimonides 1963, 3.52: 630).[21] The individual who apprehends God's being as it is "in truth" knows God not inferentially and in terms only relative to God's effects, but directly – not through mystical insight, but by intellectual acquaintance through metaphysics.[22]

"The apprehension of [God's] being as He is in truth," the knowledge of "what He is" and His "true reality": these are, of course, vague and opaque phrases. It is certainly not obvious that they commit Maimonides to saying, despite his earlier claims to the contrary, that knowledge of God's *essence* is possible for human beings. The scholarly consensus, well grounded in Maimonides' texts, while not unanimous, seems to be that they do not.[23] A less bold and perhaps more acceptable interpretation of these phrases is that Maimonides has in mind the apprehension of positive truths (and not just negative propositions characteristic of the *via negativa*) about the nature of God. These would be metaphysical truths that can in fact be demonstrated about God Himself, such as "God exists," "God is unique," "God is incorporeal," and so on.[24] But whether one opts for the strong reading (knowledge of God's essence) or the weaker reading (metaphysical knowledge about God), what does seem clear here is that we are on a different epistemic plane from the merely relational and derivative or inferential knowledge of God by analogy with human actions, and that is based on natural science, as described in the *Mishneh Torah* and the earlier chapters of the *Guide*.

That the metaphysical knowledge of God in question in *Guide* 3.51 is direct (non-inferential) and thus different from and epistemically superior to what is acquired by the individual who knows God only through a study

---

[21] In the Hebrew translation of the *Guide* made by Samuel Ibn Tibbon and reviewed and authorized by Maimonides, the phrase here is מציאות הש״י על אמתתה. Bear in mind, however, that this knowledge of God's "being as He … is in truth" does not imply a knowledge of God's *essence*.
[22] Lasker puts the distinction well: "[L]ove of God requires a twofold process: first, contemplation of God's works, namely understanding the 'whole of being as it is' and the wisdom 'as it is manifested in it', which would result in apprehension of God's actions. Then one must also apprehend 'His being as He, may He be exalted, is in truth.'" Lasker agrees that this latter achievement involves knowing "God's essential attributes, what God is" (Lasker 2006, 335).
[23] In addition to Stern (2013), see Franck (1985) and Manekin (2005); on the other side, see Lasker (2006).
[24] This is Manekin's reading (Manekin 2005, 91).

of the cosmos (natural science) is further suggested by Maimonides' introduction of the "bond" that the intellectually perfected individual enjoys with God.[25] Notice the hierarchic sequence implied in the following passage:

> If, however, you have apprehended God and His acts in accordance with what is required by the intellect, you should afterwards engage in totally devoting yourself to Him, endeavor to come closer to Him, and strengthen the bond between you and Him – that is, the intellect. (Maimonides 1963, 3.51: 620)

It is one thing to apprehend God through His actions; only after that may one "come closer to Him" and perfect one's intellect.

The bond or "cleaving" and the accompanying superior knowledge possessed by the perfected individual is a result of the divine "overflow."[26] Maimonides, in fact, explicitly identifies "the bond between us and Him" with "the intellect that overflows toward us" (Maimonides 1963, 3.52: 629). This overflow is the wisdom that emanates from God, passes through the separate intellects of the celestial spheres down to the Active Intellect (the separate intellect governing our sublunar realm), and is finally received by individuals in this world who have properly prepared minds and thus access to the Active Intellect. Maimonides explains that both true philosophers ("men of science engaged in speculation") and prophets enjoy "an overflow overflowing from God ... through the intermediation of the Active Intellect, toward the rational faculty" (Maimonides 1963, 2.36: 369) (for the prophet, the overflow continues on toward the imaginative faculty). To receive this overflow "is the highest degree of man and the ultimate term of perfection that can exist for his species" (Maimonides 1963, 2.36: 369). The perfection of the intellect thereby conferred is different from and cannot be achieved by merely mastering the empirical natural sciences. The overflow is a source of "knowledge and wisdom" not available through any other means; it immediately "renders perfect the rational faculty" (Maimonides 1963, 2.38: 377).

The content of the overflow is primarily speculative knowledge. One who is "connected" to the divine overflow and has reached this supreme level of understanding and intellectual perfection thereby enjoys a formidable cognitive union with God – what he knows reflects to a degree what God knows. To be sure, much of the content of the overflow is a deeper

---

[25] In Ibn Tibbon's translation, the term used for "bond" is *dibuk*.
[26] Maimonides introduces the "overflow" in his discussion of prophecy in *Guide* 2.32–37 and relates it to providence in *Guide* 3.51–52.

knowledge of the cosmos: an understanding of the physics of the celestial and terrestrial realms, and of the metaphysics of the spheres and the separate intellects that govern these realms. But precisely because this cosmological information now comes from God, it approximates (but does not, and cannot, replicate) the *Creator's* knowledge of the cosmos.[27]

More importantly, the overflow also reveals metaphysical truths about God not accessible to those who – to use Maimonides' metaphor – have entered the palace but do not stand in its inner court. The individual who receives the overflow to the fullest degree and experiences the consequent perfection of the rational faculty, Maimonides says, will "apprehend only divine and most extraordinary matters, will see only God and His angels" (Maimonides 1963, 2.36: 372). In the final chapter of the *Guide*, he notes that the most noble wisdom consists in "the apprehension of true realities, which have for their end the apprehension of Him" (Maimonides 1963, 3.54: 632). Maimonides does not say precisely what these metaphysical truths about God are, but suggests that they include principles about God's unity, knowledge, power, will, and eternity.

What we have here, then, is clearly an epistemic condition that surpasses the cognitive powers of all but a select few (and perhaps it remains possible even to this elite only in principle – an ideal to be aimed at and approximated but, given the weakness and infirmities of the embodied human intellect, whose powers are obstructed by the matter of the body, one that cannot actually be realized).[28] It is one thing to have obtained a relational knowledge of God through observation of the world and drawing conclusions about Him from the effects of His actions; even the masses can, at least in principle, achieve this. It is quite another thing to have a direct intellectual connection with God via the overflow; this is reserved for lovers of wisdom of the highest order and authentic prophets.

---

[27] Maimonides is perfectly clear that we cannot know things as God knows them: "A great disparity subsists between the knowledge an artificer has of the thing he has made and the knowledge someone else has of the artifact in question" (Maimonides 1963, 3.21: 484).

[28] On the role of matter here, see Stern (2013). Stern, on his nuanced "skeptical" reading, calls the state of intellectual perfection "a regulative ideal" that cannot actually be attained, but one that Maimonides nonetheless does not abandon: "Maimonides ... does not surrender the *ideal* of intellectual perfection although he holds that its achievement is not humanly realizable" (Stern 2013, 307). Again, my case is neutral on the question of whether Maimonides believes that any existing individual actually has reached or even can reach this condition. What Stern calls the "dogmatic" reading, whereby the intellectual perfection is indeed possible, is favored by Altmann (1987), Ivry (1998), and Kogan (1989).

14.6 Love and Knowledge

The intellectual bond or union with God, under the best circumstances, occupies the whole mind and leads to proper worship (and even to the enjoyment of divine providence).

> That intellect which overflowed from Him, may He be exalted, toward us is the bond between us and Him. ... You can only strengthen this bond by employing it in loving Him and in progressing toward this, just as we have explained. (Maimonides 1963, 3.51: 621)

Notice that love is now back in the picture. To so unite and bind oneself to God through receiving the divine overflow and thereby perfecting the intellect, Maimonides continues, is the true meaning of one of Judaism's central commands: "To love the Lord your God with all your heart and all your soul and all your might."

Maimonides' language here echoes the words used to describe the relationship between knowledge and the love of God in the *Mishneh Torah*. Once again he insists that "love is proportionate to apprehension" (Maimonides 1963, 3.51: 621). However, because the knowledge in question now goes beyond the knowledge of God that is possessed by those who have "understood the natural things," because it is a deeper, more intimate (metaphysical) knowledge of God, the love is correspondingly deeper, stronger, and more profound.

Indeed, Maimonides brings a new term into the *Guide* to refer to this love – a term that, while not uncommon in Judeo-Arabic literature in different contexts,[29] is found in Maimonides only in *Guide* 3.51 and nowhere else in his corpus:[30] *'ishq* (in Arabic) or *hesheq* (in Samuel Ibn Tibbon's Hebrew translation, reviewed and authorized by Maimonides himself). Zev Harvey has argued that this term denoting a passionate, all-consuming love, similar to the Greek *eros*, while a favorite of Sufi mystics to describe a human being's love of God, was typically avoided by Jewish and Muslim philosophers and religious thinkers, "who considered it too erotic for such a usage."[31] As one medieval figure puts it, the term is "applicable only to that with which one can copulate."[32] But

---

[29] See S. Harvey (1997) for an important survey.
[30] My thanks to Zev Harvey for confirming this for me.
[31] W. Z. Harvey (2014, 99); see also W. Z. Harvey (2013). S. Harvey (1997), on the other hand, believes that philosophers (especially Avicenna) are in fact Maimonides' most likely source for his use of the term.
[32] Abu'l-Faraj ibn al-Jauzi (twelfth century), quoted in S. Harvey (1997, 182).

Maimonides is not shy about using it to describe the deep and obsessive attachment to God enjoyed by the intellectually perfected individual.[33] More specifically, he employs it to refer to the cognitive condition that is the intellectual bond itself. "After apprehension, total devotion to Him and the employment of intellectual thought in passionately loving Him always should be aimed at" (Maimonides 1963, 3.51: 621).

Maimonides does continue to refer to the love of God in these latter chapters of the *Guide* also with the terms employed in the earlier chapters and in the *Mishneh Torah* – the Arabic *mahabbah* is rendered by Ibn Tibbon with the cognate *ahavah* – and in an important respect *'ishq/hesheq* is essentially a species of *mahabbah/ahavah*, namely, that whereby love is taken to its highest possible level.

> You know the difference between the terms *one who loves* [Maimonides retains the Hebrew in his Judeo-Arabic text: *ohev*] and one who loves passionately [also Hebrew: *hosheq*]; an excess of love [*mahabbah*], so that no thought remains that is directed toward a thing other than the Beloved, is passionate love [*'ishq*]. (Maimonides 1963, 3.51: 627)

Still, it is an exclusive level of love that few, if any, can reach, insofar as Maimonides reserves *'ishq/hesheq* solely for the intellectual condition described in *Guide* 3.51 (and, by implication, *Guide* 3.52–54).[34]

It is tempting to conclude, moreover, that unlike what we find in the halakhic writings, the love of God in the final chapters of the *Guide* is not *consequent* to the highest knowledge – it is *identical* with it. That is, the account of the love of God in *Guide* 3.51 suggests that this love simply *is* the highest intellectual perfection for a human being; it is constituted by the bond and thus is essentially an epistemic and intellectual state, not an

---

[33] While Maimonides does, in the passage from *Mishneh Torah, Hilkhot Teshuvah* 10.3, speak of "a very great and exceeding love" in which an individual's "soul is bound up in the love of God," he does not use the term "*hesheq*" in describing this love or the lover's union with God; this indicates that he is not speaking of the same kind of love that is the subject of *Guide* 3.51.

[34] The love of God in its intellectual version is explicitly expounded only in *Guide* 3.51. Moreover, the special term used to describe it, *'ishq/hesheq*, appears only in *Guide* 3.51, and Maimonides reverts solely to *mahabbah/ahavah* in *Guide* 3.52. However, *Guide* 3.52 is clearly a continuation of the discussion of the intellectual bond that the perfected person enjoys with God. Maimonides also explains in this chapter how "some excellent men obtain such training that they achieve human perfection", and that the love they experience "includes the apprehension of His being as He is in truth." Thus, chapter 3.52 should be seen as pursuing the same topic as chapter 3.51, and thus also as being concerned with the special (intellectual) love of God denoted by *'ishq/hesheq*, even if the term itself is absent.

affective one (although it does have an affective component).³⁵ On such a reading, at this high level of cognitive achievement, whereby one has reached an apprehension of God's "being as He is in truth," it turns out that to love God just *is* to know God: the love of God, the intellectual knowledge of God, and the cognitive bond with God are all one and the same. After telling his reader that "the intellect which overflowed from Him, may He be exalted, toward us is the bond between us and Him," Maimonides notes that "you can only strengthen this bond by employing it in loving Him" (Maimonides 1963, 3.51: 621). This would make the love of God that is the highest human perfection a purely intellectual relationship. "The exhortation [to love God]," he notes, "always refers to intellectual apprehensions, not to imagination" (Maimonides 1963, 3.51: 621). If love is – as Maimonides believes – an intense, obsessive, focused union with an object, then the ideal epistemic condition that is the philosopher's or prophet's intellectual understanding of God is itself the highest form of love attainable (at least in principle) by a human being. It is, in fact, an intellectual love insofar as the love consists in the cognitive union itself.³⁶

14.7 Conclusion

Be that as it may, for Maimonides the love of God enjoyed by the philosopher and the prophet is a deeply passionate love, a single-minded devotion that involves pleasure and joy. A consummate desire and satisfaction are an essential part of *'ishq/hesheq*. It is not a bodily pleasure, however, but a purely intellectual one. In fact, the true love of God increases as the powers of the bodily faculties diminish with age. Referring to "the perfection of the intelligibles that lead to passionate love of Him" in "pure thought," Maimonides says that "when a perfect man is stricken with years and approaches death, this apprehension increases very

---

[35] Blumenthal describes the union as an "intellectualist-mystical" one. While it involves the "communication of intellectual knowledge", he suggests that it also a mystical experience with "overtones of Sufi mysticism" (Blumenthal 1977, 52). However, he does not explain what precisely makes an experience a "mystical" one – he just mentions that it involves a "pure spiritual emanation from the divine intellect" – and so it remains unclear how the cognitive state of affairs referred to by Maimonides is both intellectual *and* mystical.

[36] Kellner disputes the idea that for Maimonides the love of God and the knowledge of God are identical (Kellner 2005, 290–293). S. Harvey, on the other hand, recognizes Maimonides' love of God in the final chapters of the *Guide* as "intellectual worship," a condition of "pure contemplation ... This highest degree of love of God *consists in* the mind's undistracted and total concentration and contemplation of God" (Harvey 1997, 180–181; my emphasis). This seems also to be Stern's reading (Stern 2013, 314–315).

powerfully, joy over this apprehension and a great love [*'ishq/hesheq*] for the object becomes stronger, until the soul is separated from the body at that moment in this state of pleasure" (Maimonides 1963, 3.51: 627).[37]

If indeed it is possible for anyone to experience the true and highest love of God – whether it be consequent to or identical with an intellectual condition – that person will be a rare and isolated individual. The more rudimentary and relational knowledge of God's actions, and the affective love of God that follows it, is something that many can attain. Knowledge of God's "being as it is in truth," however – that is, the highest human perfection that consists in a pure apprehension of God's intelligible nature which is intimately connected to the most stable and passionate love of God – is a distinct condition that is reserved for an elite. As Maimonides says, "these matters are only for a few solitary individuals of a very special sort, not for the multitude" (Maimonides 1963, 1.34: 79). Those who are not sufficiently prepared for such truths – physically, emotionally, and intellectually – should be prevented from even beginning to approach them, "just as a small baby is prevented from taking coarse foods and from lifting heavy weights" (Maimonides 1963, 1.34: 79).

---

[37] Vajda insists that the affective component here involves "tout le contraire de l'émotion" (Vajda 1957, 137). This seems right, since the affect or passion is an intellectual, not a bodily one.

Bibliography

Ackerman, Ari. 2009. "Miracles." In S. Nadler and T. M. Rudavsky, eds., *The Cambridge History of Jewish Philosophy: From Antiquity through the Seventeenth Century* (New York: Cambridge University Press), pp. 362–387.

Adamson, Peter. 2013. "From the Necessary Existent to God." In P. Adamson, ed., *Interpreting Avicenna: Critical Essays* (Cambridge: Cambridge University Press), pp. 170–189.

Al-Farabi. 1972. *The Political Regime*, ed. and trans. F. M. Najjar (Ithaca: Cornell University Press).

  1981. *Al-Farabi's Commentary and Short Treatise on Aristotle's De Interpretatione*, trans. F. W. Zimmerman (London: Oxford University Press). [= Zimmermann 1981]

  1985. *Al-Farabi on the Perfect State*, ed. and trans. R. Walzer (Oxford: Oxford University Press). [= Walzer 1985]

  2007. "Letter on the Intellect." In J. McGinnis and D. C. Reisman, eds., *Classical Arabic Philosophy: An Anthology of Sources* (Indianapolis: Hackett), pp. 68–77.

Al-Ghazali. 1997. *Incoherence of the Philosophers*, trans. M. Marmura (Provo: Brigham Young University Press).

  2000. *Maqāṣid al-Falāsifa*, ed. M. Bejou (Damascus: Miṭba'a al-Ṣabāḥ).

Altmann, Alexander. 1953. "Essence and Existence in Maimonides." *Bulletin of the John Rylands Library* 35: 294–315.

  1981 (1972). "Maimonides' Four Perfections." In Altmann, *Essays in Jewish Intellectual History* (Hanover: University Press of New England), pp. 65–76.

  1987. "Maimonides on the Intellect and the Scope of Metaphysics." In Altmann, *Von der mittelalterlichen zur modernen Aufklärung: Studien zur jüdischen Geistesgeschichte* (Tübingen: J. C. Mohr), pp. 60–129.

Amir-Muezzi, Mohammad Ali. 1994. *The Divine Guide in Early Shi'ism: The Sources of Esotericism in Islam* (Albany: SUNY Press).

Aristotle. 1984. *The Complete Works of Aristotle*, ed. J. Barnes (Princeton: Princeton University Press).

  1994. *Posterior Analytics* (2nd ed.), trans. J. Barnes (Oxford: Clarendon Press).

  1997. *Topics: Books I and VIII*, trans. R. Smith (Oxford: Clarendon Press).

  2009. *The Nicomachean Ethics*, trans. W. D. Ross, rev. L. Brown (Oxford: Oxford University Press).

Armstrong, David. 1978. *Universals and Scientific Realism* (Cambridge: Cambridge University Press).
Asper, Markus. 2013. "Narratives in (Late-Antique) Commentary." In M. Erler and J. E. Heßler, eds., *Argument und literarische Form in Antiker Philosophie* (Berlin: De Gruyter), pp. 435–456.
Assmann, Jan and Burkhard Gladigow, eds., 1995. *Text und Kommentar: Archäologie der literarischen Kommunikation IV* (Munich: Wilhelm Fink).
Averroes. 1938. *Tafsir ma Ba'ad at-Tabi'at*, vol. 1, ed. M. Bouyges (Beirut: Imprimerie Catholique).
Avicenna. 1892. *Kitab al-Isharat w'al-Tanbihat*, ed. J. Forget (Leiden: Brill).
  1949. *Avicenna's Psychology*, ed. and trans. F. Rahman (Oxford: Oxford University Press).
  1959. *Al-Najāt min al-Gharq fī Baḥr al-Ḍalālāt*, ed. M. T. Dānishpazhūh (Tehran: Dānishgāh-i Tihrān).
  2005. *The Metaphysics of the Healing (Al-Shifa)*, trans. M. Marmura (Provo: Brigham Young University Press).
Bäck, Allen. 1992. "Avicenna's Conception of the Modalities." *Vivarium* 30: 217–235.
Baneth, David H. 1935. "On the Philosophical Terminology of Maimonides." *Tarbiz* 6(3): 254–284. [Heb.]
Barnes, Jonathan. 1992. "Metacommentary." *Oxford Studies in Ancient Philosophy* 10: 267–281.
Becker, Oscar. 1952. *Untersuchungen über den Modalkalkül* (Meisenheim am Glan: Anton Hain), pp. 16–36.
Benor, Ehud. 1985. "Models for Understanding Evil in *The Guide of the Perplexed*." *Iyyun* 34: 3–33. [Heb.]
  1995. "Meaning and Reference in Maimonides' Negative Theology." *The Harvard Theological Review* 88(3): 339–360.
Ben-Sasson, Yonah. 1960. "A Study of the Doctrine of the Reasons for the Commandments in Maimonides' *Guide*." *Tarbiz* 29: 268–281. [Heb.]
Berman, Lawrence. 1961. "The Political Interpretation of the Maxim: The Purpose of Philosophy is the Imitation of God." *Studia Islamica* 15: 53–61.
  1974. "Maimonides, the Disciple of Al-Farabi." *Israel Oriental Studies* 4: 154–178.
  1980. "Maimonides on the Fall of Man." *AJS Review* 5: 1–15.
Bertolacci, Amos. 2006. *The Reception of Aristotle's* Metaphysics *in Avicenna's Kitāb al-Šifā': A Milestone of Western Metaphysical Thought* (Leiden: Brill).
Black, Deborah L. 1990. *Logic and Aristotle's Rhetoric and Poetics in Medieval Arabic Philosophy* (Leiden: Brill).
  2006. "Knowledge and Certainty in Al-Farabi's Epistemology." *Arabic Sciences and Philosophy* 16: 11–45.
  2013. "Certitude, Justification, and the Principles of Knowledge in Avicenna's Epistemology." In P. Adamson, ed., *Interpreting Avicenna: Critical Essays* (Cambridge: Cambridge University Press), pp. 120–142.

Bland, Kalman. 1982. "Moses and the Law According to Maimonides." In J. Reinharz and D. Swetschinski, eds., *Mystics, Philosophers, and Politicians: Essays in Jewish Intellectual History in Honor of Alexander Altmann* (Durham: Duke University Press), pp. 49–66.

Blumberg, Harry. 1972. "Theories of Evil in Medieval Jewish Philosophy." *Hebrew Union College Annual* 43: 149–167.

Blumenthal, David R. 1977. "Maimonides' Intellectualist Mysticism and the Superiority of the Prophecy of Moses." *Studies in Medieval Culture* 10: 51–67.

BonJour, Laurence. 1998. *In Defense of Pure Reason* (Cambridge: Cambridge University Press).

Broadie, Alexander. 1989. "Maimonides and Divine Knowledge." In R. Link-Salinger, R. J. Long, and C. Manekin, eds., *A Straight Path: Essays in Honor of Arthur Hyman* (Washington, DC: The Catholic University of America Press), pp. 47–55.

Broadie, Sarah. 1991. *Ethics with Aristotle* (Oxford: Oxford University Press).

Brunner, Peter. 1928. *Probleme der Teleologie bei Maimonides, Thomas von Aquin, und Spinoza* (Heidelberg: Carl Winter).

Bruns, Gerald. 1982. *Inventions: Writing, Textuality, and Understanding in Literary History* (New Haven: Yale University Press).

Buijs, Joseph A. 1988. "The Negative Theology of Maimonides and Aquinas." *The Review of Metaphysics* 41(4): 723–738.

Burnyeat, Myles. 1980. "Aristotle on Learning to Be Good." In A. O. Rorty, ed., *Essays on Aristotle's Ethics* (Berkeley: University of California Press), pp. 69–92.

Cappelen, Herman and Josh Dever. 2013. *The Inessential Indexical. On the Philosophical Insignificance of Perspective and the First Person* (Oxford: Oxford University Press).

Castañeda, Hector. 1974. "Thinking and the Structure of the World." *Philosophia* 4: 3–40.

Casullo, Albert. 2003. *A Priori Justification* (Oxford: Oxford University Press).

Cohen, Hermann. 1978. "Ofyah shel Torat Ha-Middot li-ha-Rambam." In Cohen, *Iyyunim bi-Yahadut u-vi-Ba'ayot ha-Dor* (Jerusalem: Mossad Bialik), pp. 17–59.

2004. *Ethics of Maimonides*, trans. with commentary by Almut Sh. Bruckstein (Madison: University of Wisconsin Press).

Crescas, Hasdai. 1990. *Or Adonai (Or Ha-Shem)*, ed. S. Fisher (Jerusalem: Ramot).

2018. *Light of the Lord*, trans. R. Weiss (Oxford: Oxford University Press).

Davidson, Herbert A. 1974. "The Study of Philosophy as a Religious Obligation." In S. Goitein, ed., *Religion in a Religious Age* (Cambridge, MA: Association for Jewish Studies), pp. 53–68.

1979. "Maimonides' Secret Position on Creation." In I. Twersky, ed., *Studies in Medieval Jewish History and Literature*, vol. 1. (Cambridge, MA: Harvard University Press), pp. 16–40.

1987. *Proofs for Eternity, Creation, and the Existence of God in Medieval Islamic and Jewish Philosophy* (New York: Oxford University Press).

1992. *Alfarabi, Avicenna, and Averroes on Intellect* (Oxford: Oxford University Press).

1992–1993. "Maimonides on Metaphysical Knowledge." *Maimonidean Studies* 3: 49–103.

2001. "The Authenticity of Works Attributed to Maimonides." In E. Fleischer et al., eds., *Me'ah She'arim: Studies in Medieval Jewish Spiritual Life in Memory of Isadore Twersky* (Jerusalem: Magnes Press), pp. 111–133.

2004. "Maimonides, Aristotle, and Avicenna." In R. Morelon and A. Hasnawi, eds., *De Zénon d'Élée a Poincaré: Recueil d'études en homage a Roshdi Rashed* (Louvain-Paris: Peeters), pp. 719–734.

2005. *Moses Maimonides: The Man and His Works* (New York: Oxford University Press).

2011. *Maimonides the Rationalist* (London: Littman).

2018. "Maimonides and the Almohads." In C. Manekin and D. Davies, eds., *Interpreting Maimonides* (Cambridge: Cambridge University Press), pp. 6–25.

Davies, Daniel. 2011. *Method and Metaphysics in Maimonides' Guide for the Perplexed* (New York: Oxford University Press).

De Souza, Igor H. 2018. *Rewriting Maimonides: Early Commentaries on the "Guide of the Perplexed"* (Berlin: De Gruyter).

Dhanani, Alnoor. 1994. *The Physical Theory of Kalam: Atoms, Space and Void in Basrian Mu'tazili Cosmology* (Leiden: Brill).

Diamond, James. 2002. *Maimonides and the Hermeneutics of Concealment: Deciphering Scripture and Midrash in* The Guide of the Perplexed (Albany: SUNY Press).

2014. *Maimonides and the Shaping of the Jewish Canon* (New York: Cambridge University Press).

Diesendruck, Zwi. 1928. "Die Teleologie bei Maimonides." *Hebrew Union College Annual* 5: 419–442.

Diogenes Laertius. 1925. *Lives of Eminent Philosophers*, trans. R. D. Hicks (Cambridge, MA: Harvard University Press).

Dutton, Blake. 2001. "Al-Ghazali on Possibility and the Critique of Causality." *Medieval Philosophy and Theology* 10: 23–46.

Eisenmann, Esti. 2007. "Remarks on the Attribute 'Corporeal' in Maimonides: In the Footsteps of Thomas Aquinas and Gersonides." In B. Ish-Shalom, ed., *Be-Darkhe Shalom: Studies in Jewish Thought Presented to Shalom Rosenberg* (Jerusalem: Beit Morasha of Jerusalem Press), pp. 265–272. [Heb.]

Epictetus. 1983. *The Handbook of Epictetus*, trans. N. White (Indianapolis: Hackett).

Even-Chen, Alexander. 2018. "On the Onkelos Translations in the *Guide of the Perplexed*." *Da'at* 85, 141–166. [Heb.]

Fackenheim, Emil. 1946/1947. "The Possibility of the Universe in Al-Farabi, Ibn Sina, and Maimonides." *Proceedings of the American Academy for Jewish Research* 16: 39–70.

Feldman, Seymour. 1968. "A Scholastic Misinterpretation of Maimonides' Doctrine of Divine Attributes." *Journal of Jewish Studies* 19: 23–39.
Fox, Marvin. 1990. *Interpreting Maimonides* (Chicago: University of Chicago Press).
Fraenkel, Carlos. 2006. "Maimonides' God and Spinoza's Deus sive Natura." *Journal of the History of Philosophy* 44(2): 169–215.
  2008. "Philosophy and Exegesis in Al-Farabi, Averroes, and Maimonides." *Laval théologique et philosophique* 64(1): 105–125.
Franck, Isaac. 1985. "Maimonides and Aquinas on Man's Knowledge of God: A Twentieth Century Perspective." *The Review of Metaphysics* 38: 591–615.
Frank, Daniel H. 1985. "The End of the *Guide*: Maimonides on the Best Life for Man." *Judaism* 34: 485–495.
  1989. "Humility as a Virtue: A Maimonidean Critique of Aristotle's Ethics." In E. Ormsby, ed., *Moses Maimonides and His Time* (Washington, DC: The Catholic University of America Press), pp. 89–99.
  1990. "Anger as a Vice: A Maimonidean Critique of Aristotle's Ethics." *History of Philosophy Quarterly* 7: 269–281.
  1992. "The Elimination of Perplexity: Socrates and Maimonides as Guides of the Perplexed." In D. H. Frank, ed., *Autonomy and Judaism: The Individual and the Community in Jewish Philosophical Thought* (Albany: SUNY Press), pp. 121–142.
  1993. "The Duty to Philosophize: Socrates and Maimonides." *Judaism* 42: 289–297.
  1994. "Reason in Action: The 'Practicality' of Maimonides' *Guide*." In D. H. Frank, ed., *Commandment and Community: New Essays in Jewish Legal and Political Philosophy* (Albany: SUNY Press), pp. 69–84.
  2006. "Ethics." In S. H. Nasr and O. Leaman, eds., *History of Islamic Philosophy* (New York: Routledge), pp. 959–968.
Frede, Michael. 1994. "Aristotle's Notion of Potentiality in *Metaphysics Theta*." In T. Scaltsas, D. Charles, and M. L. Gill, eds., *Unity, Identity, and Explanation in Aristotle's Metaphysics* (Oxford: Clarendon Press), pp. 173–193.
Freudenthal, Gad. 1993. "Maimonides' Stance on Astrology in Context: Cosmology, Physics, Medicine, and Providence." In F. Rosner and S. Kottek, eds., *Moses Maimonides: Physician, Scientist, and Philosopher* (Northvale: Jason Aronson), pp. 77–90.
  2007. "Maimonides on the Scope of Metaphysics *alias* Ma'aseh Merkavah: The Evolution of His Views." In C. del Valle, S. García-Jalón and J. P. Monferrer, eds., *Maimónides y su época* (Madrid: Ministerio de Cultura), pp. 221–230.
  2008. "Maimonides on the Knowability of the Heavens and of Their Mover: (*Guide* 2:24)." *Aleph* 8: 151–157.
Freudenthal, Gad and Mauro Zonta. 2012. "Avicenna among Medieval Jews: The Reception of Avicenna's Philosophical, Scientific and Medieval Writings in Jewish Cultures, East and West." *Arabic Sciences and Philosophy* 22: 212–287.

Galston, Miriam. 1978. "The Purpose of the Law According to Maimonides." *Jewish Quarterly Review* 69: 27–51.
  1990. *Politics and Excellence: The Political Philosophy of Alfarabi* (Princeton: Princeton University Press).
Gersonides, Levi. 1987. *The Wars of the Lord*, vol. 2, trans. S. Feldman (Philadelphia: Jewish Publication Society).
Gettier, Edmund. 1963. "Is Justified True Belief Knowledge?" *Analysis* 23: 121–123.
Glucker, Yohanan. 1959. "The Modal Problem in the Philosophy of Maimonides." *Iyyun* 10(4): 177–191. [Heb.]
Goldman, Eliezer. 1977. "On the Final End of the Universe in the *Guide of the Perplexed*." In A. Kasher and J. Levinger, eds., *Sefer Yeshayahu Leibowitz* (Tel Aviv: Student Union), pp. 164–191 (reprinted in Goldman 1996). [Heb.]
  1996. "On the Purpose of Existence in the *Guide of the Perplexed*." In Goldman, *Expositions and Inquiries: Jewish Thought in Past and Present*, ed. A. Sagi and D. Statman (Jerusalem: Magnes Press), pp. 87–114. [Heb.]
Goodman, Nelson. 1955. *Fact, Fiction, and Forecast* (Cambridge, MA: Harvard University Press).
Gregory of Nyssa. 2007. *Gregory of Nyssa: Contra Eunomium II* (Leiden, Boston: Brill).
Griffel, Frank. 2009. *Al-Ghazali's Philosophical Theology* (Oxford: Oxford University Press).
  2019. "Maimonides as a Student of Islamic Religious Thought: Revisiting Shlomo Pines' 'Translator's Introduction' and Its Comments on al-Ghazali." In J. Stern, J. Robinson, and Y. Shemesh, eds., *Maimonides' Guide of the Perplexed in Translation: A History from the Thirteenth Century to the Twentieth* (Chicago: University of Chicago Press), pp. 403–427.
Gutas, Dimitri. 2014. *Aristotle and the Aristotelian Tradition: Introduction to Reading Avicenna's Philosophical Works* (2nd ed.) (Leiden: Brill).
Guttmann, Julius. 1973. *Philosophies of Judaism* (New York: Schocken Books).
Hadad, Eliezer. 2011. *Ha-Torah ve-ha-Teva be-Kitve Ha-Rambam* (Jerusalem: Magnes Press).
Hadot, Ilsetraut. 1987. "Les introductions aux commentaires exégétiques chez les auteurs néoplatoniciens et les auteurs chrétiens." In M. Tardieu, ed., *Les règles de l'interprétation* (Paris: Cerf), pp. 99–122.
Halbertal, Moshe. 1990. "Maimonides' *Book of Commandments* and the Architecture of Halakhah and Its Theory of Interpretation." *Tarbiz* 59: 457–480. [Heb.]
  2014. *Maimonides: Life and Thought* (Princeton: Princeton University Press).
Halper, Yehuda. 2018. "Does Maimonides' *Mishneh Torah* Forbid Reading the *Guide of the Perplexed*? On Platonic Punishment for Freethinkers." *AJS Review* 42: 351–379.
Hamori, Esther. 2008. *When Gods Were Men: The Embodied God in Biblical and Near Eastern Literature* (Berlin: De Gruyter).
Hartman, David. 1976. *Maimonides: Torah and Philosophic Quest* (Philadelphia: Jewish Publication Society).

1985. "The Epistle on Martyrdom: Discussion." In *Crisis and Leadership: Epistles of Maimonides*, trans. and ann. A. Halkin; discussions by D. Hartman (Philadelphia: Jewish Publication Society).

Harvey, Elon. 2019. "Avicenna's Influence on Maimonides' Epistle on Astrology." *Arabic Sciences and Philosophy* 29: 171–183.

Harvey, Steven. 1997. "The Meaning of Terms Designating Love in Judaeo-Arabic Thought and Some Remarks on the Judaeo-Arabic Interpretation of Maimonides." In N. Golb, ed., *Judaeo-Arabic Studies* (Amsterdam: Harwood), pp. 175–196.

2004. "The Impact of Philoponus' *Commentary on the Physics* on Averroes' Three Commentaries on the *Physics*." In P. Adamson, H. Baltussen and M. W. F. Stone, eds., *Philosophy, Science and Exegesis in Greek, Arabic and Latin Commentaries* (London: Institute of Classical Studies), pp. 97–104.

2006. "The Place of the *De Anima* in the Orderly Study of Philosophy." In M. Pacheco and J. F. Meirinhos, eds., *Intellect and Imagination in Medieval Philosophy*, vol. 1 (Turnhout: Brepols), pp. 676–688.

Harvey, Warren Zev. 1979. "Maimonides and Spinoza on the Knowledge of Good and Evil." *Iyyun* 28: 67–85. [Heb.]

1981a. "A Portrait of Spinoza as a Maimonidean." *Journal of the History of Philosophy* 19: 151–172.

1981b. "A Third Approach to Maimonides' Cosmogony-Prophetology Puzzle." *Harvard Theological Review* 74: 287–301.

1986. "Ethics and Meta-Ethics, Aesthetics and Meta-Aesthetics in Maimonides." In S. Pines and Y. Yovel, eds., *Maimonides and Philosophy* (Dordrecht: Martinus Nijhoff), pp. 131–138.

1988. "Maimonides and Aquinas on Interpreting the Bible." *Proceedings of the American Academy for Jewish Research* 55: 59–77.

1994. "Political Philosophy and Halakhah in Maimonides." In J. Dan, ed., *Binah*, vol. 3 (Westport: Praeger), pp. 47–64.

1996. "Notes on Rabbi Joseph B. Soloveitchik and Maimonidean Philosophy." In A. Sagi, ed., *Faith in Changing Times: On the Teachings of Rav Joseph B. Soloveitchik* (Jerusalem: World Zionist Organization), pp. 95–107. [Heb.]

2005. "Two Approaches to Evil in Jewish History." In S. T. Katz, ed., *The Impact of the Holocaust on Jewish Theology* (New York: New York University Press), pp. 194–201.

2008a. "Maimonides' Critical Epistemology and *Guide* 2:24." *Aleph* 8: 213–235.

2008b. "Maimonides' Avicennianism." *Maimonidean Studies* 5: 107–119.

2013. "Notions of Divine and Human Love in Jewish Thought: An Interview with Warren Zev Harvey." *University of Toronto Journal of Jewish Thought* 3: 1–11.

2014. "*Ishq*, *Hesheq*, and *Amor Dei Intellectualis*." In S. Nadler, ed., *Spinoza and Medieval Jewish Philosophy* (Cambridge: Cambridge University Press), pp. 96–107.

2017. "Spinoza and Maimonides on Teleology and Anthropocentrism." In Y. Melamed, ed., *Spinoza's Ethics: A Critical Guide* (Cambridge: Cambridge University Press), pp. 43–55.

Hasnawy, Ahmad. 2004. "Réflexions sur la terminologie logique de Maimonide et son contexte Farabien: *Le Guide des Égarés* et le *Traité de Logique*." In T. Lévy and R. Rashed, eds., *Maïmonide: Perspectives arabe, hébraique, latine* (Louvain: Peeters), pp. 39–78.

Hawthorne, John and Jason Stanley. 2008. "Knowledge and Action." *Journal of Philosophy* 105(10): 571–590.

Heinemann, Isaac. 1966. *Ta'amei ha-Mitzvot be-Sifrut Isra'el* (5th ed.) (Jerusalem: ha-Histadrut ha-Tziyonit) [Heb.].

Heschel, Abraham Joshua. 1996. "Did Maimonides Believe that He had Attained the Rank of Prophecy?" In M. Faierstein, ed., *Prophetic Inspiration after the Prophets: Maimonides and Other Medieval Authorities* (Hoboken: Ktav), pp. 69–126.

Hintikka, Jaakko. 1973. *Time and Necessity: Studies in Aristotle's Theory of Modality* (Oxford: Clarendon Press).

Hourani, George. 1972. "Ibn Sina on Necessary and Possible Existence." *Philosophical Forum* 4: 74–86.

Hughes, Aaron. 2003. "Presenting the Past: The Genre of Commentary in Theoretical Perspective." *Method and Theory in the Study of Religion* 15(2): 148–168.

Hyman, Arthur. 1979–1980. "A Note on Maimonides' Classification of Law." *Proceedings of the American Academy for Jewish Research* 46–47: 323–343.

  1989. "Demonstrative, Dialectical and Sophistic Arguments in the Philosophy of Moses Maimonides." In E. Ormsby, ed., *Moses Maimonides and His Time* (Washington, DC: The Catholic University of America Press), pp. 35–51.

  1991. "Maimonides on Religious Language." In J. L. Kraemer, ed., *Perspectives on Maimonides: Philosophical and Historical Studies* (Oxford: Oxford University Press), pp. 175–191.

  2010. "Moses Maimonides, 1135–1204." In A. Hyman, J. J. Walsh, and T. Williams, eds., *Philosophy in the Middle Ages* (3rd ed.) (Indianapolis: Hackett), pp. 360–363.

Ibn al-Arabi, M. 2005. *The Meccan Revelations*, vol. 1 (New York: Pir Press).

Ibn Ezra, Abraham. 1976. *Perushei ha-Torah*, vol. 2: *Shemot* (Jerusalem: Mossad HaRav Kook).

Ibn Pakuda, Bahya ben Joseph. 1973. *The Book of Directions to the Duties of the Heart*, trans. M. Mansoor (London: Routledge and Kegan Paul).

Ibn Rushd (Averroes). 2001. *Faith and Reason in Islam: Averroes' Exposition of Religious Arguments*, trans. I. Najjar (Oxford: Oneworld).

Ibrahim, Ahmed Fekry. 2016. "Rethinking the *Taqlīd* – *Ijtihād* Dichotomy: A Conceptual-Historical Approach." *Journal of the American Oriental Society* 136: 285–303.

Ichikawa, Jonathan J. and Matthias Steup. 2018. "The Analysis of Knowledge." In E. N. Zalta, ed., *Stanford Encyclopedia of Philosophy*.

Irwin, Terence H. 1981. "Homonymy in Aristotle." *The Review of Metaphysics* 34(3): 523–544.
Ivry, Alfred L. 1982. "Maimonides on Possibility." In J. Reinharz and D. Swetschinski, eds., *Mystics, Philosophers, and Politicians: Essays in Jewish Intellectual History in Honor of Alexander Altmann* (Durham: Duke University Press), pp. 67–84.
  1998. "The Logical and Scientific Premises of Maimonides' Thought." In A. Ivry et al., eds., *Perspectives on Jewish Thought and Mysticism* (Amsterdam: Harwood), pp. 63–97.
  2005. "The *Guide* and Maimonides' Philosophical Sources." In K. Seeskin, ed., *The Cambridge Companion to Maimonides* (Cambridge: Cambridge University Press), pp. 58–81.
  2016. *Maimonides' Guide of the Perplexed: A Philosophical Guide* (Chicago: University of Chicago Press).
Jackson, Frank. 1982. "Epiphenomenal Qualia." *The Philosophical Quarterly* 32 (127): 127–136.
Jonas, Silvia. 2016. *Ineffability and Its Metaphysics: The Unspeakable in Art, Religion, and Philosophy* (New York: Palgrave Macmillan).
Judah Ha-Levi. 1905. *The Kuzari*, trans. H. Hirschfeld (London: Routledge).
  1997. *Al-Khazarī*, ed. D. H. Baneth and H. Ben-Shammai (Jerusalem: Israel Academy of Sciences and Humanities).
Kaplan, Lawrence. 2002. "An Introduction to Maimonides' 'Eight Chapters'." *The Edah Journal* 2(2).
  2016. *Maimonides: Between Philosophy and Halakhah: Rabbi Joseph B. Soloveitchik's Lectures on the Guide of the Perplexed* (Jerusalem and New York: Ktav/Urim).
  2018. "The Purpose of the *Guide of the Perplexed*, Maimonides' Theory of Parables, and Sceptical versus Dogmatic Readings of the *Guide*." In R. Haliva, ed., *Scepticism and Anti-Scepticism in Medieval Jewish Philosophy and Thought* (Berlin: De Gruyter), pp. 67–85.
Kasher, Hannah. 1998. "Biblical Miracles and the Universality of Natural Laws: Maimonides' Three Methods of Harmonization." *Journal of Jewish Thought and Philosophy* 8: 25–52.
Kellner, Menachem. 1990. *Maimonides on Human Perfection* (Atlanta: Scholars Press).
  2005. "Spiritual Life." In K. Seeskin, ed., *The Cambridge Companion to Maimonides* (Cambridge: Cambridge University Press), pp. 273–299.
Klein-Braslavy, Sara. 1986. *Maimonides' Interpretation of the Adam Stories in Genesis: A Study in Maimonides' Anthropology* (Jerusalem: Rubin Mass) [Heb.].
  1987. *Maimonides' Interpretation of the Story of Creation* (2nd ed.) (Jerusalem: Rubin Mass) [Heb.].
  2006a. "Bible Commentary." In K. Seeskin, ed., *The Cambridge Companion to Maimonides* (Cambridge: Cambridge University Press), pp. 245–272.
  2006b. "Maimonides' Exoteric and Esoteric Biblical Interpretations in the *Guide of the Perplexed*." In H. Kreisel, ed., *Study and Knowledge in Jewish Thought* (Beersheva: Ben-Gurion University of the Negev), pp. 137–164.

Knuuttila, Simo. 1993. *Modalities in Medieval Philosophy* (London: Routledge).
Kogan, Barry. 1989. "What Can We Know and When Can We Know It?: Maimonides on the Active Intelligence and Human Cognition." In E. Ormsby, ed., *Moses Maimonides and His Time* (Washington, DC: The Catholic University of America Press), pp. 121–137.
Kraemer, Joel. 1986. "Nomos and Sharia in Maimonides' Thought." *Te'uda* 4: 185–202 [Heb.].
  1989. "Maimonides on Aristotle and Scientific Method." In E. Ormsby, ed., *Moses Maimonides and His Time* (Washington, DC: The Catholic University of America Press), pp. 53–88.
  2008a. *Maimonides: The Life and World of One of Civilization's Greatest Minds* (New York: Doubleday).
  2008b. "Maimonides the Great Healer." In A. Hyman and A. Ivry, eds., *Maimonidean Studies* 5: 1–30.
  2008c. "Is There a Text in this Class?" *Aleph* 8: 247–299.
Krauss, Christina and Roy K. Gibson, eds. 2002. *The Classical Commentary: Histories, Practices, Theory* (Boston: Brill).
Kreisel, Howard. 1984. "Miracles in Medieval Jewish Philosophy." *Jewish Quarterly Review* 75: 99–133.
  1987. "Zaddik vi-Ra Lo ba-Philosophiah ha-Yehudit bimei ha-Benayim." *Da'at* 19: 17–29.
  1997. "Moses Maimonides." In D. Frank and O. Leaman, eds., *History of Jewish Philosophy* (London and New York: Routledge), pp. 245–280.
  1999. *Maimonides' Political Thought: Studies in Ethics, Law, and the Human Ideal* (Albany: SUNY Press).
  2001. *Prophecy: The History of an Idea in Medieval Jewish Philosophy* (Amsterdam: Kluwer).
  2015. *Judaism as Philosophy: Studies in Maimonides and the Medieval Jewish Philosophers of Provence* (Brighton, MA: Academic Studies Press).
Kukkonen, Taneli. 2000a. "Possible Worlds in the *Tahafut al-Tahafut*: Averroes on Plenitude and Possibility." *Journal of the History of Philosophy* 38: 329–348.
  2000b. "Possible Worlds in the *Tahafut al-Falasifa*: Al-Ghazali on Creation and Contingency." *Journal of the History of Philosophy* 38: 479–502.
Lamm, Norman. 1992–1993. "Maimonides on the Love of God." *Maimonidean Studies* 3: 131–142.
Langermann, Y. Tzvi. 1991a. "Maimonides' Repudiation of Astrology." *Maimonidean Studies* 2: 123–158.
  1991b. "The True Perplexity: *The Guide of the Perplexed* Part II, Chapter 24." In J. L. Kraemer, ed., *Perspectives on Maimonides: Philosophical and Historical Studies* (Oxford: Oxford University Press), pp. 159–174.
  2004. "Maimonides and Miracles: The Growth of a (Dis)belief." *Jewish History* 18: 147–172.
  2008. "My Truest Perplexities." *Aleph* 8: 301–317.
  2009. "Islamic Atomism and the Galenic Tradition." *History of Science* 47: 277–295.

2018. "Al-Ghazali's Purported 'Influence' on Maimonides: A Dissenting Voice in Trending Scholarship." In C. Manekin and D. Davies, eds., *Interpreting Maimonides* (Cambridge: Cambridge University Press), pp. 26–45.

Lasker, Daniel J. 2006. "Love of God and Knowledge of God in Maimonides' Philosophy." In J. Hamesse and O. Weijers, eds., *Écriture et réécriture des textes philosophiques médiévaux* (Turnhout: Brepols), pp. 329–345.

Lazarus-Yafeh, Hava. 1997. "Was Maimonides Influenced by al-Ghazali?" In M. Cogan, B. L. Eichler, and J. H. Tigay, eds., *Tehillah le-Moshe: Biblical and Judaic Studies in Honor of Moshe Greenberg* (Winona Lake: Eisenbrauns), pp. 163–169. [Heb.].

Lear, Jonathan. 1988. *Aristotle: The Desire to Understand* (Cambridge: Cambridge University Press).

Lerner, Ralph. 2000. *Maimonides' Empire of Light: Popular Enlightenment in an Age of Belief* (Chicago: University of Chicago Press).

Levinger, Jacob. 1989. *Maimonides as Philosopher and Codifier* (Jerusalem: Bialik Press) [Heb.].

Lewis, David. 1979. "Attitudes De Dicto and De Se." *The Philosophical Review* 88 (4): 513–543.

1983. "New Work for a Theory of Universals." *Australasian Journal of Philosophy* 61: 343–377.

1986. *On the Plurality of Worlds* (Oxford: Blackwell).

1988. "What Experience Teaches." *Proceedings of the Russellian Society* 13: 29–57.

Lobel, Diana. 2002. "Silence Is Praise to You." *American Catholic Philosophical Quarterly* 76(1): 25–49.

2011. "Being and the Good: Maimonides on Ontological Beauty." *Journal of Jewish Thought and Philosophy* 19(1): 1–45.

Long, A. A. and D. N. Sedley, ed. and trans. 1987. *The Hellenistic Philosophers*, vol. 1 (Cambridge: Cambridge University Press).

Lorberbaum, Yair. 2009–2010. "Maimonides on Halakhah and Aggadah and Divine Law." *Dinei Israel* 26–27: 253–297. [Heb.].

2014. "'What Would Please Them Most Is that the Intellect Would Not Find a Meaning for the Commandments and the Prohibitions': On Transcending the Rationales of the Commandments – A Close Reading of *The Guide of the Perplexed* III 31." *Da'at* 77: 17–50 [Heb.].

Lorberbaum, Yair and Haim Shapira. 2008. "Maimonides' *Epistle on Martyrdom* in the Light of Legal Philosophy." *Dine Israel* 25: 123–169.

Loux, Michael. 2006. "Aristotle's Constituent Ontology." *Oxford Studies in Metaphysics* 2: 207–250.

Lovejoy, Arthur O. 1936. *The Great Chain of Being: A Study of the History of an Idea* (Cambridge, MA: Harvard University Press).

Mackie, John. 1990. *Ethics: Inventing Right and Wrong* (London: Penguin Books).

Maïmonide. 1856–1866. *Le Guide des Égarés*, trans. S. Munk, 3 vols. (Paris: G.-P. Maisonineuve & Larose).

1996. *Traité de logique*, trans. with notes by R. Brague (Paris: Desclée de Brouwer).

Maimonides, Moses. 1931. *Dalālat al-Ḥā'irīn*, ed. S. Munk and I. Joel (Jerusalem: Junovitch).
  1938. "Treatise on Logic," ed. and trans. I. Efros. *Proceedings of the American Academy for Jewish Research* 8: 1–65 [Eng.], 1–136 [Heb].
  1963. *The Guide of the Perplexed*, trans. S. Pines (Chicago: University of Chicago Press).
  1964. *Mishnah 'im Perush R' Moshe ben Maimon, Seder Nezikin*, ed. Y. Kafih (Jerusalem: Mossad HaRav Kook).
  1966 (1912). *The Eight Chapters of Maimonides on Ethics (Shemonah Perakim)*, ed. and trans. J. Gorfinkle (New York: AMS Press).
  1966. "Maimonides' Arabic Treatise on Logic." *Proceedings of the American Academy for Jewish Research* 34: 155–160 [Eng. Introduction by I. Efros]; 1–42 [Arabic].
  1968. *The Commentary to Mishnah Aboth*, trans. A. David (New York: Bloch Publishing).
  1970–1971/1989. *The Medical Aphorisms of Moses Maimonides*, ed. and trans. F. Rosner and S. Muntner. (New York: Yeshiva University Press); rev. F. Rosner (Haifa: Maimonides Research Institute).
  1972. "Helek: Sanhedrin, Chapter 10." In I. Twersky, ed., *A Maimonides Reader* (West Orange: Behrman House), 401–423.
  1975. *Introduction to Commentary on the Mishnah*, trans. F. Rosner (New York: Feldheim).
  1975. "Eight Chapters." In R. Weiss and C. Butterworth, ed. and trans., *Ethical Writings of Maimonides* (New York: Dover Publications), pp. 60–95.
  1977. *Moreh Ha-Nevukhim*, trans. Yosef Kafih (Jerusalem: Mossad HaRav Kook) [Heb.].
  1985. *Crisis and Leadership: Epistles of Maimonides*, trans. and ann. A. Halkin; discussions by D. Hartman (Philadelphia: Jewish Publication Society).
  1992. *Haqdamot la-Mishnah*, ed. I. Shailat (Maaleh Adumim: Maaliyot) [Arabic text].
  1995. *The Guide of the Perplexed*, trans. C. Rabin (Indianapolis: Hackett).
  2000. *Moreh Nevukhim*, trans. Samuel Ibn Tibbon, with notes by Yehuda Even-Shmuel (Jerusalem: Mossad HaRav Kook) [Heb.].
  2002a. *Moreh Nevukhim*, trans. with notes, appendices, and indices by M. Schwarz (Tel Aviv: Tel Aviv University Press) [Heb.].
  2002b. *The Guide for the Perplexed*, trans. M. Friedländer (Skokie: Varda Press).
  2004. *Medical Aphorisms: Treatises 1–5. (Kitâb al-Fusûl fî al-tibb)*, ed. and trans. G. Bos (Provo: Brigham Young University Press).
  2011. *Shemonah Peraqim*, trans. M. Schwarz (Jerusalem: Ben Tzvi Institute) [Heb.].
Manekin, Charles H. 1988. "Problems of 'Plenitude' in Maimonides and Gersonides." In R. Link-Salinger, R. J. Long, and C. Manekin, eds., *A Straight Path: Essays in Honor of Arthur Hyman* (Washington, DC: The Catholic University of America Press), pp. 183–194.
  1990. "Belief, Certainty, and Divine Attributes in the *Guide of the Perplexed*." *Maimonidean Studies* 1: 117–141.

2005. *On Maimonides* (Belmont: Wadsworth).
2008a. "Divine Will in Maimonides' Later Writings." In A. Hyman and A. Ivry, eds., *Maimonidean Studies* 5: 189–222.
2008b. "The Limitations of Human Knowledge According to Maimonides: Earlier vs. Later Writings." In A. Ravitzky, ed., *Maimonides: Conservatism, Originality, Revolution* (Jerusalem: Zalman Shazar Center Press), pp. 297–316. [Heb.].
2012. "Maimonides and the Arabic Aristotelian Tradition of Epistemology." In D. M. Freidenreich and M. Goldstein, eds., *Beyond Religious Borders: Interaction and Intellectual Exchange in the Medieval Islamic World* (Philadelphia: University of Pennsylvania Press), pp. 78–95, 192–197.
2018. "Scepticism and Anti-Scepticism: The Case of Maimonides." In R. Haliva, ed., *Scepticism and Anti-Scepticism in Medieval Jewish Philosophy and Thought* (Berlin: De Gruyter), pp. 86–106.
Mansfeld, Jaap. 1994. *Prolegomena: Questions to Be Settled before the Study of an Author, or a Text* (Leiden: Brill).
Marx, Alexander. 1926. "The Correspondence between the Rabbis of Southern France and Maimonides about Astrology." *Hebrew Union College Annual* 3: 349–358 (trans. R. Lerner in *Maimonides' Empire of Light: Popular Enlightenment in an Age of Belief* (Chicago: University of Chicago Press, 2000), pp. 178–187.
Maximus the Confessor. 1985. *Maximus Confessor: Selected Writings* (Ramsay: Paulist Press).
Mayer, Toby, 2003. "Faḫr ad-Dīn ar-Rāzī's Critique of Ibn Sīnā's Argument for the Unity of God in the *Išārāt*, and Naṣīr ad-Dīn aṭ-Ṭūsī's Defence." In D. Reisman, ed., *Before and after Avicenna: Proceedings of the First Conference of the Avicenna Study Group* (Leiden: Brill), pp. 199–218.
McDaniel, Kris. 2017. *The Fragmentation of Being* (Oxford: Oxford University Press).
Meister Eckhart. 1981. *Meister Eckhart: The Essential Sermons, Commentaries, Treatises, and Defense* (Ramsay: Paulist Press).
Melamed, Yitzhak Y. 2020. "Teleology in Jewish Philosophy: Early Talmudists to Spinoza." In J. K. McDonough, ed., *Teleology: A History* (Oxford: Oxford University Press), pp. 123–149.
Michaelis, Omer. 2017. "'Even of the Philosophers': *Taqlid* in Maimonides' *Guide of the Perplexed* and Its Sources." *Da'at* 83: 7–46. [Heb.].
Miller, Alexander. 2013. *Contemporary Metaethics: An Introduction* (2nd ed.) (Malden: Polity Press).
Minnis, Alastair. 1984. *Medieval Theory of Authorship: Scholastic Literary Attitudes in the Later Middle Ages* (London: Scolar Press).
Moore, Adrian. 1997. *Points of View* (Oxford: Oxford University Press).
Most, Glenn, ed. 1999. *Commentaries=Kommentare* (Göttingen: Vandenhoeck & Ruprecht).
Nadler, Steven. 2009. "Providence and Theodicy." In S. Nadler and T. M. Rudavsky, eds., *The Cambridge History of Jewish Philosophy: From Antiquity*

through the Seventeenth Century (New York: Cambridge University Press), pp. 619–658.
Nagel, Thomas. 1974. "What Is It Like to Be a Bat?" *The Philosophical Review* 83 (4): 435–450.
Narboni, Moses. 1852. *Commentary on Moreh Nevuchim*, ed. J. Goldenthal (Vienna: Imperial Printer).
Nehorai, Michael. 1983. "Maimonides' System of the Commandments." *Da'at* 10: 29–42. [Heb.].
Novak, David. 1998. *Natural Law in Judaism* (Cambridge: Cambridge University Press).
  2014. "Natural Law and Judaism." In A. Emon, M. Levering, and D. Novak, eds., *Natural Law: A Jewish, Christian, and Islamic Trialogue* (Oxford: Oxford University Press), pp. 4–44.
Nuriel, Abraham. 1980. "Providence and Governance in *Moreh Nevukhim*." *Tarbiz* 49: 346–355. [Heb.].
Nussbaum, Martha. 2018. *The Therapy of Desire: Theory and Practice in Hellenistic Ethics* (Princeton: Princeton University Press).
Oppy, Graham. 2013 "Rowe's Evidential Arguments from Evil." In J. P. McBrayer and D. Howard-Snyder, eds., *The Blackwell Companion to the Problem of Evil* (Malden: Wiley-Blackwell), pp. 49–66.
Parens, Joshua. 2012. *Maimonides and Spinoza: Their Conflicting Views of Human Nature* (Chicago: University of Chicago Press).
Perry, John. 1977. "Frege on Demonstratives." *The Philosophical Review* 86(4): 474–497.
Pessin, Sarah. 2009. "Matter, Form, and the Corporeal World." In S. Nadler and T. M. Rudavsky, eds., *The Cambridge History of Jewish Philosophy: From Antiquity through the Seventeenth Century* (New York: Cambridge University Press), pp. 269–301.
Philo of Alexandria. 2013. *The Works of Philo: Complete and Unabridged* (Peabody: Hendrickson Publishers).
Pines, Shlomo. 1963. "Translator's Introduction: The Philosophic Sources of the *Guide of the Perplexed*." In Moses Maimonides, *The Guide of the Perplexed*, trans. with an introduction and notes by S. Pines (Chicago: University of Chicago Press), pp. lvii–cxxxiv.
  1979. "The Limitations of Human Knowledge According to Al-Farabi, Ibn Bajja, and Maimonides." In I. Twersky, ed., *Studies in Medieval Jewish History and Literature*, 2 vols. (Cambridge, MA: Harvard University Press), 1: pp. 82–109.
  1986. "The Philosophical Purport of Maimonides' Halachic Works and the Purport of the *Guide of the Perplexed*." In S. Pines and Y. Yovel, eds., *Maimonides and Philosophy* (Dordrecht: Martinus Nijhoff), pp. 1–14.
  1990. "Truth and Falsehood versus Good and Evil." In I. Twersky, ed., *Studies in Maimonides* (Cambridge, MA: Harvard University Press), pp. 95–157.
Plantinga, Alvin. 1974. *The Nature of Necessity* (Oxford: Clarendon Press).
  1983. "On Existentialism." *Philosophical Studies* 44(1): 1–20.

1993. *Warrant and Proper Function* (Oxford: Oxford University Press).
Plato. 2000. *The Republic*, trans. T. Griffith (Cambridge: Cambridge University Press).
Porphyry. 1992. *On Aristotle's Categories*, trans. S. Strange (Ithaca: Cornell University Press).
Pseudo-Dionysius. 1987. "The Mystical Theology, trans. C. Luibheid and P. Rorem." In *Pseudo-Dionysius: The Complete Works* (Ramsay: Paulist Press), 133–142.
Rabinovitch, Nahum L. 1974. "The Concept of 'Possibility' in Maimonides." *Tarbiz* 44: 159–171. [Heb.].
Raffel, Charles. 1987. "Providence as Consequent upon the Intellect: Maimonides' Theory of Providence." *AJS Review* 12(1): 25–71.
Rahman, Fazlur. 1952. *Avicenna's Psychology: An English Translation of Kitāb al-Najāt, Book II, Chapter VI, with Historico-Philosophical Notes and Textual Improvements on the Cairo Edition* (Oxford: Oxford University Press).
  1990. "Ibn Sina's Theory of the God-World Relationship." In B. McGinn and D. Burrell, eds., *God and Creation* (Notre Dame: University of Notre Dame Press), pp. 38–52.
Ravitzky, Aviezer. 1977. "The Thought of R. Zerahiah b. Isaac b. Shealtiel Hen & Maimonidean-Tibbonian Philosophy in the 13th Century." Ph.D. dissertation, Hebrew University [Heb.].
  1978–1979. "Necessary and Possible Existence: Maimonides' Ontology According to His Interpreters." *Da'at* 2–3: 67–97. [Heb.].
  1990. "The Secrets of the *Guide of the Perplexed*: Between the Thirteenth and Twentieth Centuries." In I. Twersky, ed., *Studies in Maimonides* (Cambridge, MA: Harvard University Press), pp. 159–207.
  1996. *History and Faith: Studies in Jewish Philosophy* (Amsterdam: J. C. Gieben).
  2002. "'The Ravings of Amulet Writers': Maimonides and His Disciples on Language, Nature, and Magic." In A. Sagi and N. Ilan, eds., *Jewish Culture in the Eye of the Storm: A Jubilee Book in Honor of Yosef Ahituv* (Ein Zurim: Hakibbutz Hameuhad & Jacob Herzog Center), pp. 431–458. [Heb.].
Reicher, Maria. 2019. "Nonexistent Objects." In E. N. Zalta, ed., *Stanford Encyclopedia of Philosophy*.
Reines, Alvin. 1969–1970. "Maimonides' Concept of Mosaic Prophecy." *Hebrew Union College Annual* 40/41: 325–361.
  1972. "Maimonides' Concepts of Providence and Theodicy." *Hebrew Union College Annual* 43: 169–206.
Rosenberg, Shalom. 1975. "Logic and Ontology in Jewish Philosophy in the Fourteenth Century." Ph.D. dissertation, Hebrew University [Heb.].
  1978a. "Possible and Assertoric in Medieval Logic." *Iyyun* 28(1): 57–72. [Heb.].
  1978b. "Necessary and Possible in Medieval Logic." *Iyyun* 28(2–3): 103–155. [Heb.].
Rowe, William L. 1979. "The Problem of Evil and Some Varieties of Atheism." *American Philosophical Quarterly* 16: 335–341.
Rudavsky, T.M. 2000. *Time Matters: Time, Creation, and Cosmology in Medieval Jewish Philosophy* (Albany: SUNY Press).

2010. *Maimonides* (Malden: Wiley-Blackwell).
2018. *Jewish Philosophy in the Middle Ages: Science, Rationalism, and Religion.* (Oxford: Oxford University Press).
Russell, Bertrand. 1940. *An Inquiry into Meaning and Truth* (London: Allen and Unwin).
Ryle, Gilbert. 1949. *The Concept of Mind* (Chicago: University of Chicago Press).
Rynhold, Daniel. 2005. *Two Models of Jewish Philosophy: Justifying One's Practices* (Oxford: Oxford University Press).
2009. *An Introduction to Medieval Jewish Philosophy* (London: I. B. Tauris).
Saadia Gaon. 1948. *The Book of Beliefs and Opinions*, trans. S. Rosenblatt (New Haven: Yale University Press).
Sabra, A. I. 1980. "Avicenna on the Subject Matter of Logic." *Journal of Philosophy* 77: 746–764.
1984. "The Andalusian Revolt against Ptolemaic Astronomy: Averroes and al-Bitruji." In E. Mendelsohn, ed., *Transformation and Tradition in the Sciences* (Cambridge, MA: Harvard University Press), pp. 133–153.
Salmon, Nathan. 1998. "Nonexistence." *Nous* 32(3): 277–319.
Samuel, Michael Leo. 2016. *Maimonides' Hidden Torah Commentary: Genesis 1–21* (Sarasota: First Edition Design Publishing).
Saperstein, Marc. 2005. "*Ein Li Eseq ba-Nistarot*: Saul Levi Morteira's Sermons on *Parashat Bereshit*." In R. Elior and P. Schäfer, eds., *Creation and Re-creation in Jewish Thought: Festschrift in Honor of Joseph Dan* (Tübingen: Mohr Siebeck), pp. 222–229.
Schliwski, Carsten. 2004. "Moses Ben Maimon, Šarḥ fuṣūl Abuqrāṭ: Der Kommentar des Maimonides zu den Aphorismen des Hippokrates. Kritische Edition des arabischen Textes mit Einführung und Übersetzung." Ph.D. dissertation, University of Cologne.
Schwartz, Dov. 1995. "The Debate over the Maimonidean Theory in the Thirteenth Century." *Jewish Studies Quarterly* 2: 185–196.
1999. *Astral Magic in Medieval Jewish Thought* (Ramat Gan: Bar-Ilan University Press) [Heb.].
2005. *Central Problems of Medieval Jewish Philosophy* (Leiden: Brill).
Schwarz, Michael. 1991/1992–1993. "Who Were Maimonides' Mutakallimun? Some Remarks on *Guide of the Perplexed* Part I Chapter 73." *Maimonidean Studies* 2: 159–209; 3: 143–172.
Schwarzschild, Steven. 1977. "Moral Radicalism and 'Middlingness' in the Ethics of Maimonides." *Studies in Medieval Culture* 11: 65–94.
Scott, Michael and Gabriel Citron. 2016. "What Is Apophaticism? Ways of Talking about an Ineffable God." *European Journal for Philosophy of Religion* 8(4): 23–49.
Seager, William. 2001. "The Constructed and the Secret Self." In A. Brook and R. DeVidi, eds., *Self-Reference and Self-Awareness* (Amsterdam: John Benjamins Publishing), pp. 247–268.
Seeskin, Kenneth. 2000. *Searching for a Distant God: The Legacy of Maimonides* (New York: Oxford University Press).

2005. "Metaphysics and Its Transcendence." In K. Seeskin, ed., *The Cambridge Companion to Maimonides* (Cambridge: Cambridge University Press), pp. 82–104.
Segal, Aaron. Forthcoming. "Dependence, Transcendence, and Creaturely Freedom: On the Incompatibility of Three Theistic Doctrines." *Mind*. Available at: https://academic.oup.com/mind/advance-article/doi/10.1093/mind/fzzo82/5714099
Sermoneta, Giuseppe. 1969. *Un glossario filosofico ebraico-italiano del xiii secolo* (Rome: Edizioni dell'Ateneo).
Shatz, David. 2005. "Maimonides' Moral Theory." In K. Seeskin, ed., *The Cambridge Companion to Maimonides* (Cambridge: Cambridge University Press), pp. 167–192.
2009. "'From the Depths I Have Called to You': Jewish Reflections on September 11th and Contemporary Terrorism." In Shatz, *Jewish Thought in Dialogue: Essays on Thinkers, Theologies, and Moral Theories* (Boston: Academic Studies Press), pp. 257–290.
2013. "On Constructing a Jewish Theodicy." In J. McBrayer and D. Howard-Snyder, eds., *The Blackwell Companion to the Problem of Evil* (Malden: Wiley-Blackwell), pp. 309–325.
Sider, Theodore. 2011. *Writing the Book of the World* (Oxford: Oxford University Press).
Simplicius. 2003. *On Aristotle's Categories 1–4*, trans. M. Chase (London: Duckworth).
Smith, Barry. 1991. "Textual Deference." *American Philosophical Quarterly* 28(1): 1–12.
Soloveitchik, Haym. 1980. "Maimonides' '*Iggeret Ha-Shemad*': Law and Rhetoric." In L. Landman, ed., *Joseph H. Lookstein Memorial Volume* (New York: Ktav), pp. 281–318.
Soloveitchik, Joseph B. 2002. "A Halakhic Approach to the Problem of Evil." In J. B. Soloveitchik, *Out of the Whirlwind: Essays on Suffering, Mourning, and the Human Condition* (New York: Toras HoRav Foundation), pp. 86–115.
Sosa, Ernest. 2005. "Dreams and Philosophy." *Proceedings and Addresses of the American Philosophical Association* 79(2): 7–18.
2007. *A Virtue Epistemology: Apt Belief and Reflective Knowledge*, vol. 1 (Oxford: Oxford University Press).
Spinoza, Benedict de. 1996. *Ethics*, trans. E. Curley (London: Penguin).
Stanley, Jason. 2011. *Know How* (New York: Oxford University Press).
Stanley, Jason and Timothy Williamson. 2001. "Knowing How." *Journal of Philosophy* 98(8): 411–444.
Steiner, Mark. 2019a. "Hume and Maimonides on Imaginability and Possibility." In S. Lebens, D. Rabinowitz, and A. Segal, eds., *Jewish Philosophy in an Analytic Age* (Oxford: Oxford University Press), pp. 119–134.
2019b. "A Note on Maimonides and Al-Ghazali, Leibniz and Clarke." *Iyyun* 67: 253–260.
n. d. "David Hume, the First and Last Kalamist." (unpublished manuscript).
Stern, Josef. 1997. "Philosophy or Exegesis: Some Critical Comments." In N. Golb, ed., *Judaeo-Arabic Studies* (Amsterdam: Harwood), pp. 213–228.

1998. *Problems and Parables of Law: Maimonides and Nahmanides on Reasons for the Commandments (Ta'amei Ha-Mitzvot)* (Albany: SUNY Press).
2000. "Maimonides on Language and the Science of Language." In R. S. Cohen and H. Levine, eds., *Maimonides and the Sciences* (Dordrecht: Kluwer), pp. 173–226.
2001. "Maimonides' Demonstrations: Principles and Practice." *Medieval Philosophy and Theology* 10: 47–84.
2005. "Maimonides' Epistemology." In K. Seeskin, ed., *The Cambridge Companion to Maimonides* (Cambridge: Cambridge University Press), pp. 105–133.
2008. "The Enigma of the *Guide of the Perplexed* I:68." In A. Ravitzky, ed., *Maimonides: Conservatism, Originality, Revolution* (Jerusalem: Zalman Shazar Center Press), pp. 437–451. [Heb.].
2009. "The Maimonidean Parable, the Arabic Poetics, and the Garden of Eden." *Midwest Studies in Philosophy* 33: 209–247.
2013. *The Matter and Form of Maimonides' Guide* (Cambridge, MA: Harvard University Press).
2020. "Maimonides, the Falasifa, and Al-Ghazali in *Guide* I:69." *Iyyun: The Jerusalem Philosophical Quarterly* 68: 245–279.
n. d. "Maimonides on a False Picture of Providence." (unpublished manuscript).
Stoljar, Daniel. 2017. "Physicalism." In E. N. Zalta, ed., *Stanford Encyclopedia of Philosophy*.
Strauss, Leo. 1941. "The Literary Character of the *Guide of the Perplexed*." In S. W. Baron, ed., *Essays on Maimonides* (New York: Columbia University Press), pp. 37–91.
1952. *Persecution and the Art of Writing* (Glencoe: The Free Press).
1963. "How to Begin to Study *The Guide of the Perplexed*." In Moses Maimonides, *The Guide of the Perplexed*, trans. with an introduction and notes by S. Pines (Chicago: University of Chicago Press), pp. xi–lvi.
2004. "The Place of the Doctrine of Providence According to Maimonides." *The Review of Metaphysics* 57: 537–549.
Strobino, Riccardo. Forthcoming. *Avicenna's Theory of Science: Logic, Metaphysics, Epistemology* (Berkeley: University of California Press).
Stroumsa, Sarah. 2009. *Maimonides in His World: Portrait of a Mediterranean Thinker* (Princeton: Princeton University Press).
Taylor, C. C. W. 1990. "Aristotle's Epistemology." In S. Everson, ed., *Epistemology* (Companions to Ancient Thought, vol.1) (Cambridge: Cambridge University Press), pp. 116–142.
Touati, Charles. 1968. "Le problème de l'inerrance prophétique dans la théologie juive du moyen age." *Revue de l'histoire des religions* 174(2): 169–187.
Twersky, Isadore, ed. 1972. *A Maimonides Reader* (New York: Berhman House).
1980. *Introduction to the Code of Maimonides (Mishneh Torah)* (New Haven: Yale University Press).
Tye, Michael. 2018. "Qualia." In E. N. Zalta, ed., *Stanford Encyclopedia of Philosophy*.

Ullmann-Margalit, Edna and Sidney Morgenbesser. 1977. "Picking and Choosing." *Social Research* 44: 757–785.

Urbach, Ephraim. 1975. *The Sages: Their Concepts and Beliefs*, trans. I. Abrahams (Jerusalem: Magnes Press).

Vajda, Georges. 1957. *L'Amour de Dieu dans la théologie juive du moyen age* (Paris: J. Vrin).

Van Cleve, James. 1985. "Three Versions of the Bundle Theory." *Philosophical Studies* 47(1): 95–107.

Van den Bergh. Simon. 1954. *Averroes' Tahafut al-Tahafut (The Incoherence of the Incoherence)* (London: E. J. W. Gibb Memorial Trust).

Van Gulick, Robert. 2018. "Consciousness." In E. N. Zalta, ed., *Stanford Encyclopedia of Philosophy*.

Van Inwagen, Peter. 2006. *The Problem of Evil* (Oxford: Clarendon Press).
 2011. "Relational vs. Constituent Ontologies." *Philosophical Perspectives* 25: 389–406.

Walzer, Richard, ed. and trans. 1985. *Al-Farabi on the Perfect State* (Oxford: Oxford University Press) [= Al-Farabi 1985]

Weiss, Raymond. 1991. *Maimonides' Ethics: The Encounter of Philosophic and Religious Morality* (Chicago: University of Chicago Press).

Weiss, Roslyn. 2000. "See No Evil: Maimonides on Onqelos' Translation of the Biblical Expression 'And the Lord Saw'." *Maimonidean Studies* 4: 135–162.
 2007. "Natural Order or Divine Will: Maimonides on Cosmogony and Prophecy." *Journal of Jewish Thought and Philosophy* 15(1): 1–26.

Williams, Bernard. 1985. *Ethics and the Limits of Philosophy* (London: Fontana Press).

Williams, Donald C. 1953. "The Elements of Being." *The Review of Metaphysics* 7 (2): 3–18, 171–192.

Williamson, Timothy. 2000. *Knowledge and Its Limits* (Oxford: Oxford University Press).
 2002. "Necessary Existents." In A. O'Hear, ed., *Royal Institute of Philosophy Supplement* (Cambridge University Press), pp. 269–287.
 2009. "Reply to Goldman." In P. Greenough and D. Pritchard, eds., *Williamson on Knowledge* (Oxford: Oxford University Press), pp. 305–312.

Wirmer, David. 2018. "The World and the Eye: Perplexity about Ends in the *Guide of the Perplexed* iii.13 and iii.25." In C. Manekin and D. Davies, eds., *Interpreting Maimonides* (Cambridge: Cambridge University Press), pp. 171–189.

Wisnovsky, Robert. 2002. "Final and Efficient Causality in Avicenna's Cosmology and Theology." *Quaestio* 2: 97–123.
 2003. *Avicenna's Metaphysics in Context* (Ithaca: Cornell University Press).

Wolfson, Harry A. 1934. *The Philosophy of Spinoza* (Cambridge, MA: Harvard University Press).
 1943/1973. "The Terms *Tasawwur* and *Tasdiq* in Arabic Philosophy and Their Greek, Latin, and Hebrew Equivalents." *The Moslem World* 33: 114–128; repr. in I. Twersky and G. H. Williams, eds., *Studies in the History of*

Philosophy and Religion, 2 vols. (Cambridge, MA: Harvard University Press), 1: pp. 478–492.

1966. "Maimonides on Modes and Universals." In R. Loewe, ed., *Studies in Rationalism, Judaism, and Universalism, in Memory of Leon Roth* (London: Routledge and Kegan Paul), pp. 311–321.

1976. *The Philosophy of the Kalam* (Cambridge, MA: Harvard University Press).

Wright, Crispin. 1988. "Moral Values, Projection, and Secondary Qualities." *Proceedings of the Aristotelian Society*, supp. vol. 62: 1–26.

Zimmermann, F. W., trans. 1981. *Al-Farabi's Commentary and Short Treatise on Aristotle's De Interpretatione* (London: Oxford University Press) [= Al-Farabi 1981]

Index

Abraham, 179
absolute homonymy, 117
absolute independence, 118–122
absolute nonexistence, 147–148
accidents, 107–108
Account of the Chariot (*Ma'aseh Merkavah*), 89–90, 93–101, 145, 272
   metaphysics and, 96
act-consequentialist approach to ethics, 73–76
actional attributes, 114, 121–122
Active Intellect, 54, 166, 168–172, 254–255, 280
Actual Intellect, 164
actuality, 187–190, 204–205
Adam, 30–42, 52, 55–56, 59, 228–229
   in ideal created state, 56–57
   sin of, 53–54, 61–62, 65–66
admissibility (*al-tajwiz*), 200
affirmative attributes, 176–177
Alexander of Aphrodisias, 29–30
Al-Farabi, 51, 83–85, 87, 113, 166–168, 184–186, 197, 253–254
   sublunar beings and, 93
Al-Ghazali, 85–86, 152, 189–190, 195–196, 201–202
Al-Razi, 231, 241–242
Altmann, Alexander, 84
ambiguity, 145
Ammi (Rabbi), 235–237
al-'amr al-ilāhī ("divine decree"), 97
analytic epistemology, 162
Andalusian philosophers, 205
angels, 91–92, 177–178, 180, 257
animal sacrifice, 260–261
anthropocentrism, 209–210, 217–218, 221–222, 244
   anti-, 220
   egocentrism and, 241–243
   parables (*meshalim*) and, 219–220
   theodicy and, 243

anthropomorphism, 13–14, 38–40
anti-Aristotelianism, 210
anti-atomism, 143
anti-intellectualism, 133
anti-Maimonideans, 1–2
anti-realism, 61–64, 67
apatheia (dispassion), 237–238
apodeixis (demonstration), 143–144, 149, 163, 194–195
apophatic theology, 125
apophaticism, 125, 131
   non-propositional knowledge and, 136–138
   objectivity and, 138–139
aporia (perplexity), 15–16, 211
Aquinas, Thomas, 1, 209, 215
Arabic Aristotelian philosophers, 84, 90–92, 98–99
Arabic philosophy, 88–89, 165–166
Arama, Isaac, 209
Aristotle, 4–5, 18, 22, 53, 61, 77, 83, 118–119, 191–192
   Alexander of Aphrodisias commentaries on, 29–30
   Andalusian philosophers and, 205
   anti-Aristotelianism, 210
   Arabic Aristotelian philosophers, 84, 90–92, 98–99
   arguments for eternity, 150
   authority of, 219
   cause and effect and, 152
   on causes or reasons for being, 11
   on compulsion, 127
   cosmology of, 153, 205
   creation, theory of, 159–160
   on demonstration, 143–144
   endoxa, 66–67
   epistēmē and, 78
   epistemology of, 64–65, 165
   eternity thesis of, 149, 191–192
   Galen and, 143
   human condition and, 22–23, 25–26

306

human knowledge of metaphysics and, 98
immanent intellect and, 164
interpreters of, 83–84
Late Ancient and Arabic commentators on, 197
Metaphysics, 92, 127, 197
metaphysics and, 85, 99–100
necessity and, 197
non-necessity of, 145–147
On the Soul (*De Anima*), 163–164
Plato and, 148–149
possibility and, 185–186
proof for creation, 213
providence and, 235
Socrates and, 22
on sublunar motion, 192–193
on teleology, 213–215
theory of negation, 176–177
theory of time, 150–151
on true happiness, 267
virtue ethic of, 69
arrogance, 20–21, 26
asceticism, 230–231, 239
Asharites, 235
astrology, 223, 236–237
astronomy, 205
atomism, 18, 143
  doctrine of, 146
  epistemological implications of, 145–146
attributes, 114–115, 117
  of action, 108–111, 227
  actional, 114, 121–122
  affirmative, 126
  commonality of, 118
  divine, 27, 102, 123–124, 184
  of existence, 114
  of God, 108–109, 122–123, 128–129, 267
  intrinsically disjunctive, 117–118
  moral, 72–73
  negative, 121–122
  nonactional, 107–108, 110
  positive, 112–113
Averroes, 215
Avicenna, 53, 83, 86, 166, 197
  Al-Farabi and, 166–167
  on essence of God, 119–120
  existence and, 196–200
  God and, 184–185, 199–200
  human intellective soul and, 91–92
  metaphysics and, 85–87, 92
  modalities and, 196–200
axiological shift, 237–239

Babylonian Talmud, 235–236
Balaam, 157–158

Barnes, Jonathan, 35–36
being, 109–110
  Aristotle on causes or reasons for, 11
believers, 128–129, 136–138
Benor, Ehud, 223
Berman, Lawrence, 57, 72–73
Bible, 13–14, 29, 43–44, 105–106, 126, 242
  Jewish commentary on, 33–34
  Job, 14
  secrets of, 35
  unclarity of, 36–37
biblical anthropomorphisms, 38
biblical commentary, 3
biblical exegesis, 14–15, 47, 51
biblical interpretation, 1
biblical prooftexts, 217–221
bios praktikos, 64
bios theôrêtikos, 64, 77
Blumenthal, David R., 284
Book of Beliefs and Opinions (Saadia), 271
Book of Direction to the Duties of the Heart (Ibn Pakuda), 270
Boyd, Richard, 70
Brink, David, 70
Broadie, Sarah, 70

Calvinism, 21–22
canonicity, 31
Categories (Aristotle), 176–177
causal relations, 123
causality, 6–7, 152
  exegetical argument against, 220
  final, 209, 222
celestial physics, 83–84, 167
certainty, 100–101, 159–160, 165–166
character development, 16
chayyot ha-qodesh (holy beasts), 95–96
cherubs (*keruvim*), 95–96
cognitive powers, 281
cognitivism, 78–79. *See also* non-cognitivism
  consequentialism and, 78
  moral, 61, 78
  strong, 67–72
  weak, 64–67, 71–72, 78
Cohen, Hermann, 72–73
coherence argument, 176–177
commandments, 74–75, 247–248, 258–259, 261, 271, 278
commentary
  biblical, 3
  as broader cultural phenomenon, 31–32
  clarification function of, 32–33
  conceptual, 32–40
  conceptual goals of, 42
  explanation function of, 32–33

commentary (cont.)
    formal, 40–47
    Jewish, 33–34
    non-commentary works, 45
    purposes of, 43
    on Scripture, 40–41
Commentary on the Mishnah (Maimonides), 6–7, 153–154, 156–157, 159, 210, 269
common opinion, 60–61
common sense, 23–24
community of Israel, 30
consequentialism, 71, 78
contemplative life, 267
contingency, 118–119, 199–200
    existence and, 125–126
    happiness and, 22–23
    suffering and, 23–24
    vulnerability and, 25
conventional morality, 71–72
conversion, 223
correlations, 198–199
corruptibility, 211
corruption, 57, 199–200, 214
cosmic determinism, 18–19
cosmology, 2–3, 11–12, 18, 95, 143
    of Aristotle, 153, 205
    metaphysics and, 95–97
courage, 268
creation, 6, 145–151, 184, 258–259
    Aristotle proof for, 213
    creation/eternity debate, 256–257
    divine law and, 256–259
    esoteric view of, 148–149
    eternal, 149–150
    ex nihilo, 144, 155–156, 159–160
    miracles and, 151–159
    Scriptural account of, 218
    Six Days of, 217–218
creaturely foreknowledge, 120–121
Crescas, Hasdai, 209
cruelty, 249–250

daily prayers, 126–127
Dalalat al-Ha'irin (Maimonides), 1
Daniel, 157–158, 177–178
Davidson, Herbert, 86, 188–189
Davies, Daniel, 96
Day of Atonement, 216
De Anima (On the Soul) (Aristotle), 163–164
decrees (*hukkim*), 259
definitions, categories of, 107–108
demonstration (*apodeixis*), 143–144, 149, 163, 194–195
determinism, 71, 152–153, 155–156
Dhanani, Alnoor, 143

dialectical arguments, 149
dialectical reasoning, 53–54
disorder, 226
divination, 170
divine actions, 228
divine attributes, 27, 102, 123–124, 184
divine commandments, 139
"divine decree" (*al-'amr al-ilāhī*), 97
divine emanation, 168–169
divine existence, 119
divine foreknowledge, 120–121, 225
divine governance, 97
divine incorporeality, 38–39
divine justice, 98–99
divine law
    creation and, 256–259
    idolatry and, 259–262
    source and goal of, 247–256
divine matters (*'inyanim elohiyim*), 92–93
    certainty and, 100–101
    scientific knowledge of, 100
divine mercy, 176–177
divine names, 263–265
divine possibility, 157
divine retribution, 235
divine sciences, 4, 8, 87–88, 92–93, 99–100, 145
    apprehension of God and, 93–94
    Arabic Aristotelian philosophers and, 90–91
    explanation of, 90
    human perfection and, 90
    metaphysics and, 87
    Rabbis and, 95
divine secrets, 89
divine unity, 37, 196–197
divine will, 154–155, 196
divine wisdom, 57, 196
dreams, 173–174, 177–178, 183, 254–255

egocentrism, 241–244
Eliezer, 179
elitism, 88–89
elohim, 51–53
emanation, 164–165, 169, 172
emet (truth), 30–42, 230
endoxa (generally-accepted beliefs), 66–67, 78
Epictetus, 237–238
Epicurus, 12, 224–225
    atomism and, 18
    providence and, 235
episteme (knowledge), 64–65, 69–70, 78
epistemic norms, 182
epistemological skepticism, 148–150

epistemology, 2–3, 5, 11–12, 165–168
  analytic, 162
  Aristotelian, 64–65, 165
  of prophecy, 5–6, 181–183
equanimity, 11–12
equivocity, 225
  pure, 5, 116–118, 123, 198
eschatology, 63
esoteric doctrines, 210
esoteric names, 263
Essay on Resurrection (Maimonides), 152–153
essence-attributes, 198
eternal creation, 149–150
eternally beginningless universe, 147
eternally existing universe, 143
eternity, 184, 187, 195
  arguments for, 150
  Aristotle and, 149, 191–192
  creation/eternity debate, 256–257
  natural science and, 213
  of time, 147
ethics, 2–3, 11–12, 87
  act-consequentialist approach to, 73–76
  of intellectual perfection, 72–77
  metaethics, 61–62, 78
  normative, 61
  Stoics and, 18–19
  virtue, 60, 69, 71
Ethics (Aristotle), 18
Ethics (Spinoza), 2–4, 12, 209
Euthyphro (Plato), 16–17
Eve, 30–42, 53, 228–229
evil (*ra'*), 30–42, 223–224, 241–242, 244. *See also* good and evil
  God and, 224–225
  inexorability of, 230–235
  as privation, 230–232
  unjustified, 224
exegesis, 33, 42–43, 221–222
  anti-teleological, 218–219
  biblical, 14–15, 47, 51
exegetical commentaries, 126
existence, 106–107, 109, 113–114, 119–120
  attributes of, 114
  Avicenna and, 196–200
  divine, 119
  of God, 85, 109–111, 184, 242–243
  necessity of, 197
  possibility of, 197
existence-attributes, 198
existential import, 122–123
exoteric explanations, 37
explanation function of commentary, 32–33
extended parable argument, 177–178
external meaning (*zāhir*), 173–174, 215–216, 220

externalism, 162
extralinguistic reality, 104–105
extramental reality, 104–105
Ezekiel, 89, 92–101, 176–177

faith, 128–129
falasifa (philosophers), 6, 127, 184, 187, 189–190, 200–205
  Mutakallimun and, 201–202
falsafa (philosophy), 193
falsafa al-ūlā (first philosophy), 92
false beliefs, 181–182
falsehood (*sheqer*), 30–42
felicity, 24–25
final causality, 209, 222
final cause, 212
final end (*al-ghāya*), 212
First Cause, 164
first intelligence, 164
first intelligibles, 166
first philosophy (*falsafa al-ūlā*), 92
forbidden tree, 30–42
form, 54–55
four causes, 212
four-globe model, 95–96
Fox, Marvin, 52, 63–64
free will, 75–76, 225
Freudenthal, Gad, 95–96

Galen, 143, 154–155
Galileo Galilei, 143–144
Garden of Eden, 30–42, 51
  expulsion from, 55–57
  good and evil and, 61–62
  Kreisel, Haim, on, 53
  material element in, 59
  Midrash and, 54–55
  Onqelos on, 51–52
generation, 214–215
generosity, 268
Genesis, 6–7, 89, 159–160, 218, 221–222
  first words of, 147
  heavenly bodies and, 218–219
  Six Days of Creation, 217–218
gentiles, 87–88
geometry, 85–86
Gersonides, Levi, 209
Gettier, Edmund, 162
Gettier-proof formulation, 130–132
al-ghāya (final end), 212
al-ghāya al-akhīra (ultimate final end), 212–214
al-ghāya al-aula (proximate final end), 213–214
God, 4, 24, 37–38, 55–56, 102, 106–107
  acts of, 156–157
  Adam created in image of, 52, 59

God (cont.)
   anthropomorphic conceptions of, 171
   apprehension of, 93–95, 274, 285
   attributes of, 108–109, 122–123, 128–129, 267
   Avicenna and, 184–185, 199–200
   characteristics of, 126
   comprehension of, 129
   divine will of, 154–155
   doctrinal truths about, 87–88
   essence of, 57–58, 119–120, 273–274
   evil and, 224–225
   existence of, 85, 109–111, 184, 242–243
   goodness of, 227–228
   governance of, 96–97
   humans distinguished from, 233–234
   incorporeality of, 105–106
   indirect descriptions of, 128
   ineffability of, 125
   intervention by, 152
   knowledge of, 5, 99, 128–129, 136, 138–139, 275–281
   known but not comprehended, 136
   love of, 12, 269–271, 275–277, 282–285
   moral attributes of, 72–73
   nature of, 8, 102–103, 108, 139, 176–177
   necessary existence of, 198–199
   nonactional attributes and, 107–108
   as noncompound, 108, 126–128
   omnipotence of, 152, 225–227
   positive descriptions of, 126–127
   praise of, 128–129
   pure equivocation and, 116–118
   revelation by, 252–253
   simplicity of, 126–128
   suffering allowed by, 223
   Torah and, 256–257, 261
   as Unmoved Mover, 164
   ways of speaking of, 128
   will of, 256, 262
   world created by, 127
God's actions (*ma'asim*), 272
good (*tov*), 30–42
good action, 68
good and evil, 53, 60, 64
   Garden of Eden and, 61–62
   knowledge of, 30–42, 55
   subjective nature of, 228–229
   truths about, 229
good life, 267
goodness, 227–228
   subjective nature of, 228–229
graciousness, 227

"grue-like" predicates, 115

haecceity ('thisness'), 120
halakhah, 139, 223, 239
halakhic system, 64
halakhic writings, 8, 152–153, 269–271, 273, 275–276, 283–284
Halevi, Judah, 264–265
hallucination, 176
happiness, 21–23
Harvey, Warren Zev, 65, 68, 70–71, 234–235, 282–283
hashgahah peratit (individual providence), 235
heavenly bodies, 194–195, 218–219
Hebrew Bible, 29–31, 38, 43–44, 126
Hebrew-Aramaic/Judeo-Arabic distinction, 44
heresy, 90
hermeneutics, 29
Hilkhot Teshuvah (*Laws of Repentance*) (Maimonides), 273
Hilkhot Yesodei ha-Torah (*Laws of the Foundations of the Torah*) (Maimonides), 271
Hippocrates, 29–30
holy beasts (*chayyot ha-qodesh*), 95–96
homonymy, 117–118
hukkim (decrees), 259
human actions, 127
human cognition, 84
human condition, 8, 22, 25–26
human finitude, 6–7
human frailty, 112–113
human good, 2–3, 7–8, 18–19
human intellect, 97–99, 148–149, 195, 281
human intellective soul, 91–92
human intellectual capabilities, 136–137
human knowledge, 98, 195, 204–205
human mercy, 176–177
human perfection, 8, 12, 63–64, 87–88, 110, 250
   discrete stages of, 268
   divine science and, 90
   love of God and, 269
   pure contemplation and, 267
   social order and, 250–251
human soul, 163–164
Hume, David, 190, 224–225
humility, 27
Hyman, Arthur, 70, 103–105
hypothetical necessity, 127, 194–195

Ibn Ezra, Abraham, 264–265, 271
Ibn Pakuda, Bahya, 270
Ibn Rushd, 38

Index

Ibn Tibbon, Samuel, 1, 92–93, 240
idolatry, 87–88, 90, 250–251, 259–262, 264–265
imagination, 54–55, 157, 164, 172, 200, 202, 232–233
  as corporeal faculty, 230
  dominance of, 250–251
  perfect, 171–172
  products of, 229
  sensory impressions and, 172–173
imaginative faculty, 53–54
imaginative prophecy, 167
imitatio Dei, 57–59, 72–73, 268–269
imitation, 87–88
immanent intellect, 164
impetuosity, 20, 26
impossibility, 184–186
The Incoherence of the Philosophers (Al-Ghazali), 152
incomprehensible knowledge, 129–132
incorporealism, 105–106
incorruptibility, 211
indexical knowledge, 135
individual providence (*hashgahah peratit*), 235
ineffability, 125
intellection, 110–111
intellectual error, 236–237
intellectual insight, 11–12
intellectual norms, 4
intellectual perfection, 57–58, 69–71, 75, 253–254
  achievement of, 70–72
  ethics of, 72–77
  highest level of, 278–279
  Stern, Josef, on, 281–282
intellectual prophecy, 167
Intelligences, 155–156
intelligibles, 229
intention, 233–234
Intentions of the Philosophers (Al-Ghazali), 85–86
internal meaning (*bāṭin*), 173–174
interpretation, 1, 31–32, 44–45, 180
  esoteric, 39–40
  Maimonidean, 43–44, 46
  obscurity and, 36
  by Onqelos, 51–52
  of Scripture, 38–39, 45–47
intuition, 133, 170
intuitive faculty, 170
'*inyanim elohiyim* (divine matters), 92–93
  certainty and, 100–101
  scientific knowledge of, 100
Isaiah, 221–222, 225
'*ishq/hesheq* (intense love), 284–285

Islam, 38, 64, 143
Ivry, Alfred, 232

Jackson, Frank, 134
Jacob, 157–158, 173–174
Jeremiah, 221–222
Jewish philosophy, 1, 11–12
Jewish religious canon, 39–40
Job, 20–28, 77, 224, 238
Job, 14, 29–30, 55–56
Joshua, 159
Judaic law, 64
Judaism, 1–2, 17–18, 37, 87–88, 239
  alleviating suffering, 242–243
  foundations of, 151, 256–258
  rabbinic, 20
  science and, 152
justified true belief, 130–132, 136

Kabbalists, 234
Kalam, 143, 189–190, 193, 200–204, 258–259
  arguments, 146
  Avicenna and, 197
  Al-Ghazali and, 201
  metaphysics and, 146
  theologians, 93–94, 145–146, 153
Kaplan, Lawrence, 74
Kellner, Menachem, 284–285
keruvim (cherubs), 95–96
Klein-Braslavy, Sara, 51, 54–55, 148–149
knowledge of good and evil, 30–42, 55
knowledge-how, 133
Kraemer, Joel, 143–144
Kreisel, Haim, 53, 65–66, 68, 153

Langermann, Y. Tzvi, 143
Laqish, R. Simeon b., 54–55
Law of Moses, 146–147, 211–212, 215–217
Laws of Repentance (*Hilkhot Teshuvah*) (Maimonides), 273
Laws of the Foundations of the Torah (*Hilkhot Yesodei ha-Torah*) (Maimonides), 91–92, 118–119, 271
Leibniz, Gottfried Wilhelm, 1, 209
Lewis, David, 115, 135
life, power, and knowledge, 106–107
logos, 56–57
love and knowledge, 282–284
lovingkindness, 227

Ma'aseh Bereshit (Account of Creation), 272
Ma'aseh Merkavah (Account of the Chariot), 89–90, 93–101, 145, 272
  metaphysics and, 96

ma'asim (God's actions), 272
Mackie, John, 61, 67
"Maimonides on Religious Language" (Hyman), 103–104
Manekin, Charles, 165–166
mashal (parable), 36–37, 42–43
al-mashhūrāt (generally-accepted beliefs), 66–67
matter, 54–55, 230–235
Mayer, Toby, 85
Medical Aphorisms (Maimonides), 154–156
memory, 176
mental representations, 204–205
mental unease, 11–12, 14–15
merciful characteristics, 127
mercy, 227, 276–277
meshalim (parables), 29, 33–34, 36–37, 277
    anthropocentrism and, 219–220
    nonextended parable argument, 178–179
    nonparabolic prophecy, 179–181
    types of, 173–174
    use of, 36–37
metaethics, 61–62, 78
metaphysics, 2–4, 11–12, 91–92, 94–95, 167, 278–279
    Account of the Chariot (*Ma'aseh Merkavah*) and, 96
    Arabic Aristotelian philosophers and, 84
    Aristotle and, 85, 99–100
    Avicenna and, 85–87, 92
    biblical exegesis and, 47
    certainty in, 100–101
    cosmology and, 95–97
    disagreements in matters of, 149
    divine sciences and, 87
    false metaphysical beliefs, 4–5
    human knowledge of, 98, 195, 204–205
    Kalam and, 146
    limitations to, 97–98
    metaphysical truths, 5
    modalities in, 205
    rabbinic esoteric wisdom and, 89
    science and, 92
    subject-matter of, 95
    theology and, 83–85
    ultimate goal of, 8
Metaphysics (Aristotle), 92, 127, 197
Metaphysics of the Healing (Avicenna), 120
method individuation, 162–163, 171–172
Mezuzah, 263–265
Midrash, 54–56
miracles, 6, 144
    creation and, 151–159
    existence of, 159–160
    putative, 5–6

Mishnah, 14, 30, 44–45, 89
Mishneh Torah (Maimonides), 1, 60, 63, 66, 91–92, 95–96, 100, 261, 269, 271, 275
mitzvah, 74–75
modalities, 184–187, 205
    Avicenna and, 196–200
    determination of, 202–203
modality, 6, 195–196
monotheism, 1–2, 252–253
moral attributes, 72–73
moral cognitivism, 61, 78
moral dispositions, 72–73
moral judgements, 59, 64–65, 67
moral non-cognitivism, 62, 66
moral perfection, 68–69
moral realism, 61
moral reform, 16
moral virtue, 20–22, 24, 57, 267–268
Moreh Nevukim (Maimonides), 1
Morteira, Saul, 209
Mosaic prophecy, 161, 182–183
Moses, 24–25, 75, 154–155, 251–252
    Galen and, 155
    Law of, 146–147, 211–212, 215–217
    prophecy and, 257–258
Mutakallimun, 6, 143, 146, 149, 184, 188, 190, 194–195, 200–205
Mutazilites, 143, 235
mystical experience, 284

Nadler, Steven, 241–242
Nagel, Thomas, 134
Narboni, Moses, 209, 240
natural law, 61, 152, 249
natural sciences, 4, 145, 214, 279
    aporia in, 211
    eternity and, 213
naturalism, 6–7, 257–258
naturalistic justice, 235–241
nature, 249, 261
    uniformity of, 190
    will and, 248–249
necessarily existent being in itself, 196–200
necessary existence of God, 198–199
necessary-existence, 118–119, 122
necessitation, 191–196, 204–205
necessity, 184, 187–190, 204–205
    Aristotle and, 197
    hypothetical, 127, 194–195
    nonnecessity, 145–147
negative attributes, 112–114
negative predications, 111–112
negative theology, 5, 103, 176–177, 224–225, 228–230, 238

Index

Neoplatonic ontology, 220
Neoplatonism, 224
nonactional attributes, 107–108, 110
non-cognitivism, 61–64, 66–67, 78
nonexistence, 195
nonextended parable argument, 178–179
non-Mosaic prophecy, 6, 161–162, 182–183
nonparabolic prophecy, 172–175, 179–181
non-propositional knowledge, 132, 135–136, 138–139
   apophaticism and, 136–138
   indexical knowledge, 135
   knowledge-how, 133
   phenomenal knowledge, 134
normative ethics, 61

obedience, 247–248
objective standards of value, 79
objectivity, 138–139
obscurity, 35–36
occult powers, 263–265
On the Soul (De Anima) (Aristotle), 163–164
Onqelos, 43–44, 51–52, 55–56
The Order of Nabatean Worship, 259–260
overflow, 280–281

pagan literature, 259
parables (*meshalim*), 29, 33–34, 36–37, 277
   anthropocentrism and, 219–220
   nonextended parable argument, 178–179
   nonparabolic prophecy, 179–181
   use of, 36–37
parabolic prophecies, 179
particularization, 200
peace of mind, 11–12, 18–19
perception, 172–173
perceptual beliefs, 163
perfect imagination, 171–172
perfection, 214–215, 268. *See also specific types*
perplexity, 11–18, 221
   arrogance and, 26
   attempts to overcome, 18–19
   erroneous readings of Scripture and, 36–37
   impetuosity and, 26
   Plato and, 16–17
   root cause of, 27–28
   Socrates and, 17–18
Perry, John, 135
phenomenal knowledge, 134
philosophical psychology, 2–3, 11–12
philosophy of language, 2–3, 11–12, 123–124
philosophy of law, 2–3, 11–12
philosophy of mind, 5
physicalism, 134

physics, 86–87, 89, 91–92, 94–95
Pines, Shlomo, 1–2, 12, 19, 97
Plato, 1–3, 12, 15–16
   Aristotle and, 148–149
   authority of, 148
   foundations of Judaism and, 151
   on male and female, 54–55
   Neoplatonic ontology, 220
   Neoplatonic version of eternal creation, 149–150
   Neoplatonism, 224
   perplexity and, 16–17
   view for understanding creation, 6, 146–147
political leaders, 253–254
political philosophy, 11–12
positive attributes, 112–113
possibility, 184–190
possible of existence in themselves and necessary of existence through a cause, 196–200
Posterior Analytics (Aristotle), 191–192
postlapsarian state, 59
potentiality, 187–190, 204–205
practical intellect, 53
practical life, 267
practical philosophy, 11–12
prayer, 260–261, 270
preamble (*tamhīd*), 210–212
presumption, 20
Principle of Plenitude, 186–189, 202–203, 232–233
privation, 111–112, 224, 231–234
prohairesis (choice), 69
prohibition, 52
prophecy, 99–100, 157–158, 162–163, 184, 253–254. *See also* non-Mosaic prophecy
   agents of, 172–173
   belief-forming method employed in cases of, 6
   epistemology of, 5–6, 181–183
   false beliefs from, 181–182
   imaginative, 167
   intellectual, 167
   meaning of, 179
   Mosaic, 161, 182–183
   Moses and, 257–258
   nonparabolic, 172–175, 179–181
   parabolic, 172–176, 179
   rational faculty in context of, 170
   revelation of, 254–255
   sufficient conditions for, 168–169
prophetic beliefs, 176
prophetic method, 161, 181–183
   Avicenna and, 167–168
   emanation, 168–169
   general argument, 179–181
   output beliefs, 176

prophetic method (cont.)
  perfect imagination, 171
  rationalized emanation, 169–171
  rationalized impressions, 171–176
  scope of, 161–162
propositional knowledge, 132, 136–137
Proverbs, 41, 217–218
providence, 99–100, 184
  general, 235
  naturalistic, 239
  suffering and, 223–224, 244
  theories of, 235
proximate final end (al-ghāya al-aula), 213–214
psychic immunity, 238–239, 241
Ptolemy, 164, 205
pure intellects, 232–233
purposeful particularization, 191–196
putative miracles, 5–6

Quran, 255–256

R. Joseph (dedicatee of Maimonides' Guide), 86–89, 266
  dedicatory epistle to, 19
  Job and, 20–28
  perplexity of, 12–18
ra' (evil), 30–42, 223–224, 241–242, 244. See also good and evil
  God and, 224–225
  inexorability of, 230–235
  as privation, 230–232
  unjustified, 224
Rabbi Ammi, 7
rabbinic esoteric wisdom, 89
rabbinical legal canon, 30
radical dependence, 121
Raffel, Charles, 235, 237–238
Railton, Peter, 70
rational animality, 199
rational faculty, 54, 163–164, 166, 280
  Active Intellect and, 171–172
  in context of prophecy, 170
  perfect, 171–172
rationalized emanation, 172
rationalized impressions, 175–178
rectilinear motion of bodies, 194
Red Sea, 153–154, 156–157
relational predicates, 115
relations, 107–108
religion, foundations of, 100
religious knowledge, 139
religious language, 105–106, 123–124, 126–127
Republic (Plato), 2–3, 12

revelation, 252–253, 265
  authoritativeness of, 257–258
  of prophecy, 254–255
  of Quran, 255–256
Revelation at Sinai, 157–158
reward and punishment (*sakhar va-onesh*), 7, 235
riddles, 145
righteousness, 23–24
rule-consequentialism, 75–76, 78–79
Rynhold, Daniel, 227

Saadia, 29–30, 271
Sabians, 259–260
Sages, 145
sakhar va-onesh (reward and punishment), 7, 235
Sammael, 54–55
Samuel, 172–173
Satan, 54–55, 234–235
Schwartz, Michael, 116
science. See also divine sciences; natural sciences
  Judaism and, 152
  metaphysics and, 92
  speculative, 84–86
  subject and goals of, 85–86
scientific certainty, 159–160
scientific curriculum, 87–88
scientific knowledge, 100, 143–144, 163, 238–239, 241
scientific naturalism, 159–160
Scotus, John Duns, 189–190
Scripture, 35, 41, 44–45, 47, 95, 157–158
  Account of Creation, 218
  authority of, 40
  commentary on, 40–41
  concealment in, 94–95
  erroneous readings of, 36–37
  interpretation of, 38–39, 45–47
  Mosaic doctrine in, 149–150
  philosophicality of, 16, 18–19, 26
  plausibility of, 145–147
  rereading, 42–43
  scientific certainty and, 159–160
  textual difficulty in, 41–42
  uneducated readers of, 37
  valid readings of, 33–34
  view for understanding creation, 6, 146–147
semantics, 11–12
sense perception, 134
sensory modalities, 172–173
sexuality, 249–250
shame, 230–231

Shatz, David, 64
Shema, 270
Shemonah Perakim (Maimonides), 55–56, 60
sheqer (falsehood), 30–42
sickness of the soul, 247–248
silence, 128–129
sin, 53–54, 61–62, 65–66, 235–236
Six Days of Creation, 217–218
Skeptic phenomenalism, 18
skepticism, 61, 148–150, 204–205
social order, 250–251
sociology of knowledge, 31
Socrates, 15–18, 22
Sokol, Moshe, 223
Soloveitchik, Joseph, 64
Sosa, Ernest, 176
spatio-temporal location, 135
special providence, 99–100
speculative sciences, 84–86
Spinoza, Baruch, 1–4, 11–12, 181–182, 209
spiritual extinction, 90
spiritual maturity, 128
spiritual perfection, 275
Stern, Josef, 89, 111–113, 117, 165, 167
  on disorder, 226
  divine existence and, 119
  on intellectual perfection, 281–282
  on matter, 231
Stoics, 18–19, 21–22, 238
Strauss, Leo, 19, 83
Sturgeon, Nicholas, 70
sublunar motion, 192–193
sublunar sphere, 145–147, 153
  primary qualities of, 194
  rectilinear motion of bodies in, 194
sublunar substances, 197
sublunar world, 96, 168–169
suffering, 242
  allowed by God, 223
  antidote to, 24
  contingency and, 23–24
  Judaism alleviating, 242–243
  providence and, 223–224, 244
supernatural events, 144, 153–154

al-tajwiz (admissibility), 200
Talmud, 7, 44–45
  Babylonian, 235–236
  exegetical commentaries of, 126
teleology, 209–210, 215–217, 221–222
  anti-teleological exegesis, 218–219
  Aristotle on, 213–215
  cosmologies and, 70

telos (goal), 68–69, 77
temporal model, 204–205
temporal/statistical model, 186–187
theodicy, 7, 20–21, 223–225, 228–229, 232–233, 241–242
  anthropocentrism and, 243
  axiological-shift, 239
theology, 47, 90–91, 128–129, 137–138
  apophatic, 125
  metaphysics and, 83–85
  negative, 5, 103, 176–177, 224–225, 228–230, 238
Theorems and Axioms (Avicenna), 53
time, 185–186
Torah, 30, 74–75, 96–97, 250–251, 255–256, 258–259
  authoritativeness of, 257–258
  characteristics of God in, 126
  God and, 256–257, 261
  laws of, 248–249
  study of, 266
Touati, Charles, 181–182
tov (good), 30–42
Tractate Avot, 74
Tractatus Theologico-Politicus (Spinoza), 1
traditional authority, 23–24
transcendent intellect, 164
transgression, 235–236
Treatise on the Art of Logic (Maimonides), 66, 116, 184–185
tree of knowledge, 52
tree of life, 55–57
truth (*emet*), 30–42, 230
tzelem elohim (image of God), 52, 59

ultimate final end (*al-ghāya al-akhīra*), 212–214
ultimate perfection, 72
Unmoved Mover, 164
utilitarianism, 68

virtue, 15–16, 23–24
  ethics, 60, 69, 71
  moral, 20–22, 24, 57, 267–268
vita activa, 58
vita contemplativa, 58
vulnerability, 25

Weiss, Roslyn, 152
will, 248
  divine will, 154–155, 196
  free, 75–76, 225
  of God, 256, 262
  nature and, 248–249

Williamson, Timothy, 163
wisdom, 21–22, 248
  divine, 57
  lack of, 25–26
World to Come, 62–64

worship, 247–248, 260, 282–283

Zachariah, 177–178
ẓāhir (external meaning), 173–174, 215–216, 220

CAMBRIDGE CRITICAL GUIDES

Titles published in this series (continued):

Aristotle's *Politics*
EDITED BY THORNTON LOCKWOOD AND THANASSIS SAMARAS

Aristotle's *Physics*
EDITED BY MARISKA LEUNISSEN

Kant's *Lectures on Ethics*
EDITED BY LARA DENIS AND OLIVER SENSEN

Kierkegaard's *Fear and Trembling*
EDITED BY DANIEL CONWAY

Kant's *Lectures on Anthropology*
EDITED BY ALIX COHEN

Kant's *Religion within the Boundaries of Mere Reason*
EDITED BY GORDON MICHALSON

Descartes' *Meditations*
EDITED BY KAREN DETLEFSEN

Augustine's *City of God*
EDITED BY JAMES WETZEL

Kant's *Observations and Remarks*
EDITED BY RICHARD VELKLEY AND SUSAN SHELL

Nietzsche's *On the Genealogy of Morality*
EDITED BY SIMON MAY

Aristotle's *Nicomachean Ethics*
EDITED BY JON MILLER

Kant's *Metaphysics of Morals*
EDITED BY LARA DENIS

Spinoza's *Theological-Political Treatise*
EDITED BY YITZHAK Y. MELAMED and MICHAEL A. ROSENTHAL

Plato's *Laws*
EDITED BY CHRISTOPHER BOBONICH

Plato's *Republic*
EDITED BY MARK L. MCPHERRAN

Kierkegaard's *Concluding Unscientific Postscript*
EDITED BY RICK ANTHONY FURTAK

Wittgenstein's *Philosophical Investigations*
EDITED BY ARIF AHMED

Kant's *Critique of Practical Reason*
EDITED BY ANDREWS REATH and JENS TIMMERMANN

Kant's *Groundwork of the Metaphysics of Morals*
EDITED BY JENS TIMMERMANN

Kant's *Idea for a Universal History with a Cosmopolitan Aim*
EDITED BY AMÉLIE OKSENBERG RORTY and JAMES SCHMIDT

Mill's *On Liberty*
EDITED BY C. L. TEN

Hegel's *Phenomenology of Spirit*
EDITED BY DEAN MOYAR and MICHAEL QUANTE

For EU product safety concerns, contact us at Calle de José Abascal, 56–1°, 28003 Madrid, Spain or eugpsr@cambridge.org.

www.ingramcontent.com/pod-product-compliance
Ingram Content Group UK Ltd.
Pitfield, Milton Keynes, MK11 3LW, UK
UKHW022115130426
469895UK00017B/223